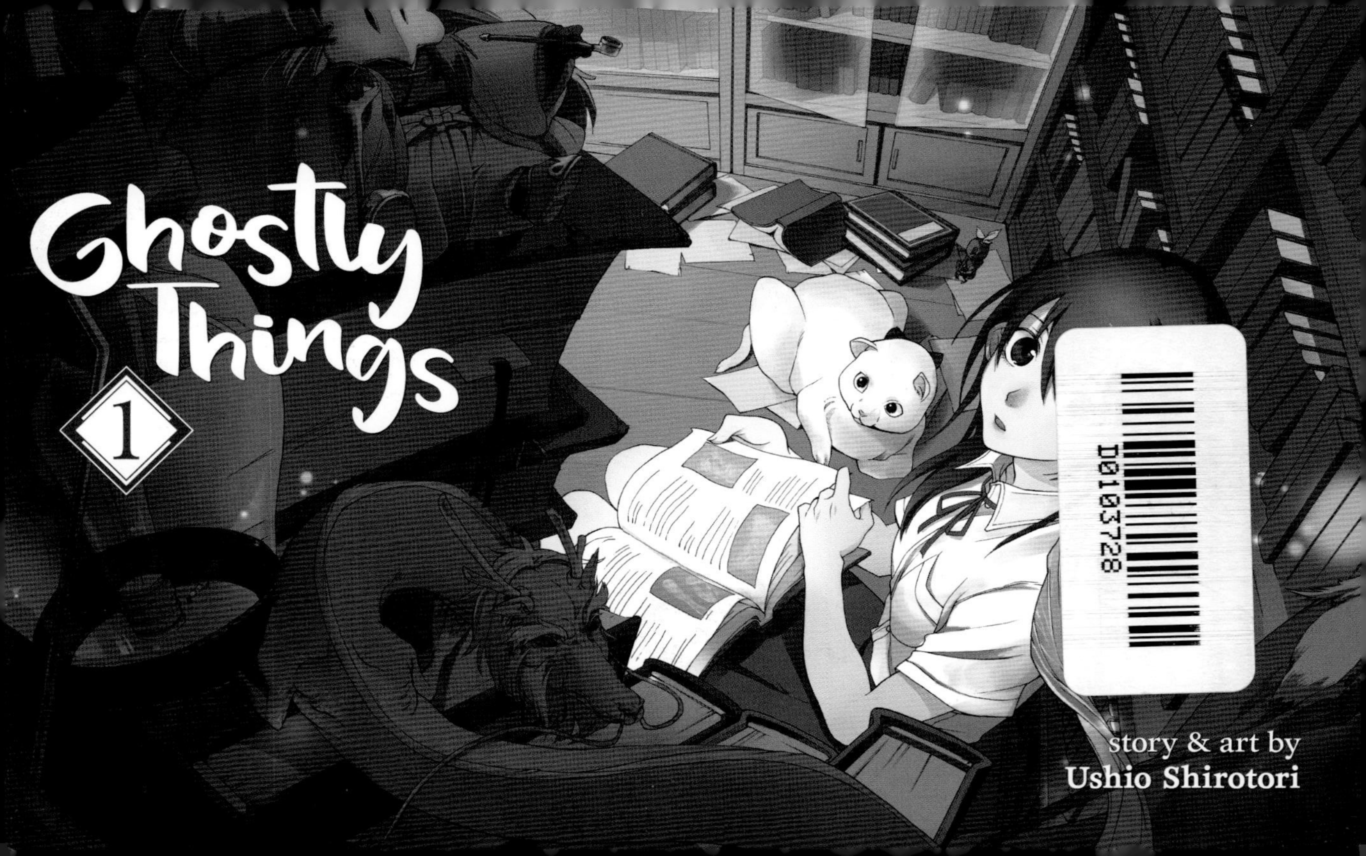
Ghostly Things
1
story & art by
Ushio Shirotori

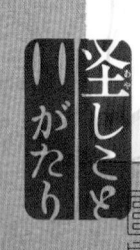

目次

怪しこといがたり

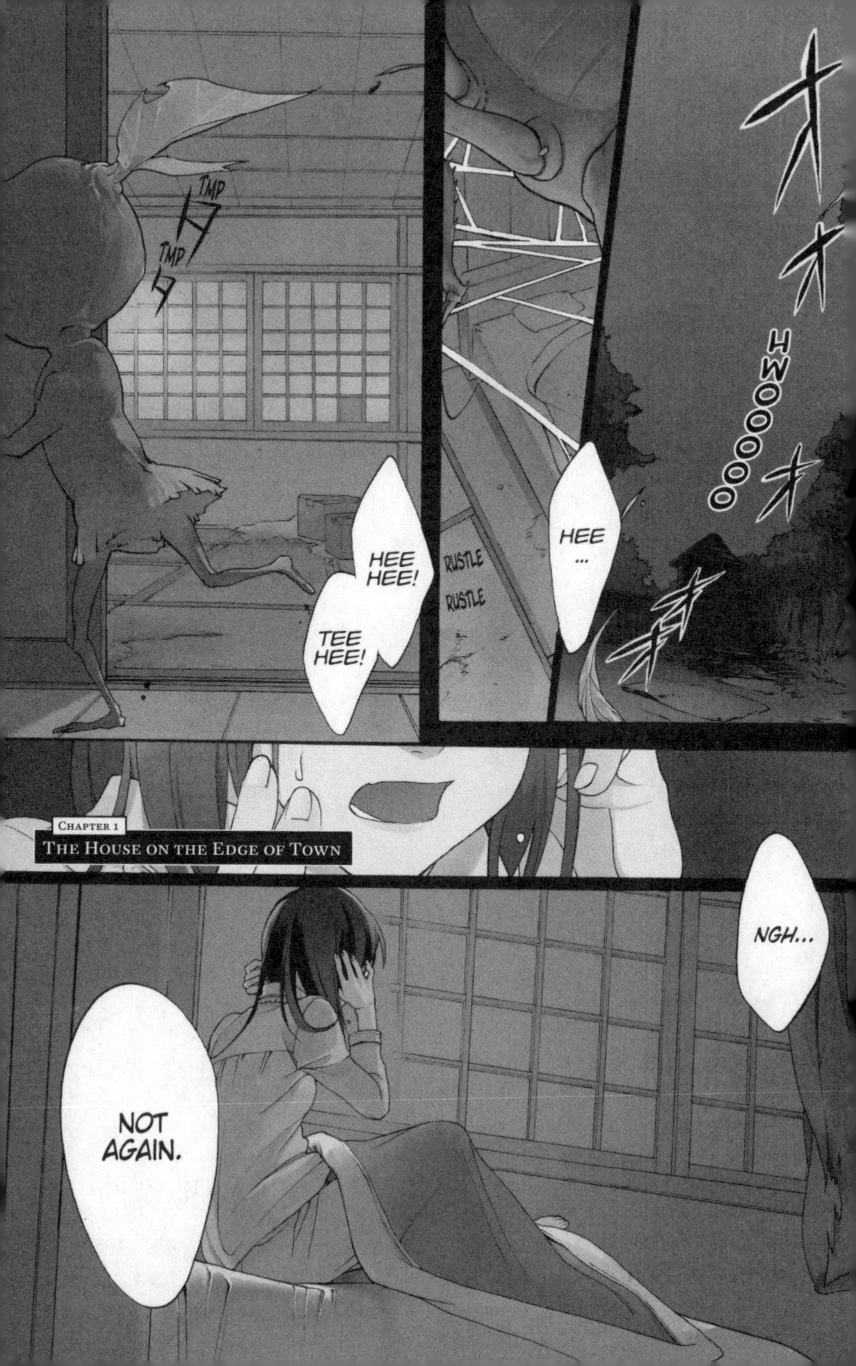
HWOOOOO
HEE...
RUSTLE
RUSTLE
TMP
TMP
HEE HEE!
TEE HEE!
CHAPTER 1
THE HOUSE ON THE EDGE OF TOWN
NGH...
NOT AGAIN.

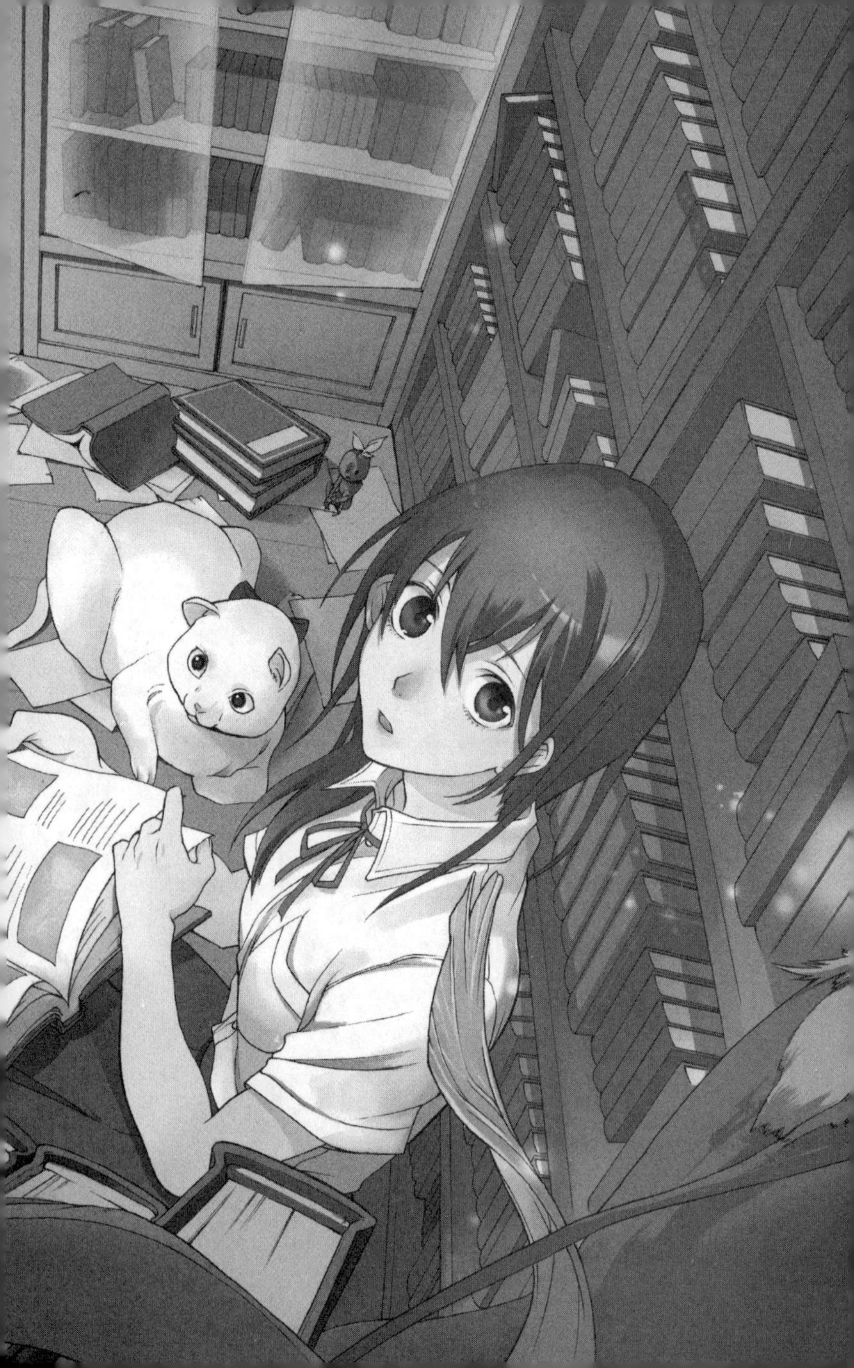

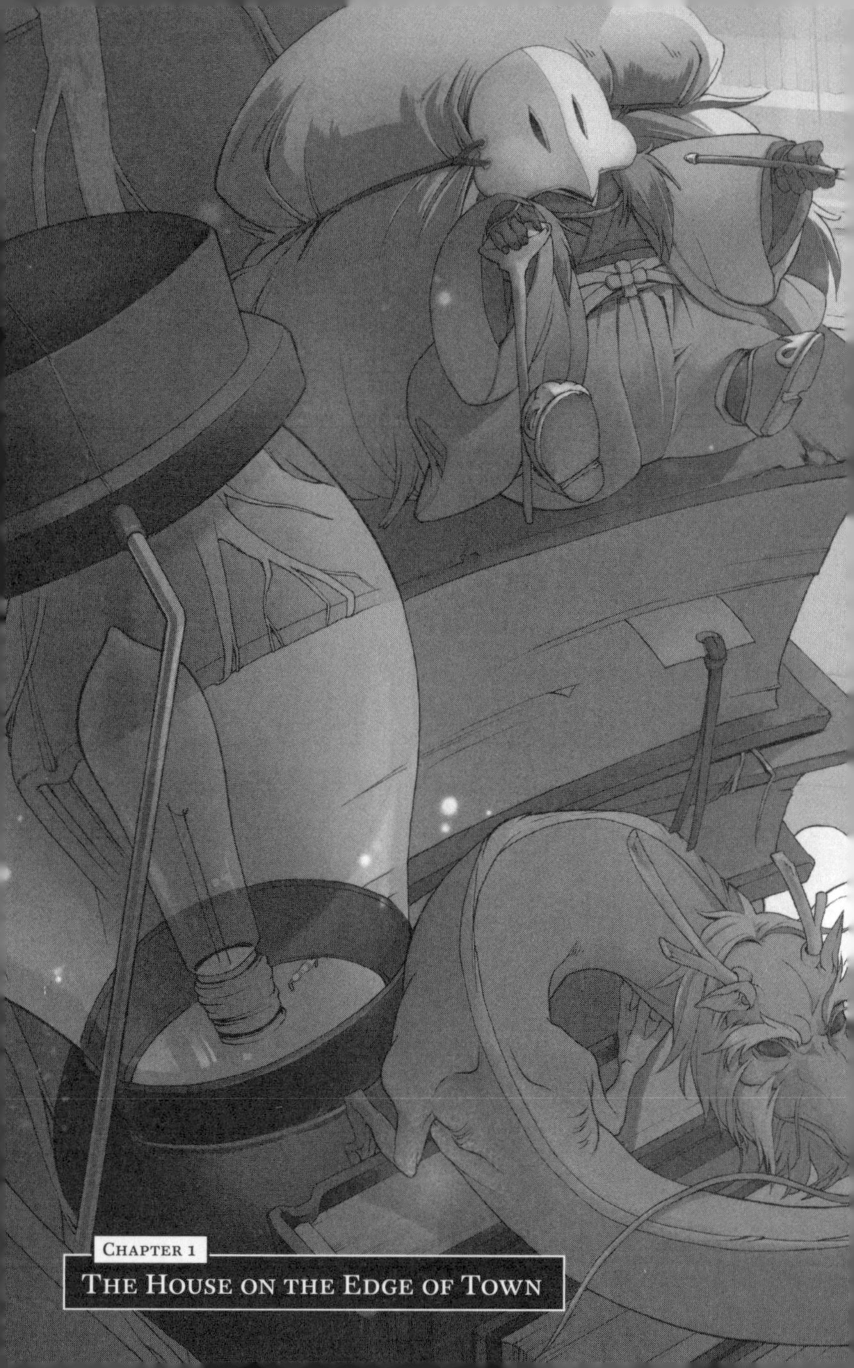

Chapter 1

The House on the Edge of Town

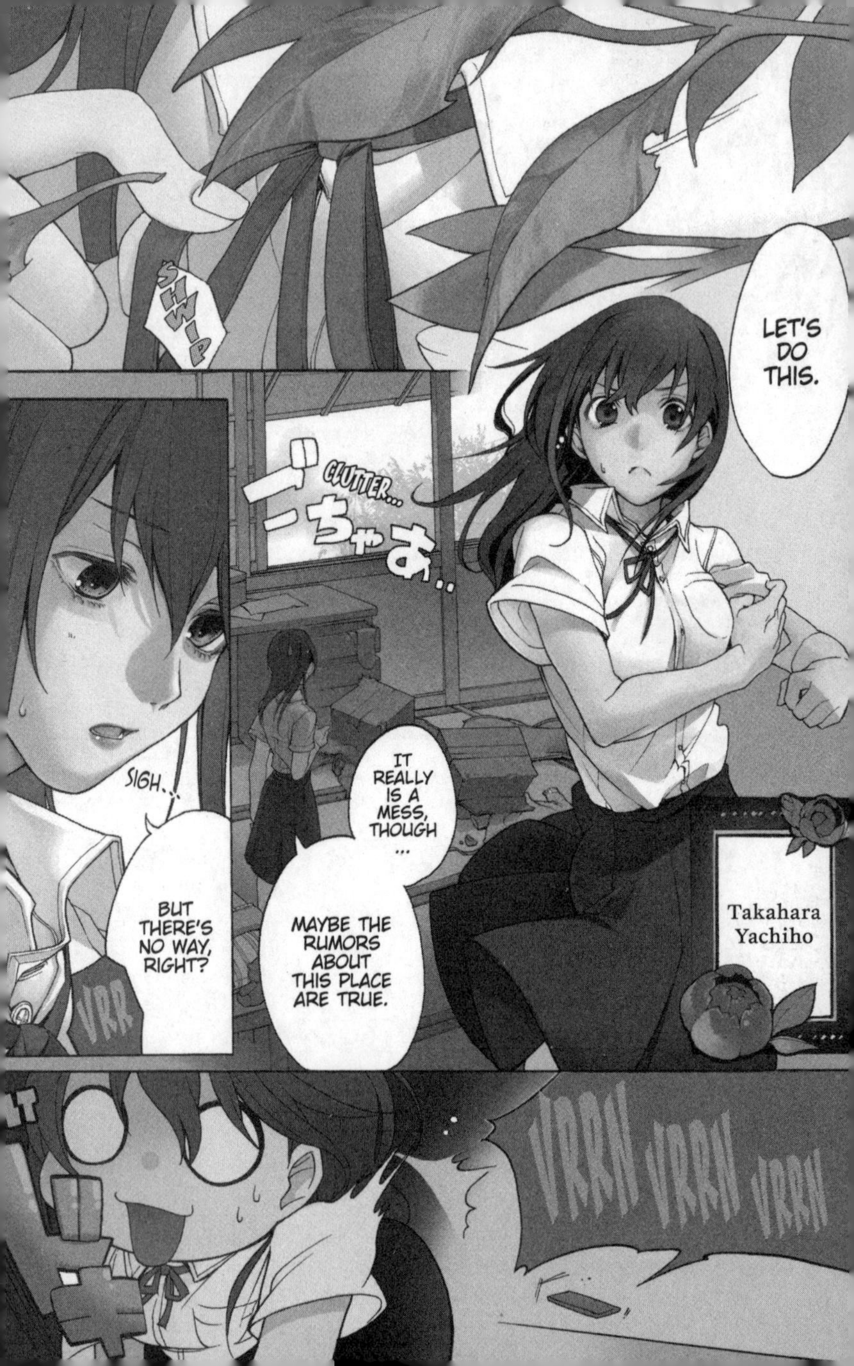
SHWIP
LET'S DO THIS.
Takahara Yachiho
CLUTTER...
ごーちゃあ..
IT REALLY IS A MESS, THOUGH ...
MAYBE THE RUMORS ABOUT THIS PLACE ARE TRUE.
SIGH...
BUT THERE'S NO WAY, RIGHT?
VRR
VRRN VRRN VRRN

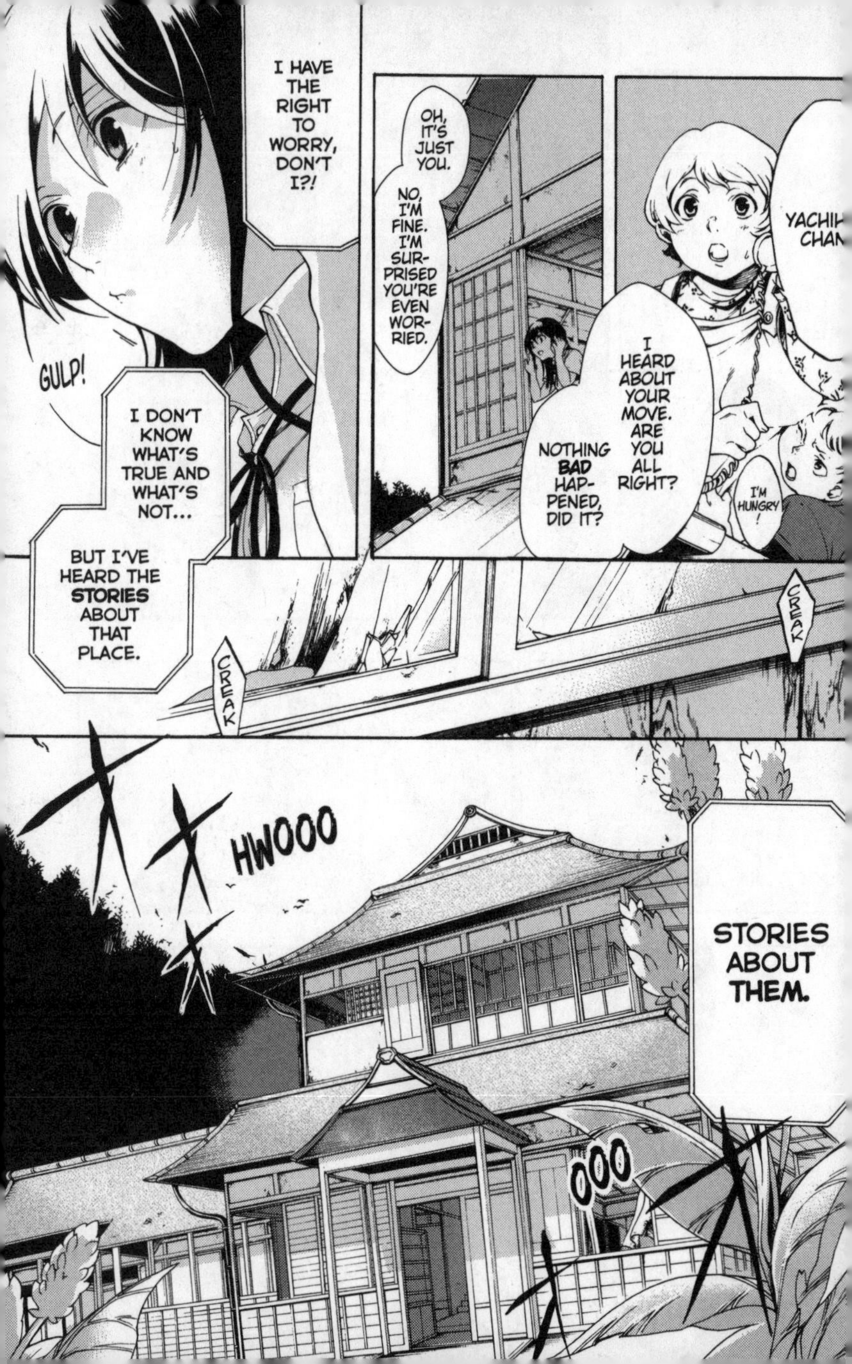
YACHIH
CHAN
I HEARD ABOUT YOUR MOVE. ARE YOU ALL RIGHT?
NOTHING BAD HAPPENED, DID IT?
I'M HUNGRY!
OH, IT'S JUST YOU.
NO, I'M FINE. I'M SURPRISED YOU'RE EVEN WORRIED.
I HAVE THE RIGHT TO WORRY, DON'T I?!
GULP!
I DON'T KNOW WHAT'S TRUE AND WHAT'S NOT...
BUT I'VE HEARD THE STORIES ABOUT THAT PLACE.
CREAK
CREAK
STORIES ABOUT THEM.
HWOOO
OOO

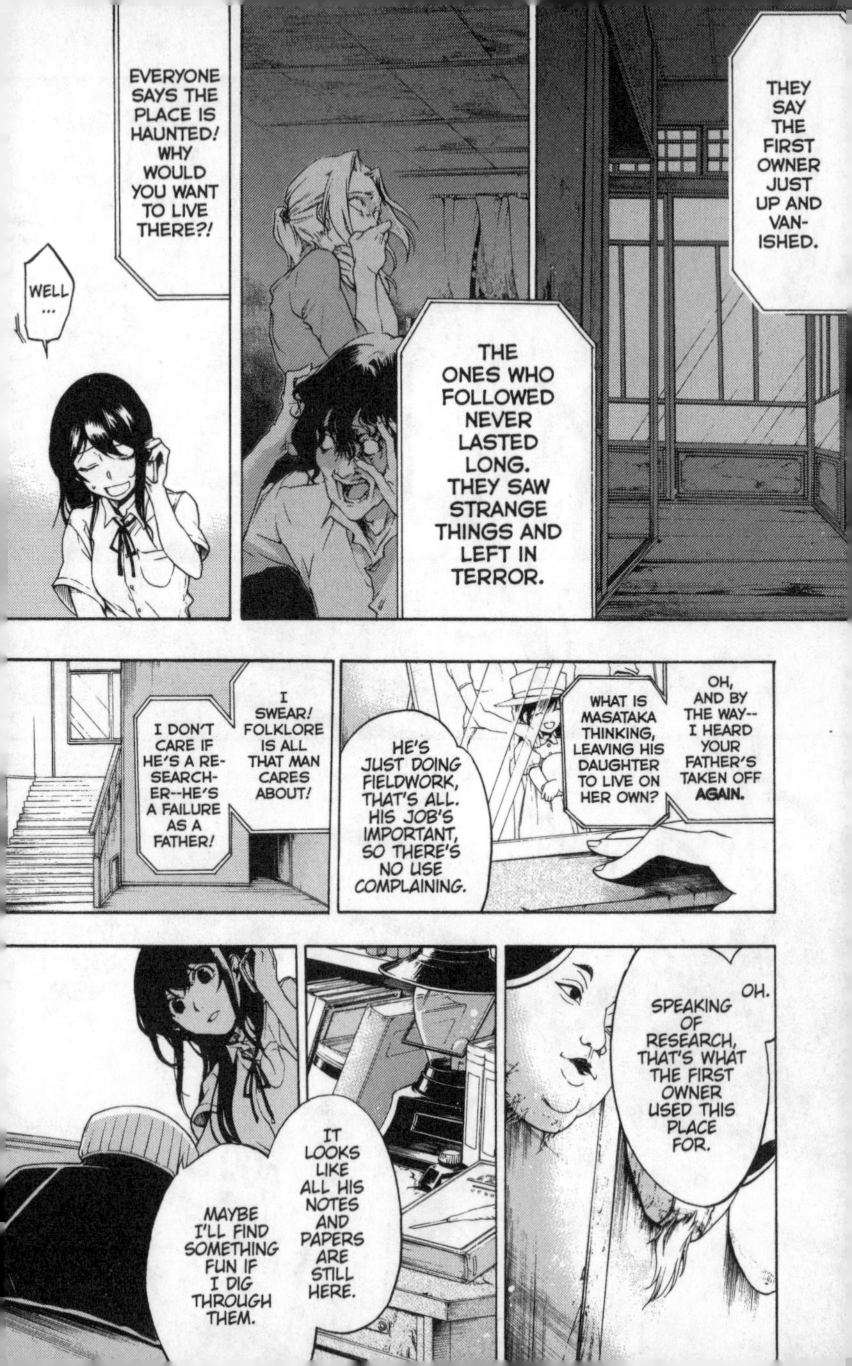
THEY SAY THE FIRST OWNER JUST UP AND VAN-ISHED.
THE ONES WHO FOLLOWED NEVER LASTED LONG. THEY SAW STRANGE THINGS AND LEFT IN TERROR.
EVERYONE SAYS THE PLACE IS HAUNTED! WHY WOULD YOU WANT TO LIVE THERE?!
WELL...
OH, AND BY THE WAY-- I HEARD YOUR FATHER'S TAKEN OFF **AGAIN.**
WHAT IS MASATAKA THINKING, LEAVING HIS DAUGHTER TO LIVE ON HER OWN?
HE'S JUST DOING FIELDWORK, THAT'S ALL. HIS JOB'S IMPORTANT, SO THERE'S NO USE COMPLAINING.
I SWEAR! FOLKLORE IS ALL THAT MAN CARES ABOUT!
I DON'T CARE IF HE'S A RE-SEARCH-ER--HE'S A FAILURE AS A FATHER!
OH.
SPEAKING OF RESEARCH, THAT'S WHAT THE FIRST OWNER USED THIS PLACE FOR.
IT LOOKS LIKE ALL HIS NOTES AND PAPERS ARE STILL HERE.
MAYBE I'LL FIND SOMETHING FUN IF I DIG THROUGH THEM.

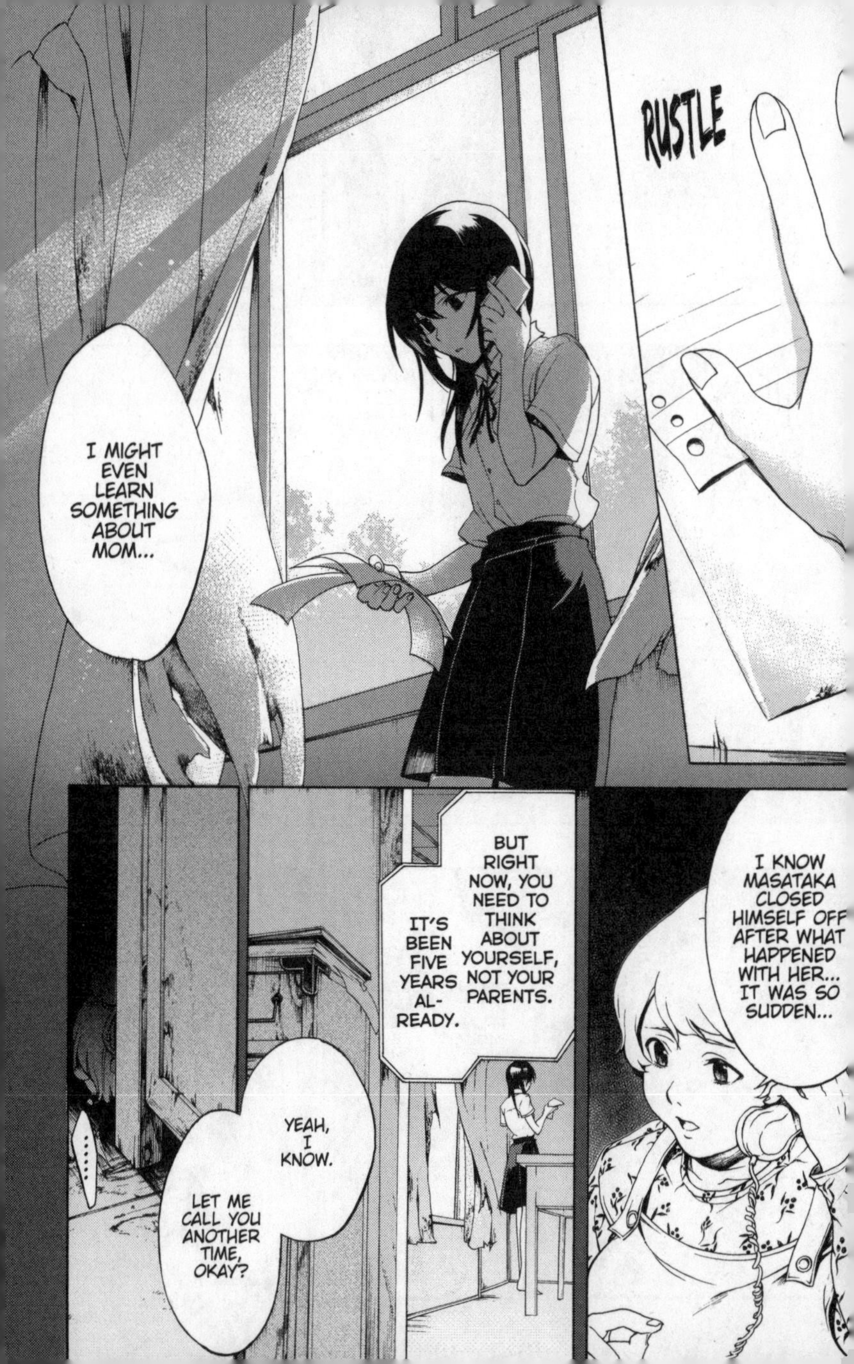
RUSTLE
I MIGHT EVEN LEARN SOMETHING ABOUT MOM...
I KNOW MASATAKA CLOSED HIMSELF OFF AFTER WHAT HAPPENED WITH HER... IT WAS SO SUDDEN...
BUT RIGHT NOW, YOU NEED TO THINK ABOUT YOURSELF, NOT YOUR PARENTS.
IT'S BEEN FIVE YEARS AL-READY.
YEAH, I KNOW.
LET ME CALL YOU ANOTHER TIME, OKAY?
......

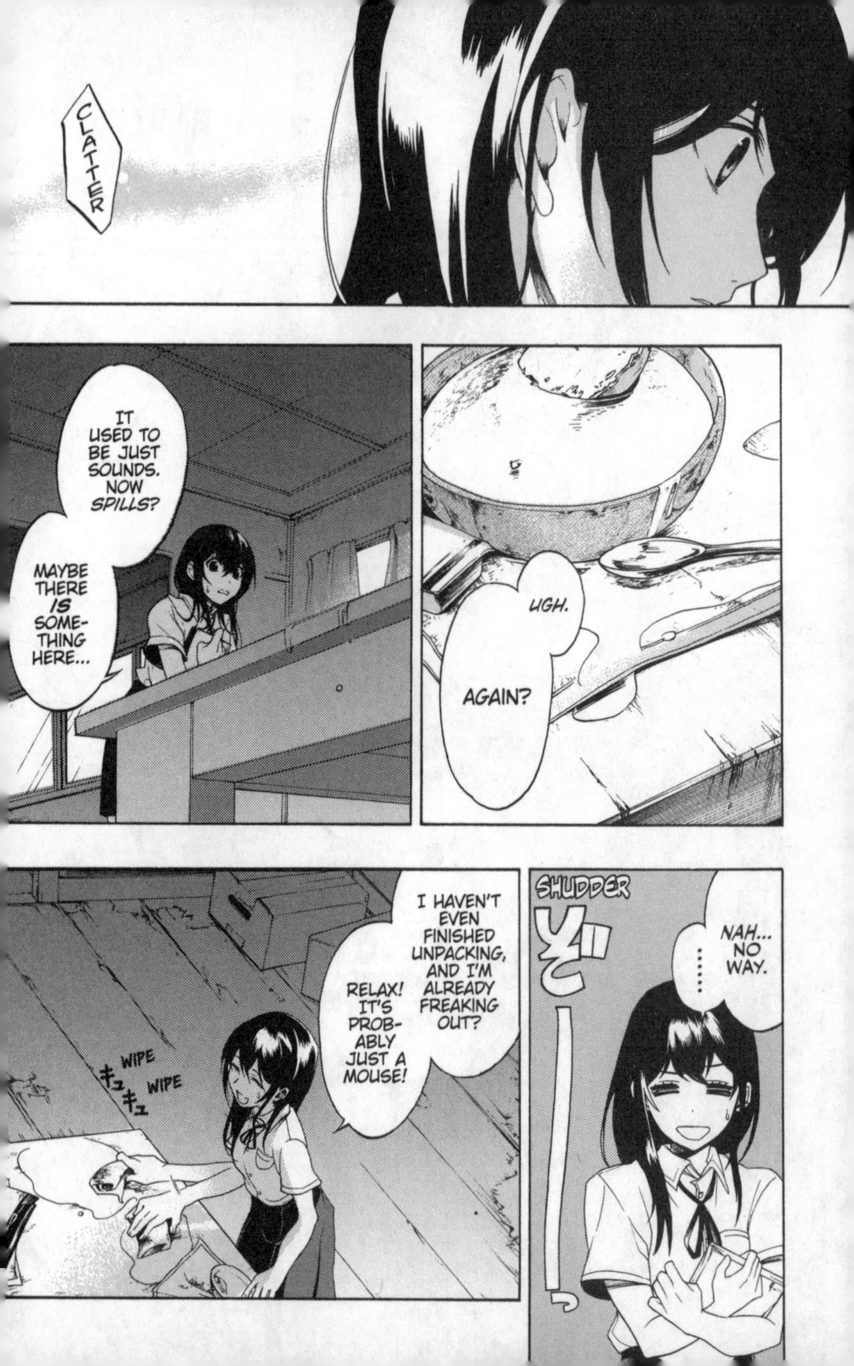
CLATTER
UGH.
AGAIN?
IT USED TO BE JUST SOUNDS. NOW *SPILLS*?
MAYBE THERE *IS* SOMETHING HERE...
SHUDDER
......
NAH... NO WAY.
I HAVEN'T EVEN FINISHED UNPACKING, AND I'M ALREADY FREAKING OUT?
RELAX! IT'S PROBABLY JUST A MOUSE!
WIPE WIPE

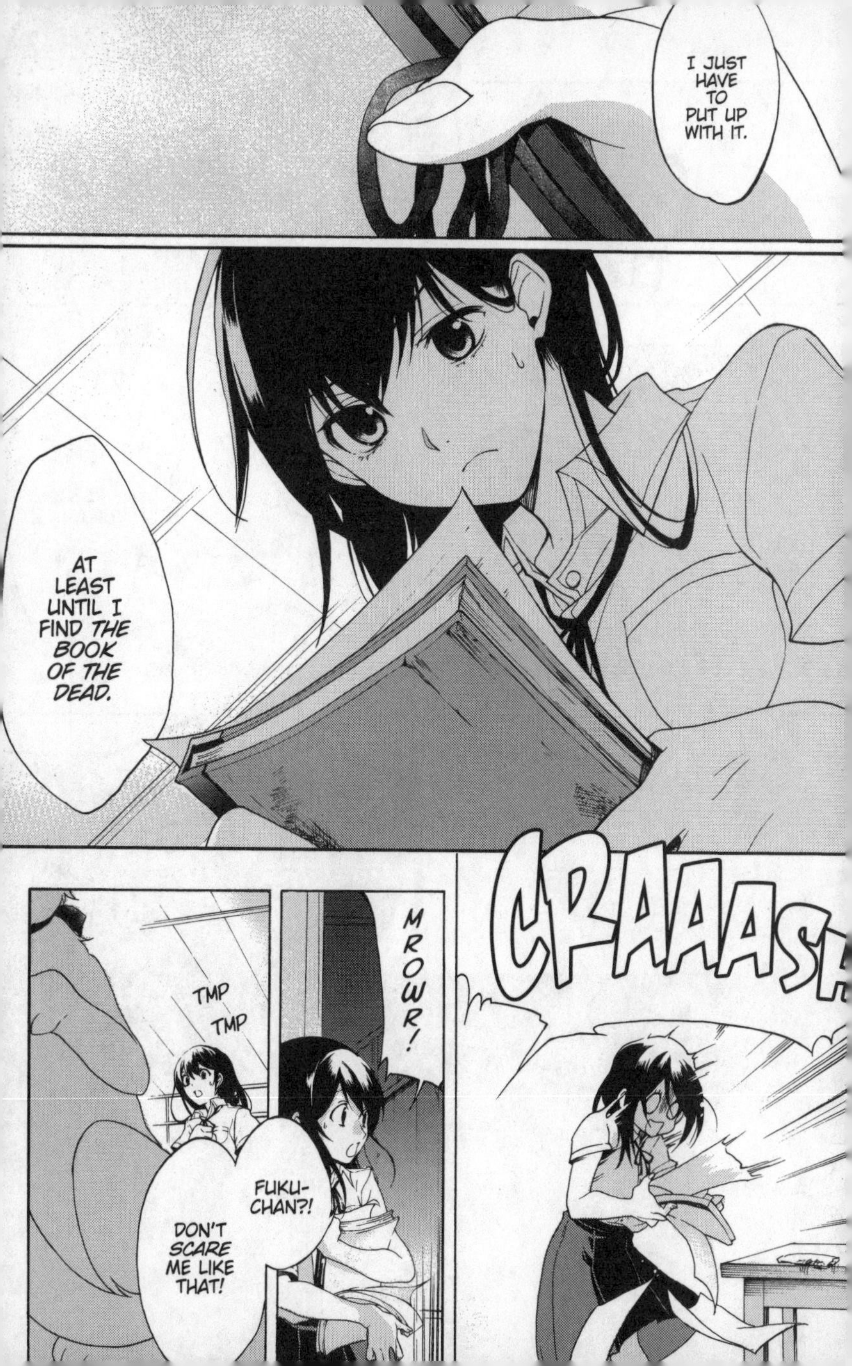
I JUST HAVE TO PUT UP WITH IT.
AT LEAST UNTIL I FIND *THE BOOK OF THE DEAD.*
CRAAASH
MROWR!
TMP
TMP
FUKU-CHAN?!
DON'T *SCARE* ME LIKE THAT!

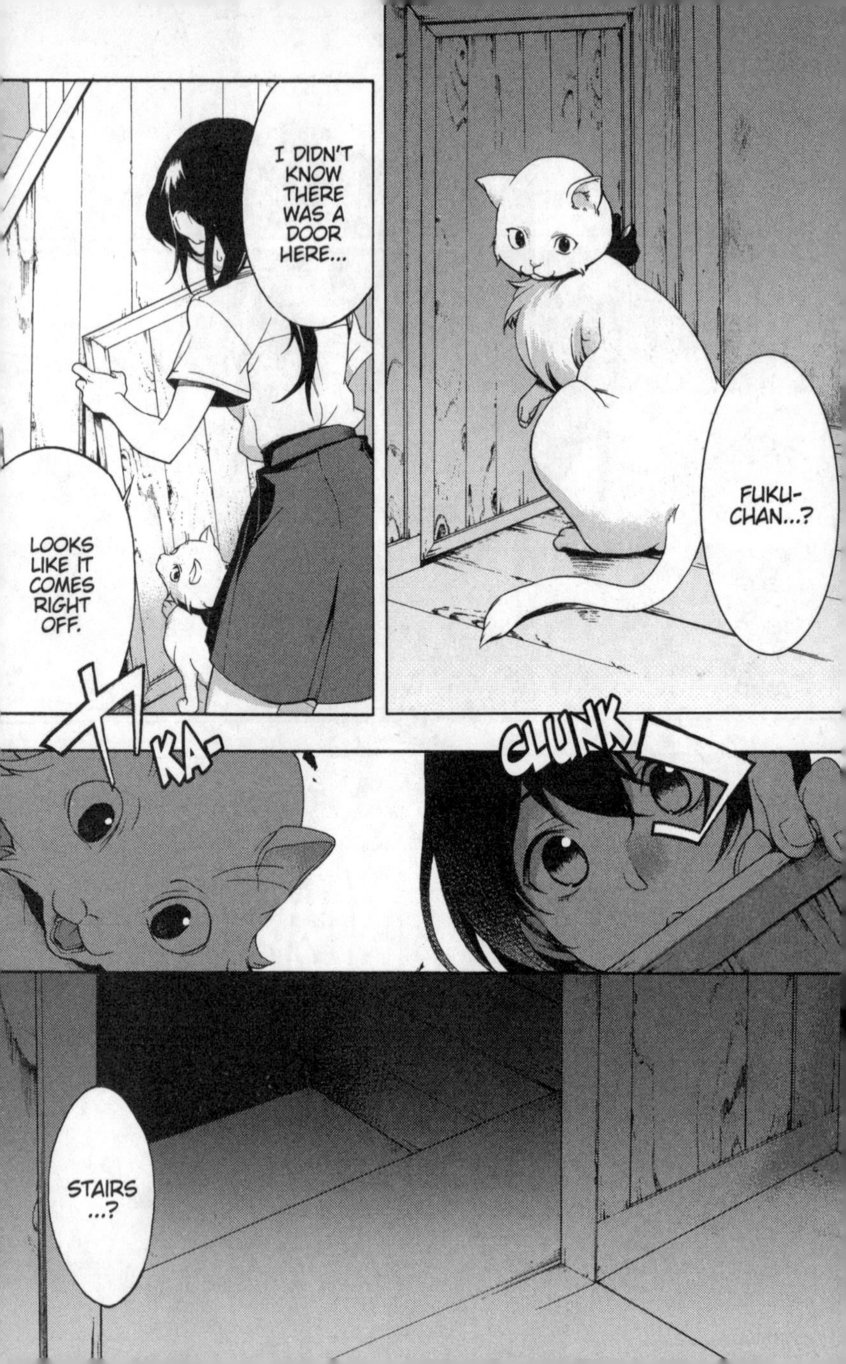
FUKU-CHAN...?
I DIDN'T KNOW THERE WAS A DOOR HERE...
LOOKS LIKE IT COMES RIGHT OFF.
CLUNK
KA-
STAIRS ...?

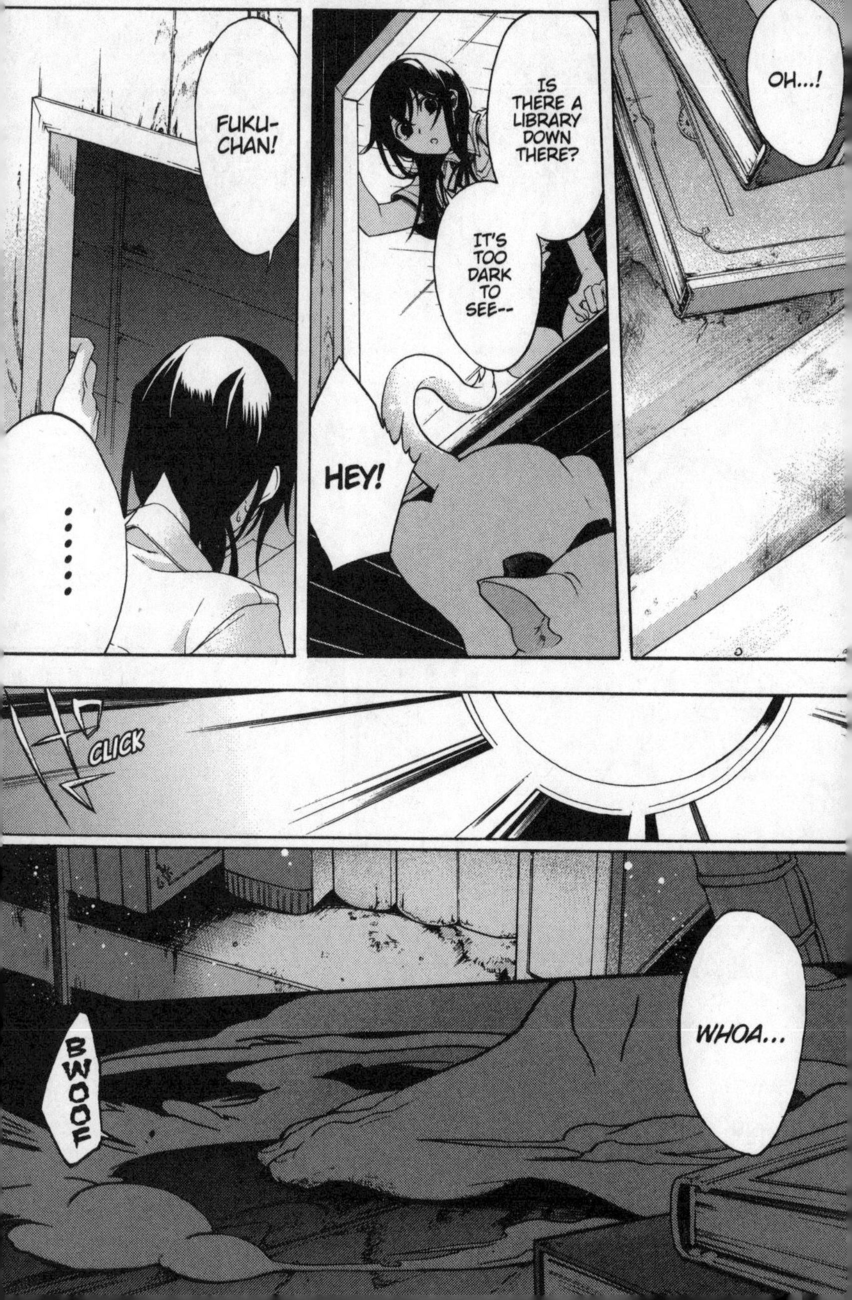
OH...!
IS THERE A LIBRARY DOWN THERE?
IT'S TOO DARK TO SEE--
HEY!
FUKU-CHAN!
......
CLICK
WHOA...
BWOOF

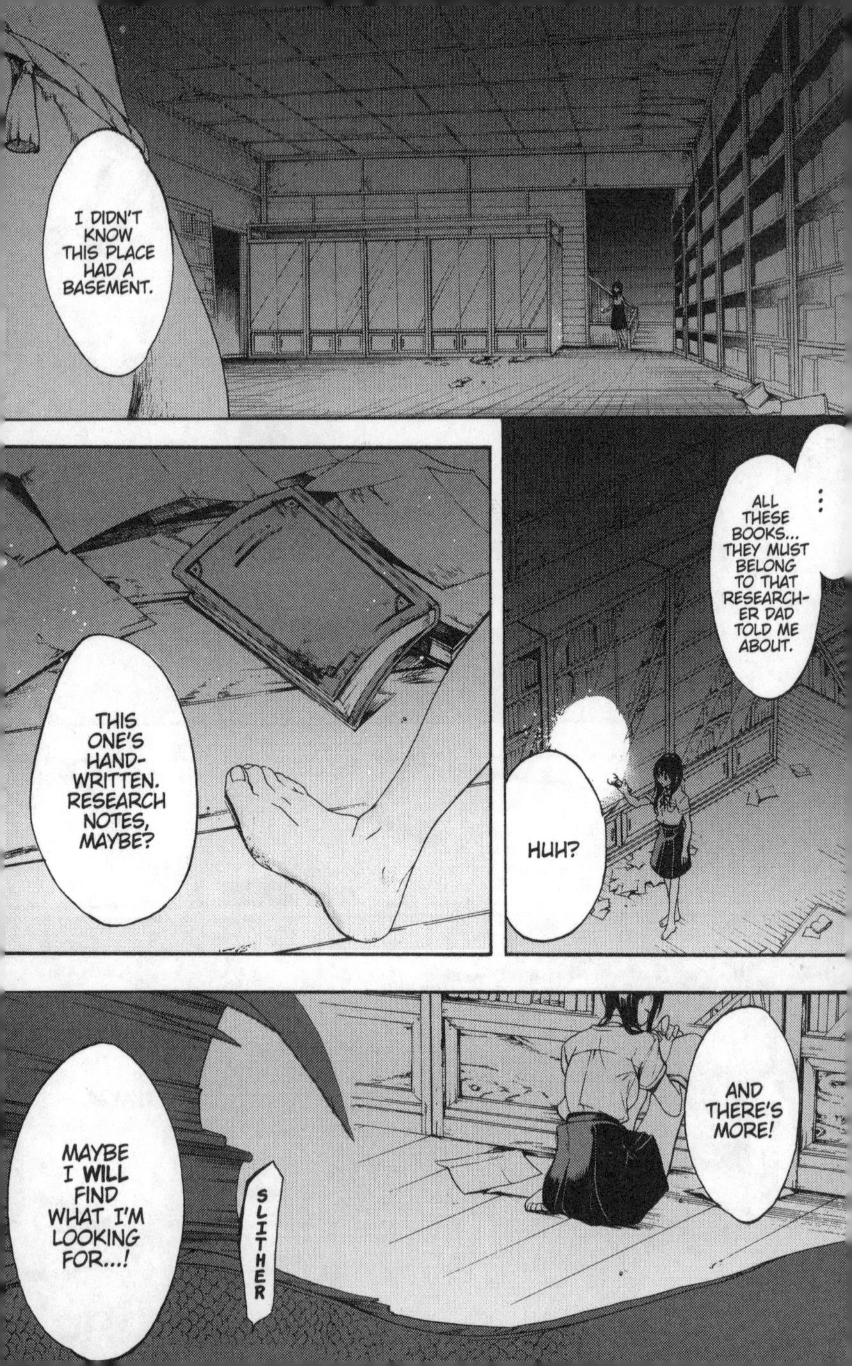
I DIDN'T KNOW THIS PLACE HAD A BASEMENT.
...
ALL THESE BOOKS... THEY MUST BELONG TO THAT RESEARCHER DAD TOLD ME ABOUT.
HUH?
THIS ONE'S HAND-WRITTEN. RESEARCH NOTES, MAYBE?
AND THERE'S MORE!
SLITHER
MAYBE I **WILL** FIND WHAT I'M LOOKING FOR...!

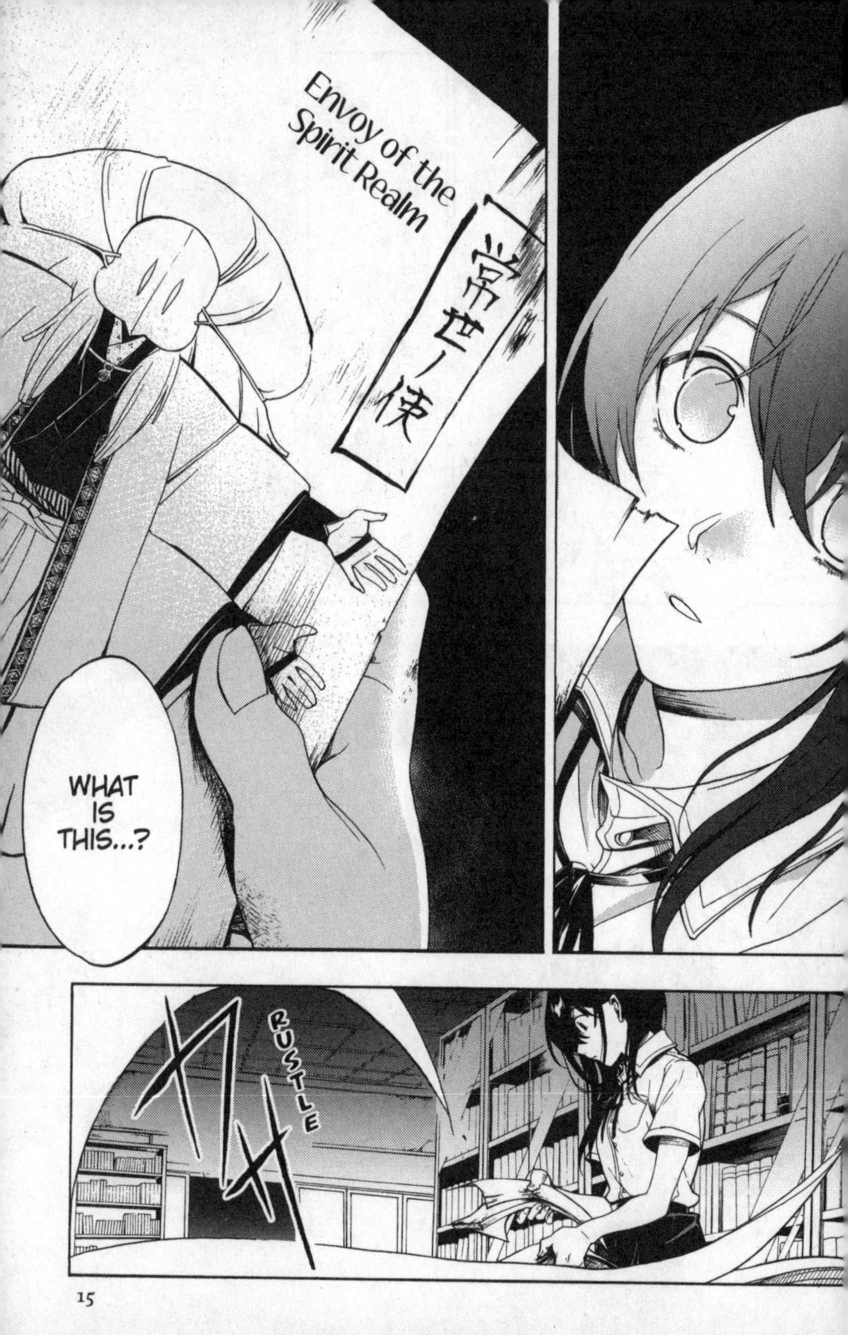
Envoy of the Spirit Realm
常世ノ使
WHAT IS THIS...?
RUSTLE

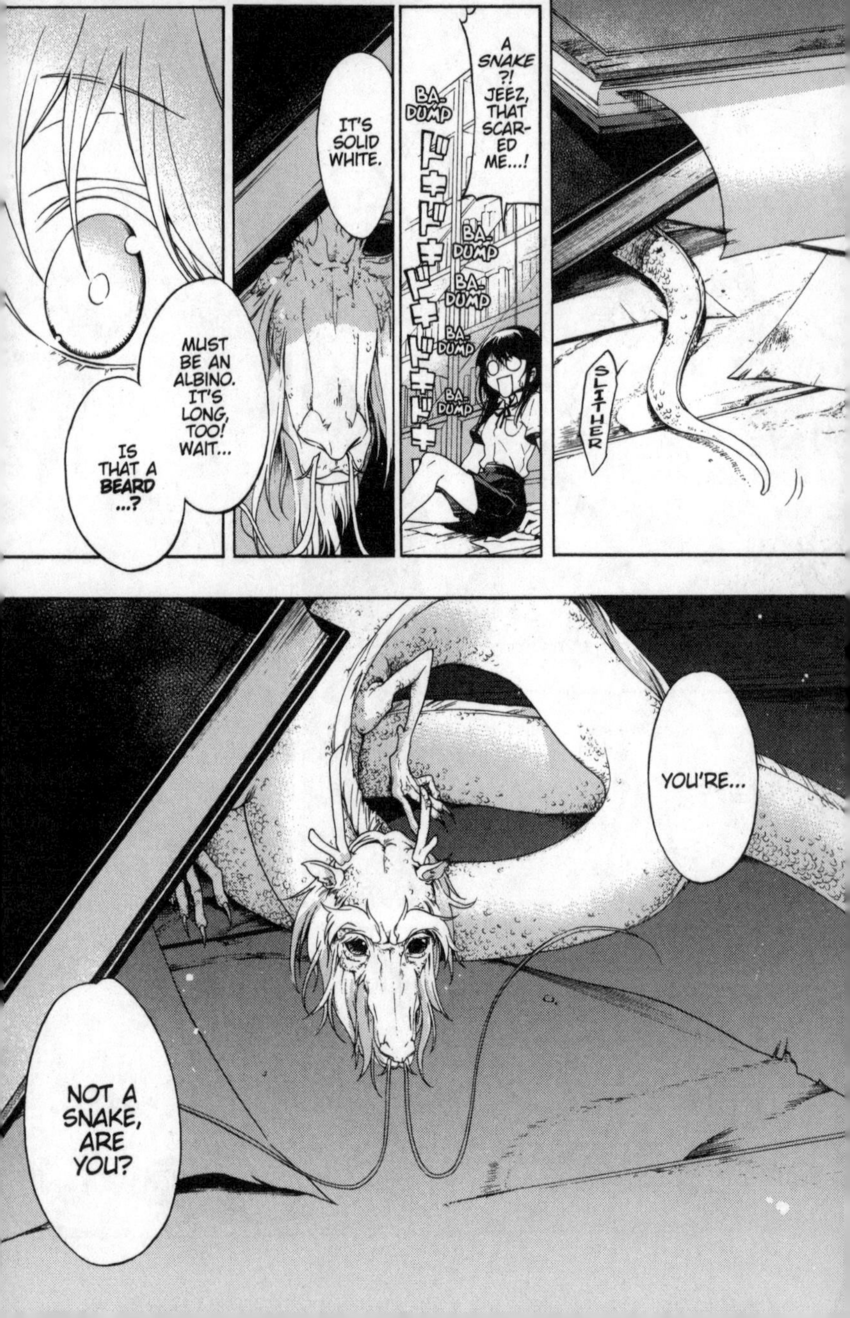
SLITHER
A SNAKE?! JEEZ, THAT SCARED ME...!
BA-DUMP
ドキドキドキドキ
BA-DUMP
BA-DUMP
BA-DUMP
BA-DUMP
IT'S SOLID WHITE.
MUST BE AN ALBINO. IT'S LONG, TOO! WAIT...
IS THAT A BEARD...?
YOU'RE...
NOT A SNAKE, ARE YOU?

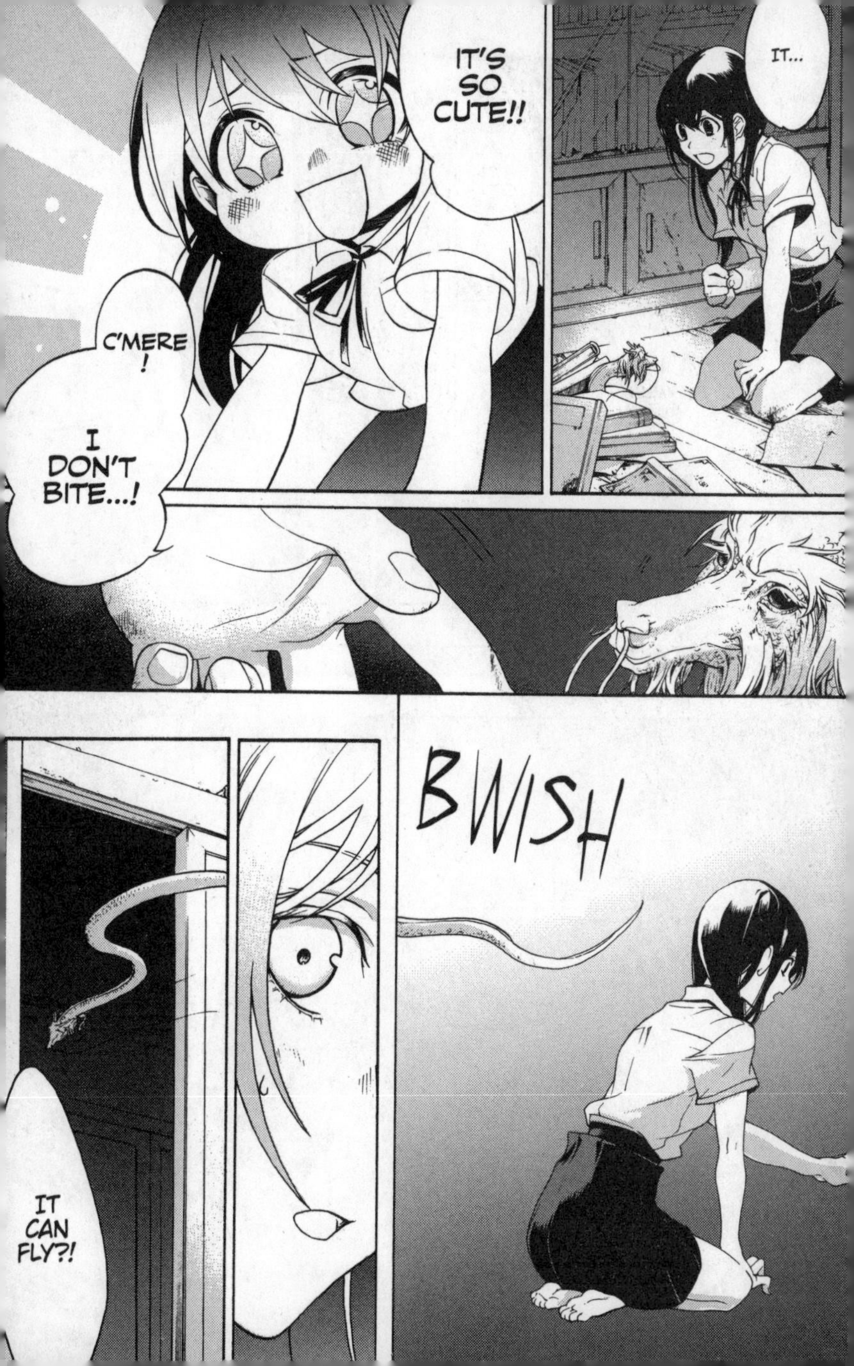
IT...
IT'S SO CUTE!!
C'MERE!
I DON'T BITE...!
BWISH
IT CAN FLY?!

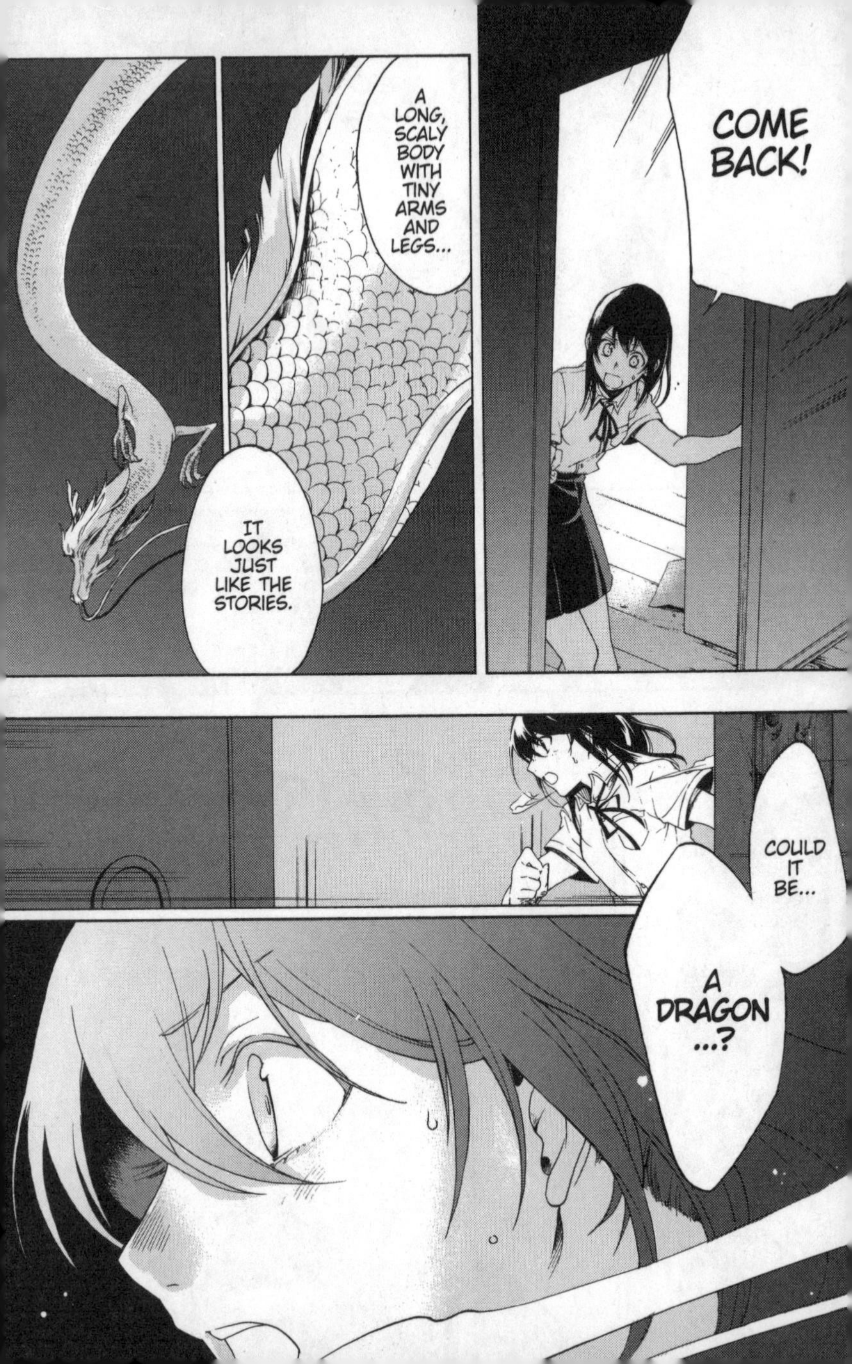
COME BACK!
A LONG, SCALY BODY WITH TINY ARMS AND LEGS...
IT LOOKS JUST LIKE THE STORIES.
COULD IT BE...
A DRAGON ...?

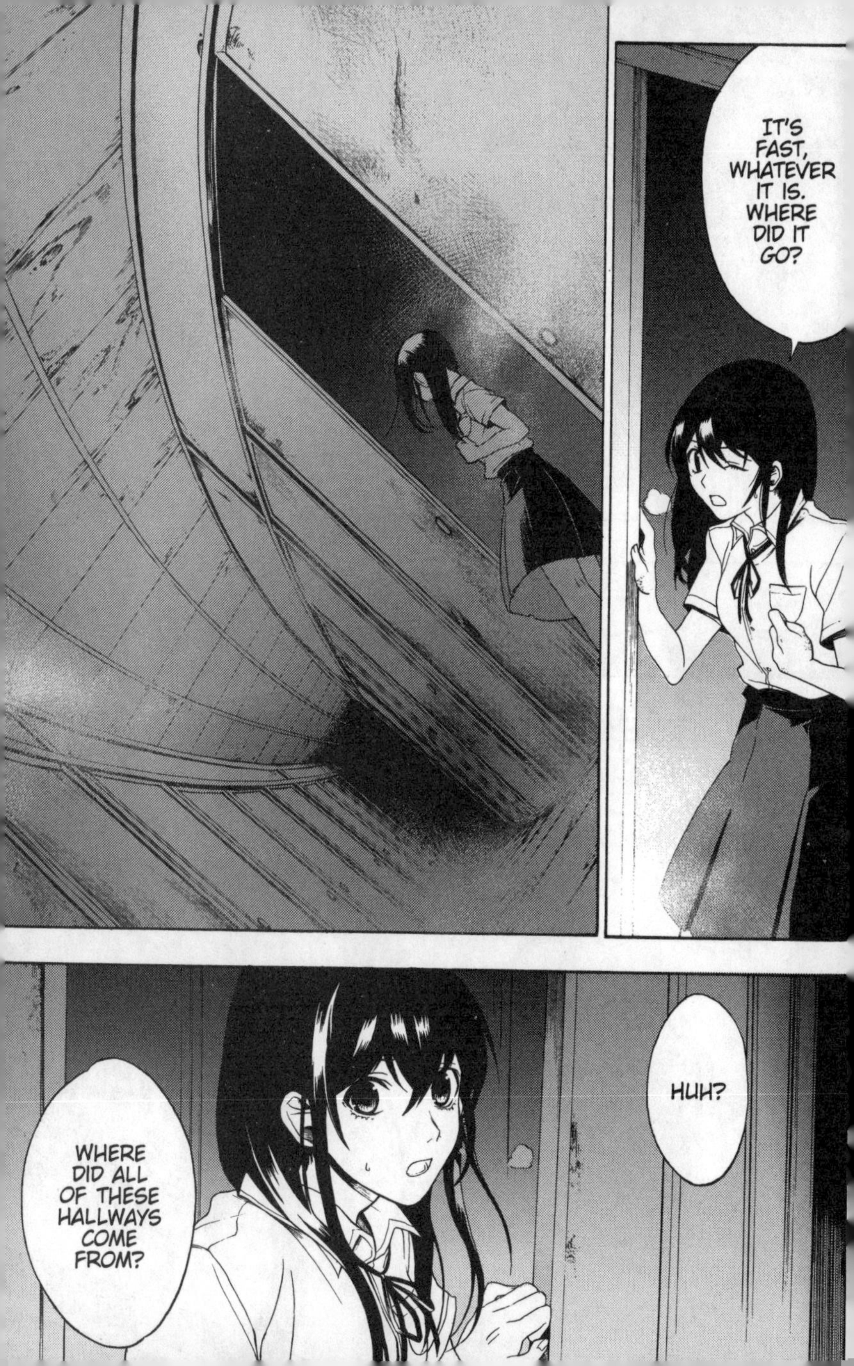
IT'S FAST, WHATEVER IT IS. WHERE DID IT GO?
HUH?
WHERE DID ALL OF THESE HALLWAYS COME FROM?

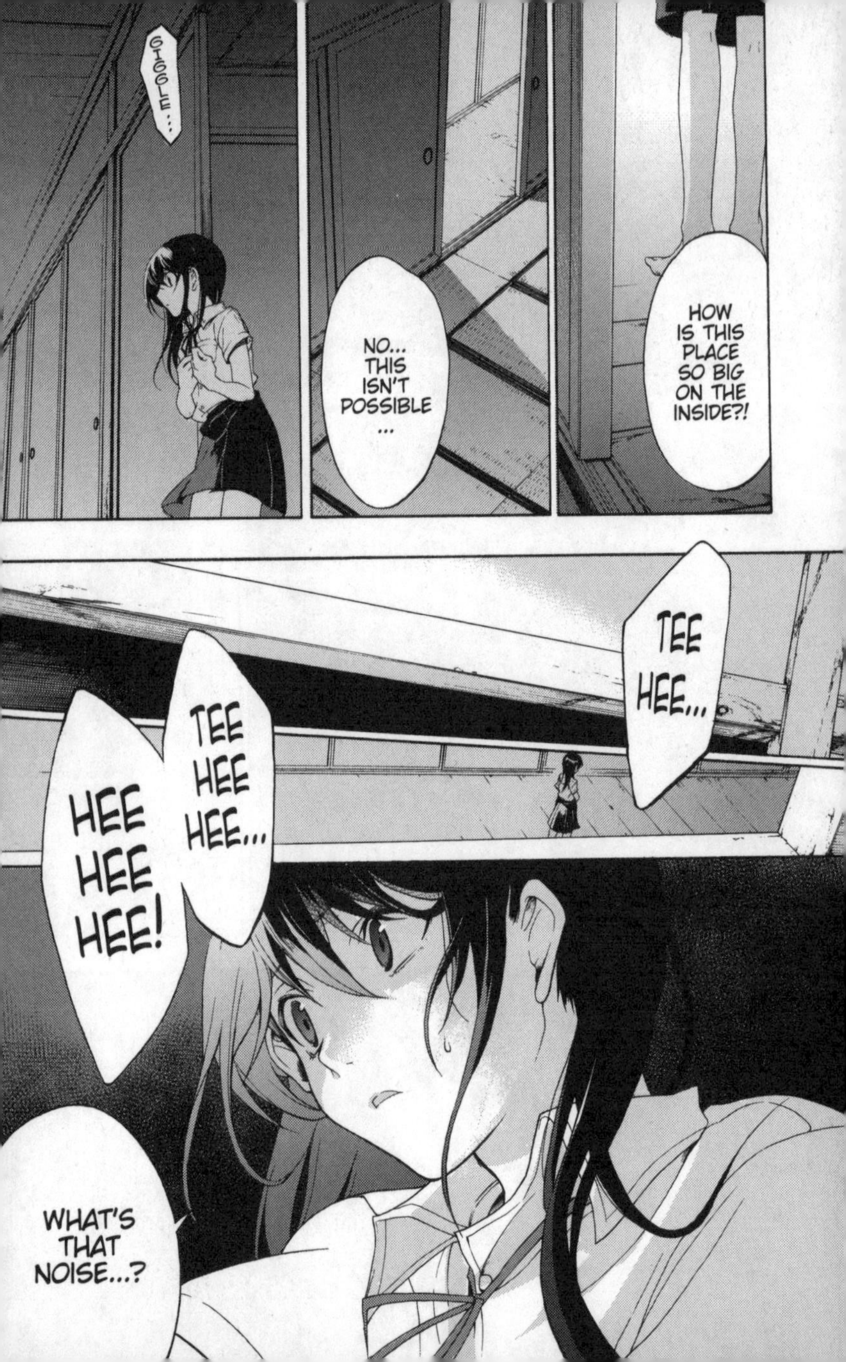
HOW IS THIS PLACE SO BIG ON THE INSIDE?!
NO... THIS ISN'T POSSIBLE ...
GIGGLE...
TEE HEE...
TEE HEE HEE...
HEE HEE HEE!
WHAT'S THAT NOISE...?

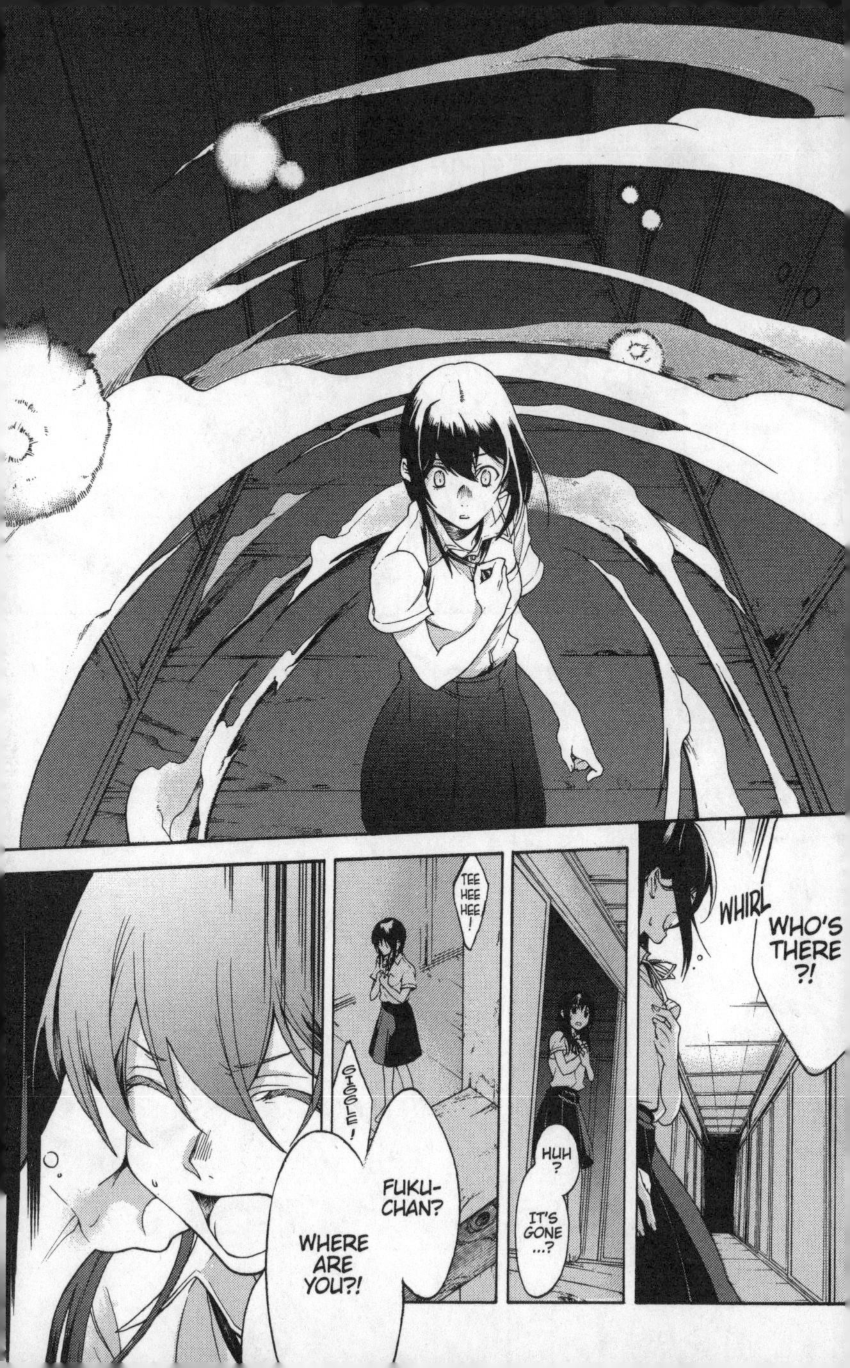
WHIRL
WHO'S THERE?!
HUH?
IT'S GONE...?
TEE HEE HEE!
GIGGLE!
FUKU-CHAN?
WHERE ARE YOU?!

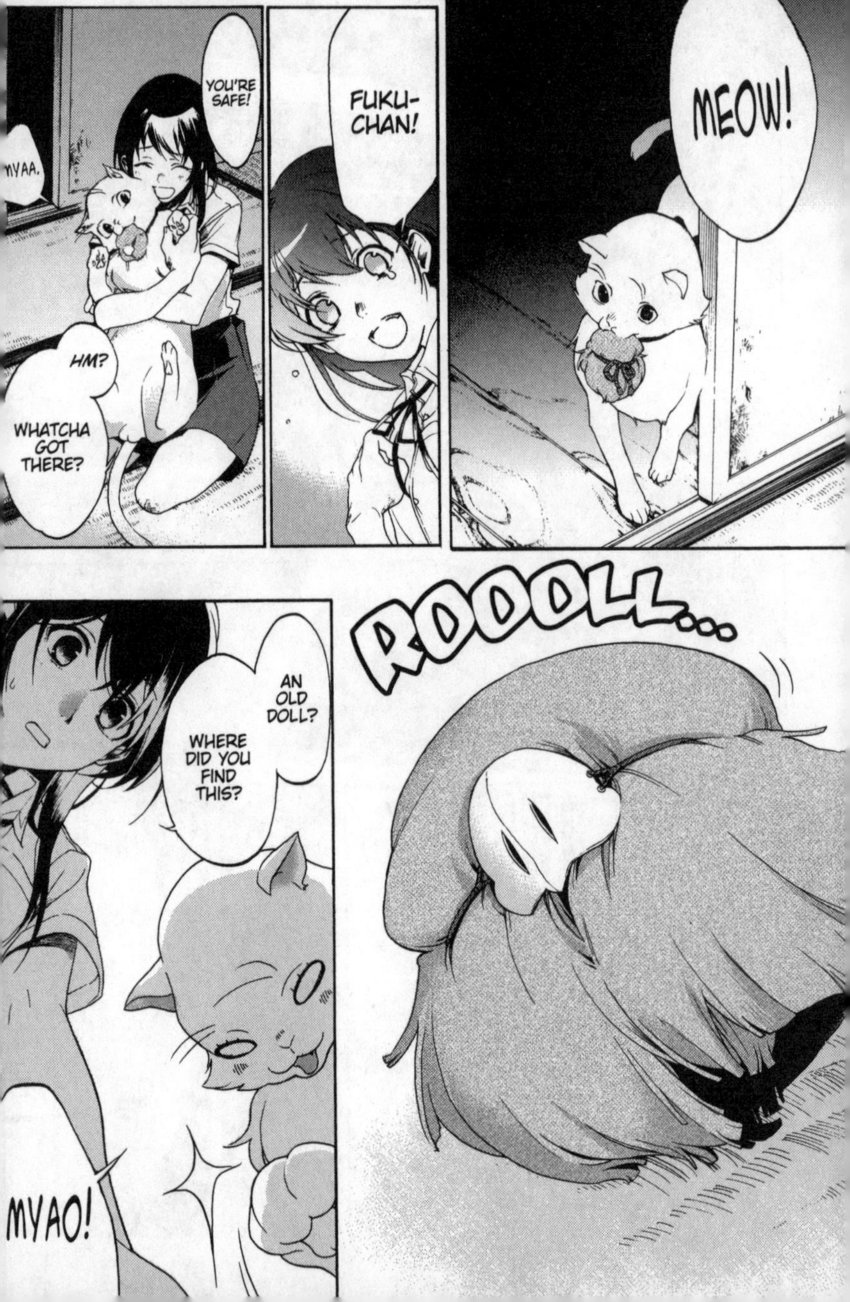
MEOW!
FUKU-CHAN!
YOU'RE SAFE!
MYAA.
HM?
WHATCHA GOT THERE?
ROOOLL...
AN OLD DOLL?
WHERE DID YOU FIND THIS?
MYAO!

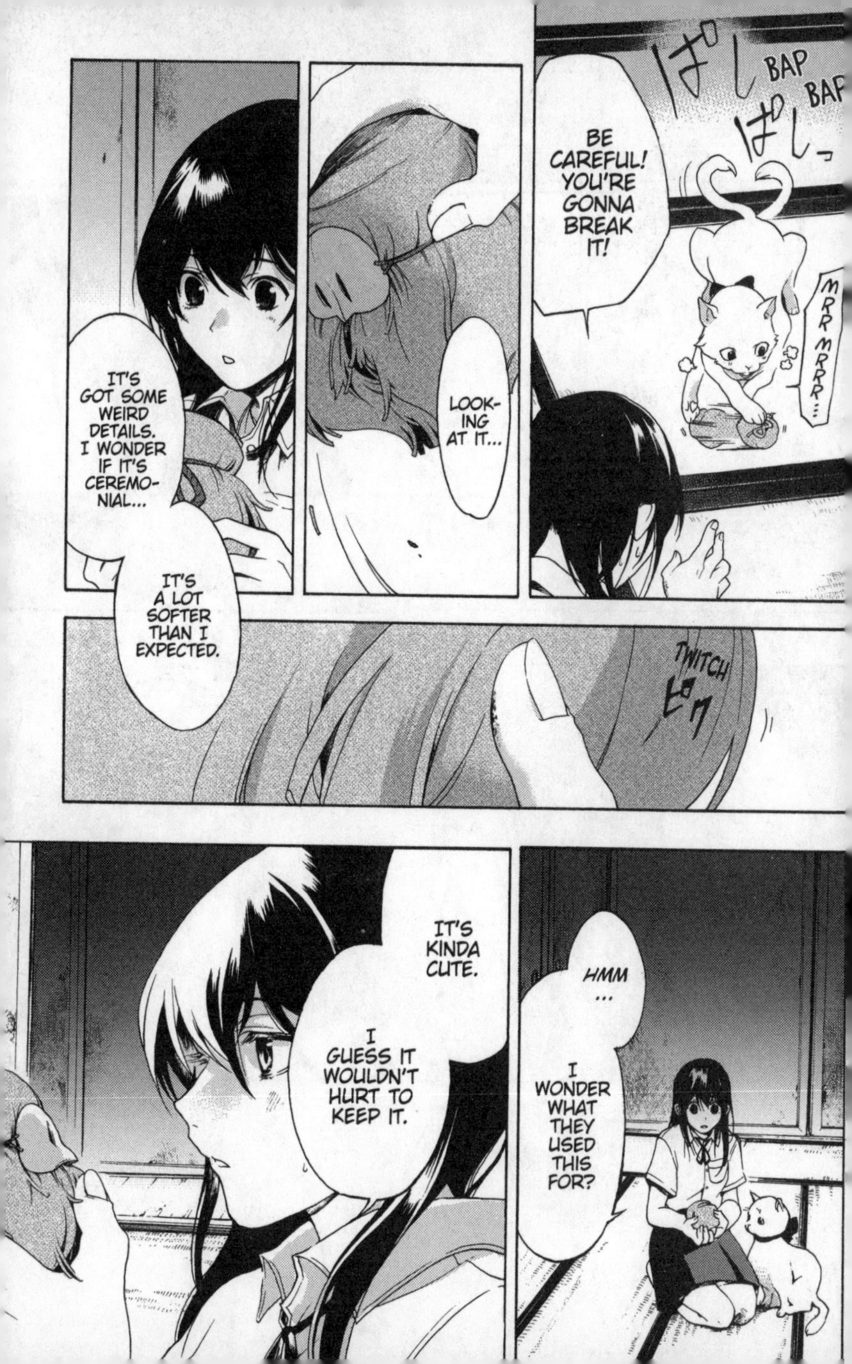
ぱし
BAP
ぱしっ
BAP
BE CAREFUL! YOU'RE GONNA BREAK IT!
MRR MRRR...
LOOKING AT IT...
IT'S GOT SOME WEIRD DETAILS. I WONDER IF IT'S CEREMONIAL...
IT'S A LOT SOFTER THAN I EXPECTED.
TWITCH
ピク
HMM...
I WONDER WHAT THEY USED THIS FOR?
IT'S KINDA CUTE.
I GUESS IT WOULDN'T HURT TO KEEP IT.

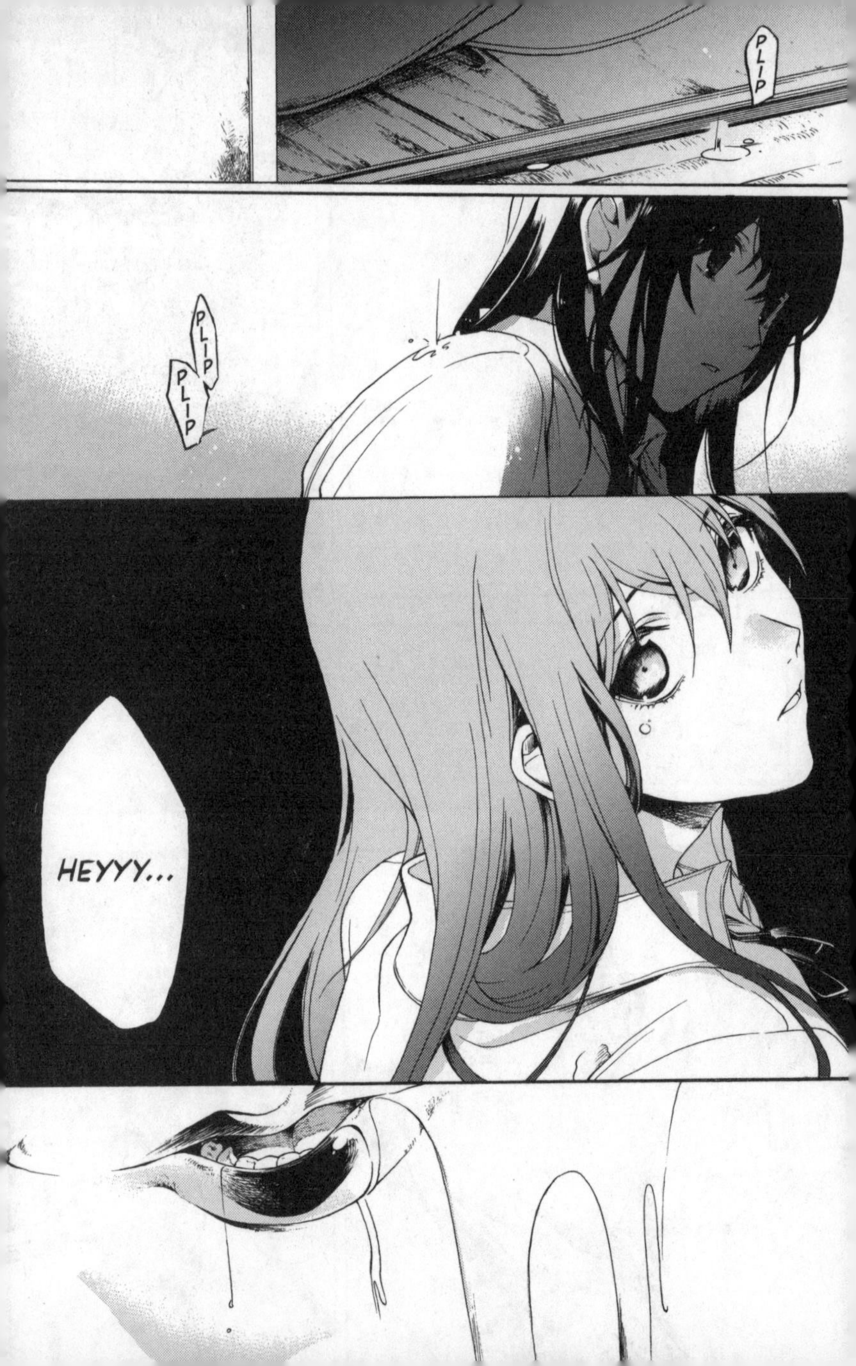
PLIP
PLIP
PLIP
HEYYY...

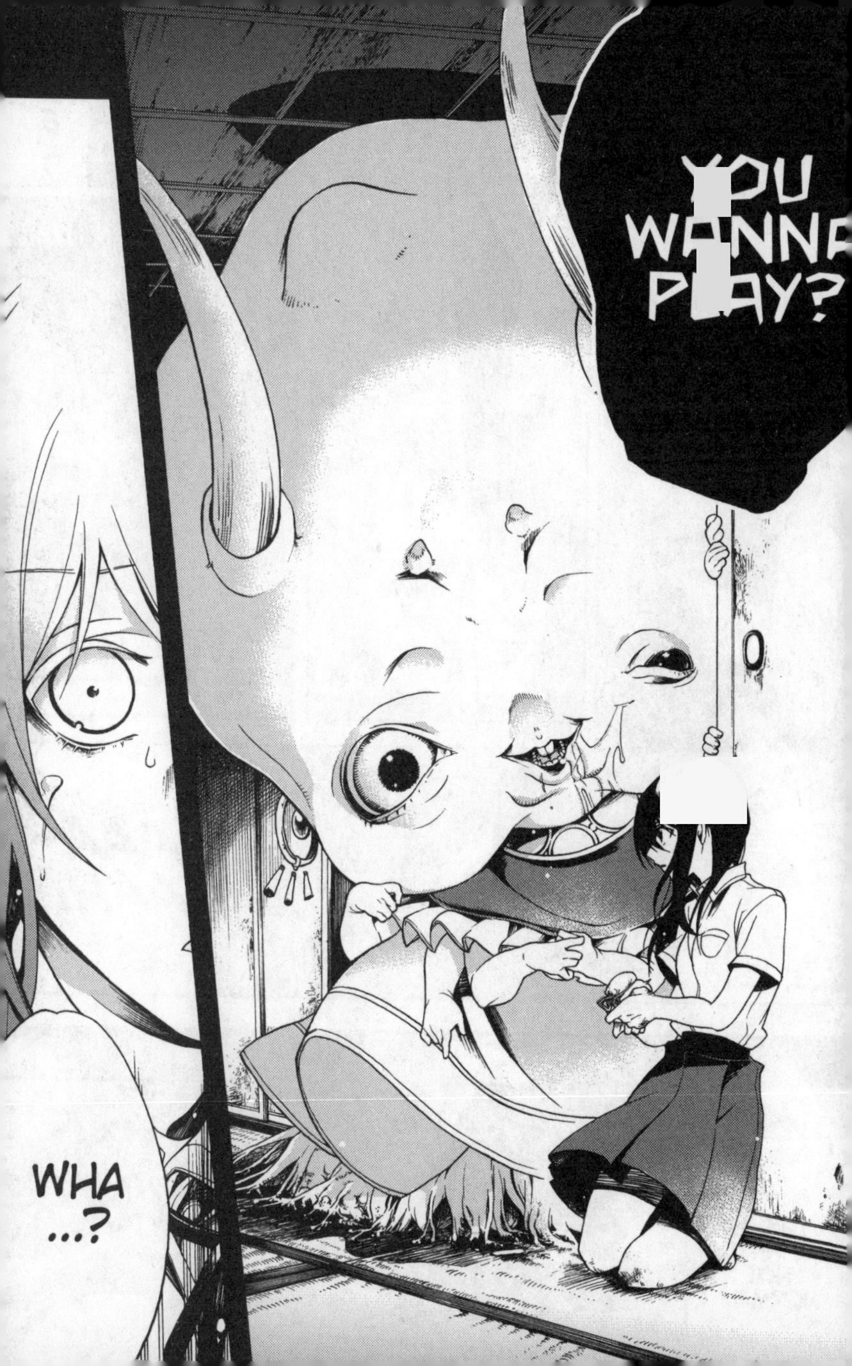
YOU WANNA PLAY?
WHA ...?

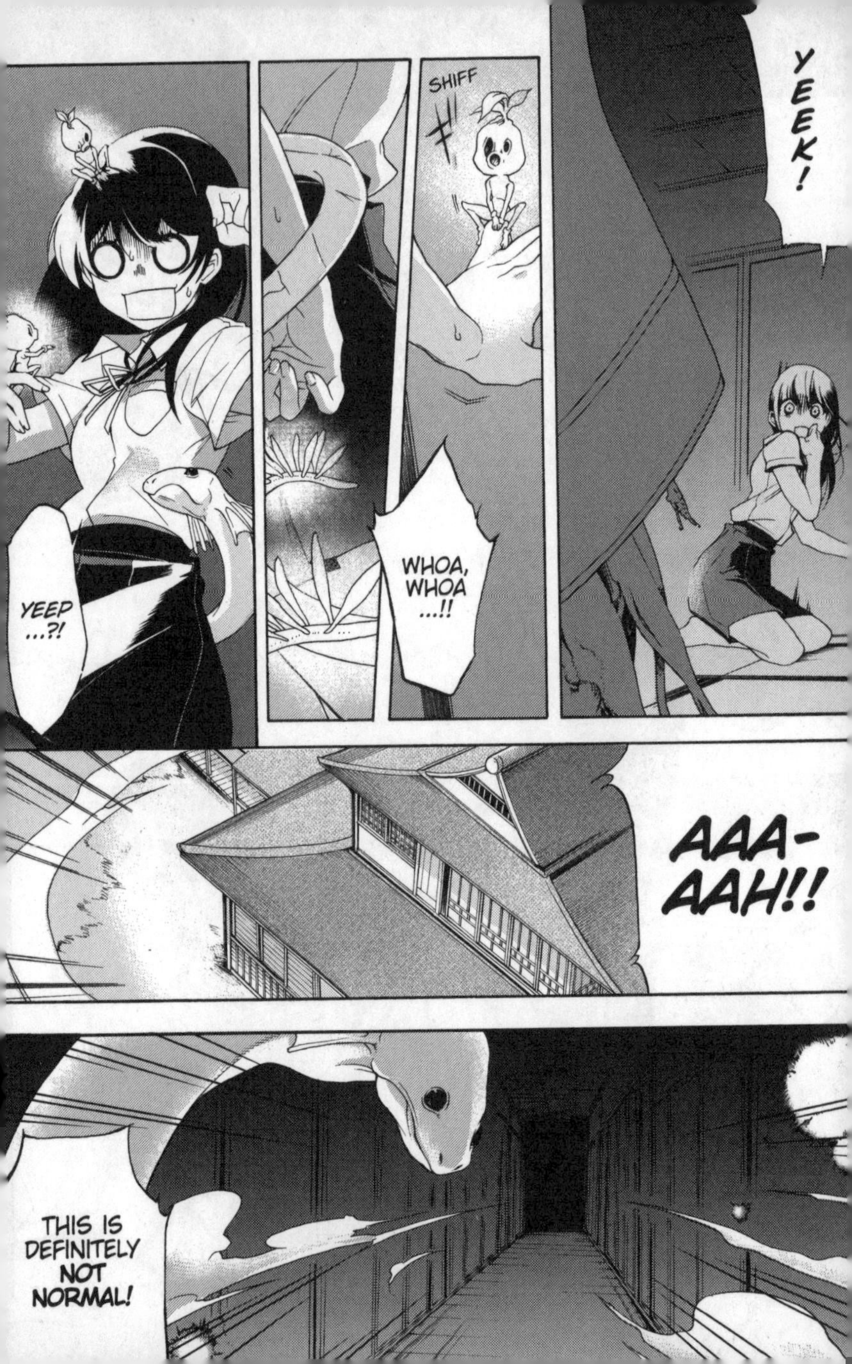

YEEK!
SHIFF
WHOA, WHOA ...!!
YEEP ...?!
AAA-AAH!!
THIS IS DEFINITELY NOT NORMAL!

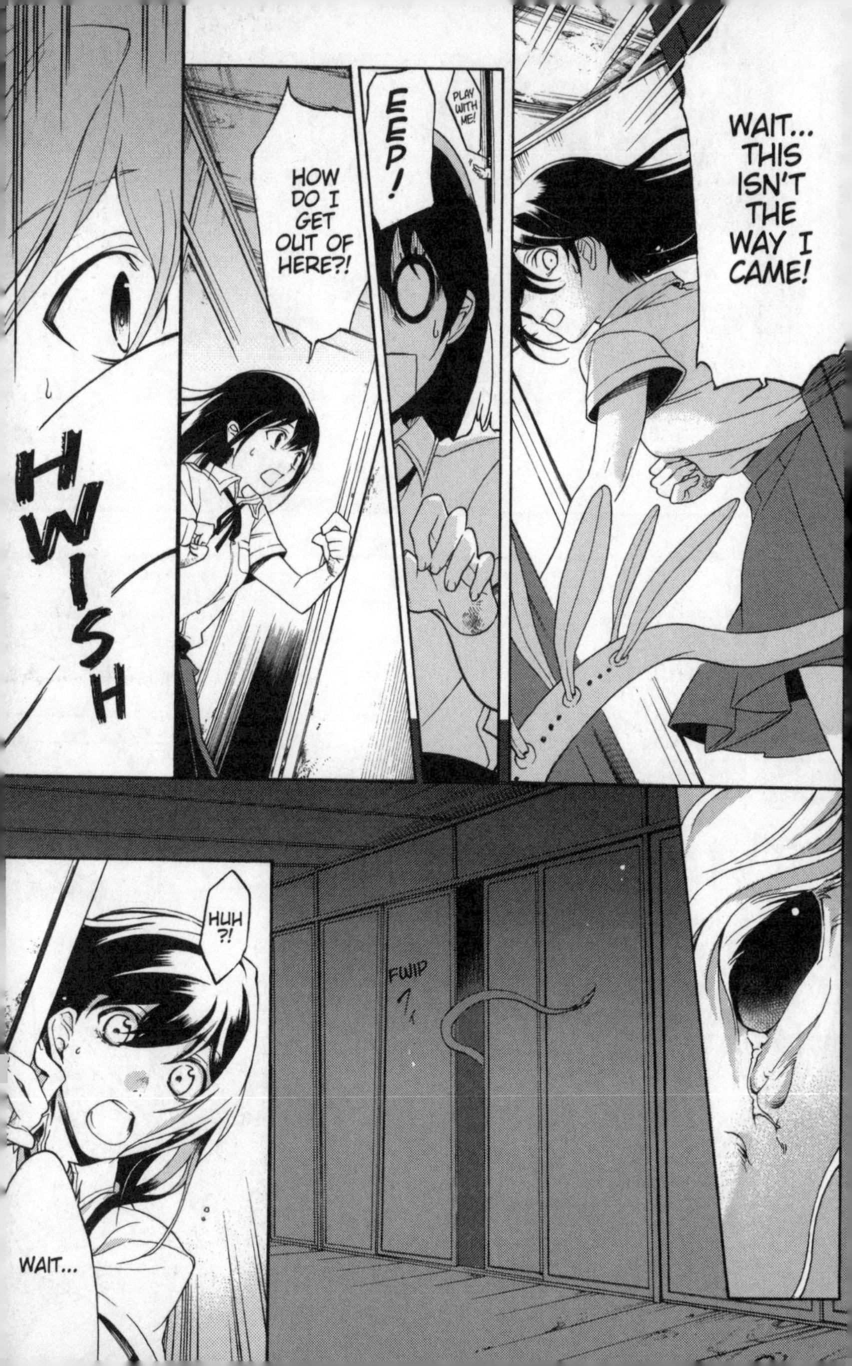
WAIT... THIS ISN'T THE WAY I CAME!
PLAY WITH ME!
EEP!
HOW DO I GET OUT OF HERE?!
HWISH
FWIP
HUH?!
WAIT...

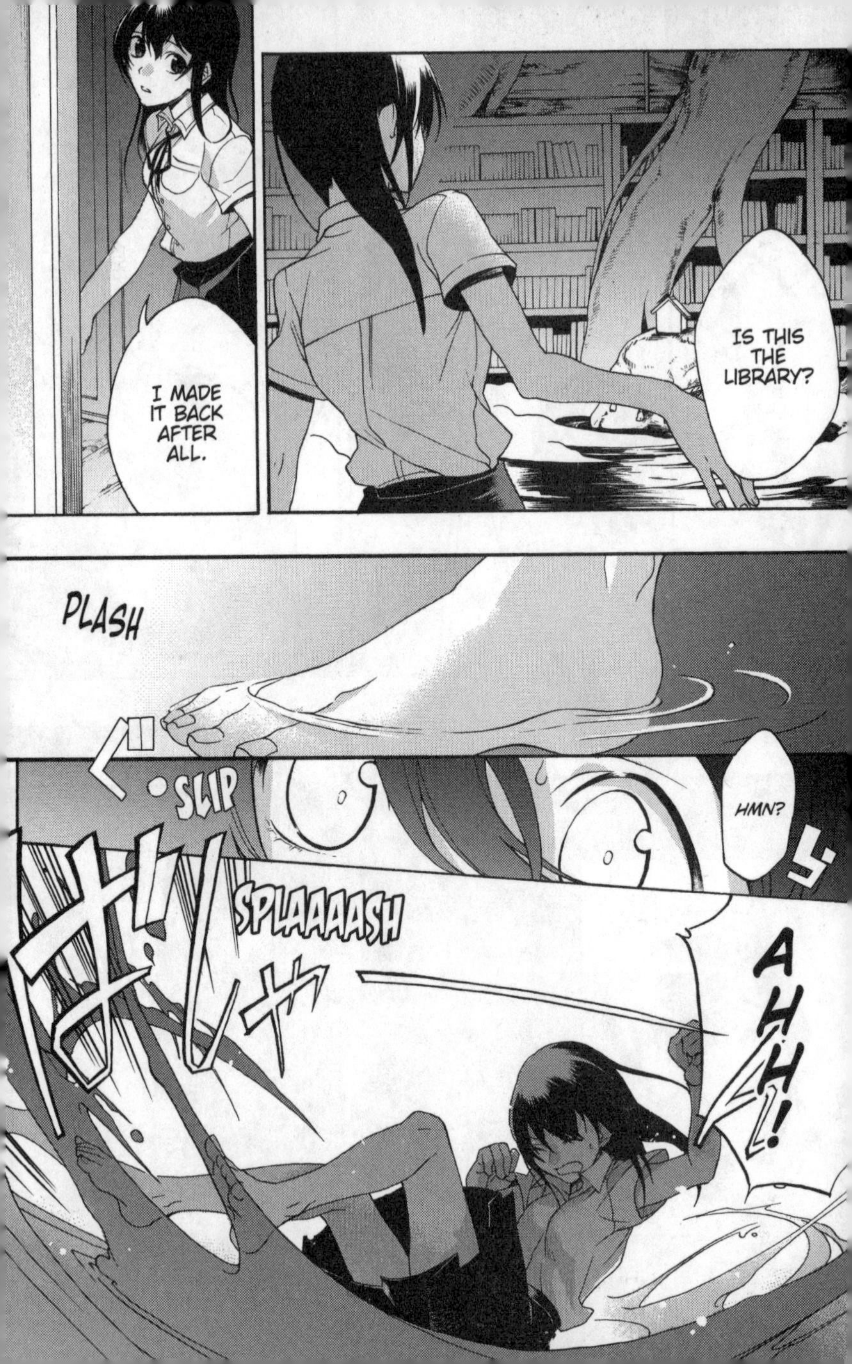
IS THIS THE LIBRARY?
I MADE IT BACK AFTER ALL.
PLASH
HMN?
SLIP
AHH!
SPLAAAASH

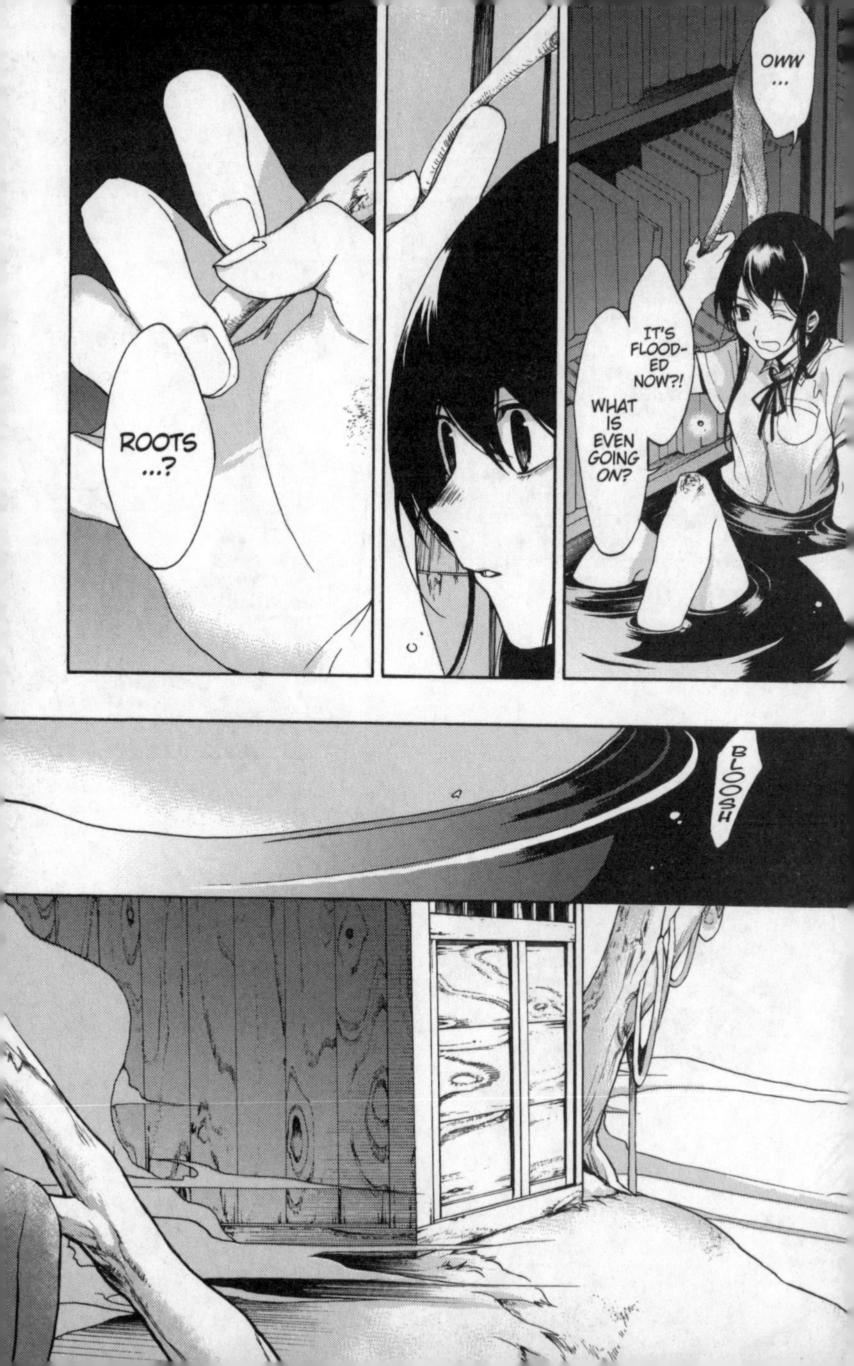
OWW ...
IT'S FLOOD-ED NOW?!
WHAT IS EVEN GOING ON?
ROOTS ...?
BLOOSH

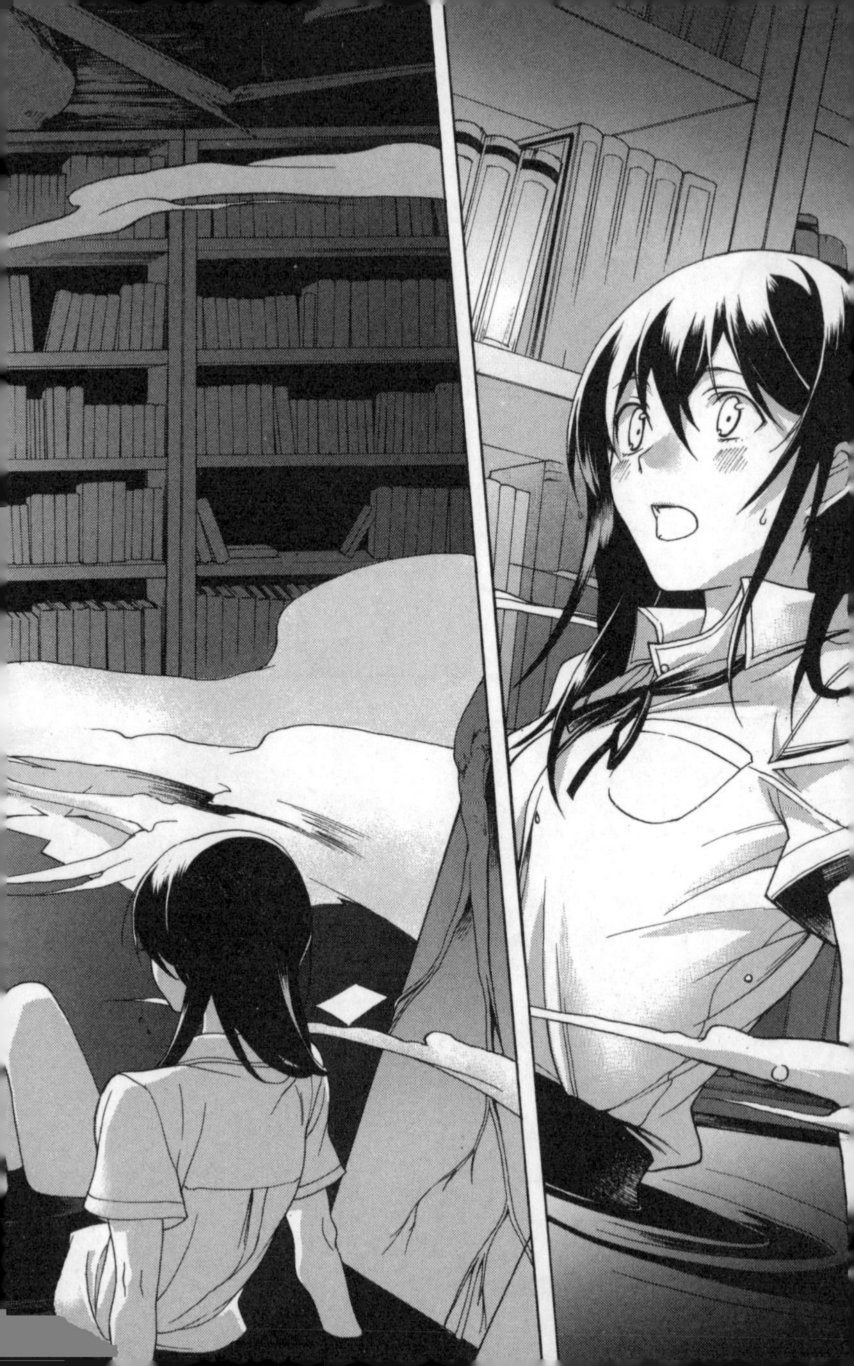

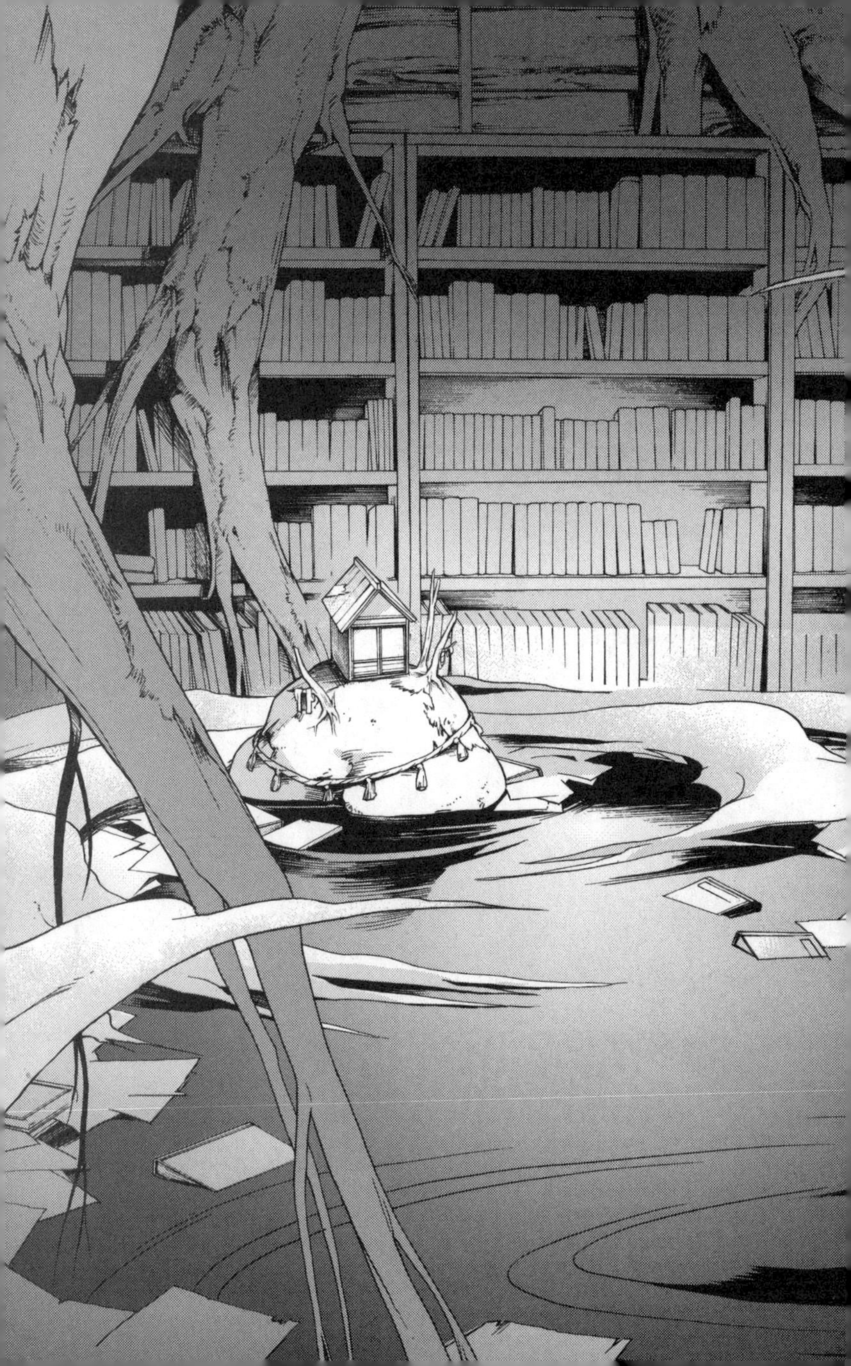

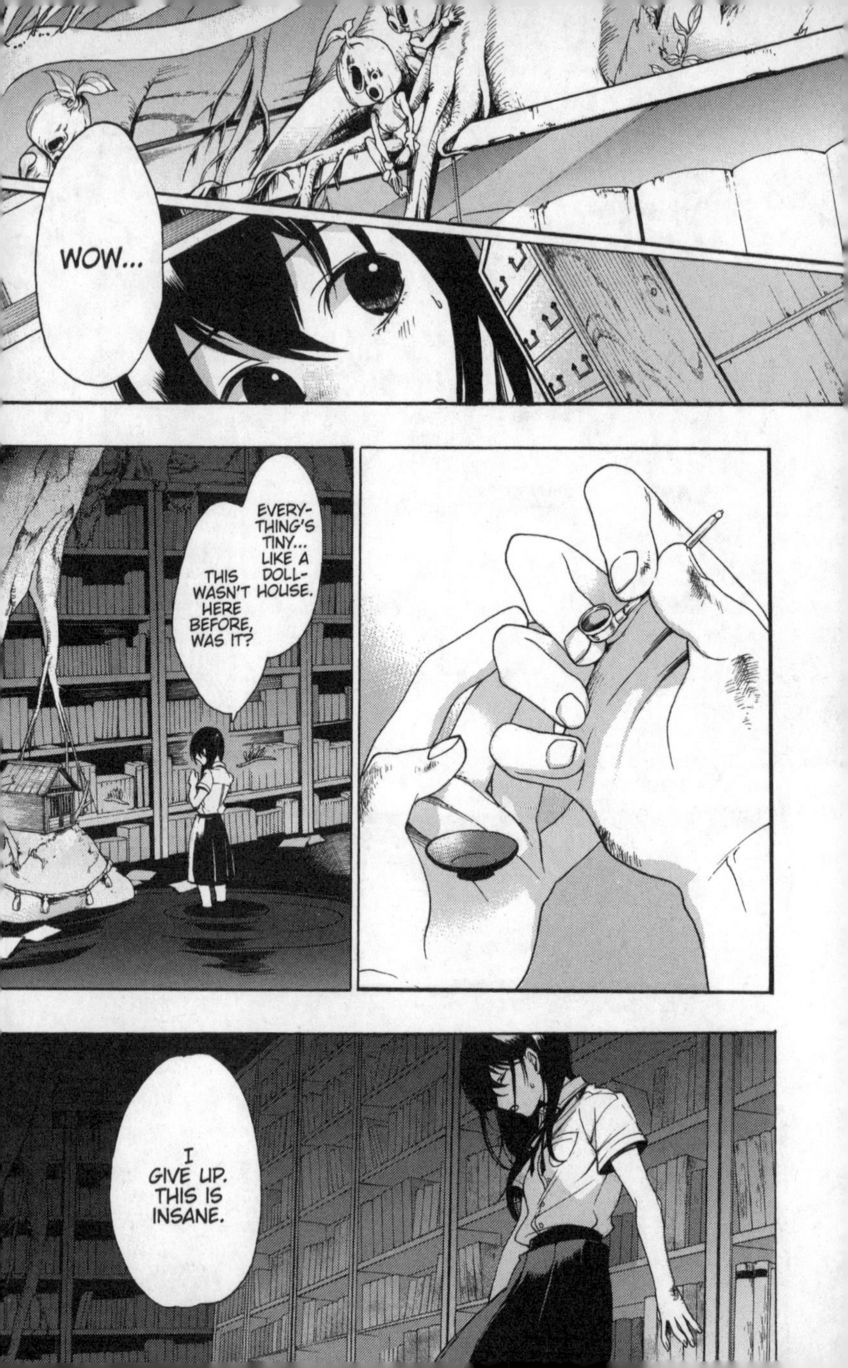
WOW...
EVERYTHING'S TINY... LIKE A DOLL-HOUSE.
THIS WASN'T HERE BEFORE, WAS IT?
I GIVE UP. THIS IS INSANE.

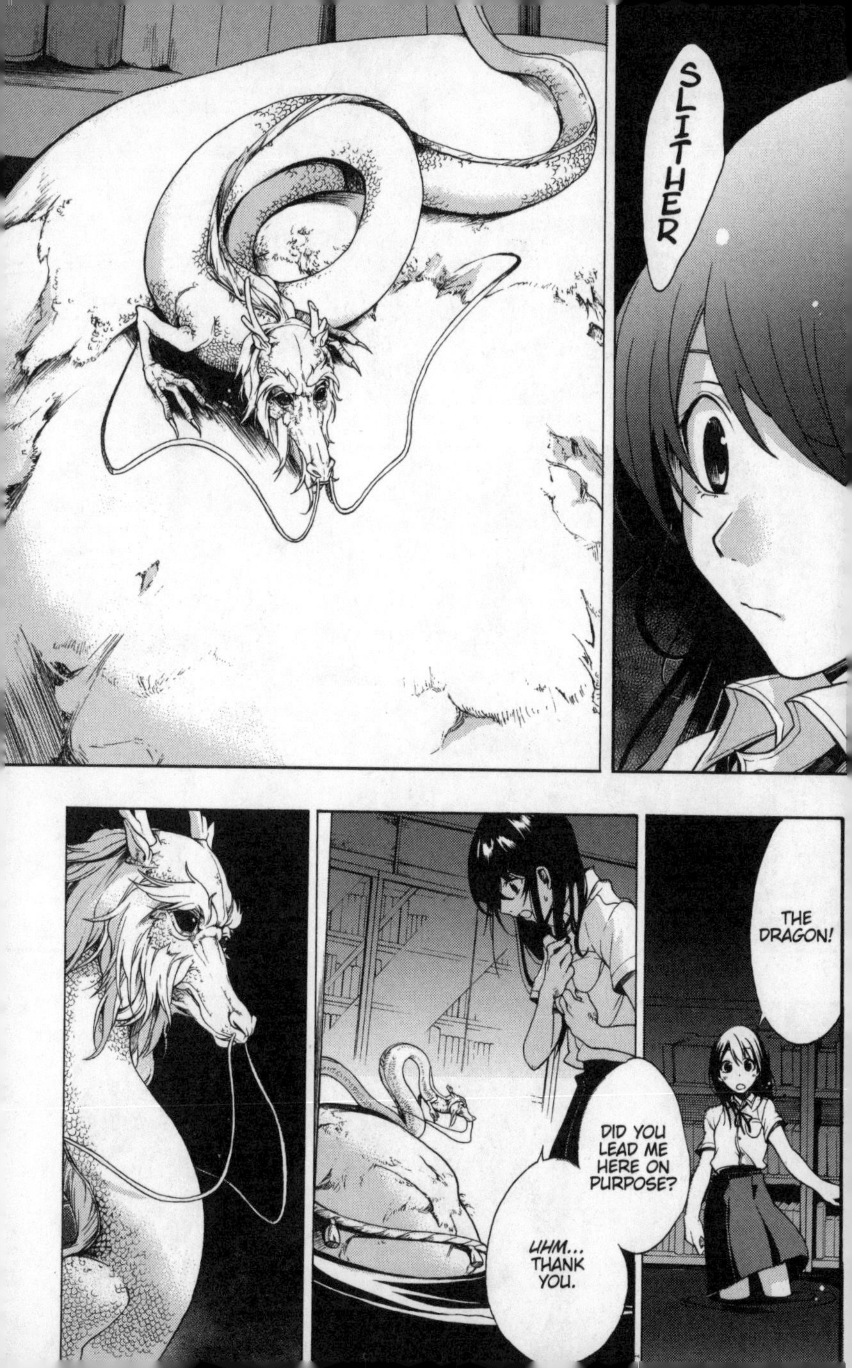
SLITHER
THE DRAGON!
DID YOU LEAD ME HERE ON PURPOSE?
UHM... THANK YOU.

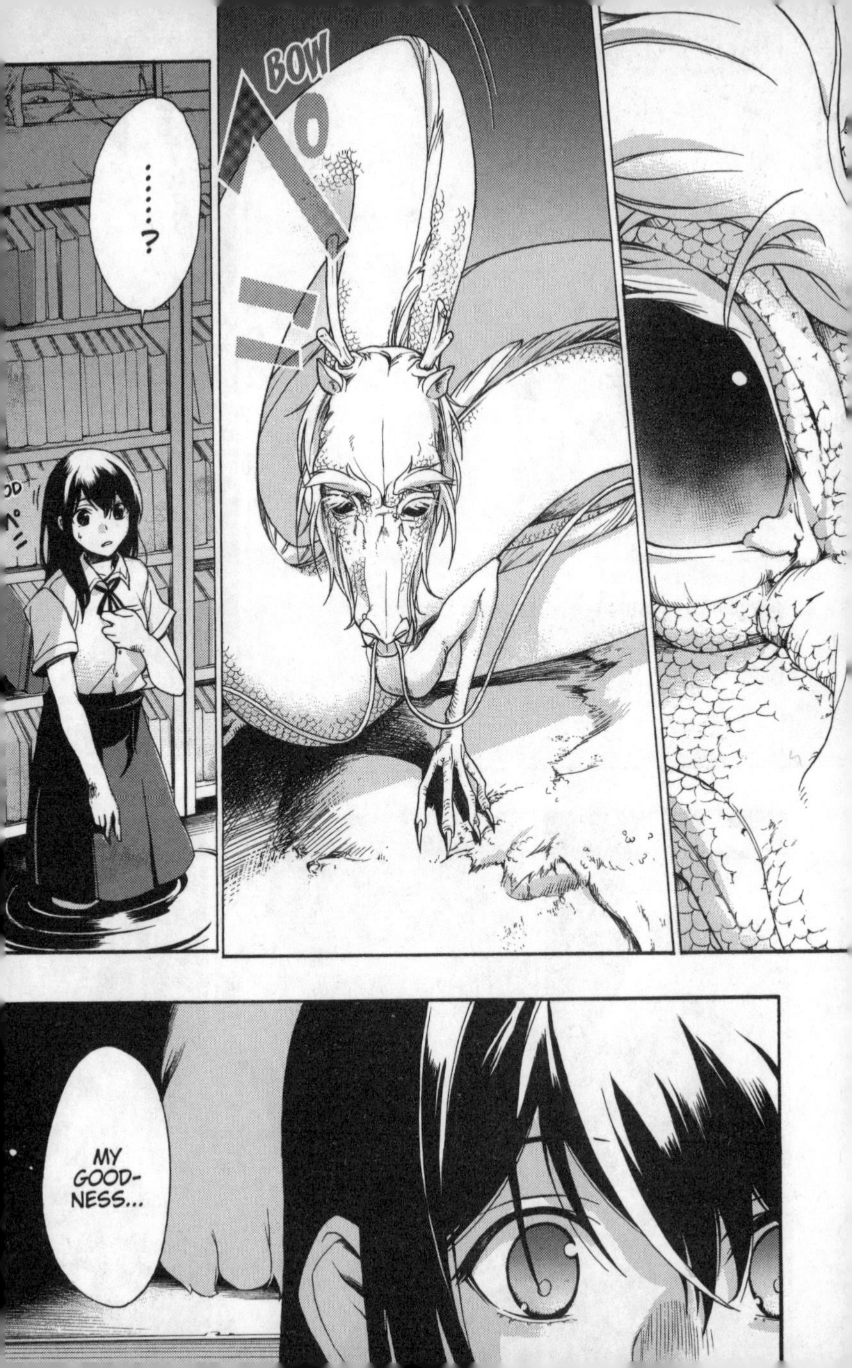
BOW
......?
MY GOOD-NESS...

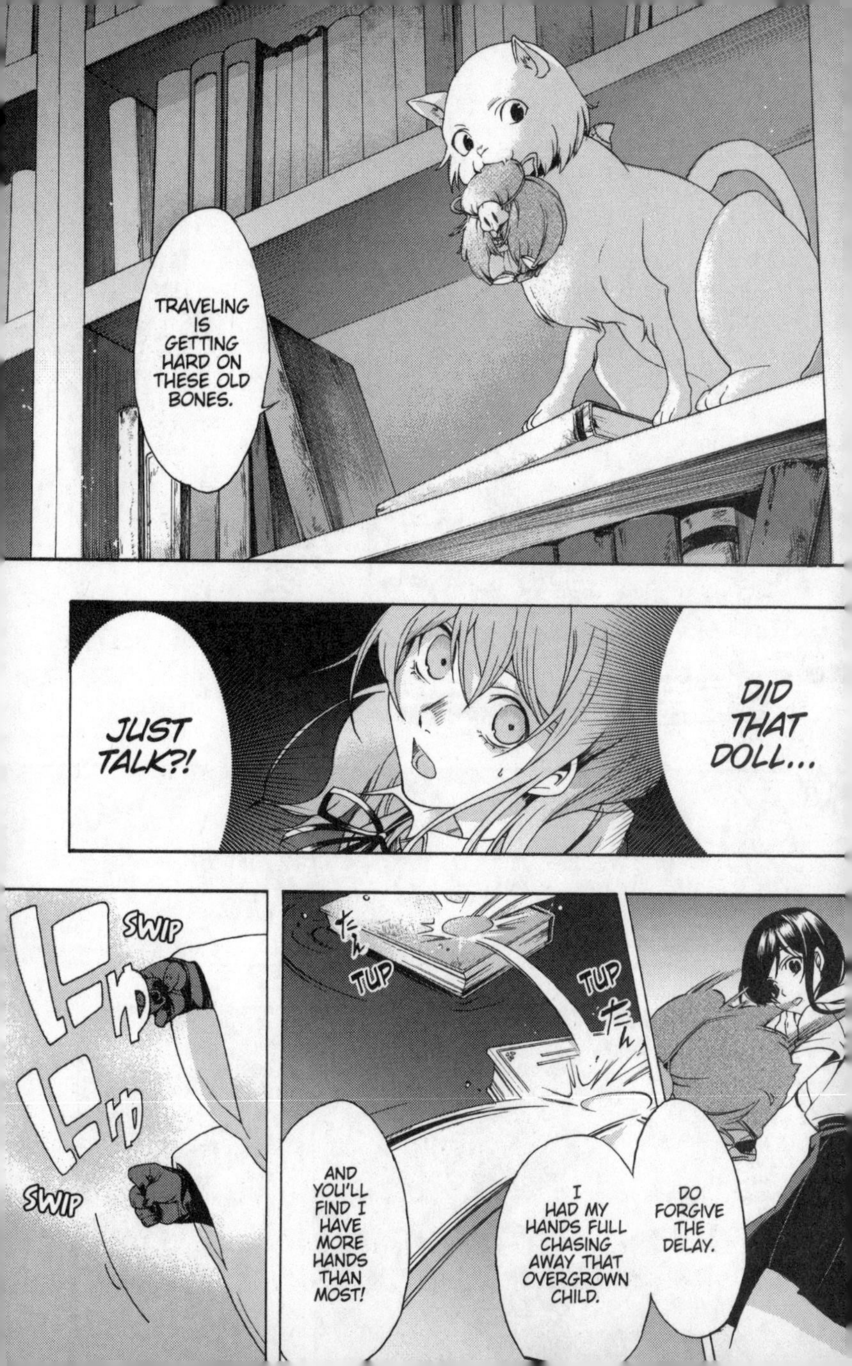
TRAVELING IS GETTING HARD ON THESE OLD BONES.
DID THAT DOLL...
JUST TALK?!
TUP
たん
TUP
たん
DO FORGIVE THE DELAY.
I HAD MY HANDS FULL CHASING AWAY THAT OVERGROWN CHILD.
AND YOU'LL FIND I HAVE MORE HANDS THAN MOST!
SWIP
にゅ
にゅ
SWIP

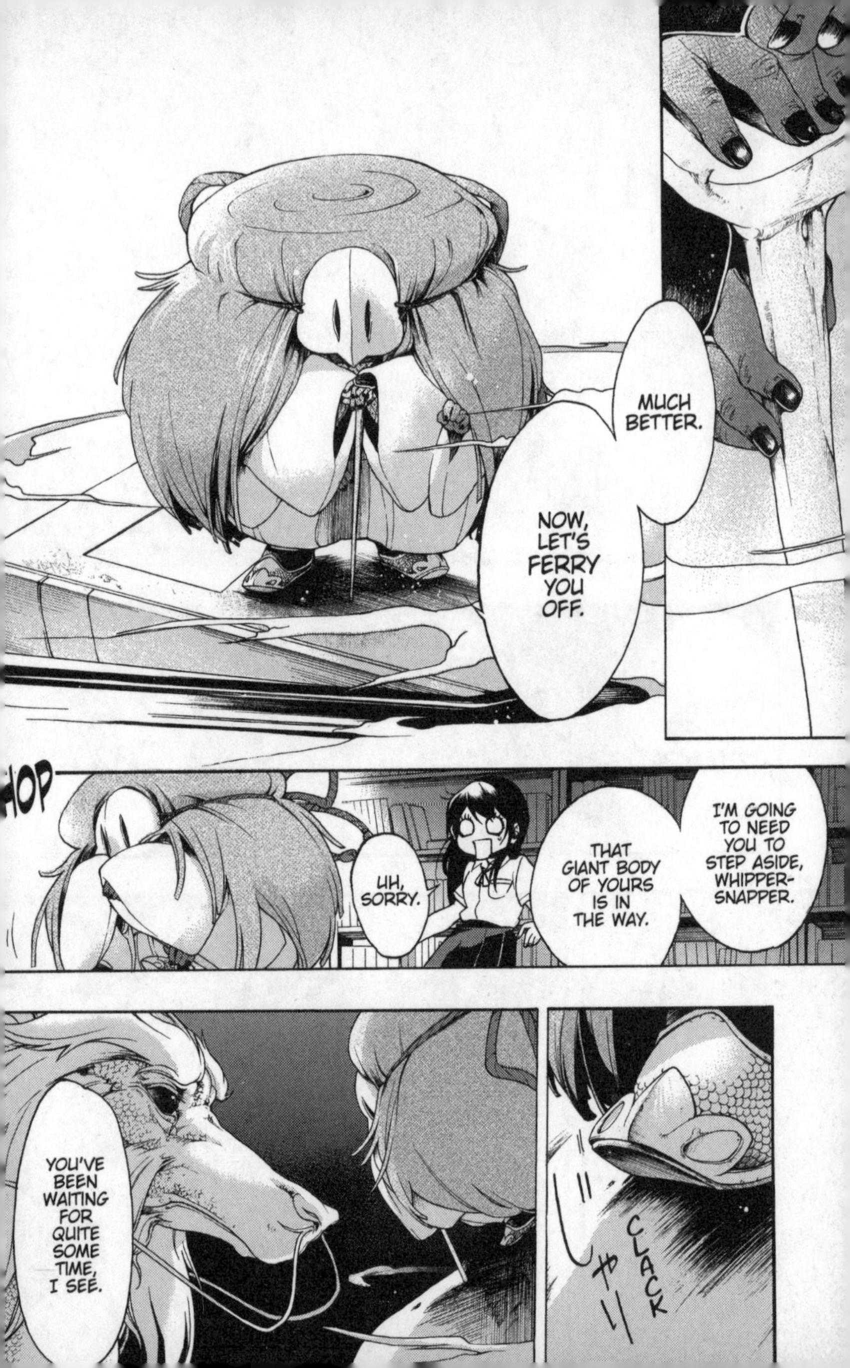
MUCH BETTER.
NOW, LET'S FERRY YOU OFF.
HOP
I'M GOING TO NEED YOU TO STEP ASIDE, WHIPPER-SNAPPER.
THAT GIANT BODY OF YOURS IS IN THE WAY.
UH, SORRY.
CLACK
YOU'VE BEEN WAITING FOR QUITE SOME TIME, I SEE.

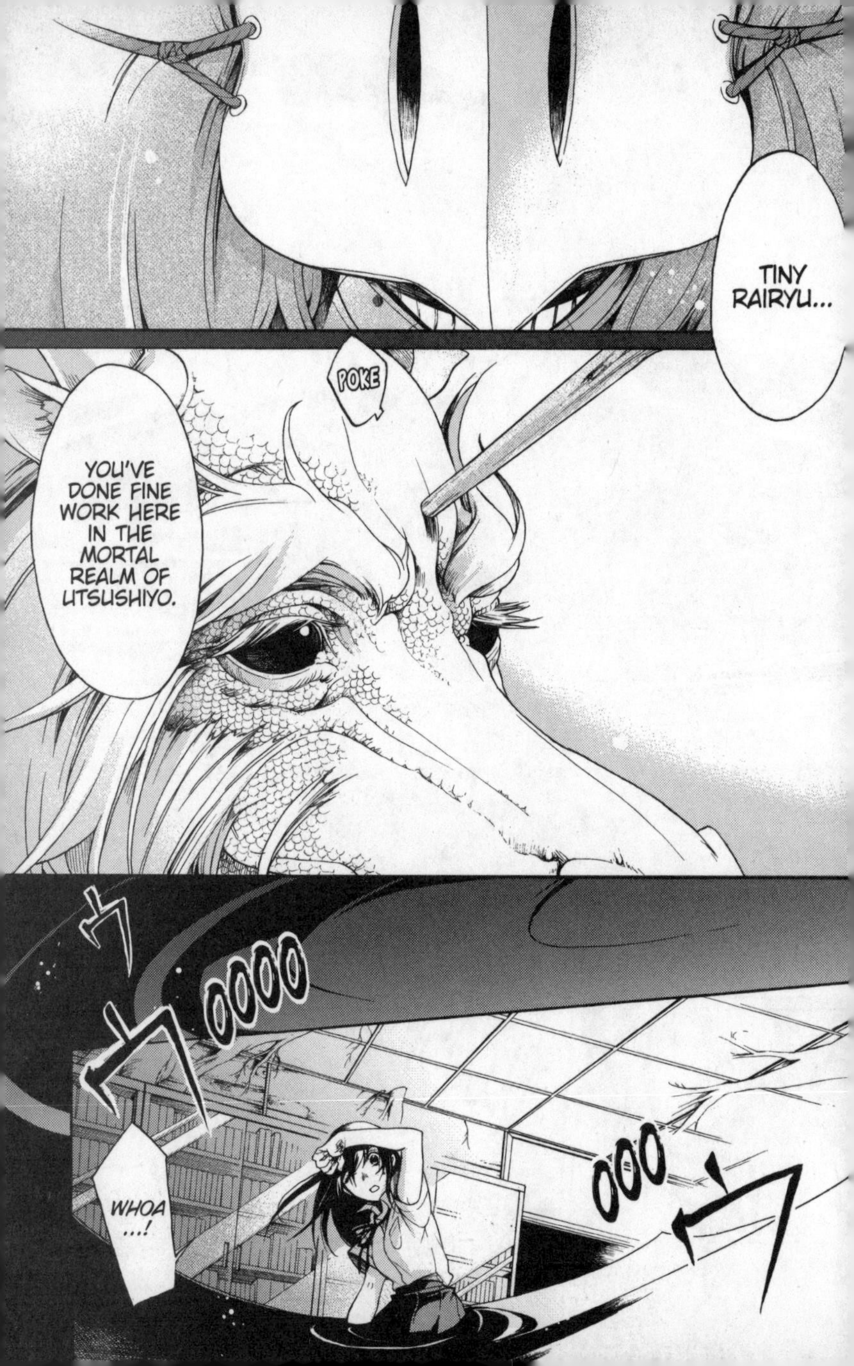
TINY RAIRYU...
POKE
YOU'VE DONE FINE WORK HERE IN THE MORTAL REALM OF UTSUSHIYO.
DOOO
DOOOO
WHOA ...!

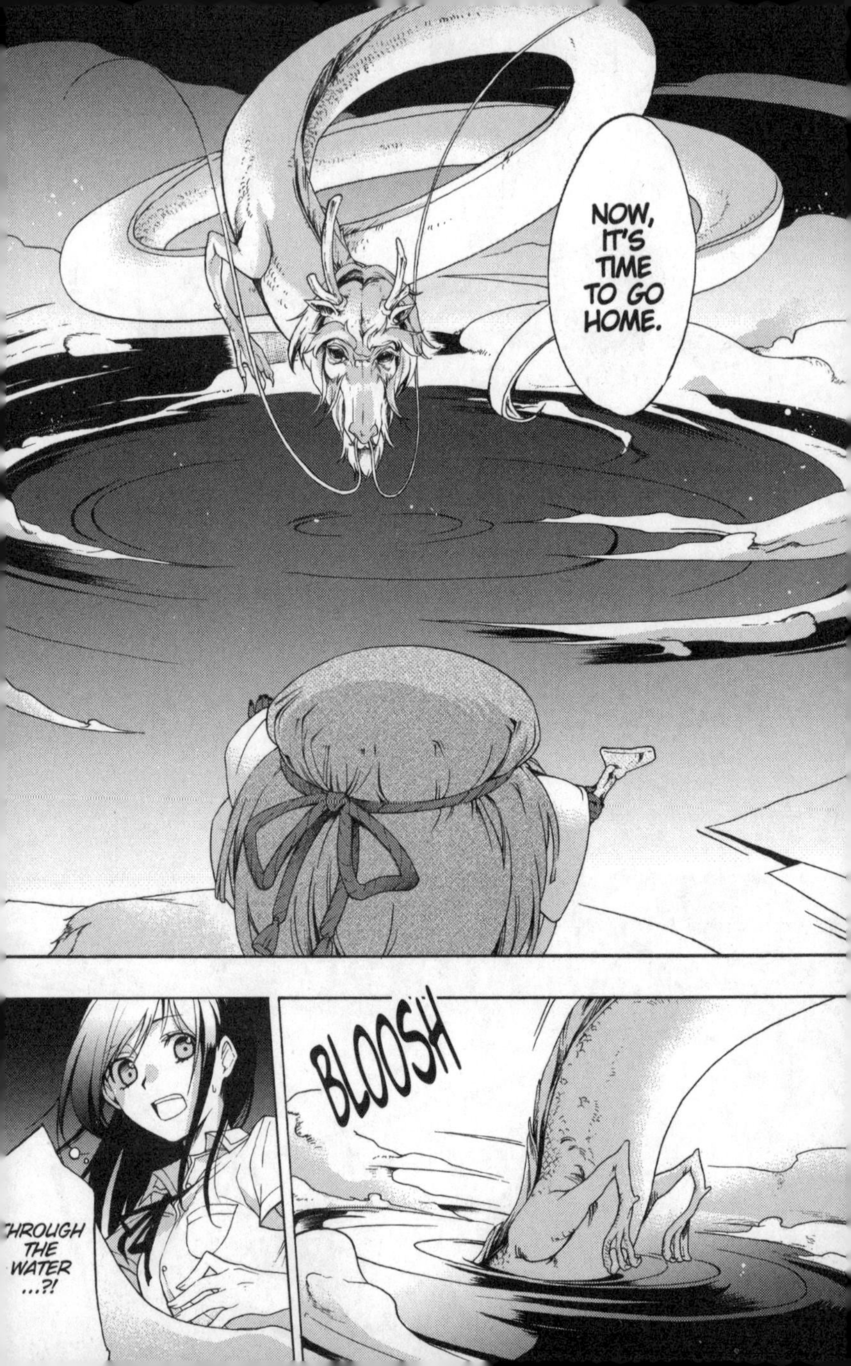
NOW, IT'S TIME TO GO HOME.
BLOOSH
THROUGH THE WATER ...?!

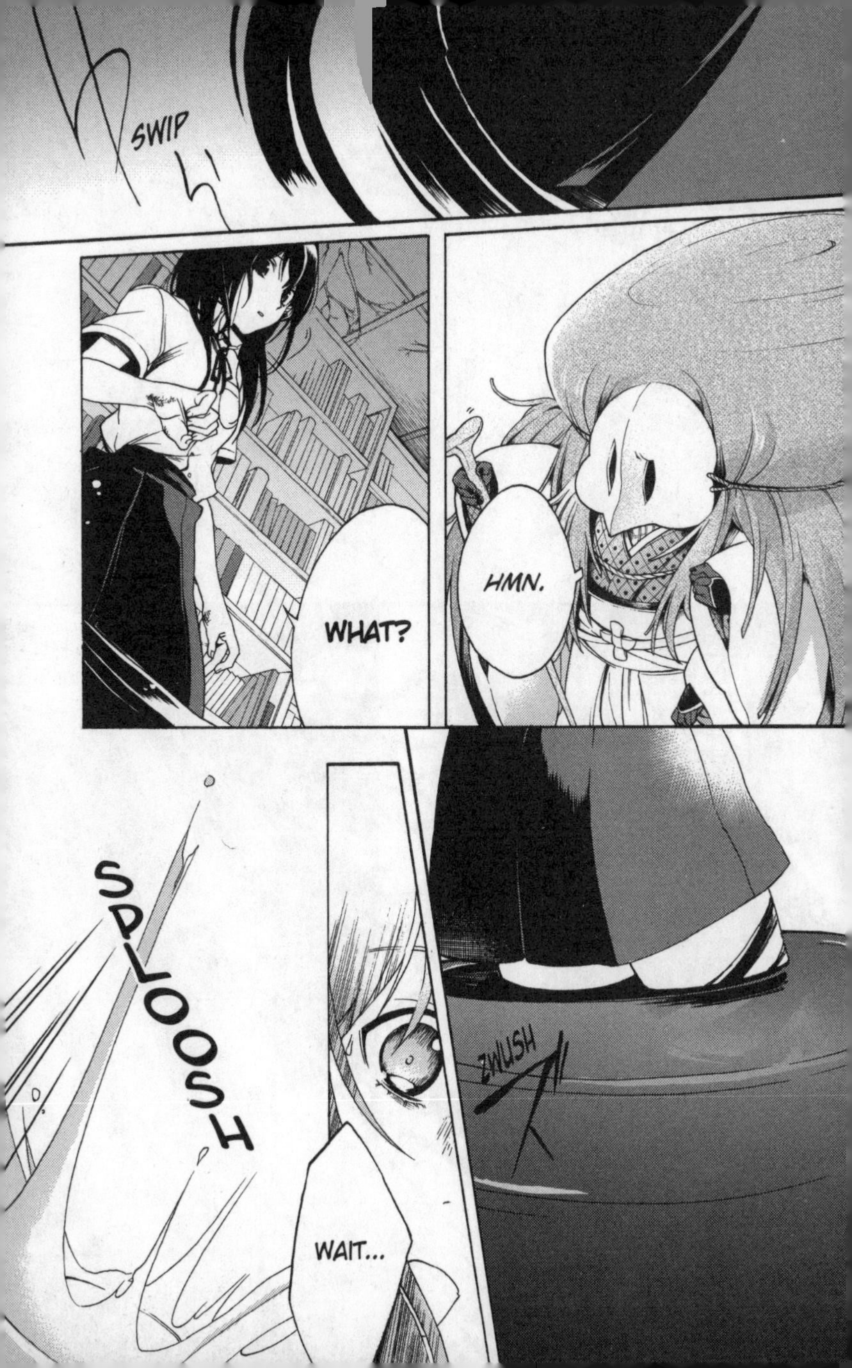
SWIP
HMN.
WHAT?
ZWUSH
SPLOOSH
WAIT...

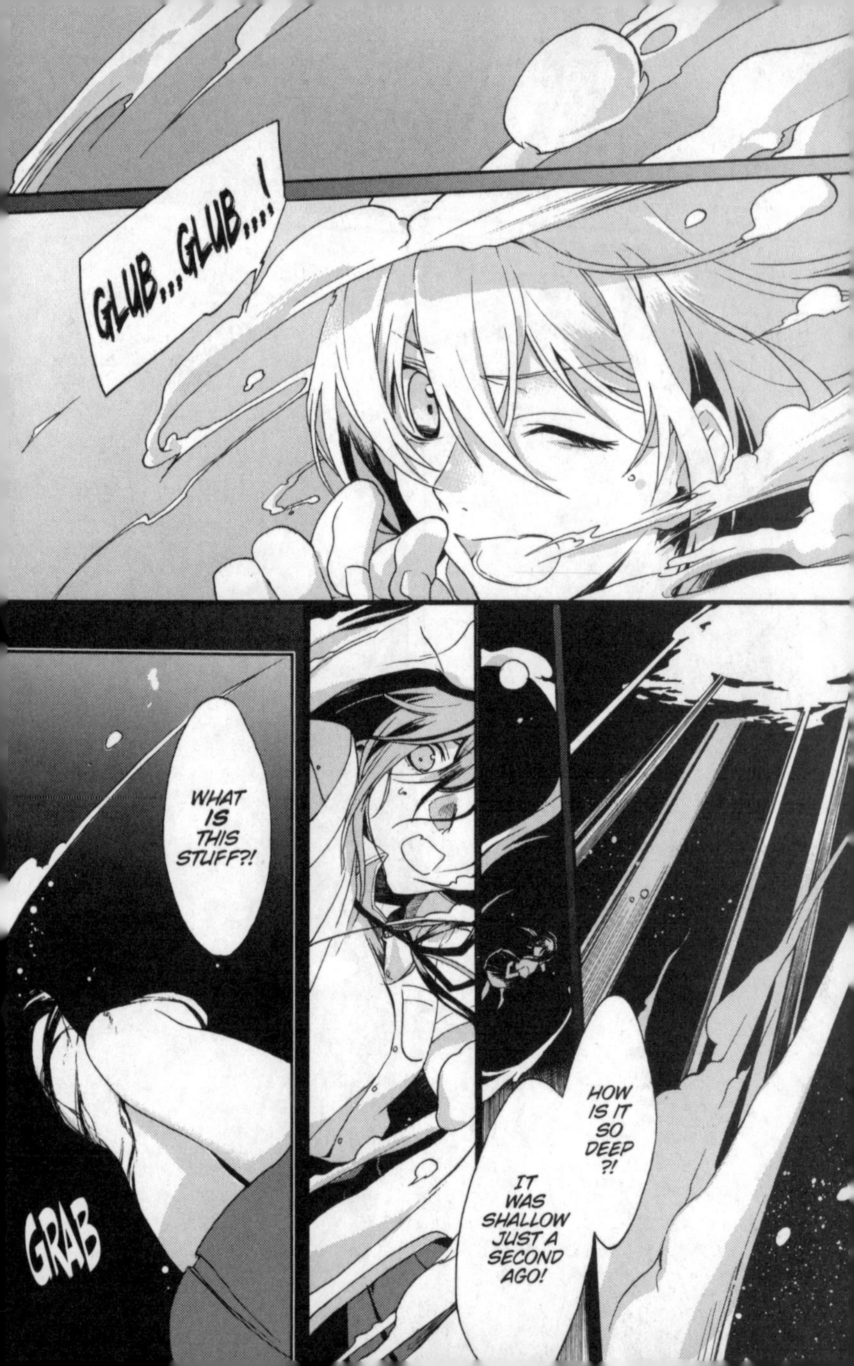
GLUB...GLUB...!
HOW IS IT SO DEEP?!
IT WAS SHALLOW JUST A SECOND AGO!
WHAT IS THIS STUFF?!
GRAB

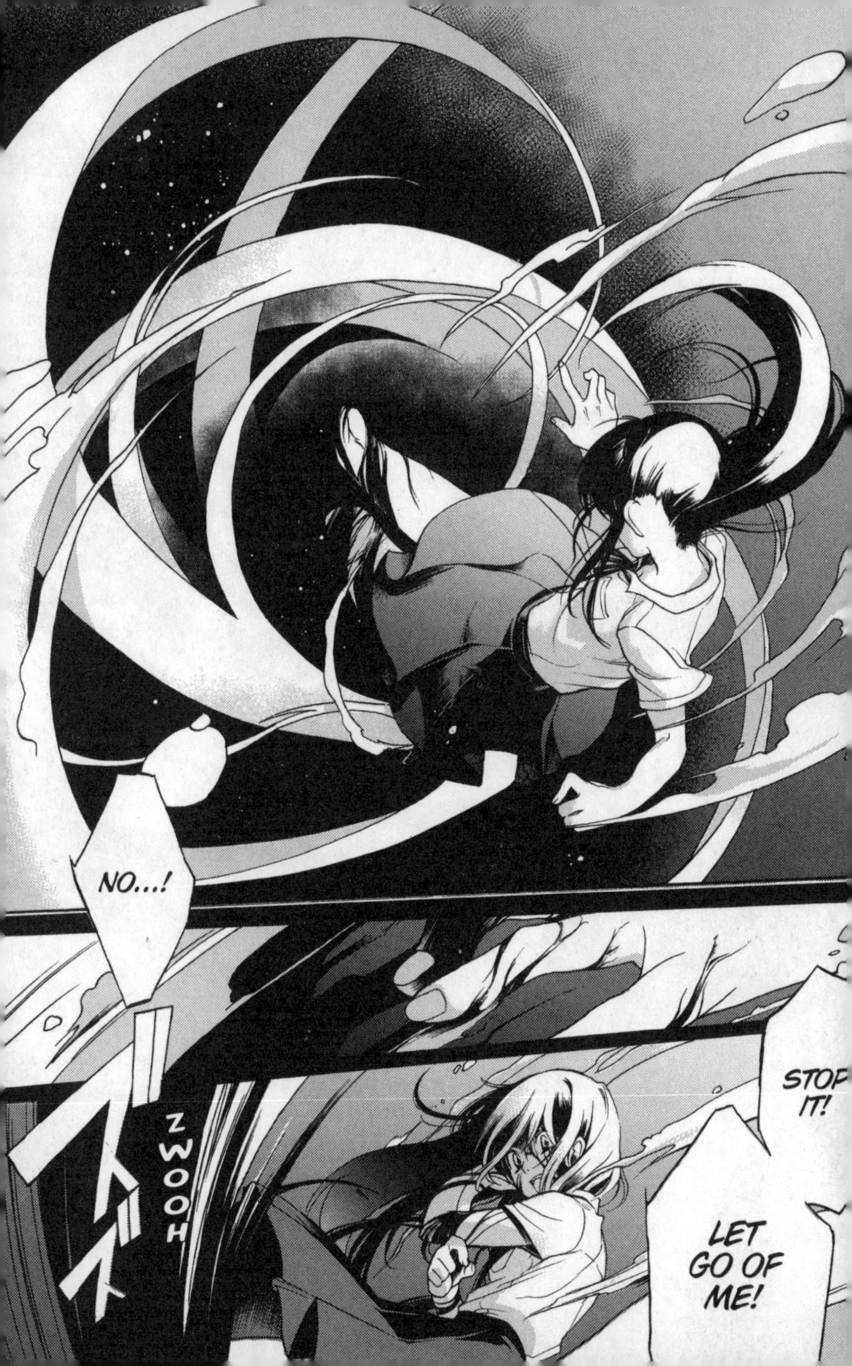
NO...!
STOP IT!
LET GO OF ME!
ZWOOH

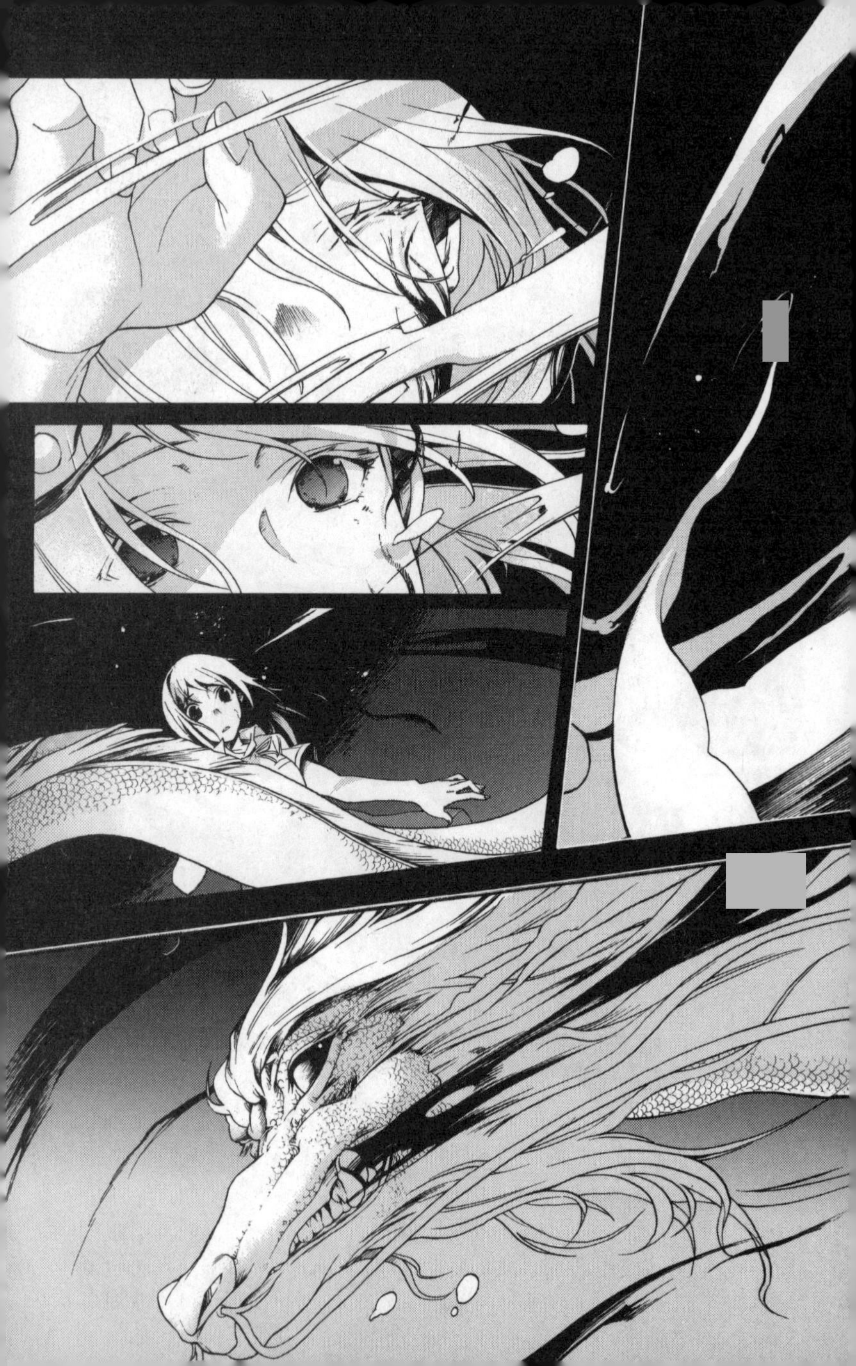

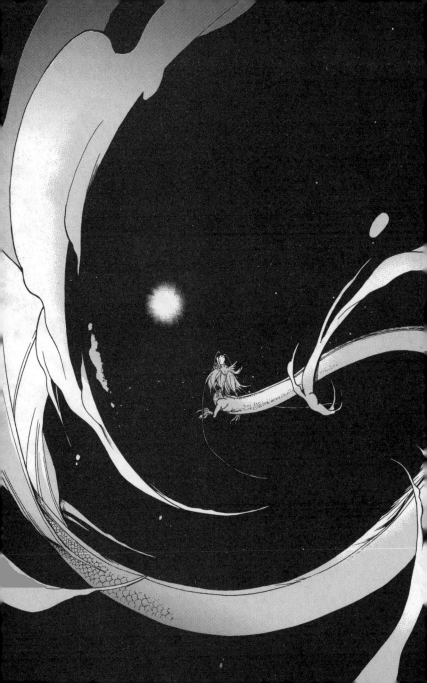

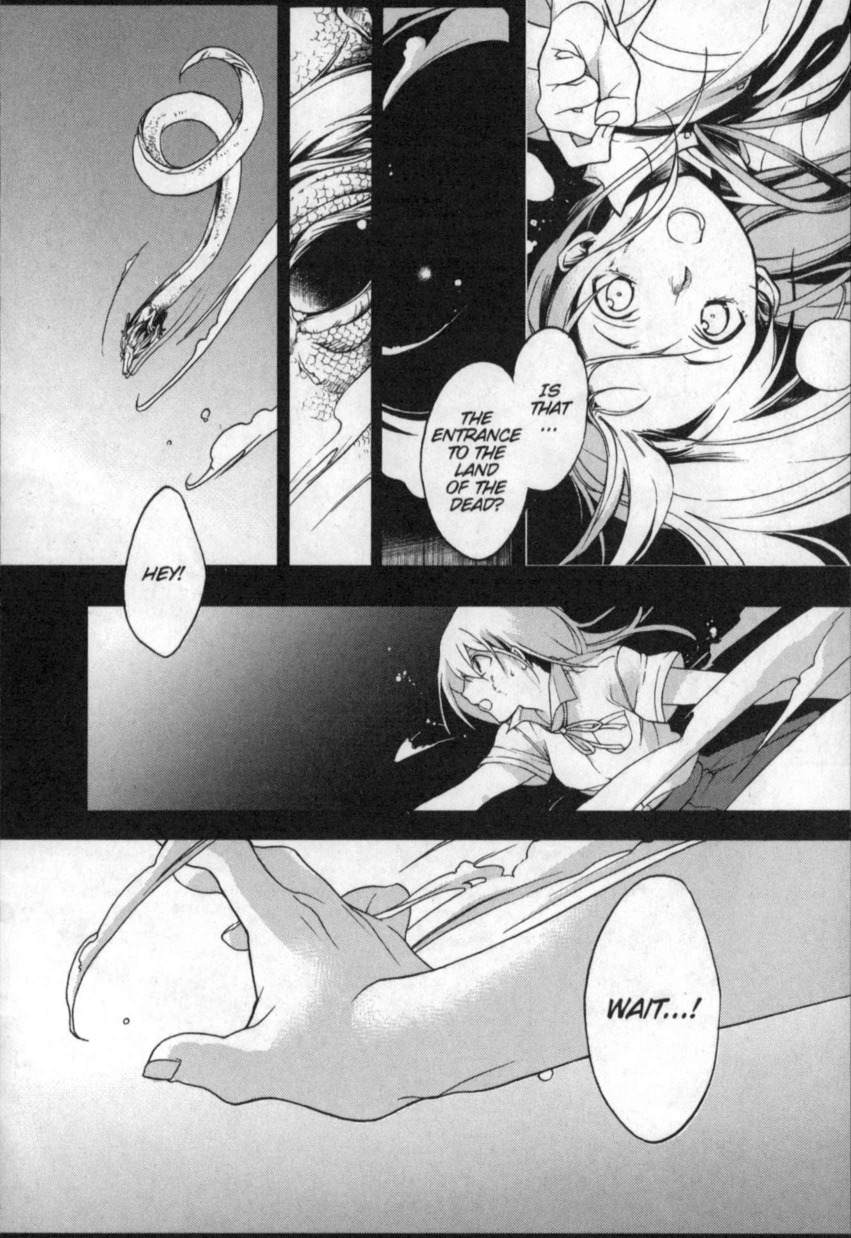
IS THAT ...
THE ENTRANCE TO THE LAND OF THE DEAD?
HEY!
WAIT...!

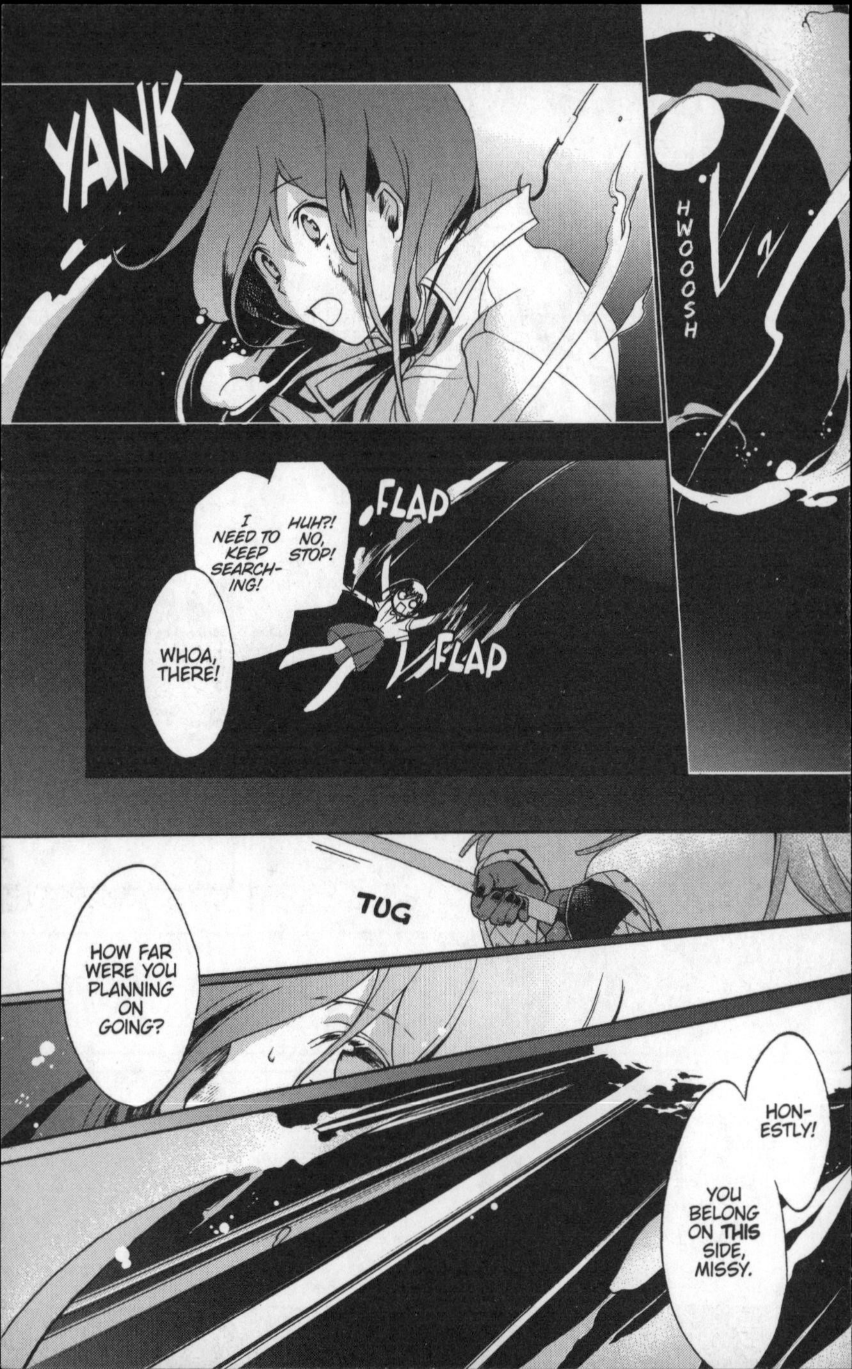
HWOOOSH
YANK
FLAP
HUH?! NO, STOP!
I NEED TO KEEP SEARCHING!
FLAP
WHOA, THERE!
TUG
HOW FAR WERE YOU PLANNING ON GOING?
HON-ESTLY!
YOU BELONG ON **THIS** SIDE, MISSY.

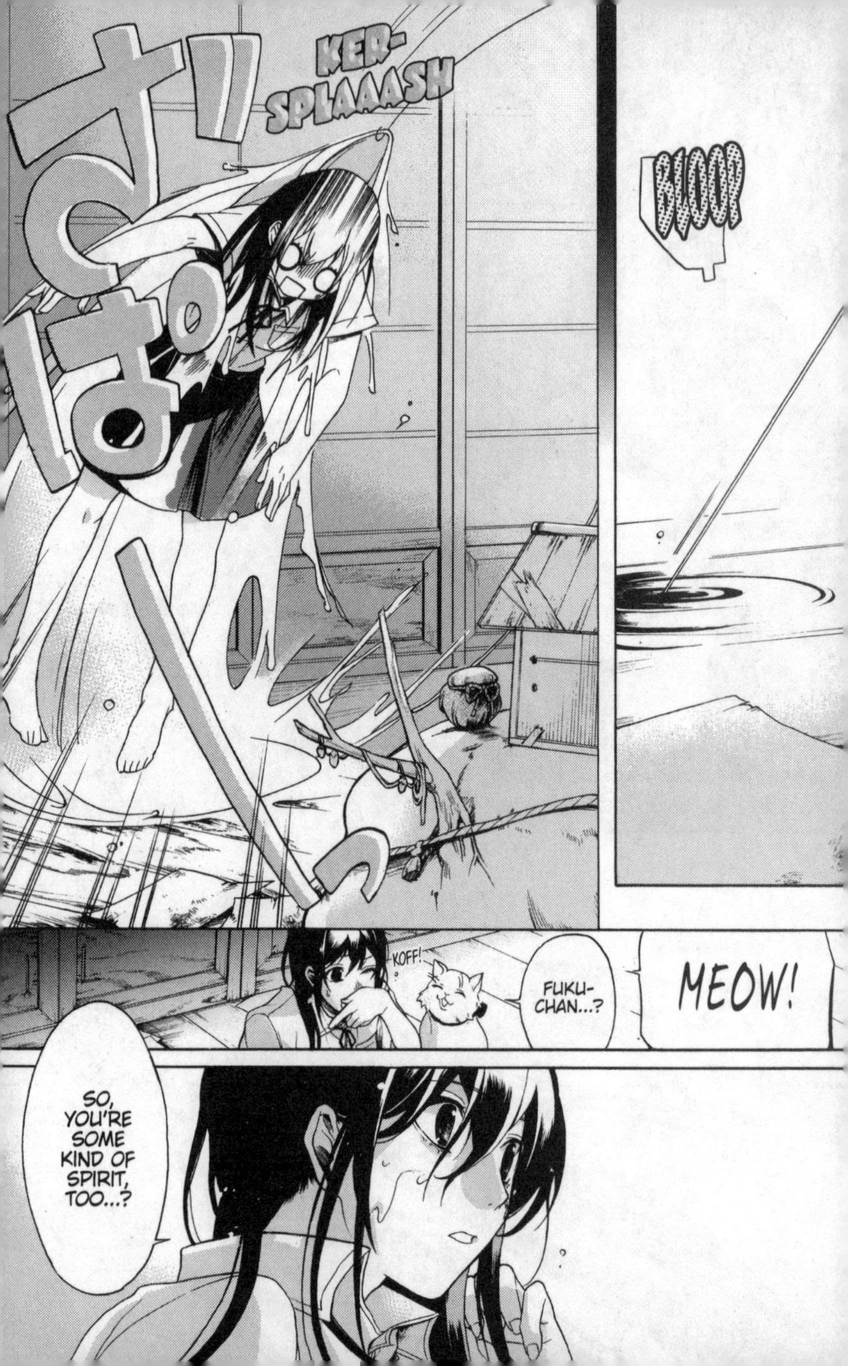
BLOOP
KER-SPLAAASH
MEOW!
FUKU-CHAN...?
KOFF!
SO, YOU'RE SOME KIND OF SPIRIT, TOO...?

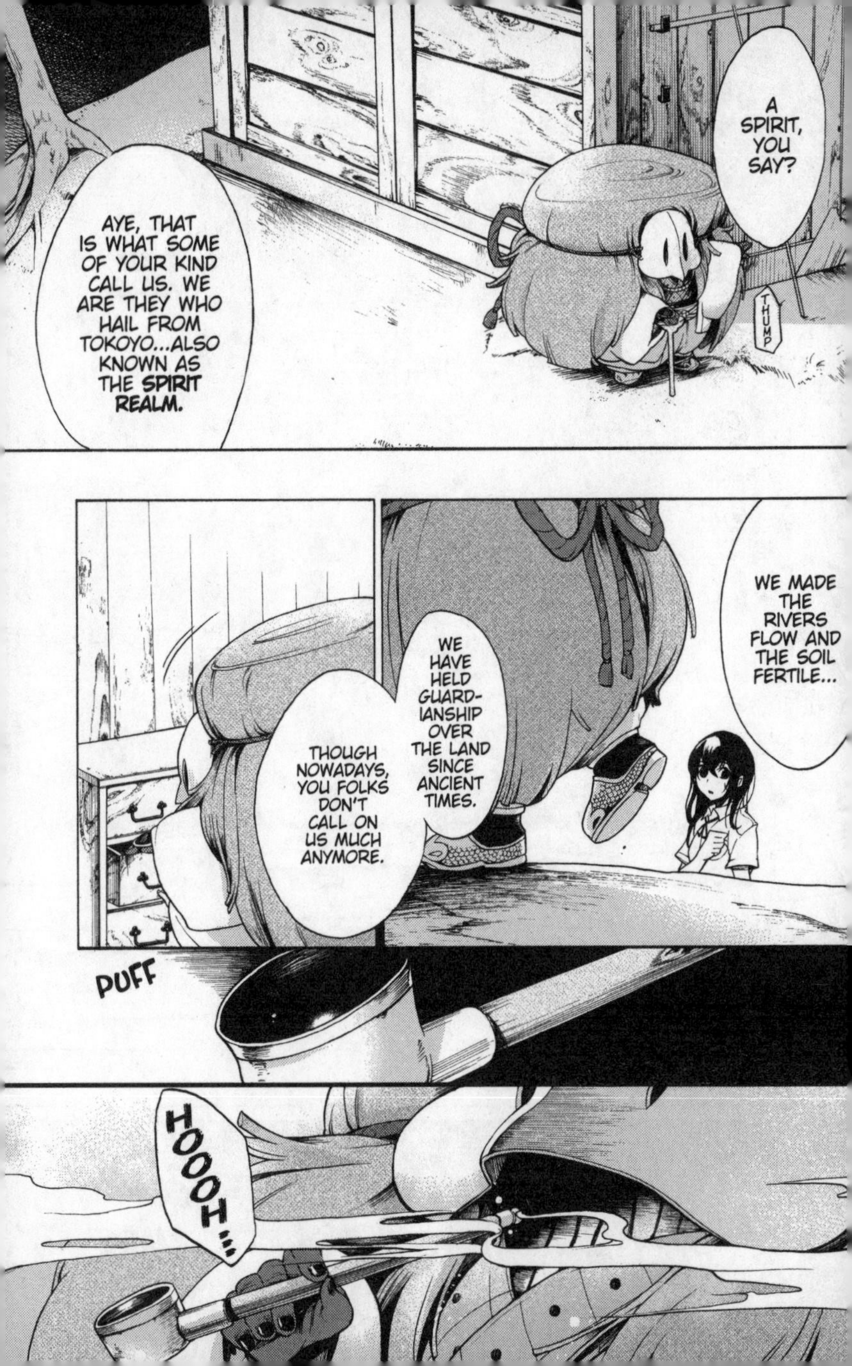
A SPIRIT, YOU SAY?
THUMP
AYE, THAT IS WHAT SOME OF YOUR KIND CALL US. WE ARE THEY WHO HAIL FROM TOKOYO...ALSO KNOWN AS THE SPIRIT REALM.
WE MADE THE RIVERS FLOW AND THE SOIL FERTILE...
WE HAVE HELD GUARD-IANSHIP OVER THE LAND SINCE ANCIENT TIMES.
THOUGH NOWADAYS, YOU FOLKS DON'T CALL ON US MUCH ANYMORE.
PUFF
HOOOH...

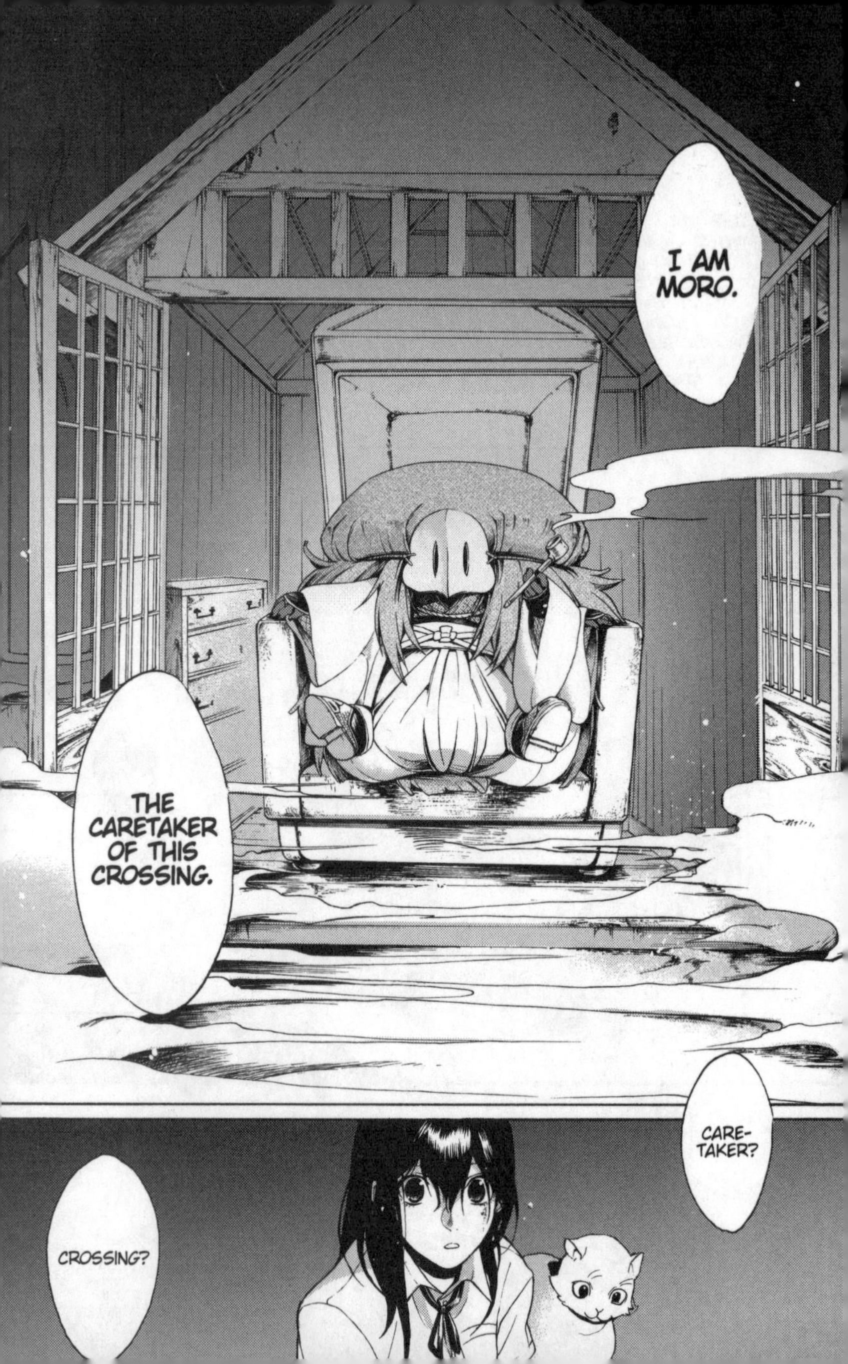
I AM MORO.
THE CARETAKER OF THIS CROSSING.
CARE-TAKER?
CROSSING?

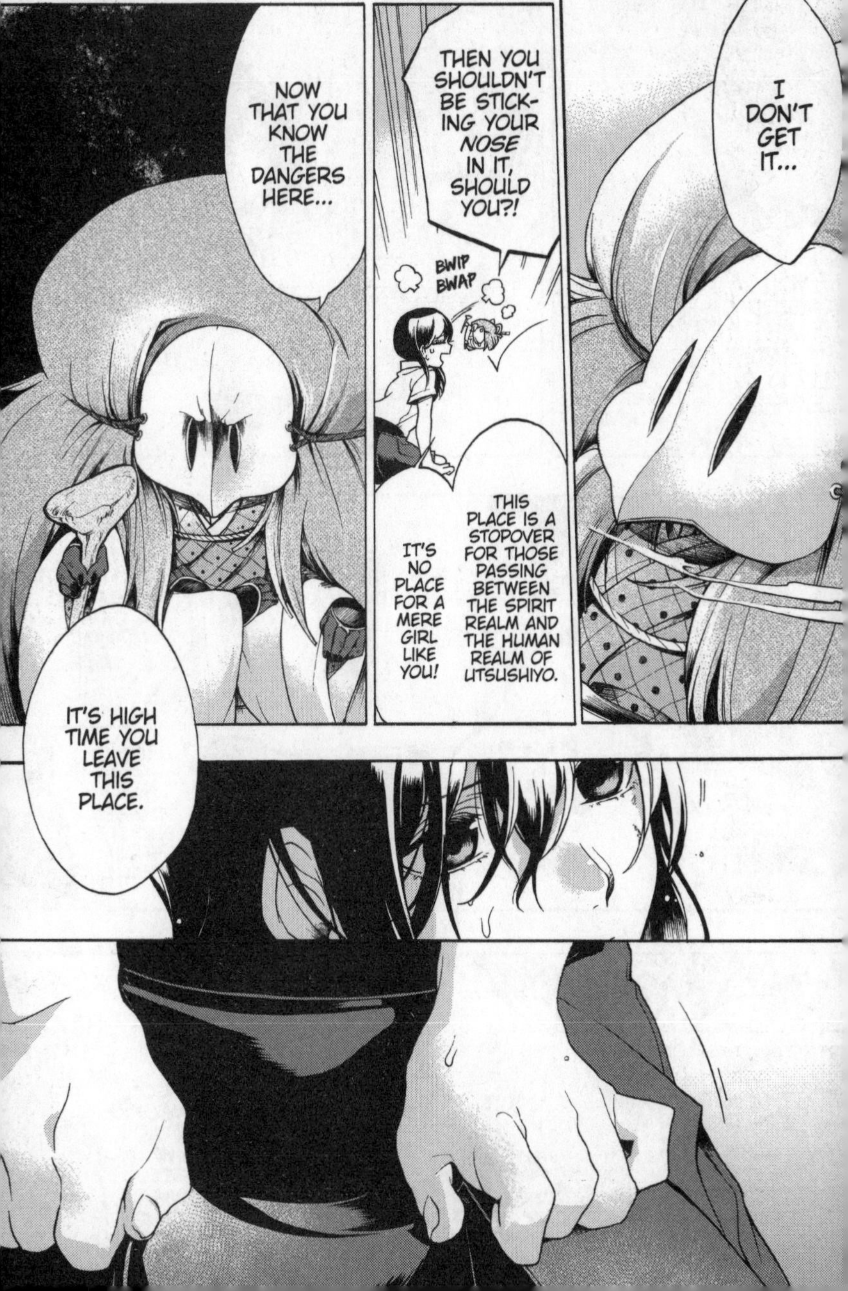
I DON'T GET IT...
THEN YOU SHOULDN'T BE STICKING YOUR *NOSE* IN IT, SHOULD YOU?!
BWIP BWAP
THIS PLACE IS A STOPOVER FOR THOSE PASSING BETWEEN THE SPIRIT REALM AND THE HUMAN REALM OF UTSUSHIYO.
IT'S NO PLACE FOR A MERE GIRL LIKE YOU!
NOW THAT YOU KNOW THE DANGERS HERE...
IT'S HIGH TIME YOU LEAVE THIS PLACE.

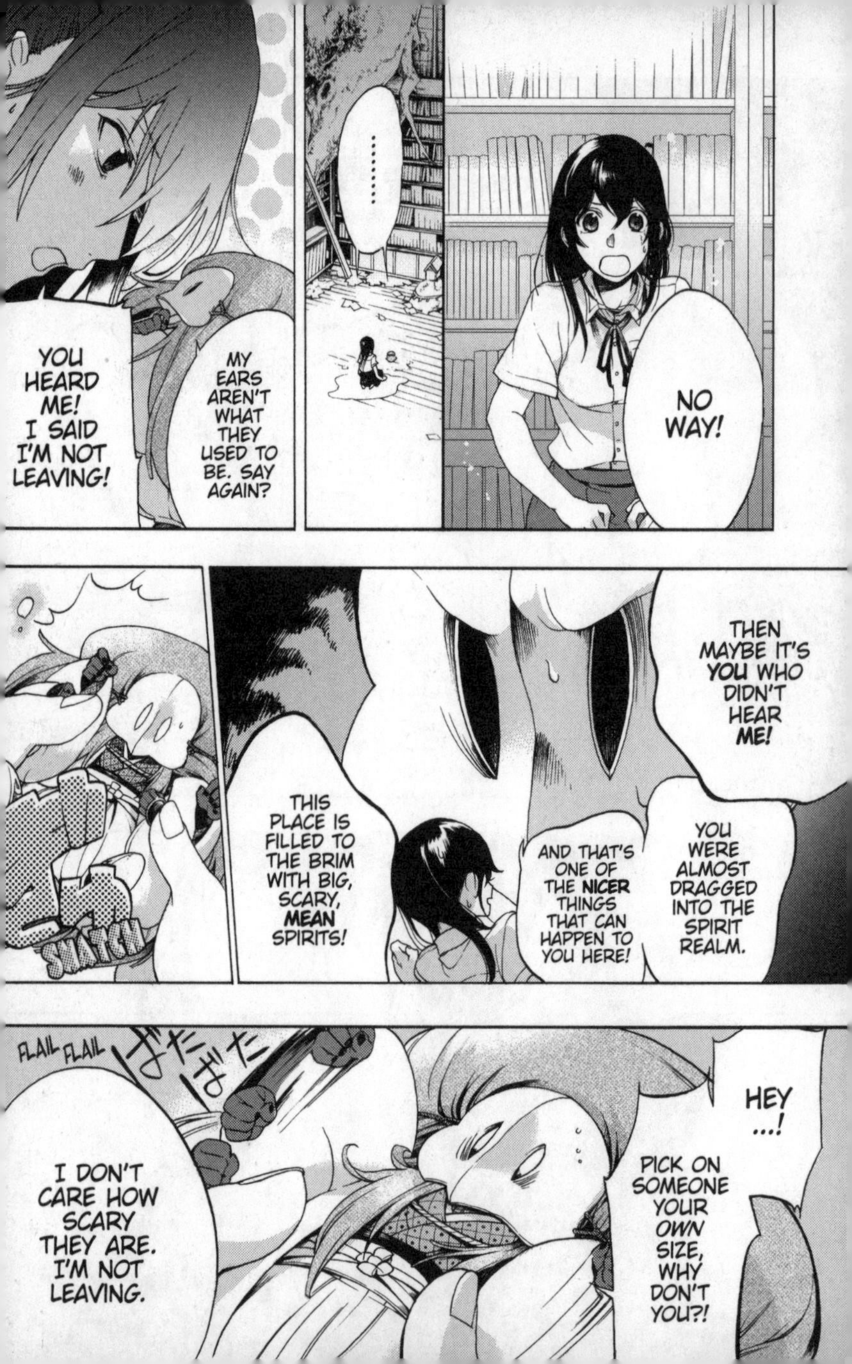
NO WAY!
......
MY EARS AREN'T WHAT THEY USED TO BE. SAY AGAIN?
YOU HEARD ME! I SAID I'M NOT LEAVING!
THEN MAYBE IT'S YOU WHO DIDN'T HEAR ME!
YOU WERE ALMOST DRAGGED INTO THE SPIRIT REALM.
AND THAT'S ONE OF THE NICER THINGS THAT CAN HAPPEN TO YOU HERE!
THIS PLACE IS FILLED TO THE BRIM WITH BIG, SCARY, MEAN SPIRITS!
SNATCH
HEY ...!
PICK ON SOMEONE YOUR OWN SIZE, WHY DON'T YOU?!
FLAIL FLAIL
ばたばた
I DON'T CARE HOW SCARY THEY ARE. I'M NOT LEAVING.

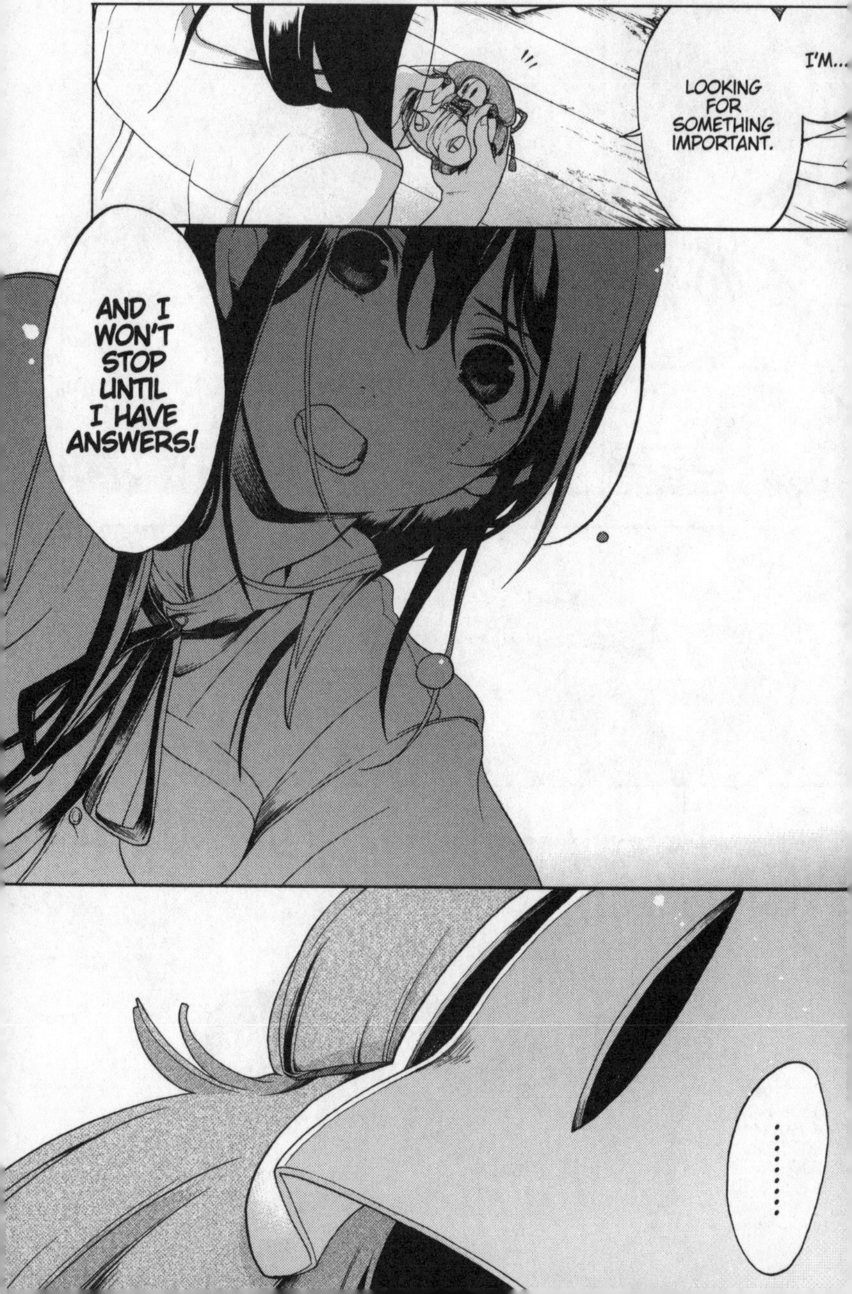
I'M...
LOOKING FOR SOMETHING IMPORTANT.
AND I WON'T STOP UNTIL I HAVE ANSWERS!
....

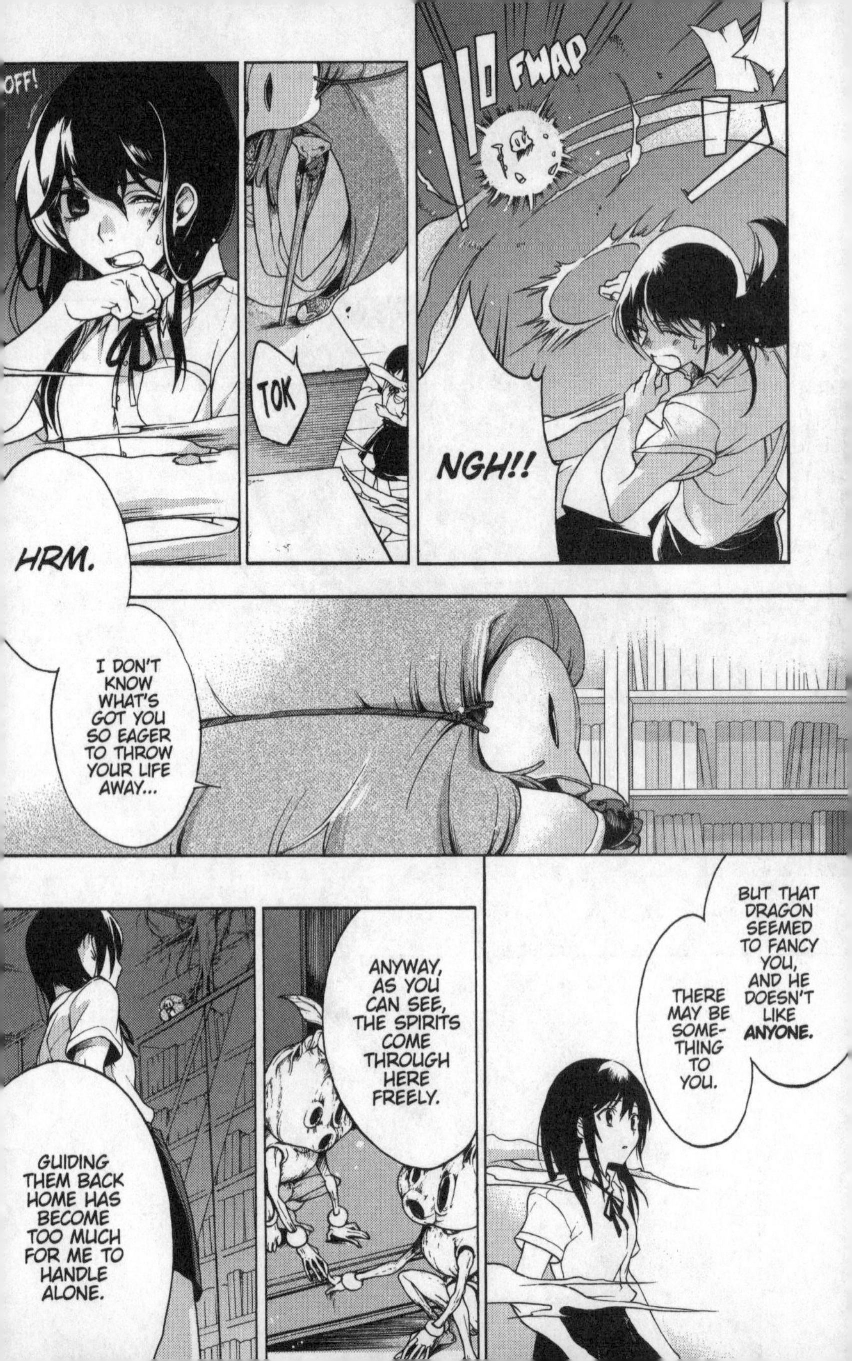
FWAP
NGH!!
TOK
OFF!
HRM.
I DON'T KNOW WHAT'S GOT YOU SO EAGER TO THROW YOUR LIFE AWAY...
BUT THAT DRAGON SEEMED TO FANCY YOU, AND HE DOESN'T LIKE ANYONE.
THERE MAY BE SOME-THING TO YOU.
ANYWAY, AS YOU CAN SEE, THE SPIRITS COME THROUGH HERE FREELY.
GUIDING THEM BACK HOME HAS BECOME TOO MUCH FOR ME TO HANDLE ALONE.

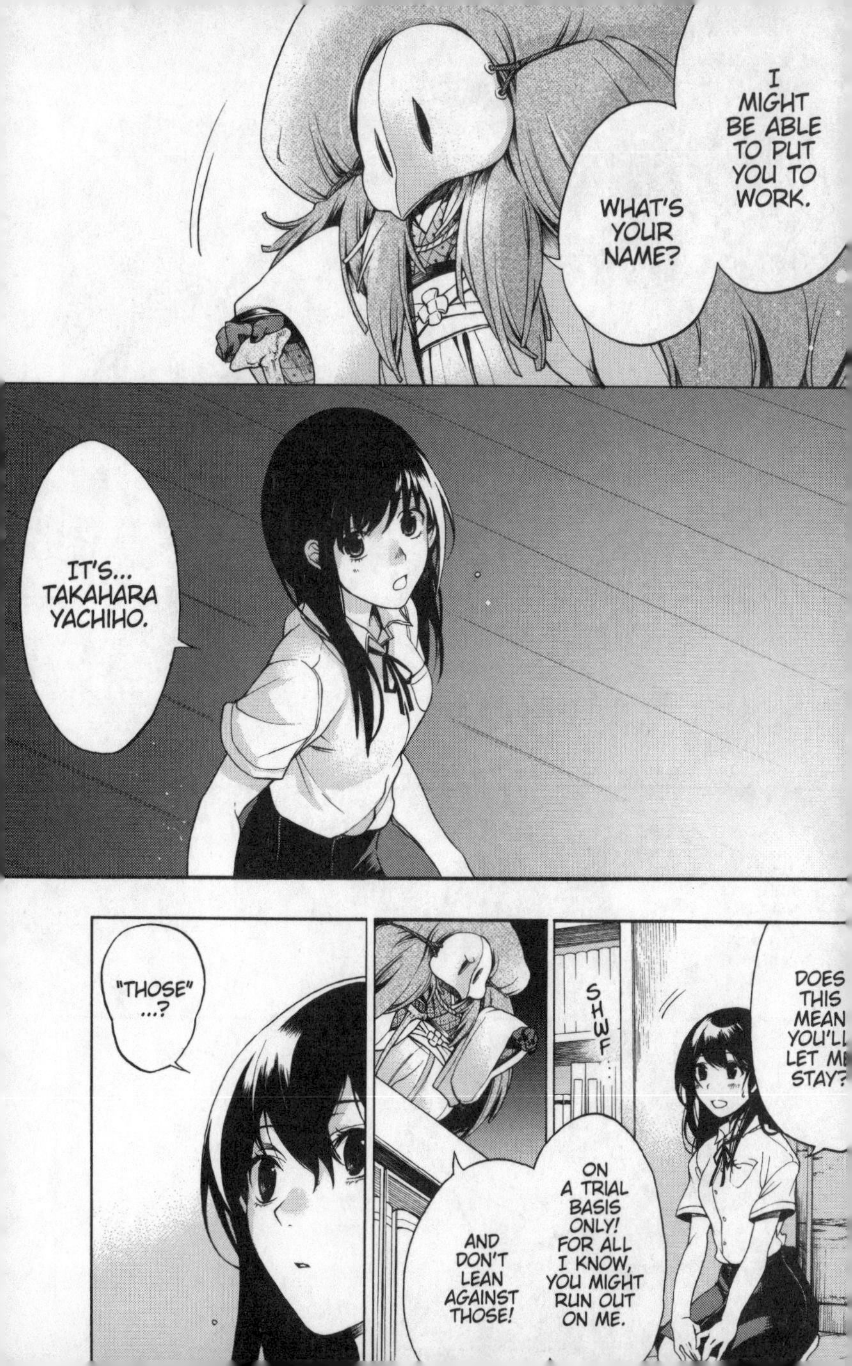
I MIGHT BE ABLE TO PUT YOU TO WORK.
WHAT'S YOUR NAME?
IT'S... TAKAHARA YACHIHO.
DOES THIS MEAN YOU'LL LET ME STAY?
SHWF
ON A TRIAL BASIS ONLY! FOR ALL I KNOW, YOU MIGHT RUN OUT ON ME.
AND DON'T LEAN AGAINST THOSE!
"THOSE" ...?

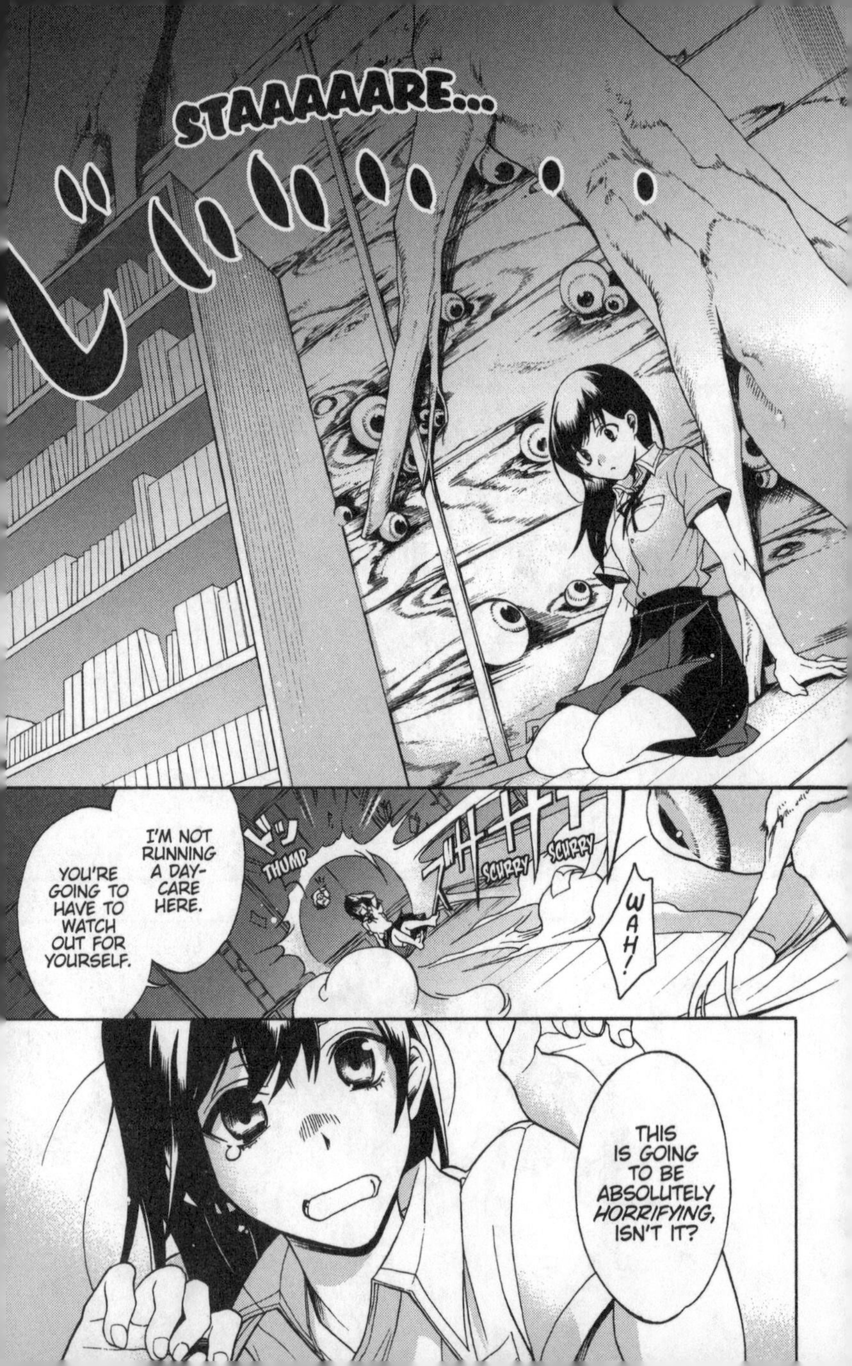
STAAAAAARE...
WAH!
SCURRY SCURRY
THUMP
ドッ
I'M NOT RUNNING A DAY-CARE HERE.
YOU'RE GOING TO HAVE TO WATCH OUT FOR YOURSELF.
THIS IS GOING TO BE ABSOLUTELY *HORRIFYING,* ISN'T IT?

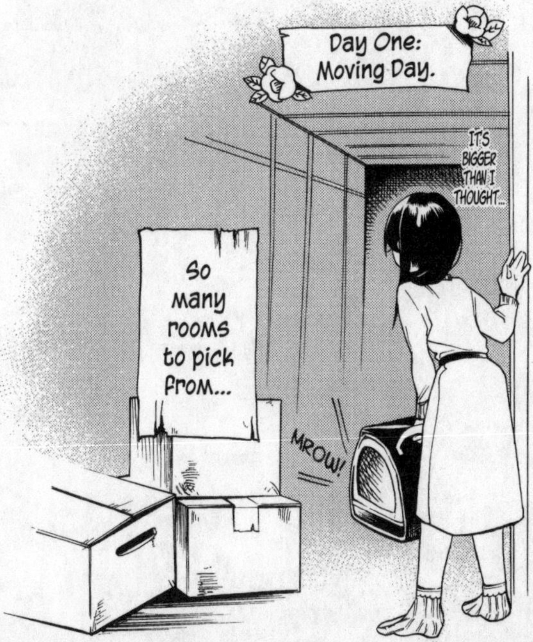
Day One: Moving Day.
IT'S BIGGER THAN I THOUGHT...
So many rooms to pick from...
MROW!

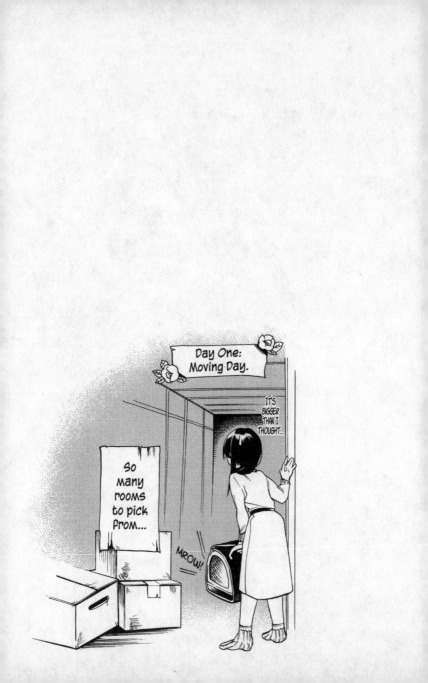

Ghostly
Things

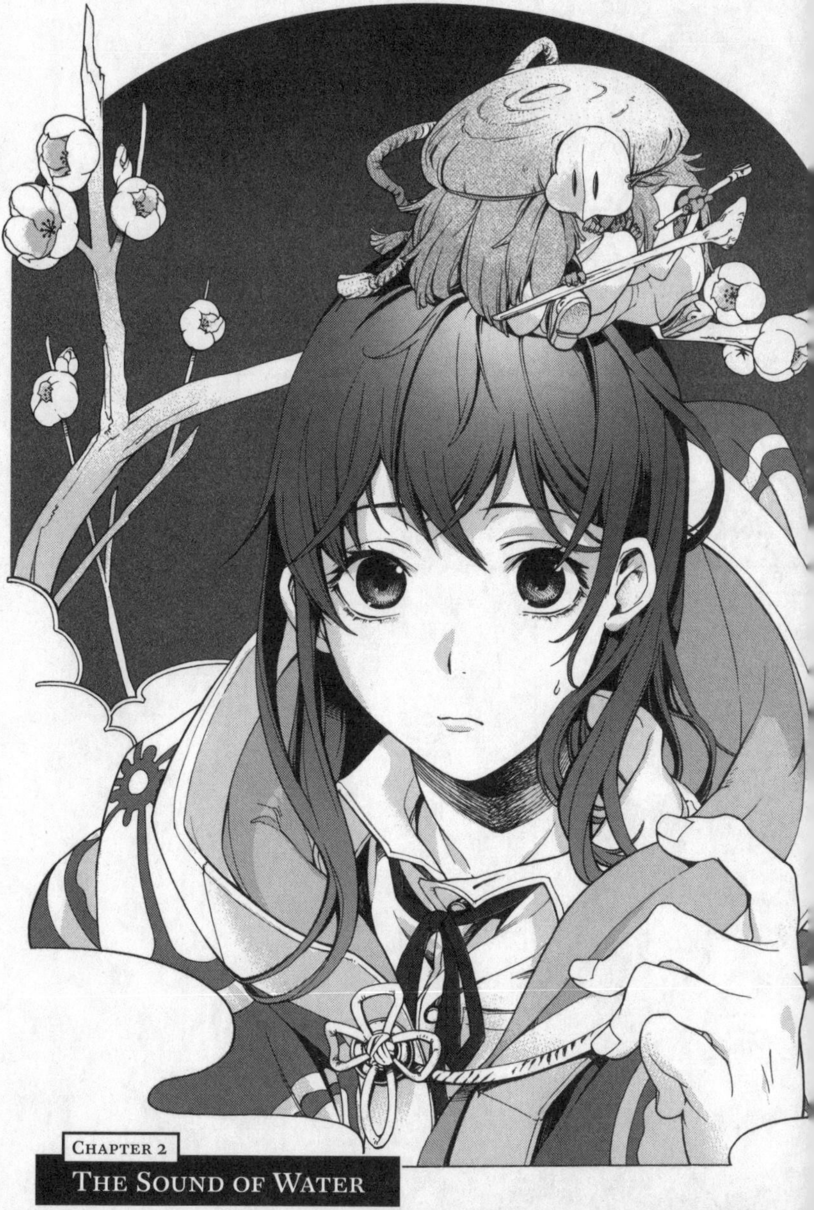

CHAPTER 2

THE SOUND OF WATER

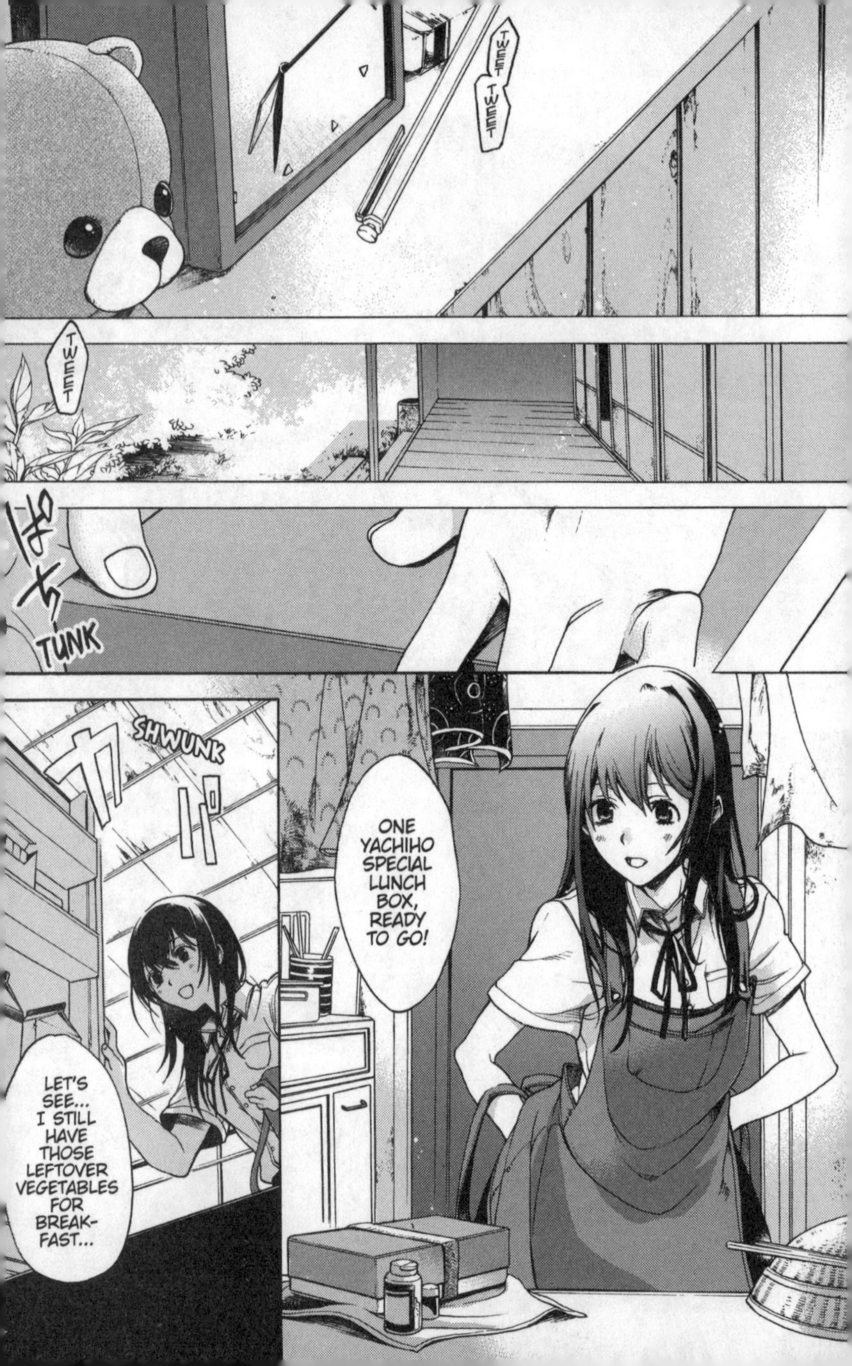
TWEET TWEET
TWEET
ぱち
TUNK
ONE YACHIHO SPECIAL LUNCH BOX, READY TO GO!
ガパ
SHWUNK
LET'S SEE... I STILL HAVE THOSE LEFTOVER VEGETABLES FOR BREAK-FAST...

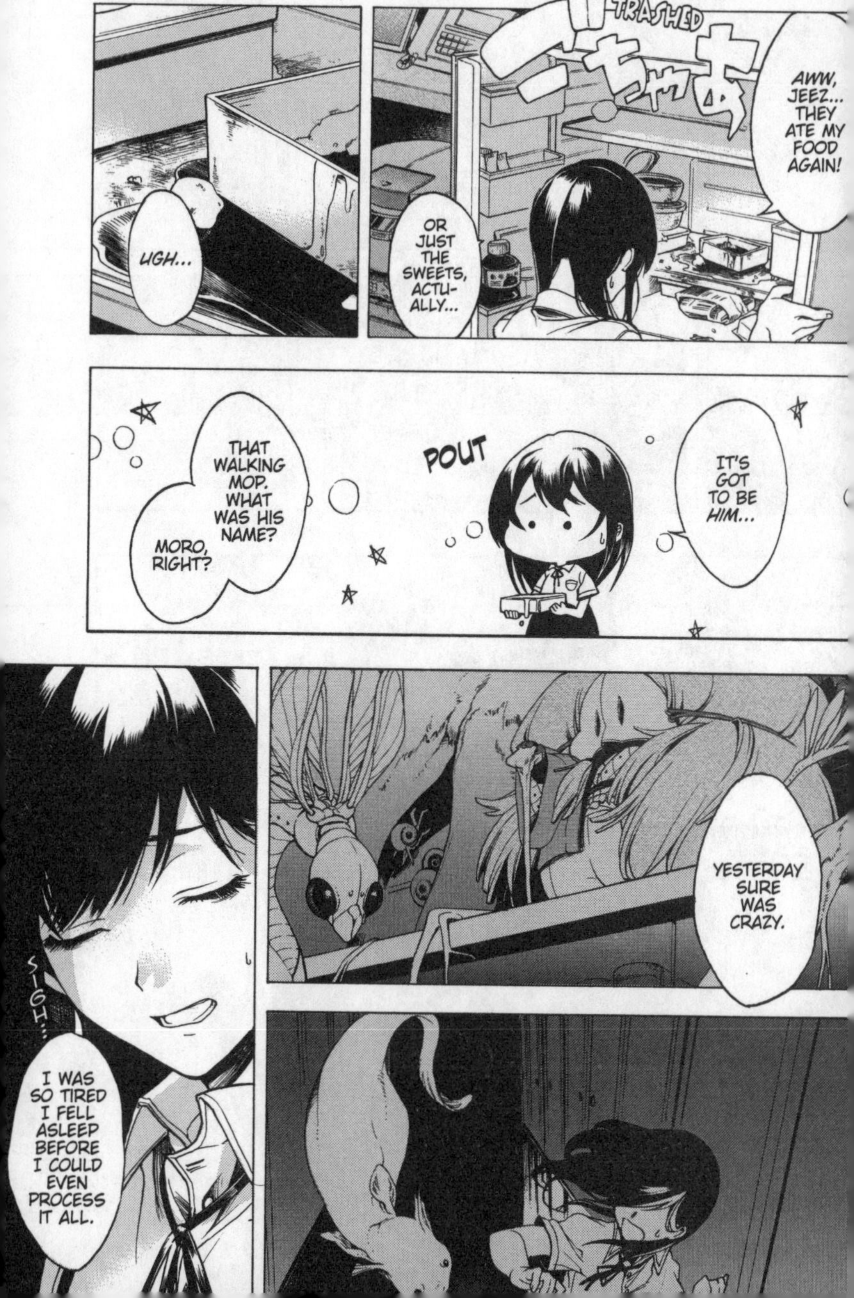
TRASHED
AWW, JEEZ... THEY ATE MY FOOD AGAIN!
OR JUST THE SWEETS, ACTUALLY...
UGH...
IT'S GOT TO BE HIM...
POUT
THAT WALKING MOP. WHAT WAS HIS NAME?
MORO, RIGHT?
YESTERDAY SURE WAS CRAZY.
SIGH...
I WAS SO TIRED I FELL ASLEEP BEFORE I COULD EVEN PROCESS IT ALL.

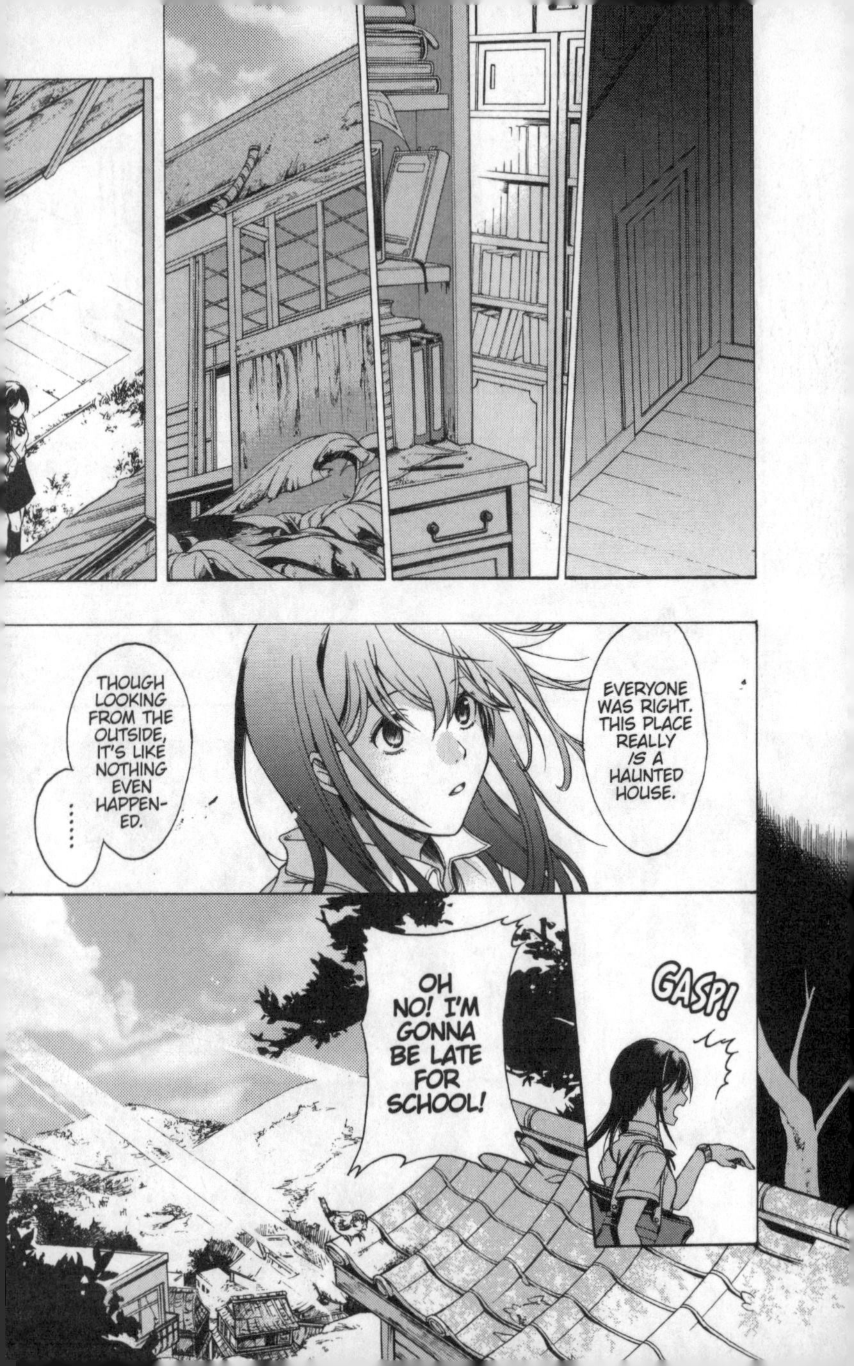
EVERYONE WAS RIGHT. THIS PLACE REALLY IS A HAUNTED HOUSE.
THOUGH LOOKING FROM THE OUTSIDE, IT'S LIKE NOTHING EVEN HAPPEN-ED. ......
GASP!
OH NO! I'M GONNA BE LATE FOR SCHOOL!

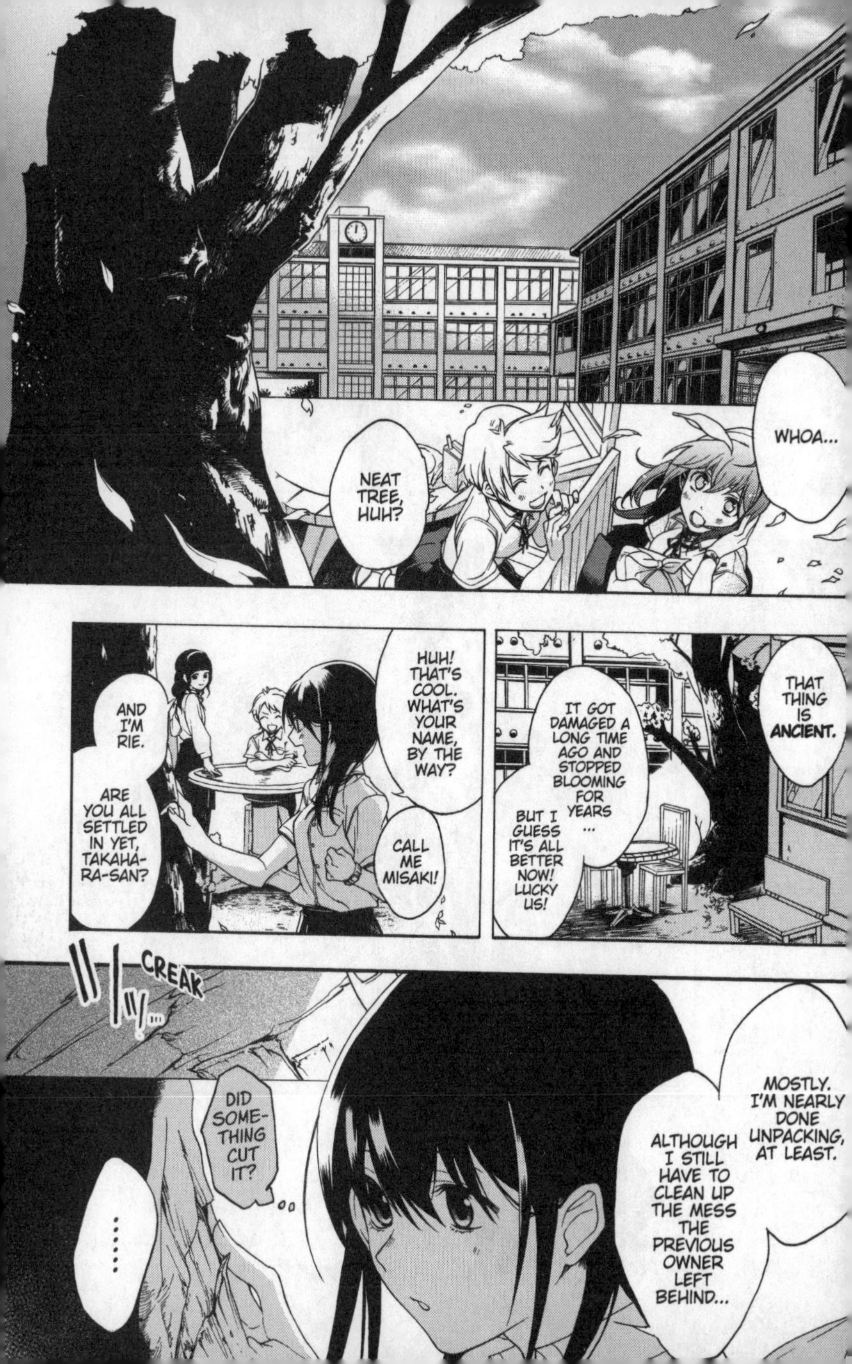
WHOA...
NEAT TREE, HUH?
THAT THING IS **ANCIENT.**
IT GOT DAMAGED A LONG TIME AGO AND STOPPED BLOOMING FOR YEARS...
BUT I GUESS IT'S ALL BETTER NOW! LUCKY US!
HUH! THAT'S COOL. WHAT'S YOUR NAME, BY THE WAY?
CALL ME MISAKI!
AND I'M RIE.
ARE YOU ALL SETTLED IN YET, TAKAHARA-SAN?
CREAK
MOSTLY. I'M NEARLY DONE UNPACKING, AT LEAST.
ALTHOUGH I STILL HAVE TO CLEAN UP THE MESS THE PREVIOUS OWNER LEFT BEHIND...
DID SOMETHING CUT IT?
......

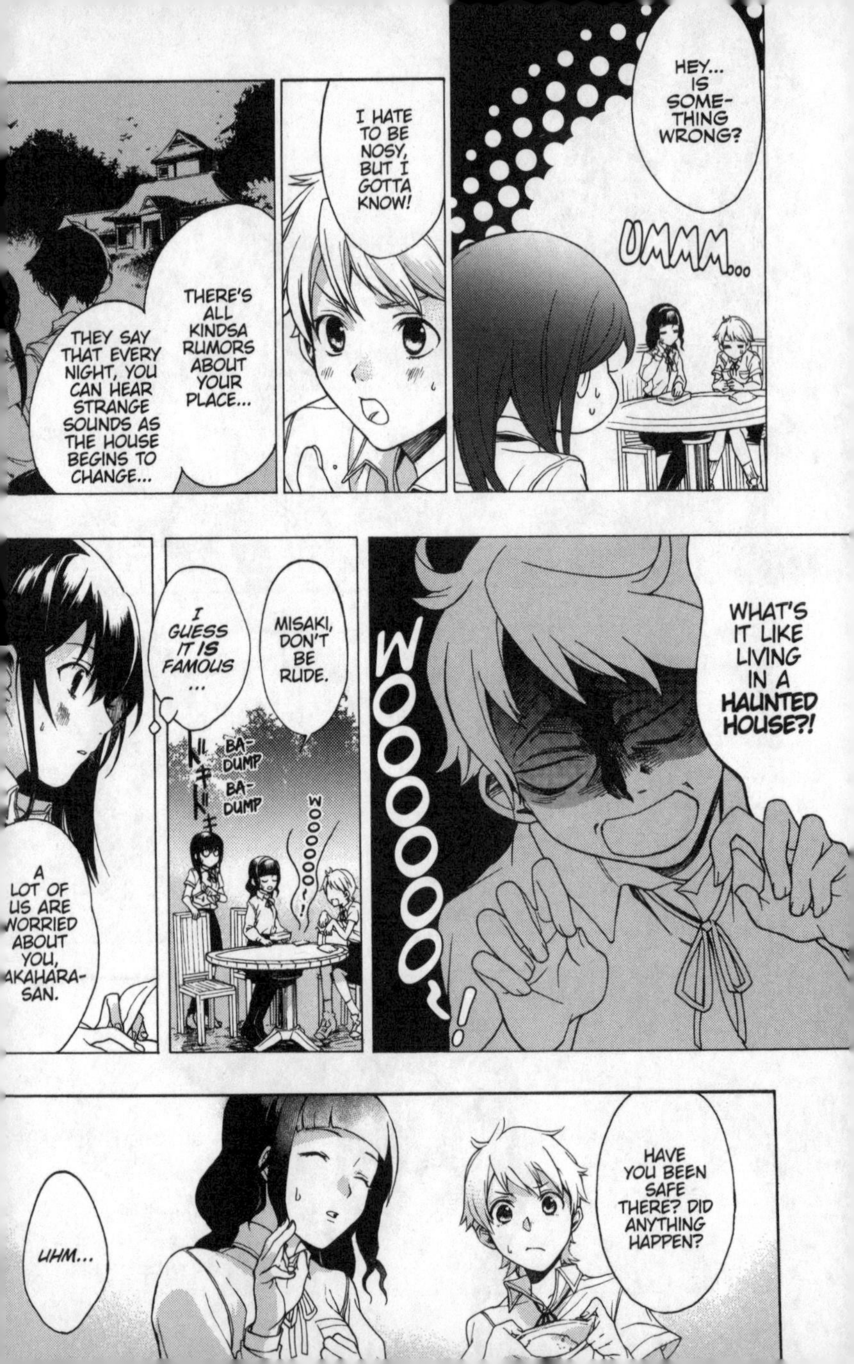
HEY... IS SOMETHING WRONG?
UMMM...
I HATE TO BE NOSY, BUT I GOTTA KNOW!
THERE'S ALL KINDSA RUMORS ABOUT YOUR PLACE...
THEY SAY THAT EVERY NIGHT, YOU CAN HEAR STRANGE SOUNDS AS THE HOUSE BEGINS TO CHANGE...
WHAT'S IT LIKE LIVING IN A HAUNTED HOUSE?!
WOOOOOO~!
MISAKI, DON'T BE RUDE.
WOOOOOOO~!
BA-DUMP BA-DUMP
I GUESS IT IS FAMOUS...
A LOT OF US ARE WORRIED ABOUT YOU, AKAHARA-SAN.
HAVE YOU BEEN SAFE THERE? DID ANYTHING HAPPEN?
UHM...

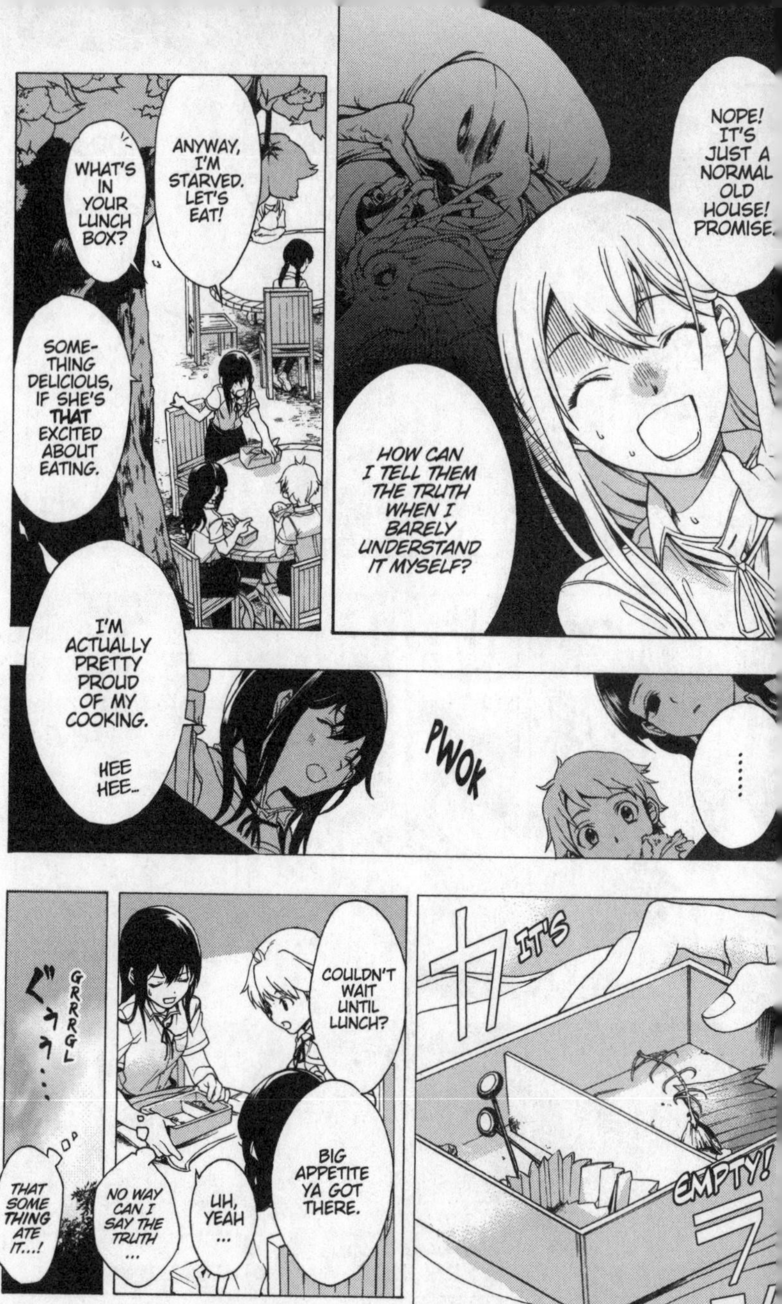
NOPE! IT'S JUST A NORMAL OLD HOUSE! PROMISE.
HOW CAN I TELL THEM THE TRUTH WHEN I BARELY UNDERSTAND IT MYSELF?
ANYWAY, I'M STARVED. LET'S EAT!
WHAT'S IN YOUR LUNCH BOX?
SOMETHING DELICIOUS, IF SHE'S **THAT** EXCITED ABOUT EATING.
I'M ACTUALLY PRETTY PROUD OF MY COOKING.
HEE HEE..
PWOK
......
IT'S
EMPTY!
COULDN'T WAIT UNTIL LUNCH?
BIG APPETITE YA GOT THERE.
UH, YEAH...
NO WAY CAN I SAY THE TRUTH...
THAT SOMETHING ATE IT...!
GRRRGL...

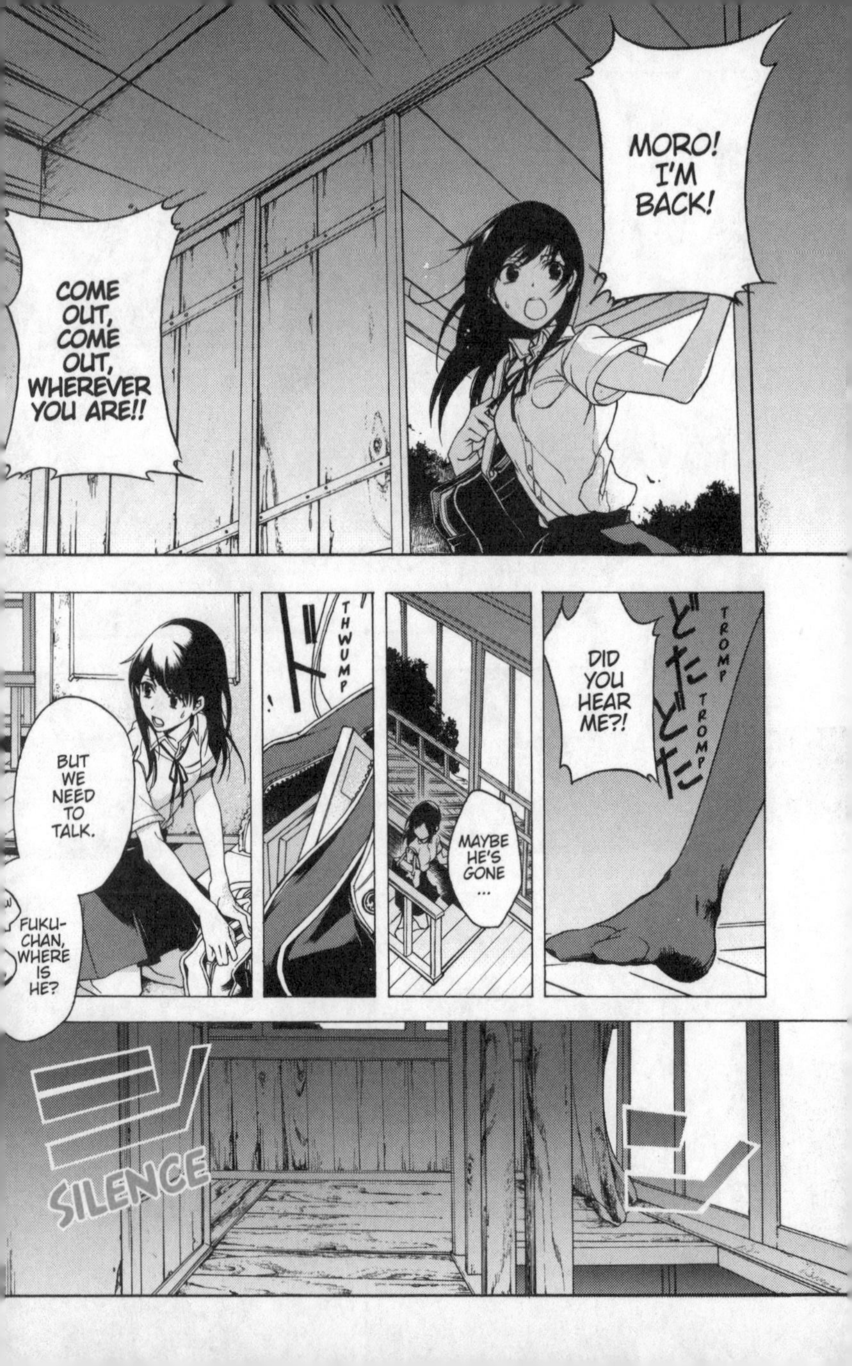
MORO! I'M BACK!
COME OUT, COME OUT, WHEREVER YOU ARE!!
どたどた
TROMP TROMP
DID YOU HEAR ME?!
MAYBE HE'S GONE...
THWUMP
BUT WE NEED TO TALK.
FUKU-CHAN, WHERE IS HE?
SILENCE

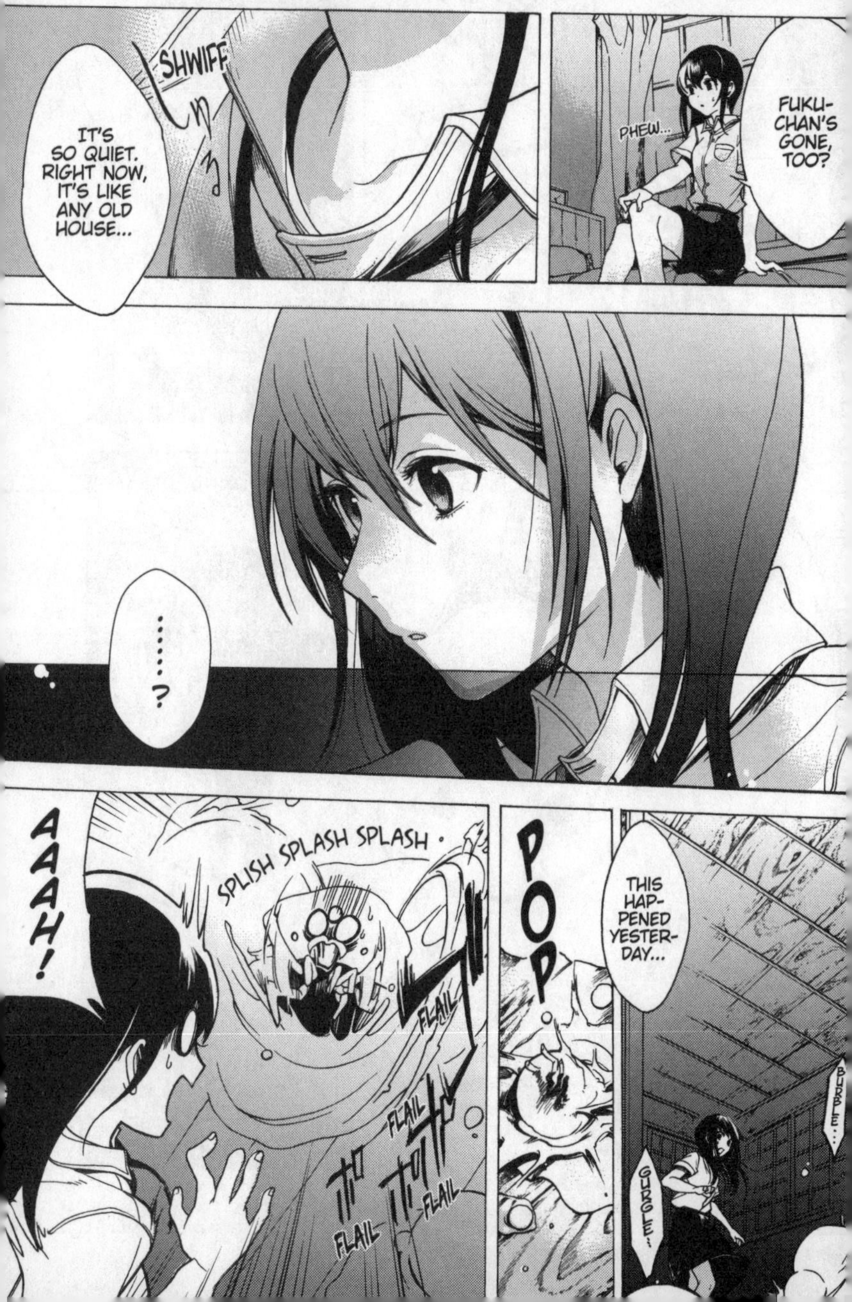
FUKU-CHAN'S GONE, TOO?
PHEW...
SHWIFF
IT'S SO QUIET. RIGHT NOW, IT'S LIKE ANY OLD HOUSE...
......?
THIS HAP-PENED YESTER-DAY...
BURBLE...
GURGLE...
POP
SPLISH SPLASH SPLASH
FLAIL
FLAIL
FLAIL
FLAIL
AAAH!

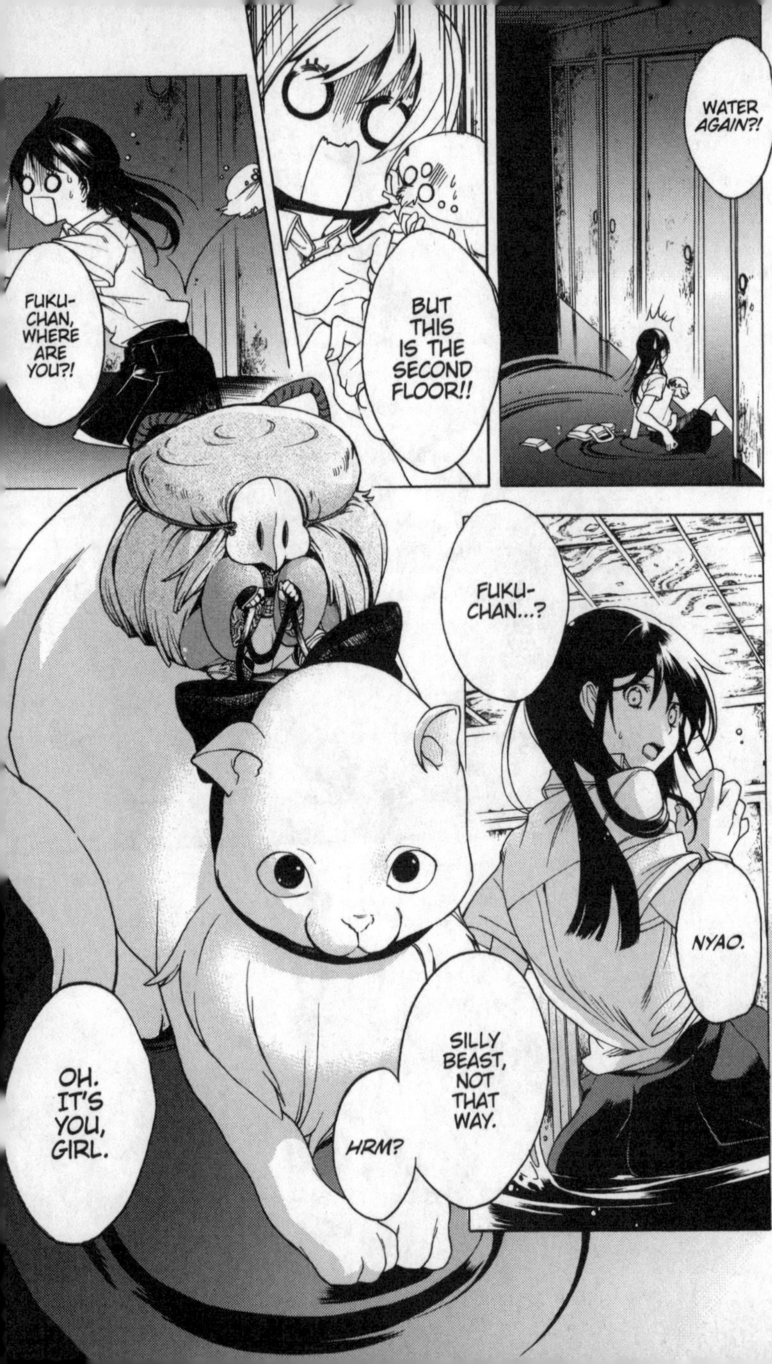
WATER AGAIN?!
BUT THIS IS THE SECOND FLOOR!!
FUKU-CHAN, WHERE ARE YOU?!
FUKU-CHAN...?
NYAO.
SILLY BEAST, NOT THAT WAY.
HRM?
OH. IT'S YOU, GIRL.

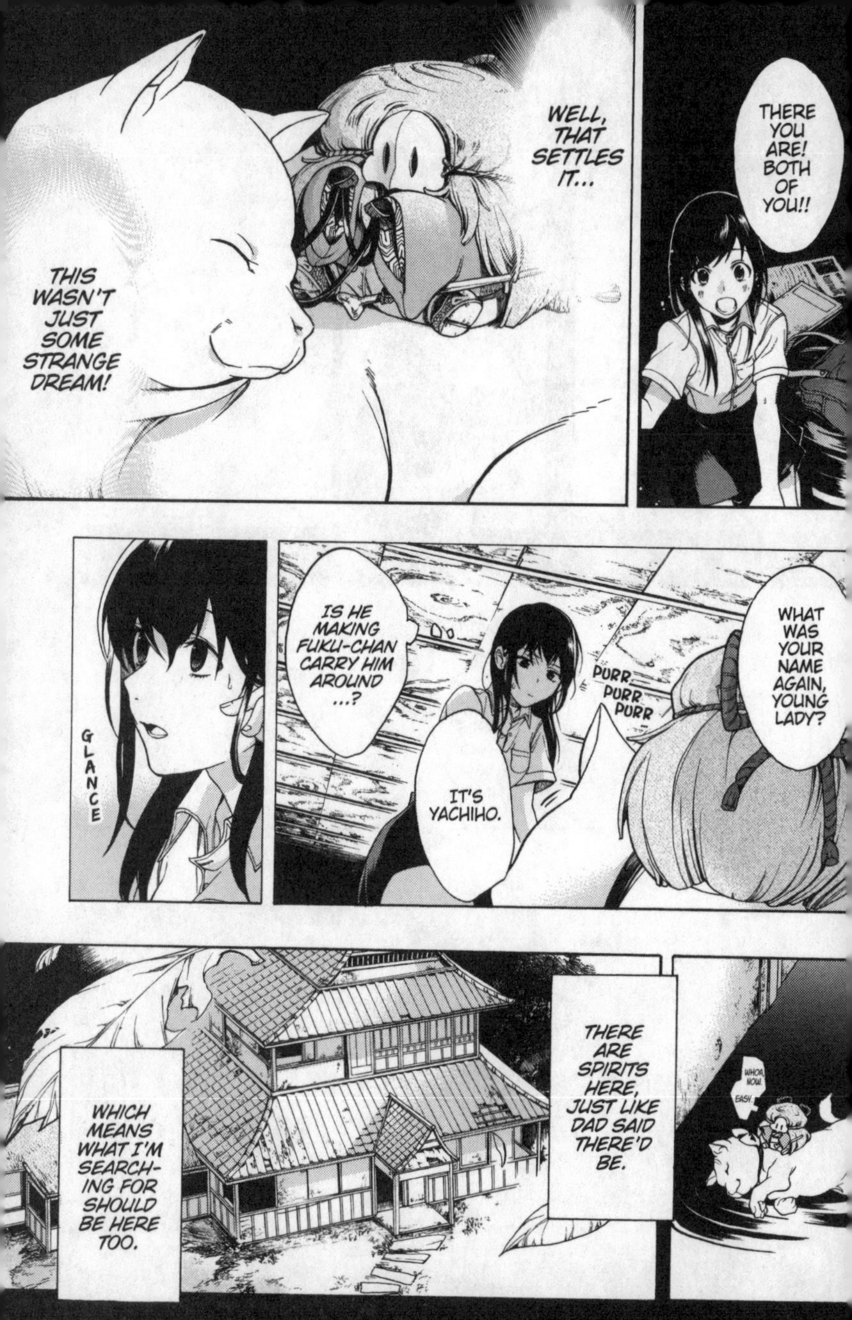
THERE YOU ARE! BOTH OF YOU!!
WELL, THAT SETTLES IT...
THIS WASN'T JUST SOME STRANGE DREAM!
WHAT WAS YOUR NAME AGAIN, YOUNG LADY?
PURR PURR PURR
IT'S YACHIHO.
IS HE MAKING FUKU-CHAN CARRY HIM AROUND ...?
GLANCE
WHOA, NOW.
EASY.
THERE ARE SPIRITS HERE, JUST LIKE DAD SAID THERE'D BE.
WHICH MEANS WHAT I'M SEARCHING FOR SHOULD BE HERE TOO.

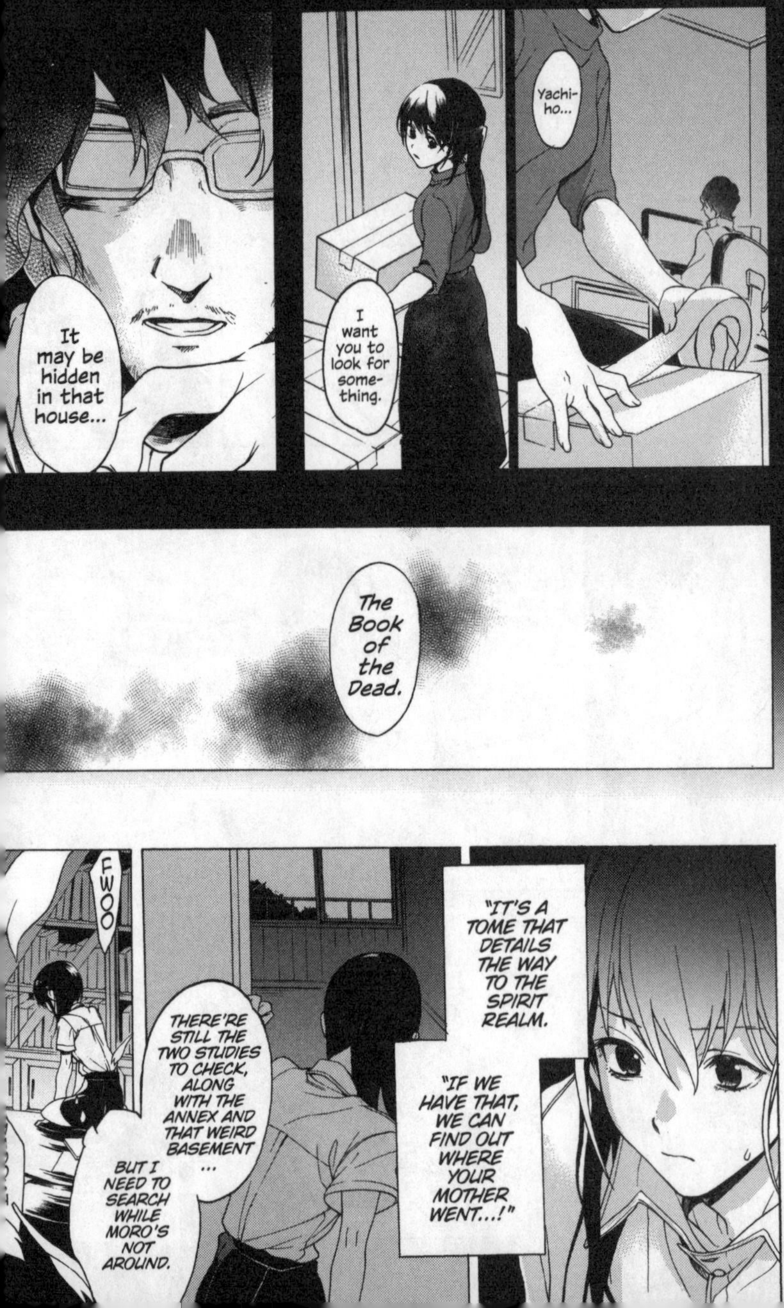

Yachi-ho...
I want you to look for some-thing.
It may be hidden in that house...
The Book of the Dead.
"IT'S A TOME THAT DETAILS THE WAY TO THE SPIRIT REALM.
"IF WE HAVE THAT, WE CAN FIND OUT WHERE YOUR MOTHER WENT...!"
THERE'RE STILL THE TWO STUDIES TO CHECK, ALONG WITH THE ANNEX AND THAT WEIRD BASEMENT...
BUT I NEED TO SEARCH WHILE MORO'S NOT AROUND.
FWOO

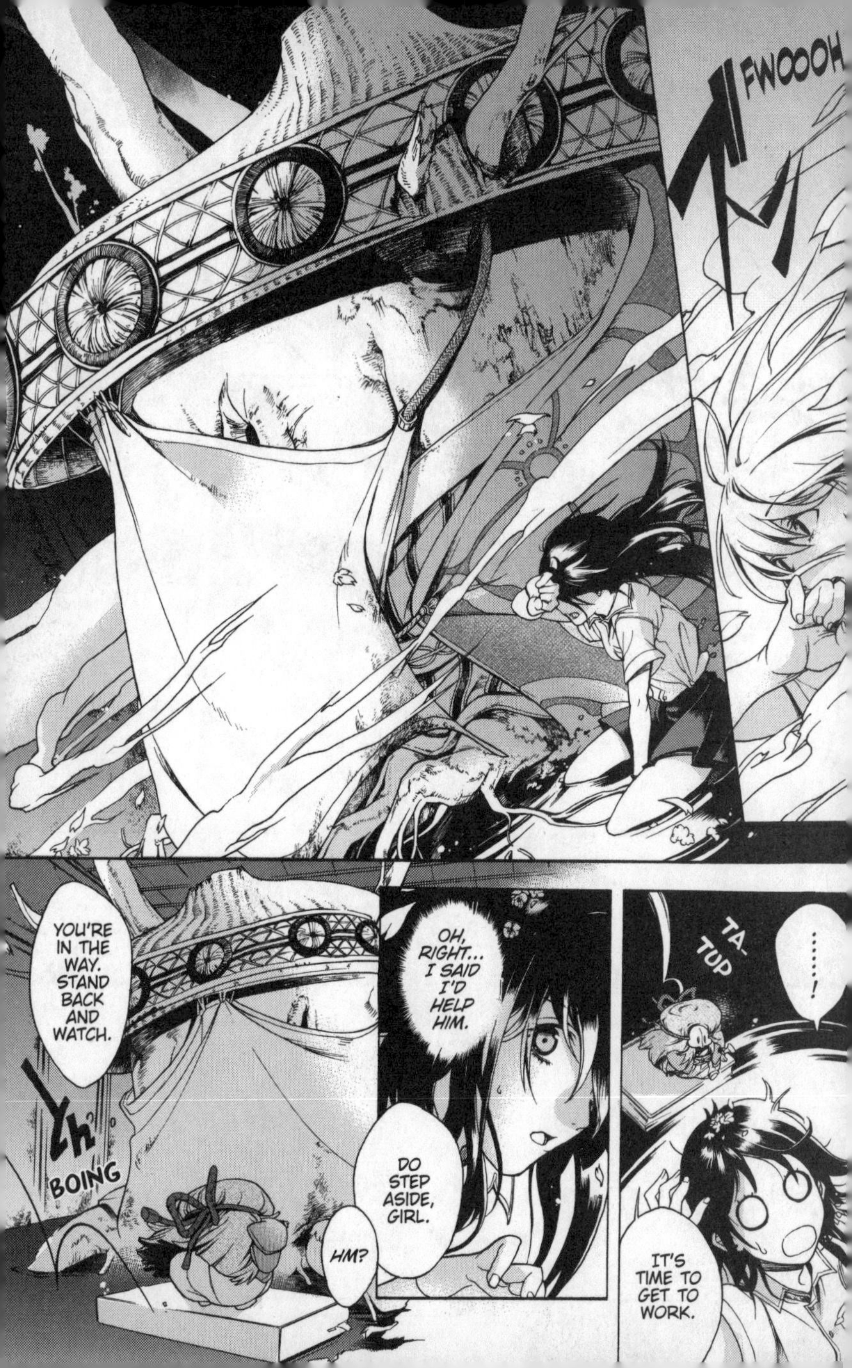
FWOOOH
......!
TA-TUP
IT'S TIME TO GET TO WORK.
OH, RIGHT... I SAID I'D HELP HIM.
DO STEP ASIDE, GIRL.
HM?
YOU'RE IN THE WAY. STAND BACK AND WATCH.
BOING

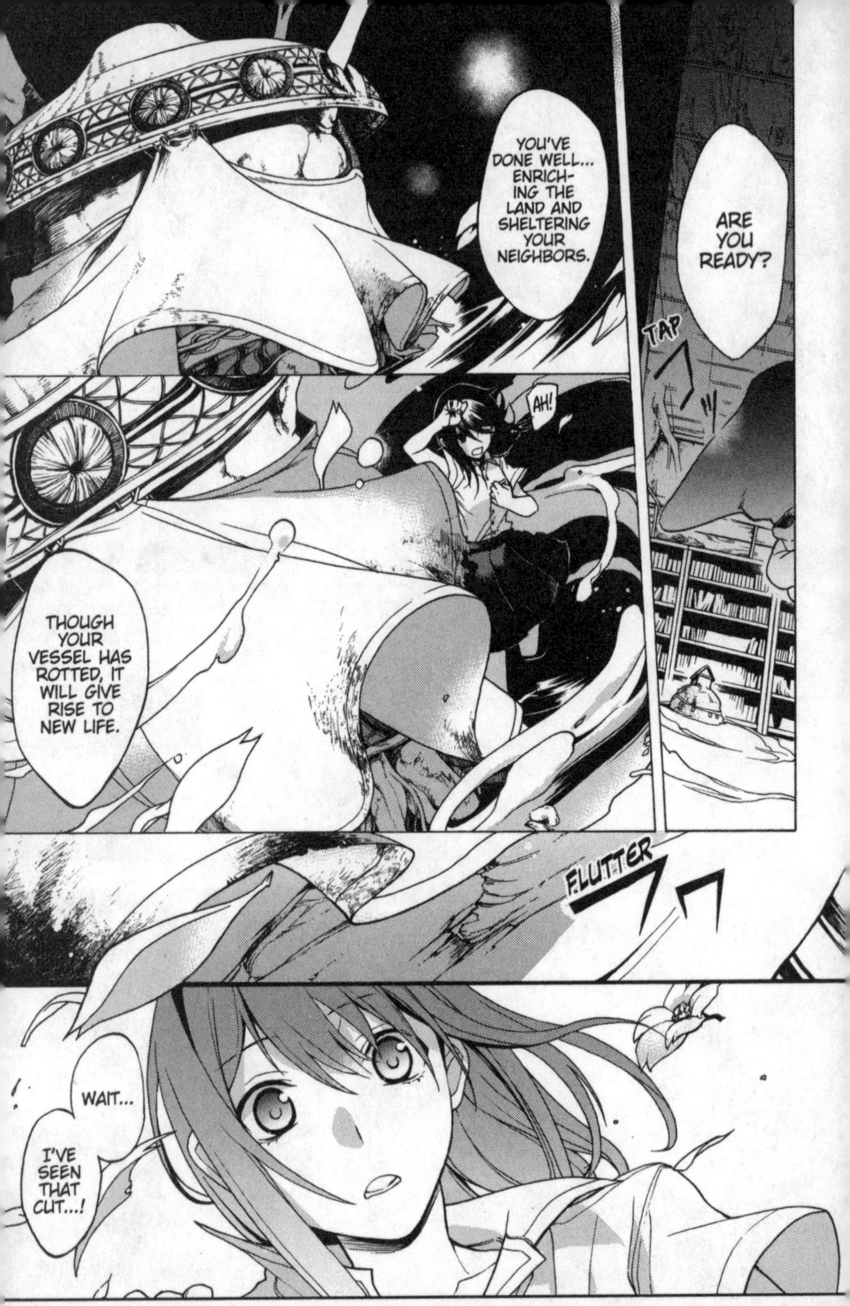
ARE YOU READY?
TAP
YOU'VE DONE WELL... ENRICHING THE LAND AND SHELTERING YOUR NEIGHBORS.
AH!
THOUGH YOUR VESSEL HAS ROTTED, IT WILL GIVE RISE TO NEW LIFE.
FLUTTER
WAIT...
I'VE SEEN THAT CUT...!

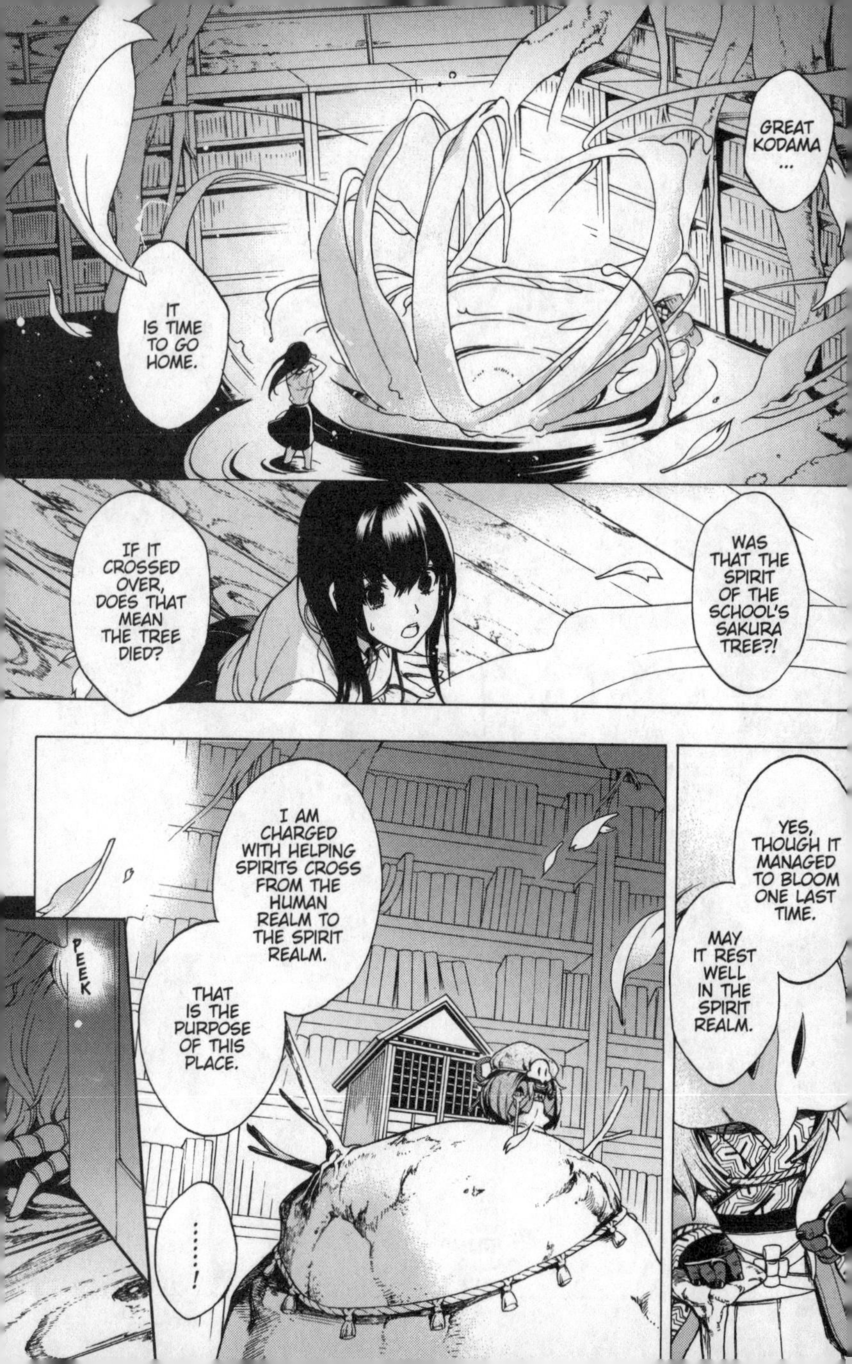
GREAT KODAMA ...
IT IS TIME TO GO HOME.
WAS THAT THE SPIRIT OF THE SCHOOL'S SAKURA TREE?!
IF IT CROSSED OVER, DOES THAT MEAN THE TREE DIED?
YES, THOUGH IT MANAGED TO BLOOM ONE LAST TIME.
MAY IT REST WELL IN THE SPIRIT REALM.
I AM CHARGED WITH HELPING SPIRITS CROSS FROM THE HUMAN REALM TO THE SPIRIT REALM.
THAT IS THE PURPOSE OF THIS PLACE.
PEEK
......!

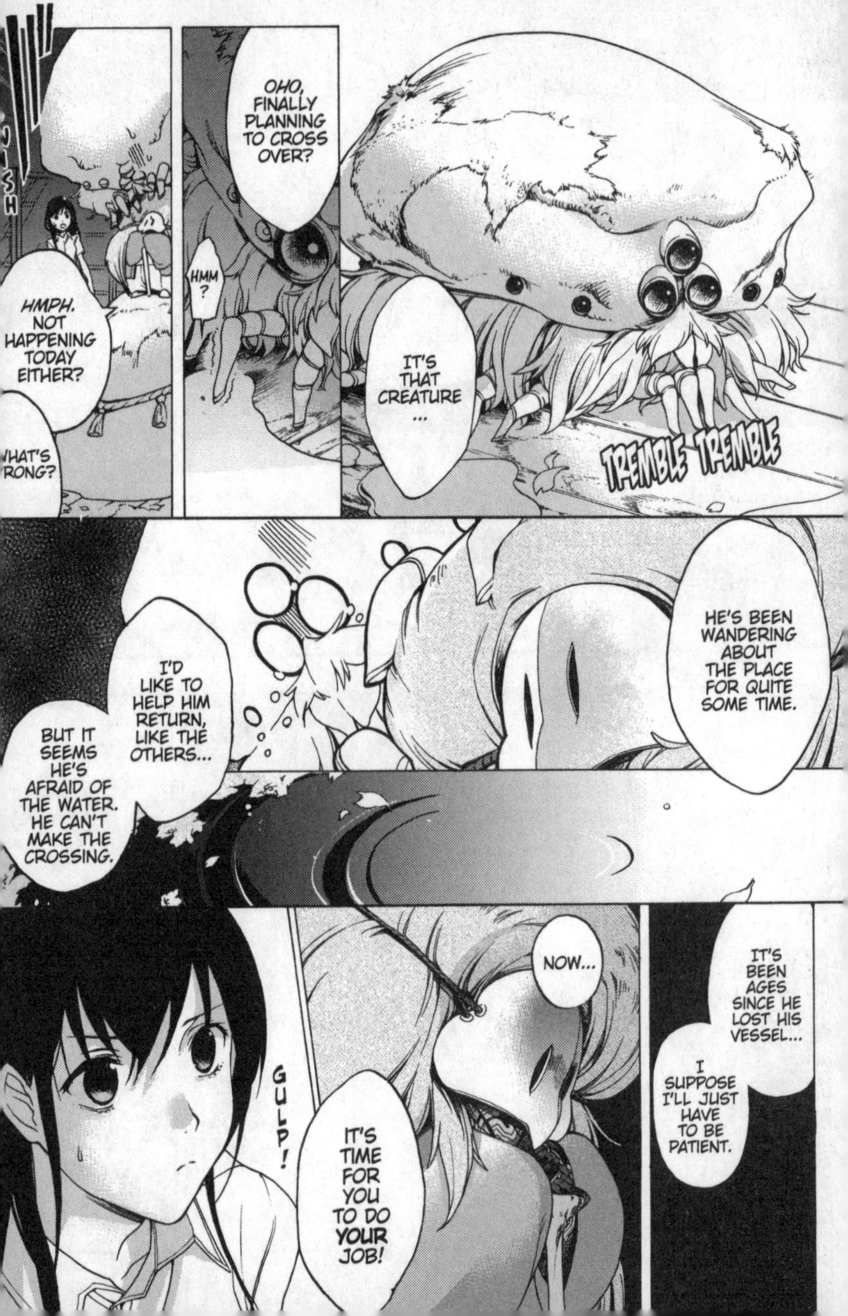
IT'S THAT CREATURE...
TREMBLE TREMBLE
OHO, FINALLY PLANNING TO CROSS OVER?
HMM?
HMPH. NOT HAPPENING TODAY EITHER?
HAT'S RONG?
HE'S BEEN WANDERING ABOUT THE PLACE FOR QUITE SOME TIME.
I'D LIKE TO HELP HIM RETURN, LIKE THE OTHERS...
BUT IT SEEMS HE'S AFRAID OF THE WATER. HE CAN'T MAKE THE CROSSING.
IT'S BEEN AGES SINCE HE LOST HIS VESSEL...
I SUPPOSE I'LL JUST HAVE TO BE PATIENT.
NOW...
IT'S TIME FOR YOU TO DO **YOUR** JOB!
GULP!

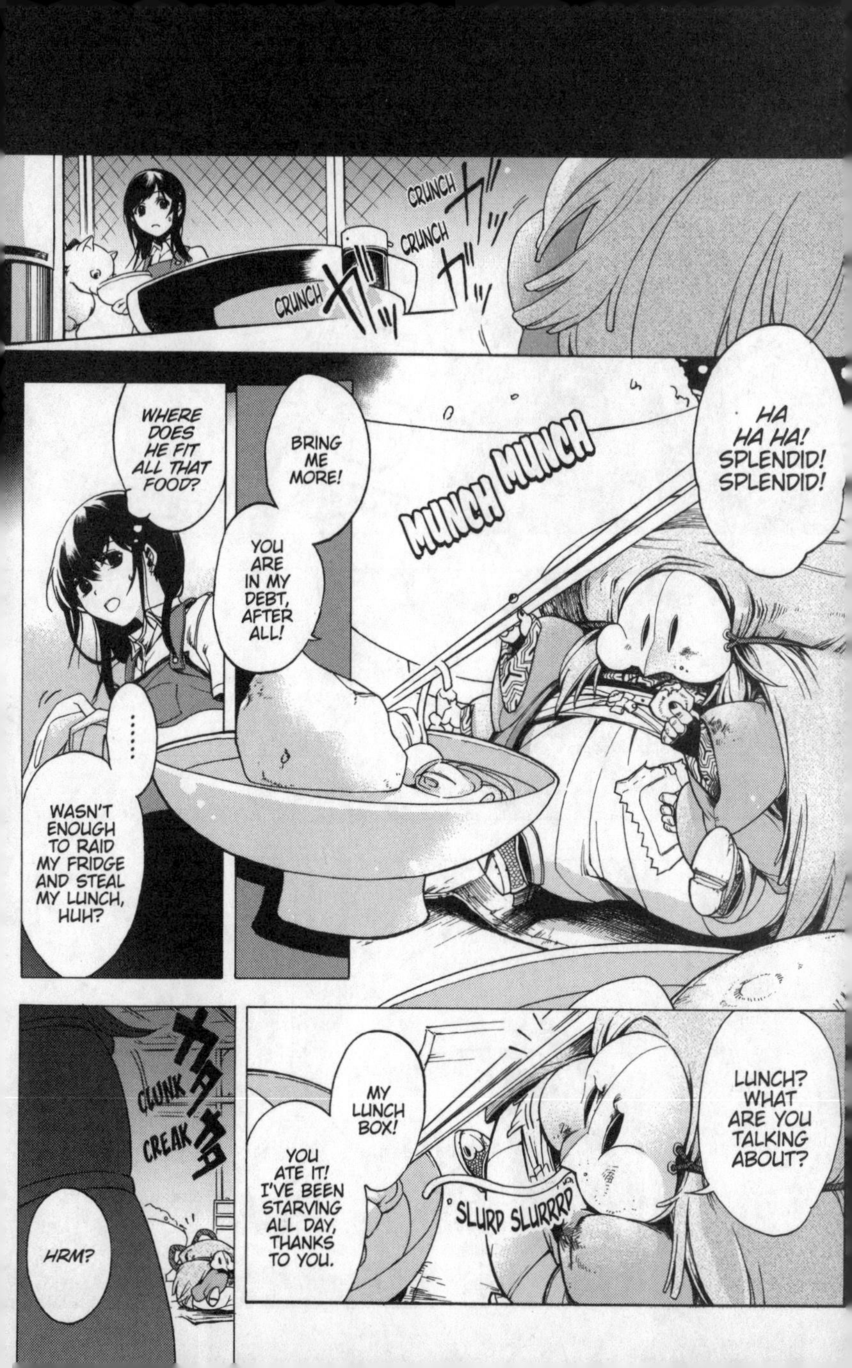
CRUNCH
CRUNCH
CRUNCH
HA HA HA! SPLENDID! SPLENDID!
MUNCH MUNCH
BRING ME MORE!
YOU ARE IN MY DEBT, AFTER ALL!
WHERE DOES HE FIT ALL THAT FOOD?
......
WASN'T ENOUGH TO RAID MY FRIDGE AND STEAL MY LUNCH, HUH?
LUNCH? WHAT ARE YOU TALKING ABOUT?
SLURP SLURRRP
MY LUNCH BOX!
YOU ATE IT! I'VE BEEN STARVING ALL DAY, THANKS TO YOU.
CLUNK
CREAK
HRM?

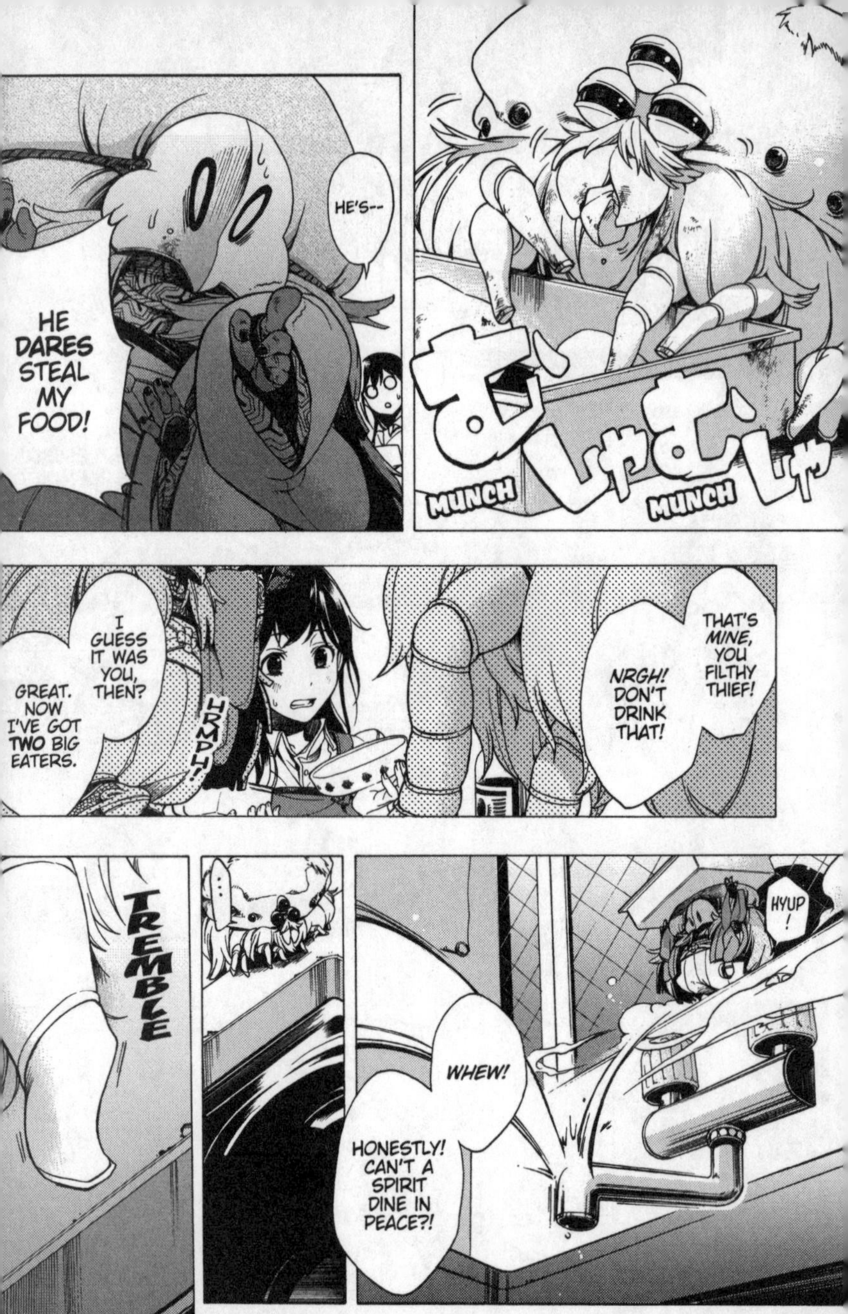
むしゃむしゃ
MUNCH MUNCH
HE'S--
HE DARES STEAL MY FOOD!
NRGH! DON'T DRINK THAT!
THAT'S *MINE*, YOU FILTHY THIEF!
HRMPH!
I GUESS IT WAS YOU, THEN?
GREAT. NOW I'VE GOT **TWO** BIG EATERS.
HYUP!
WHEW!
HONESTLY! CAN'T A SPIRIT DINE IN PEACE?!
...
TREMBLE

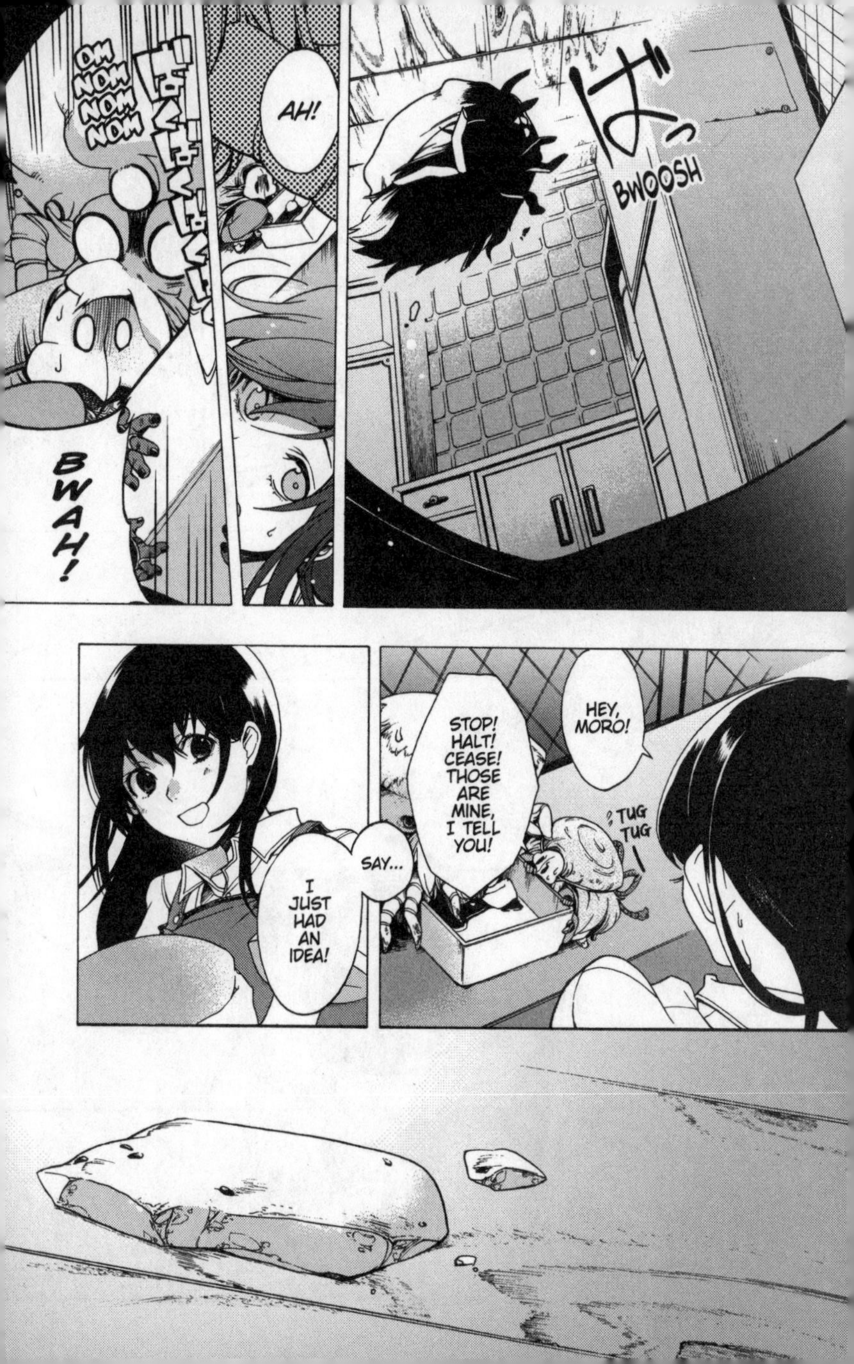
ばっ
BWOOSH
AH!
OM NOM NOM NOM
BWAH!
HEY, MORO!
STOP! HALT! CEASE! THOSE ARE MINE, I TELL YOU!
TUG TUG
SAY...
I JUST HAD AN IDEA!

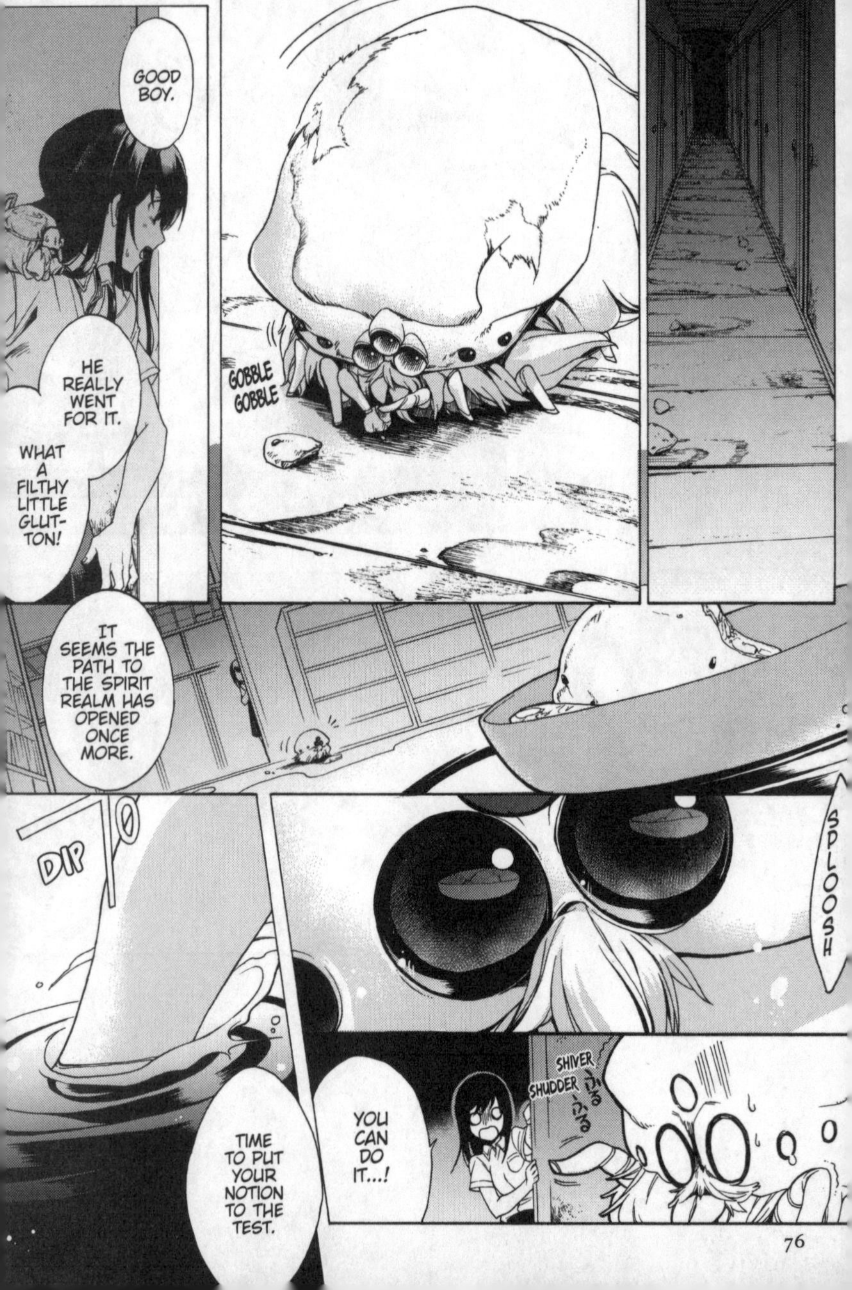
GOBBLE GOBBLE
GOOD BOY.
HE REALLY WENT FOR IT.
WHAT A FILTHY LITTLE GLUTTON!
IT SEEMS THE PATH TO THE SPIRIT REALM HAS OPENED ONCE MORE.
SPLOOSH
DIP
SHIVER ふる
SHUDDER ふる
YOU CAN DO IT...!
TIME TO PUT YOUR NOTION TO THE TEST.

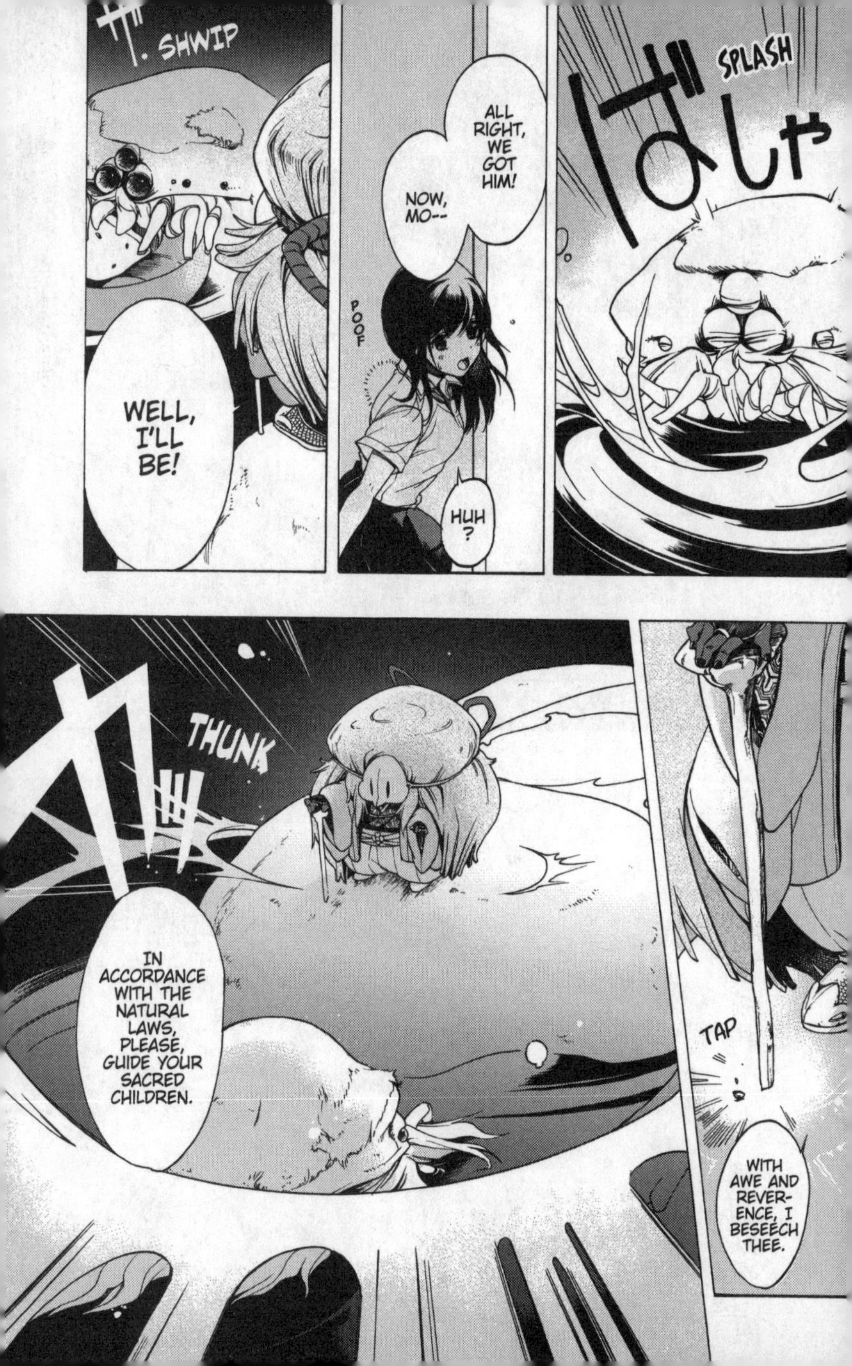

ばしゃ
SPLASH
ALL RIGHT, WE GOT HIM!
NOW, MO--
POOF
HUH?
SHWIP
WELL, I'LL BE!
TAP
WITH AWE AND REVERENCE, I BESEECH THEE.
THUNK
IN ACCORDANCE WITH THE NATURAL LAWS, PLEASE, GUIDE YOUR SACRED CHILDREN.

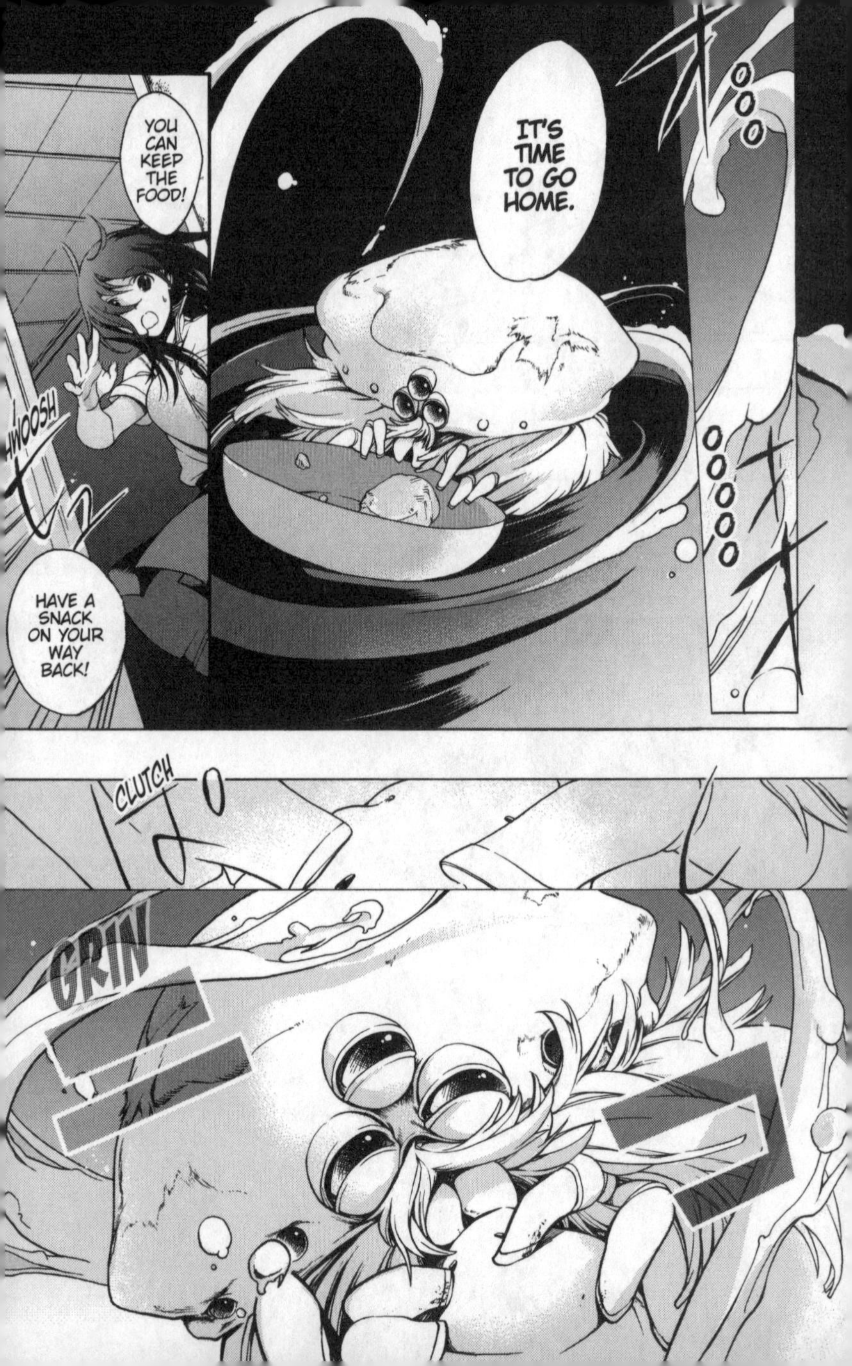

OOO
OOOOOO
IT'S TIME TO GO HOME.
YOU CAN KEEP THE FOOD!
HWOOSH
HAVE A SNACK ON YOUR WAY BACK!
CLUTCH
GRIN

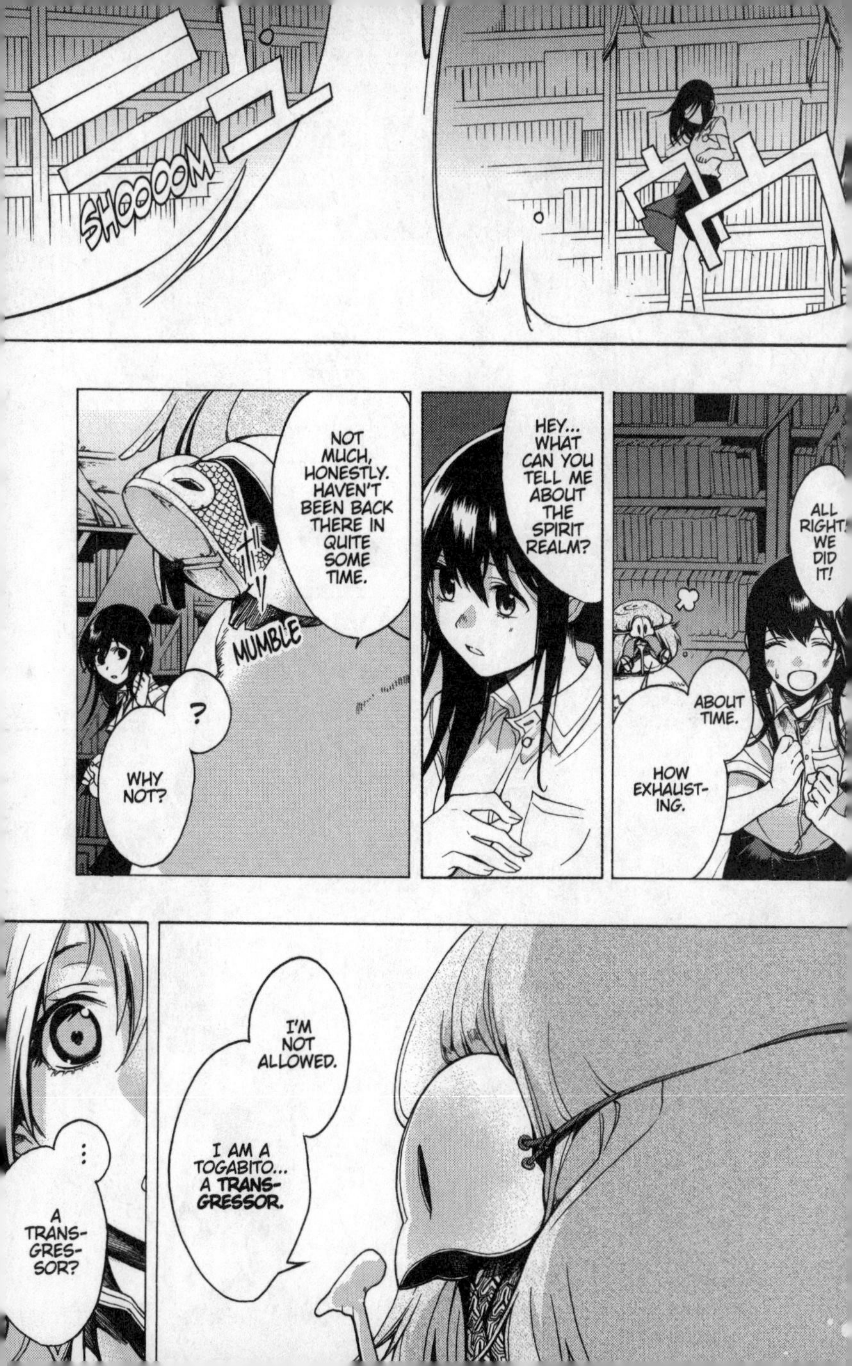
SHOOOOM
ALL RIGHT! WE DID IT!
ABOUT TIME.
HOW EXHAUST-ING.
HEY... WHAT CAN YOU TELL ME ABOUT THE SPIRIT REALM?
NOT MUCH, HONESTLY. HAVEN'T BEEN BACK THERE IN QUITE SOME TIME.
MUMBLE
?
WHY NOT?
I'M NOT ALLOWED.
I AM A TOGABITO... A **TRANS-GRESSOR.**
...
A TRANS-GRES-SOR?

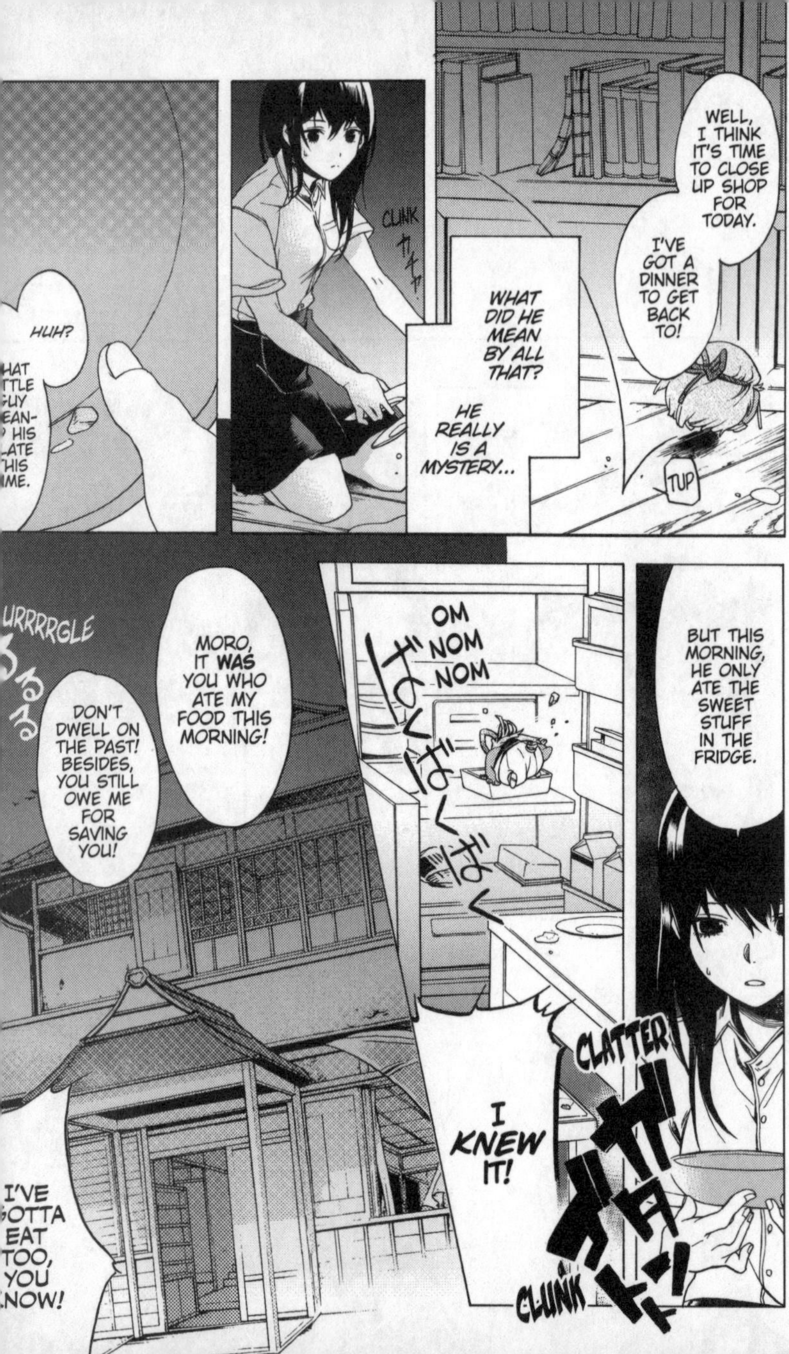
WELL, I THINK IT'S TIME TO CLOSE UP SHOP FOR TODAY.
I'VE GOT A DINNER TO GET BACK TO!
TUP
CLINK
WHAT DID HE MEAN BY ALL THAT?
HE REALLY IS A MYSTERY...
HUH?
BUT THIS MORNING, HE ONLY ATE THE SWEET STUFF IN THE FRIDGE.
CLATTER
I KNEW IT!
CLUNK
OM NOM NOM
URRRRGLE
MORO, IT WAS YOU WHO ATE MY FOOD THIS MORNING!
DON'T DWELL ON THE PAST! BESIDES, YOU STILL OWE ME FOR SAVING YOU!
I'VE OTTA EAT TOO, YOU NOW!

SCHOOL UNIFORM

THE SCHOOL REQUIRES A SPECIFIC TYPE OF SKIRT, PANTS, AND JACKET, BUT YOU'RE GIVEN A LOT OF FREEDOM TO CUSTOMIZE YOUR LOOK.

YOUR CHOICE OF SWEATER OR VEST. (COMES WITH A JACKET)

SHIRT — HAS TO BE WHITE. NO COLORED SHIRTS.

YOU CAN LEAVE THE TOP TWO BUTTONS OPEN.

RIBBON — CHOOSE ANY COLOR.

YACHIHO USUALLY GOES WITH RED.

SKIRT

POCKET

ZIPPER

FRONT

BACK

KNEE LENGTH. ANYTHING SHORTER AND YOU'LL GET A WARNING.

YOUR CHOICE OF SOCKS. TIGHTS ARE OKAY.

(YACHIHO WEARS KNEE-HIGHS.)

WHITE, NAVY, AND EMBROIDERED SOCKS ARE ALLOWED.

KNEE-HIGH   ANKLET   TURN-CUFF   STOCKINGS

Ghostly
Things

Chapter 3
New Growth

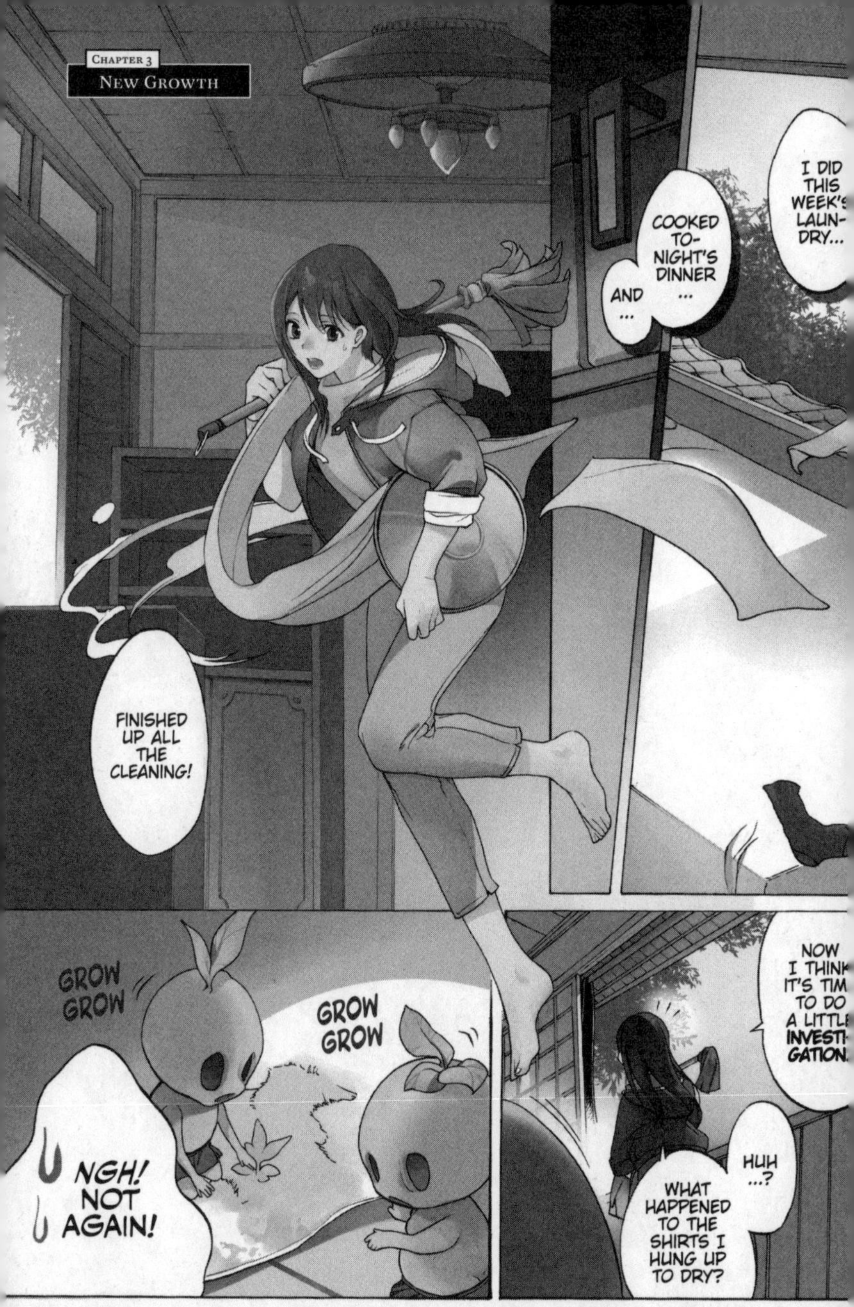

I DID THIS WEEK'S LAUNDRY...
COOKED TONIGHT'S DINNER...
AND...
FINISHED UP ALL THE CLEANING!
NOW I THINK IT'S TIM TO DO A LITTLE INVESTIGATION.
HUH...?
WHAT HAPPENED TO THE SHIRTS I HUNG UP TO DRY?
GROW GROW
GROW GROW
NGH! NOT AGAIN!

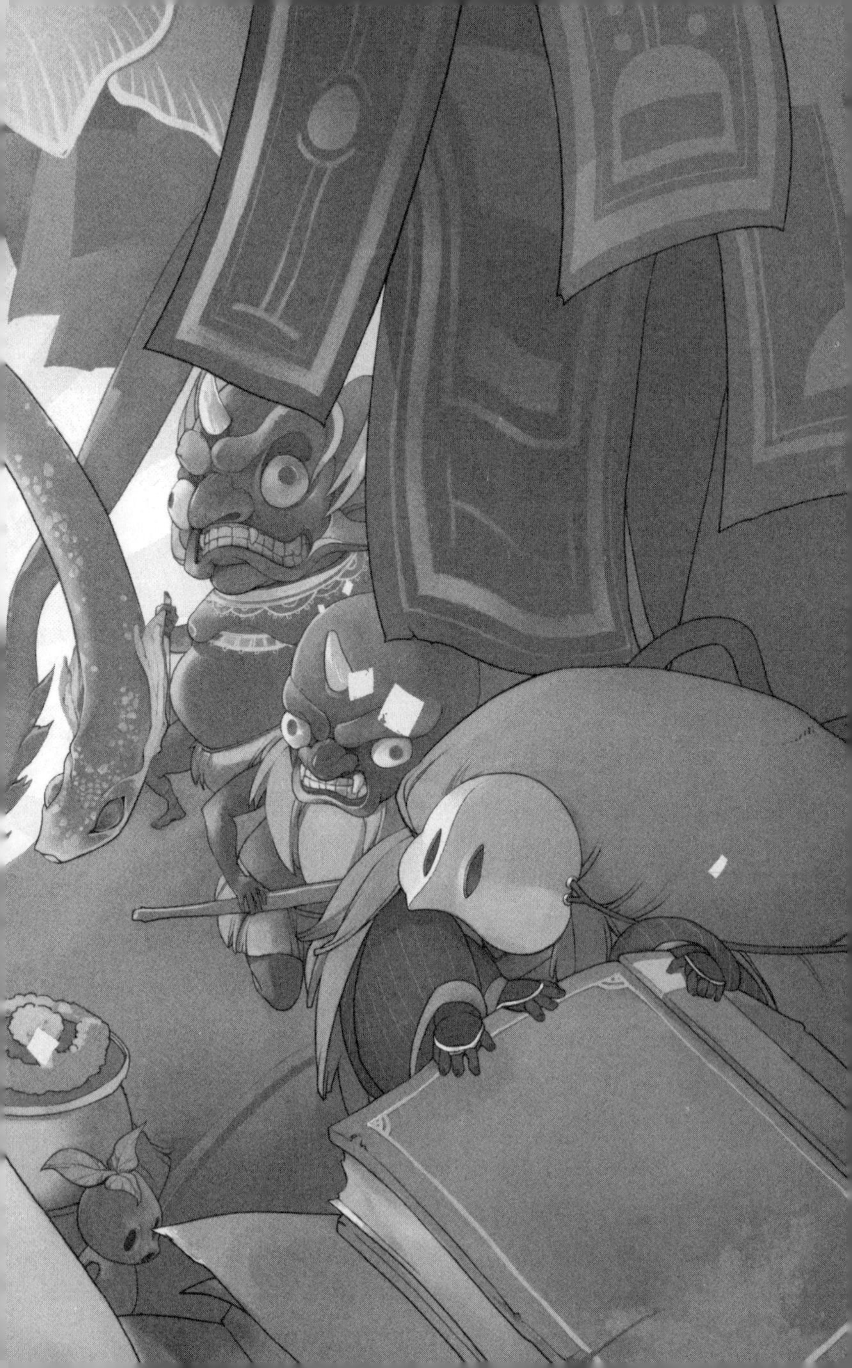

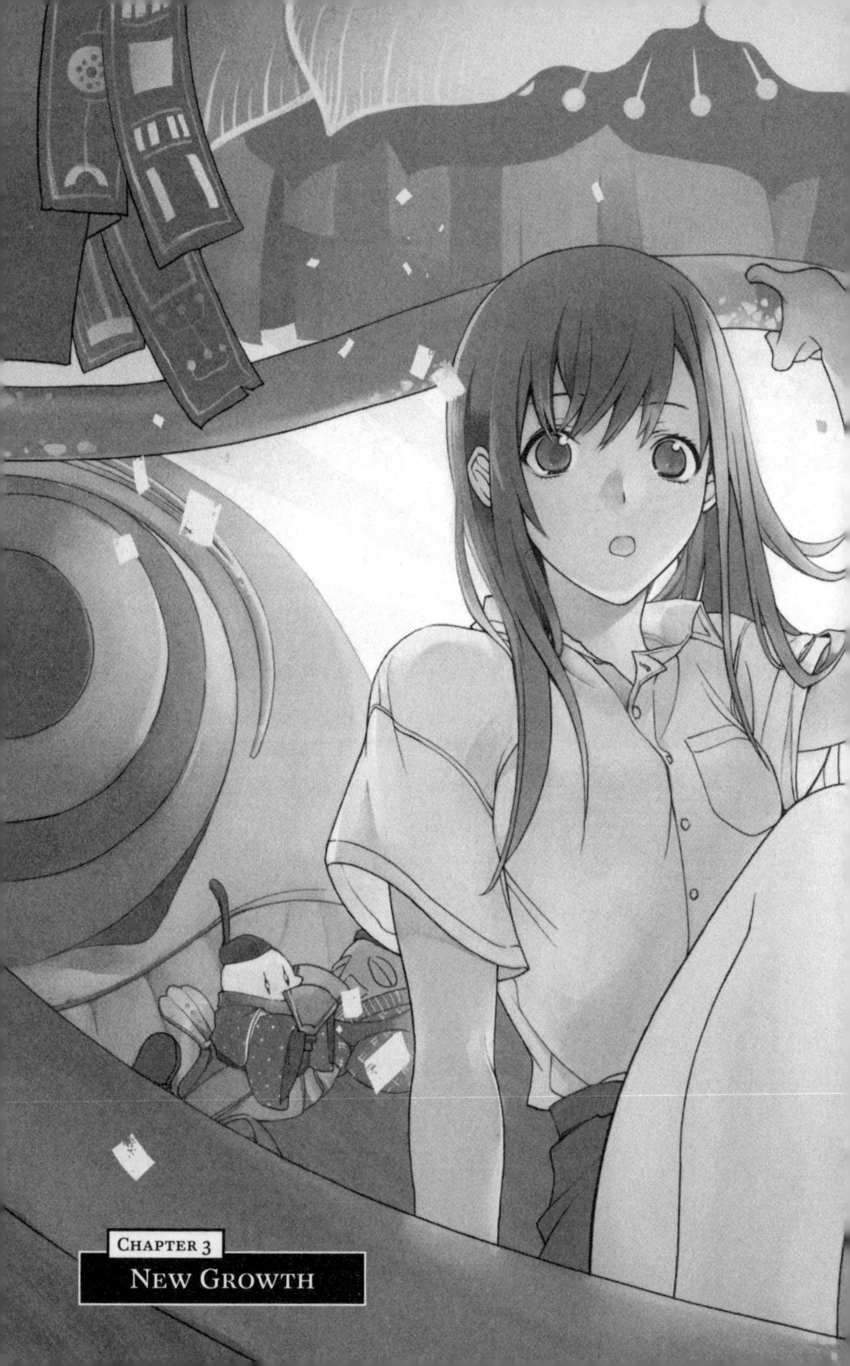

Chapter 3
New Growth

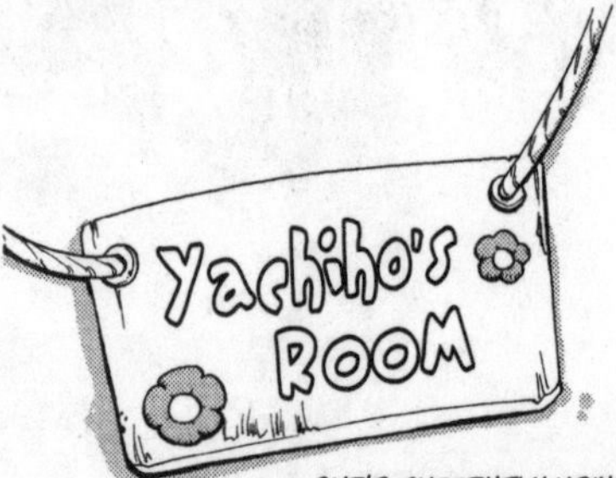
Yachiho's Room

SHE'S CURRENTLY USING AN 11X11 FOOT ROOM ON THE SECOND FLOOR AS A BEDROOM. IT GETS PLENTY OF LIGHT, BUT SHE DOESN'T LIKE THE DUST.

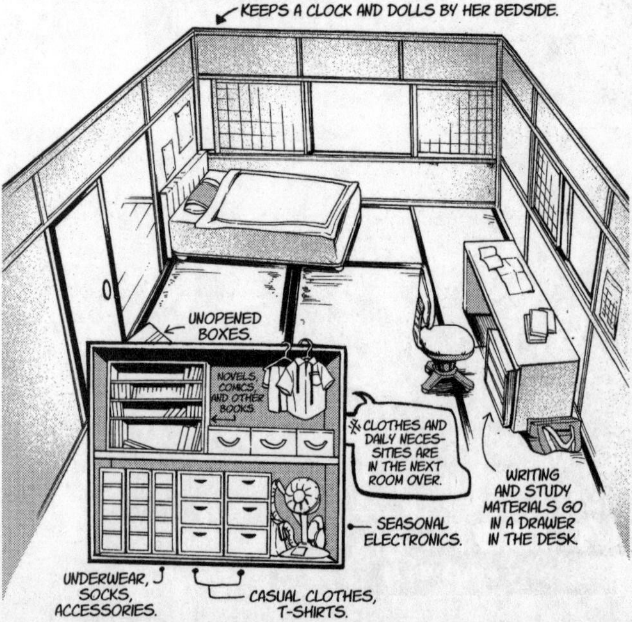
KEEPS A CLOCK AND DOLLS BY HER BEDSIDE.
UNOPENED BOXES.
NOVELS, COMICS, AND OTHER BOOKS
※CLOTHES AND DAILY NECES-SITIES ARE IN THE NEXT ROOM OVER.
WRITING AND STUDY MATERIALS GO IN A DRAWER IN THE DESK.
SEASONAL ELECTRONICS.
UNDERWEAR, SOCKS, ACCESSORIES.
CASUAL CLOTHES, T-SHIRTS.

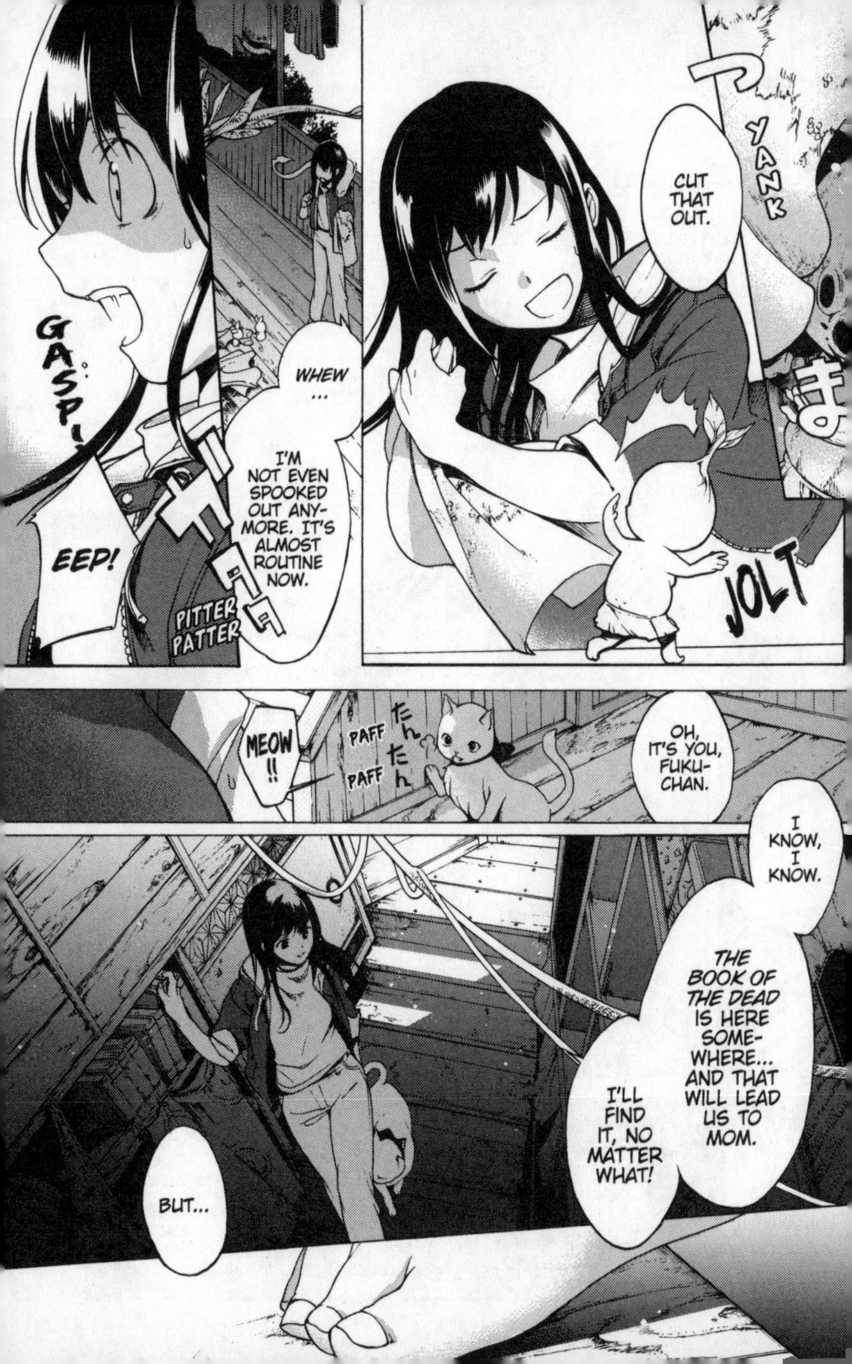
つ
YANK
CUT THAT OUT.
ま
JOLT
GASP!
EEP!
WHEW...
I'M NOT EVEN SPOOKED OUT ANYMORE. IT'S ALMOST ROUTINE NOW.
PITTER PATTER
OH, IT'S YOU, FUKU-CHAN.
たん たん
PAFF PAFF
MEOW!!
I KNOW, I KNOW.
THE BOOK OF THE DEAD IS HERE SOMEWHERE... AND THAT WILL LEAD US TO MOM.
I'LL FIND IT, NO MATTER WHAT!
BUT...

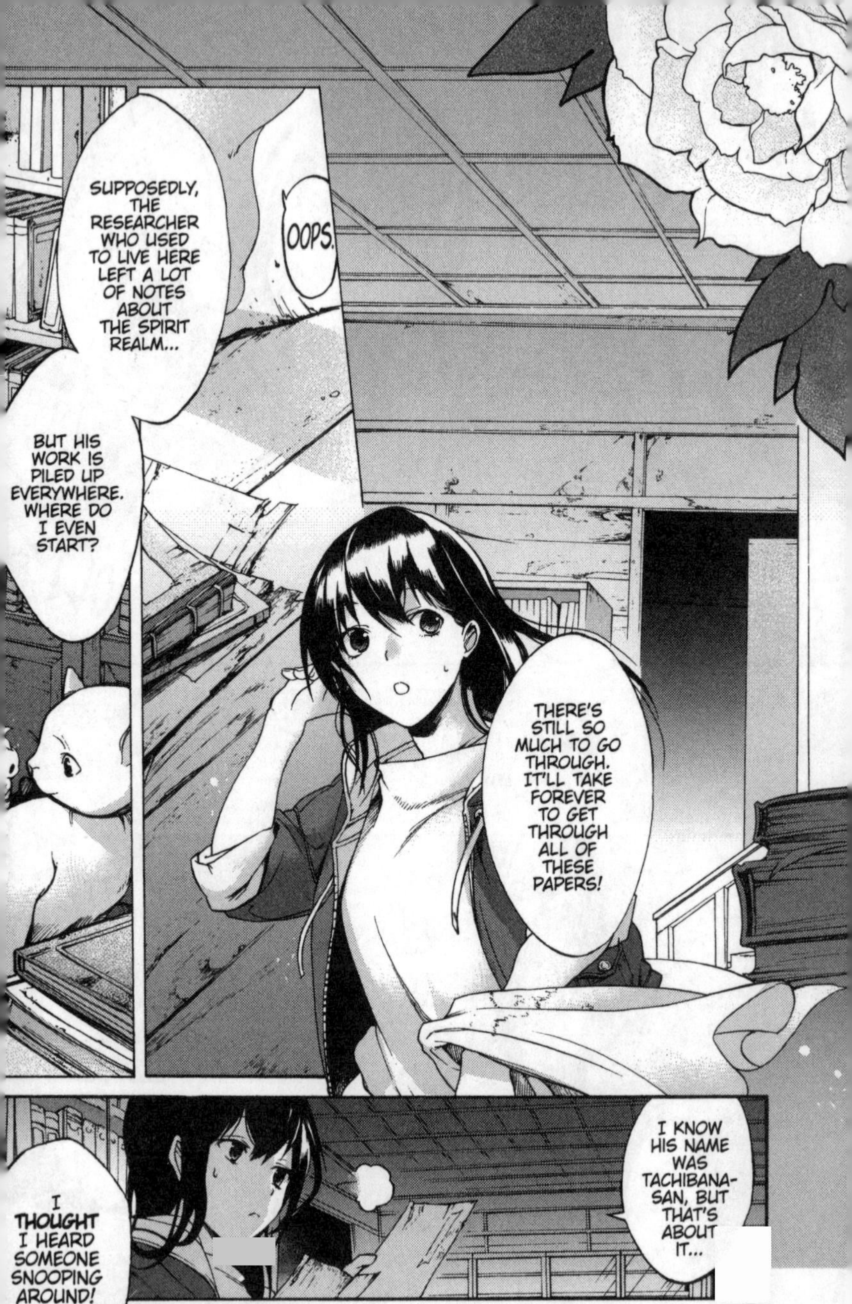
OOPS.
THERE'S STILL SO MUCH TO GO THROUGH. IT'LL TAKE FOREVER TO GET THROUGH ALL OF THESE PAPERS!
SUPPOSEDLY, THE RESEARCHER WHO USED TO LIVE HERE LEFT A LOT OF NOTES ABOUT THE SPIRIT REALM...
BUT HIS WORK IS PILED UP EVERYWHERE. WHERE DO I EVEN START?
I KNOW HIS NAME WAS TACHIBANA-SAN, BUT THAT'S ABOUT IT...
I THOUGHT I HEARD SOMEONE SNOOPING AROUND!

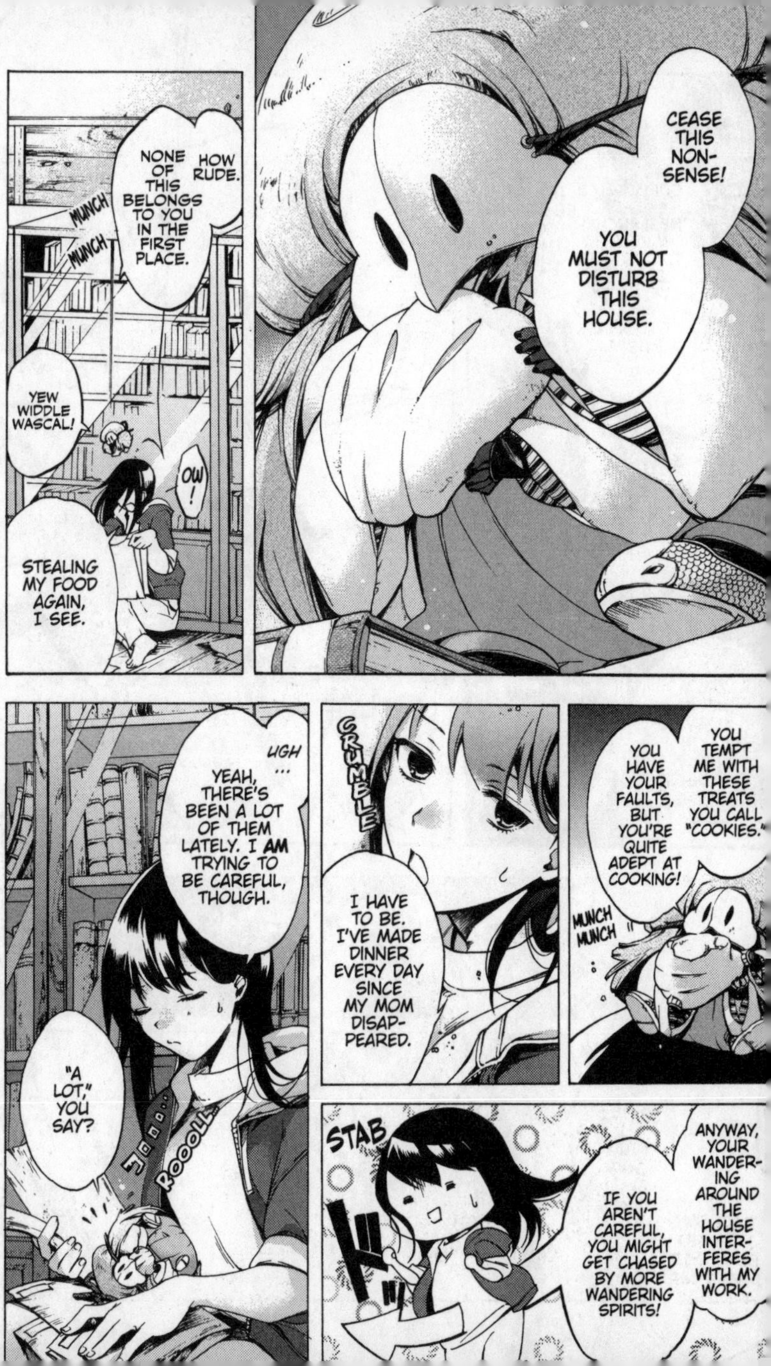
CEASE THIS NON-SENSE!
YOU MUST NOT DISTURB THIS HOUSE.
HOW RUDE.
NONE OF THIS BELONGS TO YOU IN THE FIRST PLACE.
MUNCH MUNCH
YEW WIDDLE WASCAL!
OW!
STEALING MY FOOD AGAIN, I SEE.
YOU TEMPT ME WITH THESE TREATS YOU CALL "COOKIES."
YOU HAVE YOUR FAULTS, BUT YOU'RE QUITE ADEPT AT COOKING!
MUNCH MUNCH
CRUMBLE
I HAVE TO BE. I'VE MADE DINNER EVERY DAY SINCE MY MOM DISAP-PEARED.
STAB
ANYWAY, YOUR WANDER-ING AROUND THE HOUSE INTER-FERES WITH MY WORK.
IF YOU AREN'T CAREFUL, YOU MIGHT GET CHASED BY MORE WANDERING SPIRITS!
UGH...
YEAH, THERE'S BEEN A LOT OF THEM LATELY. I **AM** TRYING TO BE CAREFUL, THOUGH.
ROOOLL
"A LOT," YOU SAY?

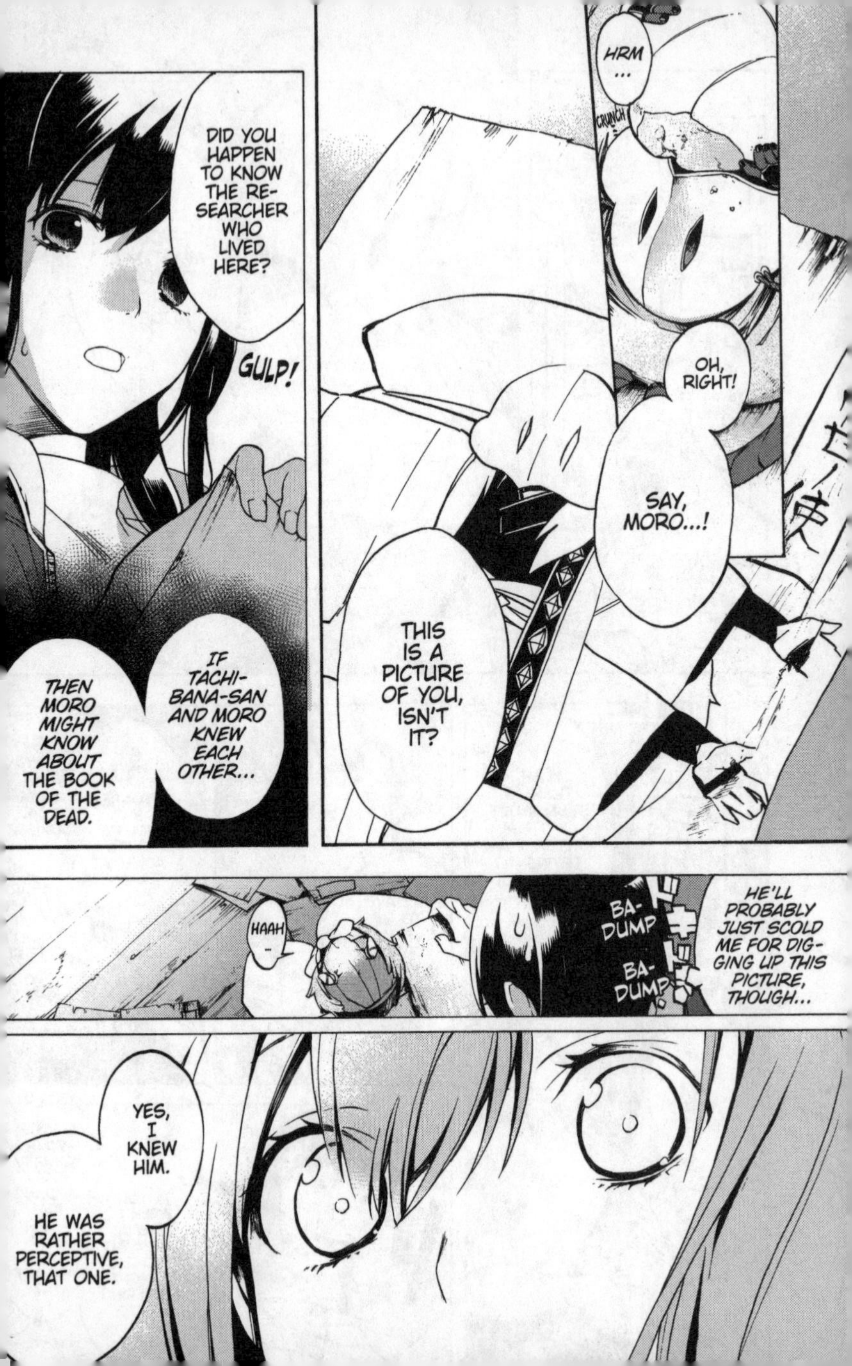
HRM ...
CRUNCH
OH, RIGHT!
SAY, MORO...!
THIS IS A PICTURE OF YOU, ISN'T IT?
DID YOU HAPPEN TO KNOW THE RE-SEARCHER WHO LIVED HERE?
GULP!
IF TACHI-BANA-SAN AND MORO KNEW EACH OTHER...
THEN MORO MIGHT KNOW ABOUT THE BOOK OF THE DEAD.
HE'LL PROBABLY JUST SCOLD ME FOR DIG-GING UP THIS PICTURE, THOUGH...
BA-DUMP
BA-DUMP
HAAH ...
YES, I KNEW HIM.
HE WAS RATHER PERCEPTIVE, THAT ONE.

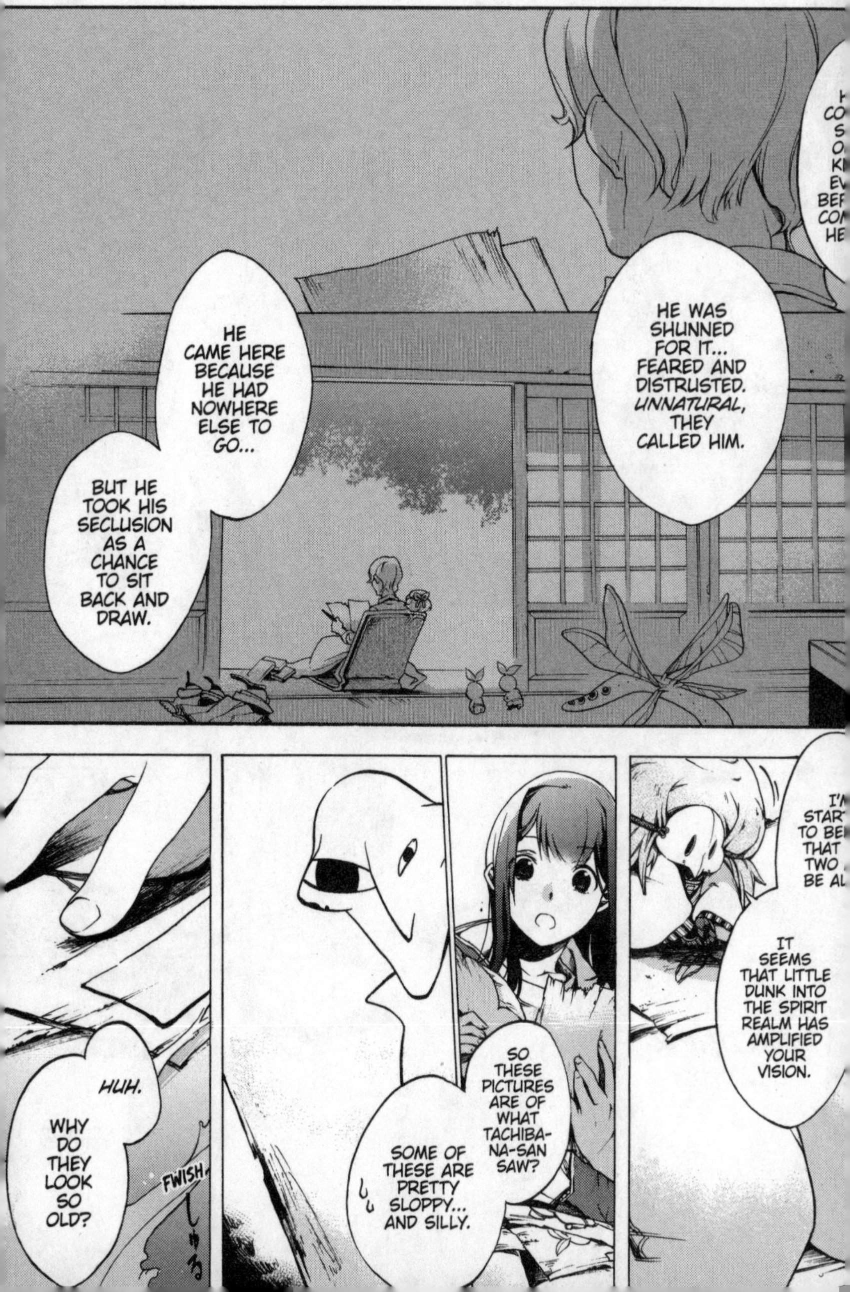
HE WAS SHUNNED FOR IT... FEARED AND DISTRUSTED. *UNNATURAL*, THEY CALLED HIM.
HE CAME HERE BECAUSE HE HAD NOWHERE ELSE TO GO...
BUT HE TOOK HIS SECLUSION AS A CHANCE TO SIT BACK AND DRAW.
IT SEEMS THAT LITTLE DUNK INTO THE SPIRIT REALM HAS AMPLIFIED YOUR VISION.
SO THESE PICTURES ARE OF WHAT TACHIBANA-SAN SAW?
SOME OF THESE ARE PRETTY SLOPPY... AND SILLY.
HUH.
WHY DO THEY LOOK SO OLD?
FWISH

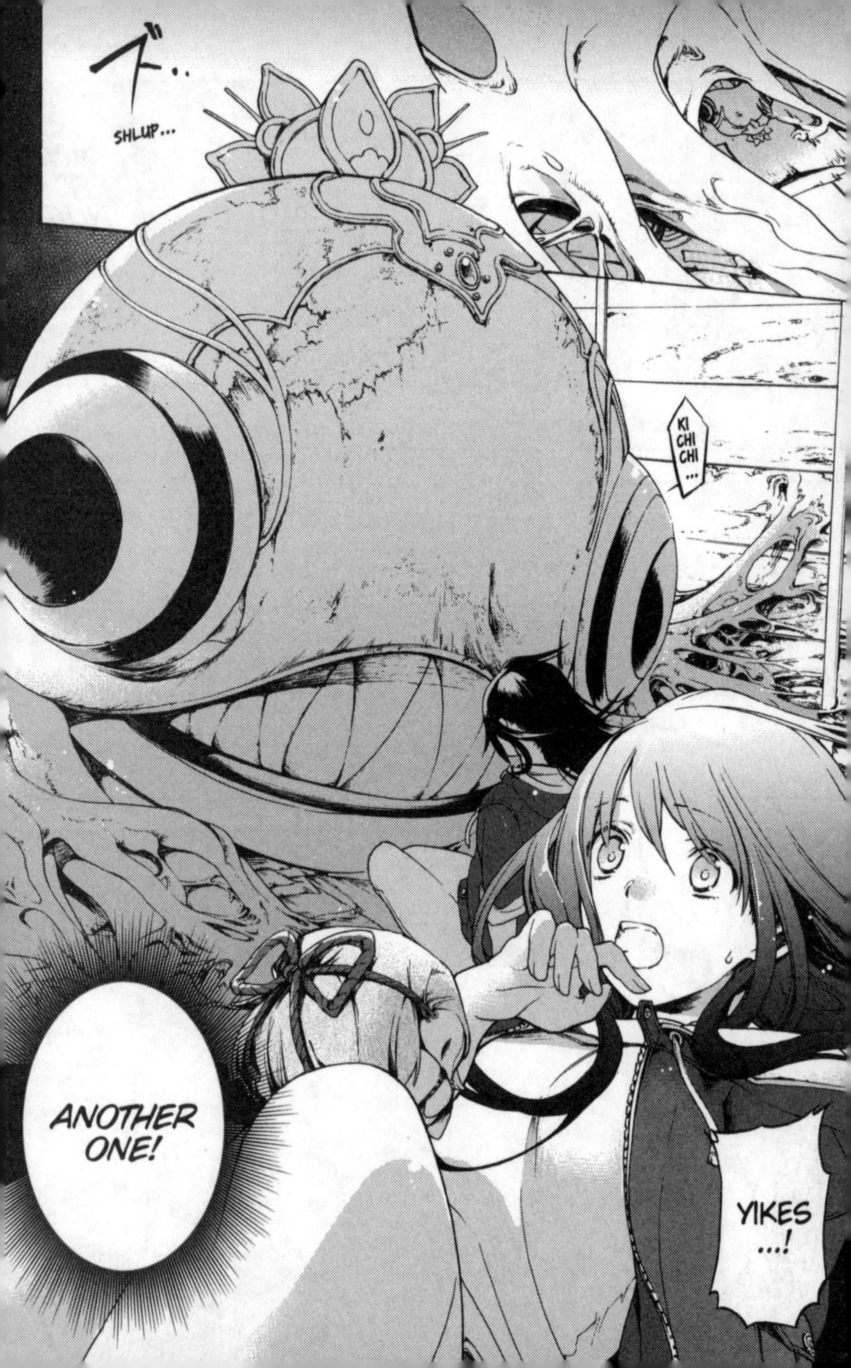
ズ..
SHLUP...
KI CHI CHI ...
YIKES ...!
ANOTHER ONE!

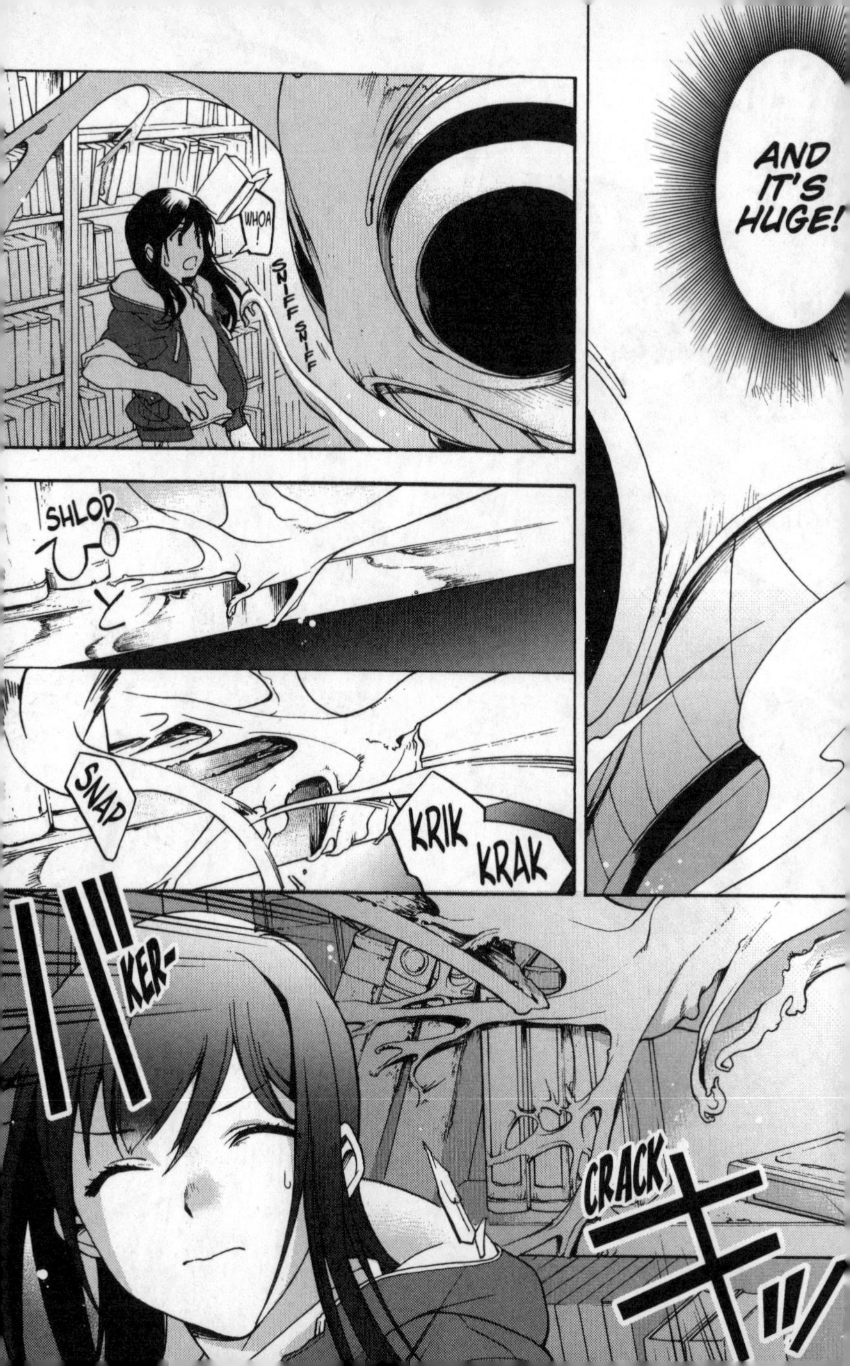
AND IT'S HUGE!
WHOA!
SNIFF SNIFF
SHLOP
KRIK KRAK
SNAP
KER-
CRACK

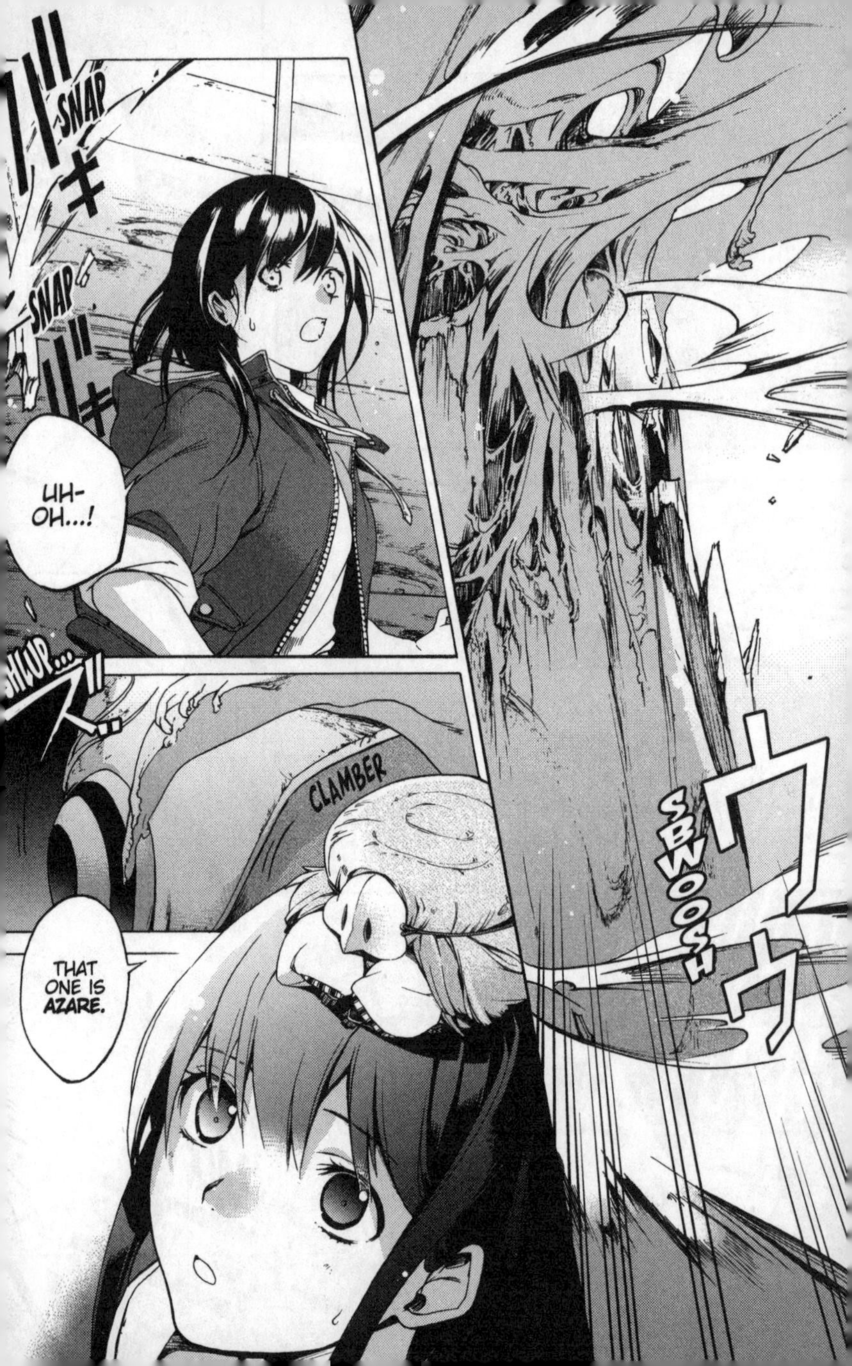
SBWOOSH
SNAP
SNAP
UH-OH...!
SHLUP...
CLAMBER
THAT ONE IS AZARE.

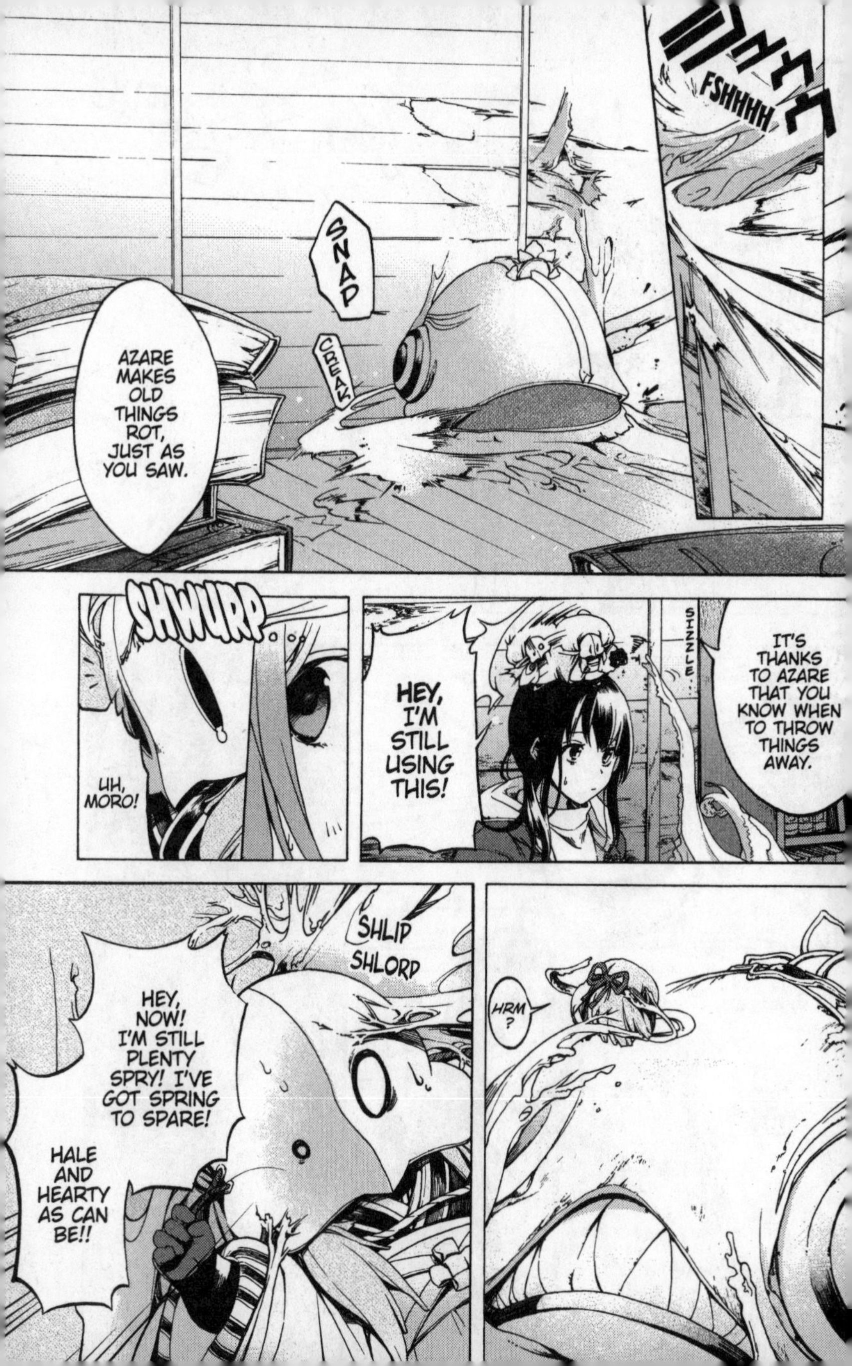
FSHHHH
SNAP
CREAK
AZARE MAKES OLD THINGS ROT, JUST AS YOU SAW.
IT'S THANKS TO AZARE THAT YOU KNOW WHEN TO THROW THINGS AWAY.
SIZZLE
HEY, I'M STILL USING THIS!
SHWURP
UH, MORO!
HRM?
SHLIP
SHLORP
HEY, NOW! I'M STILL PLENTY SPRY! I'VE GOT SPRING TO SPARE!
HALE AND HEARTY AS CAN BE!!

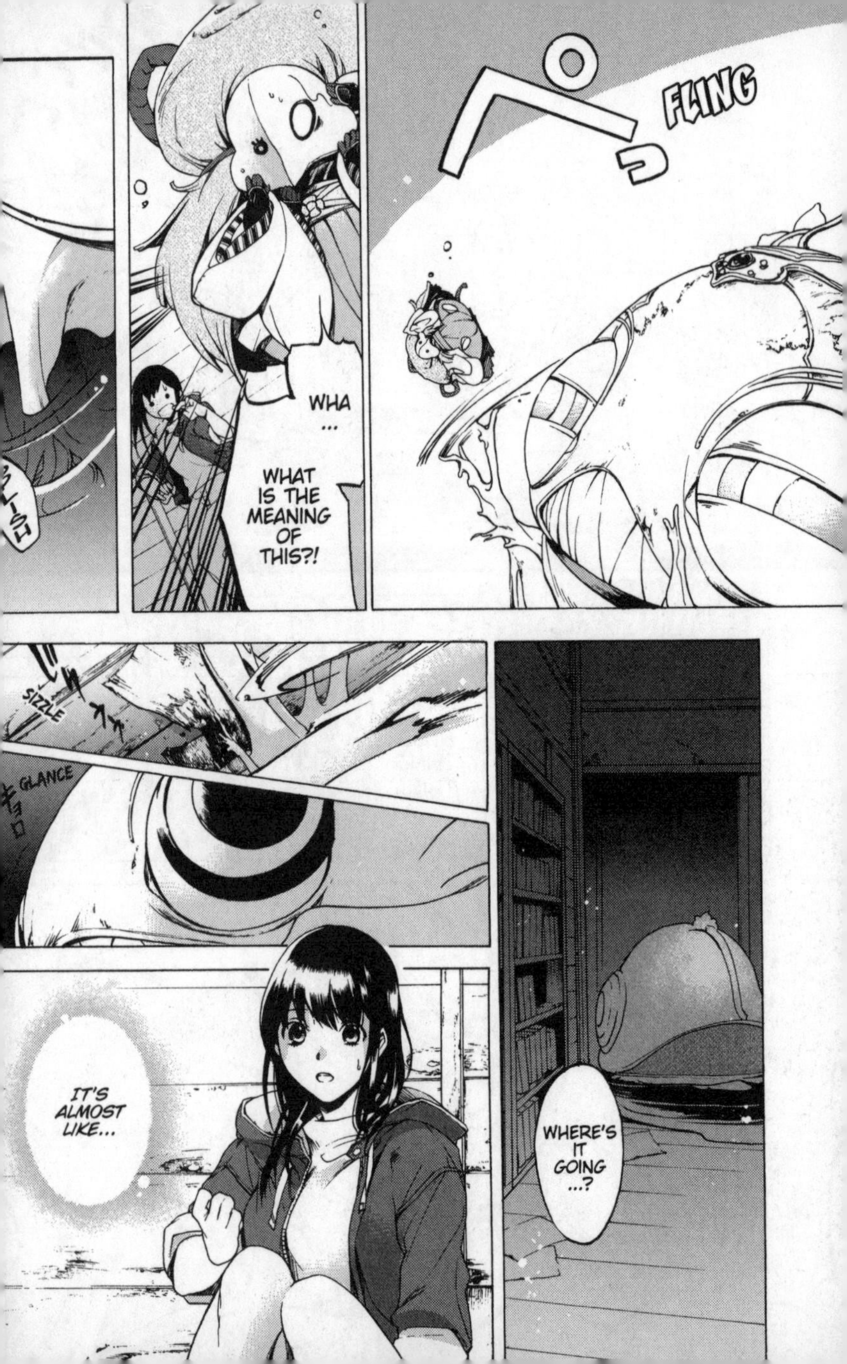
FLING
WHA ...
WHAT IS THE MEANING OF THIS?!
SLISH
WHERE'S IT GOING ...?
SIZZLE
GLANCE
IT'S ALMOST LIKE...

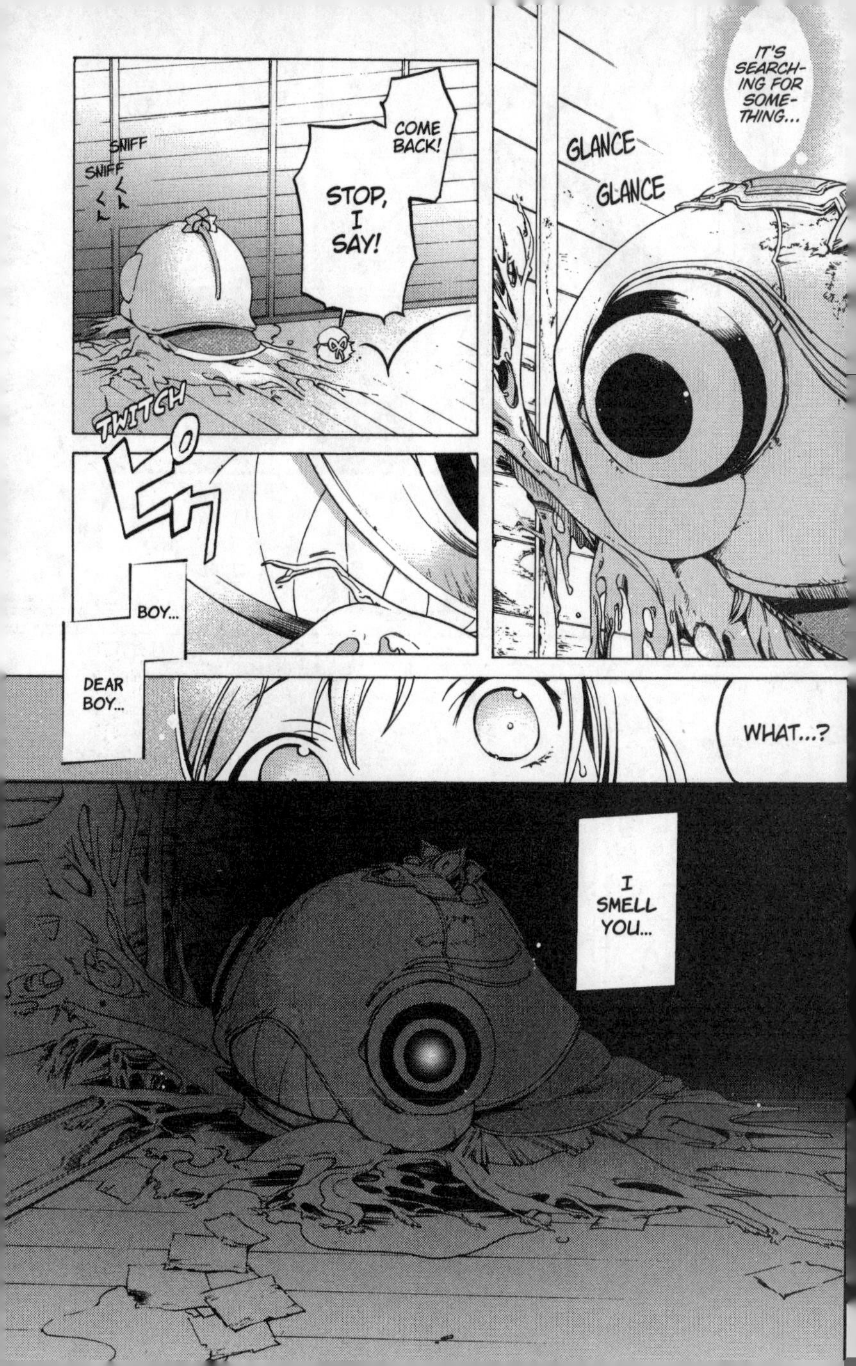

IT'S SEARCHING FOR SOMETHING...
GLANCE
GLANCE
SNIFF
SNIFF
くんくん
COME BACK!
STOP, I SAY!
TWITCH
ピク
BOY...
DEAR BOY...
WHAT...?
I SMELL YOU...

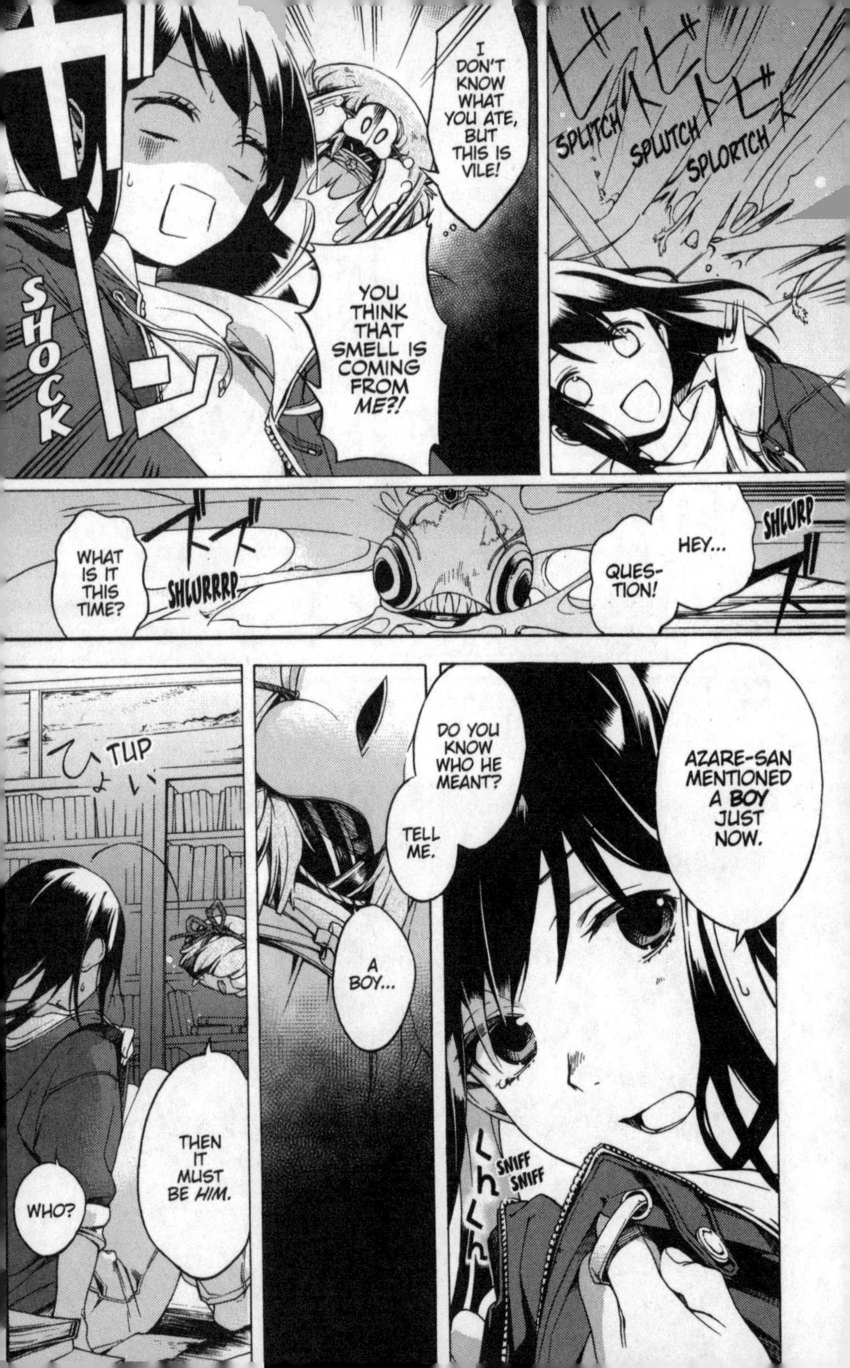
SPLUTCH
SPLUTCH
SPLORTCH
I DON'T KNOW WHAT YOU ATE, BUT THIS IS VILE!
YOU THINK THAT SMELL IS COMING FROM *ME*?!
SHOCK
SHLURP
HEY... QUES-TION!
SHLURRRP
WHAT IS IT THIS TIME?
AZARE-SAN MENTIONED A **BOY** JUST NOW.
SNIFF SNIFF
DO YOU KNOW WHO HE MEANT?
TELL ME.
A BOY...
TUP
THEN IT MUST BE *HIM*.
WHO?

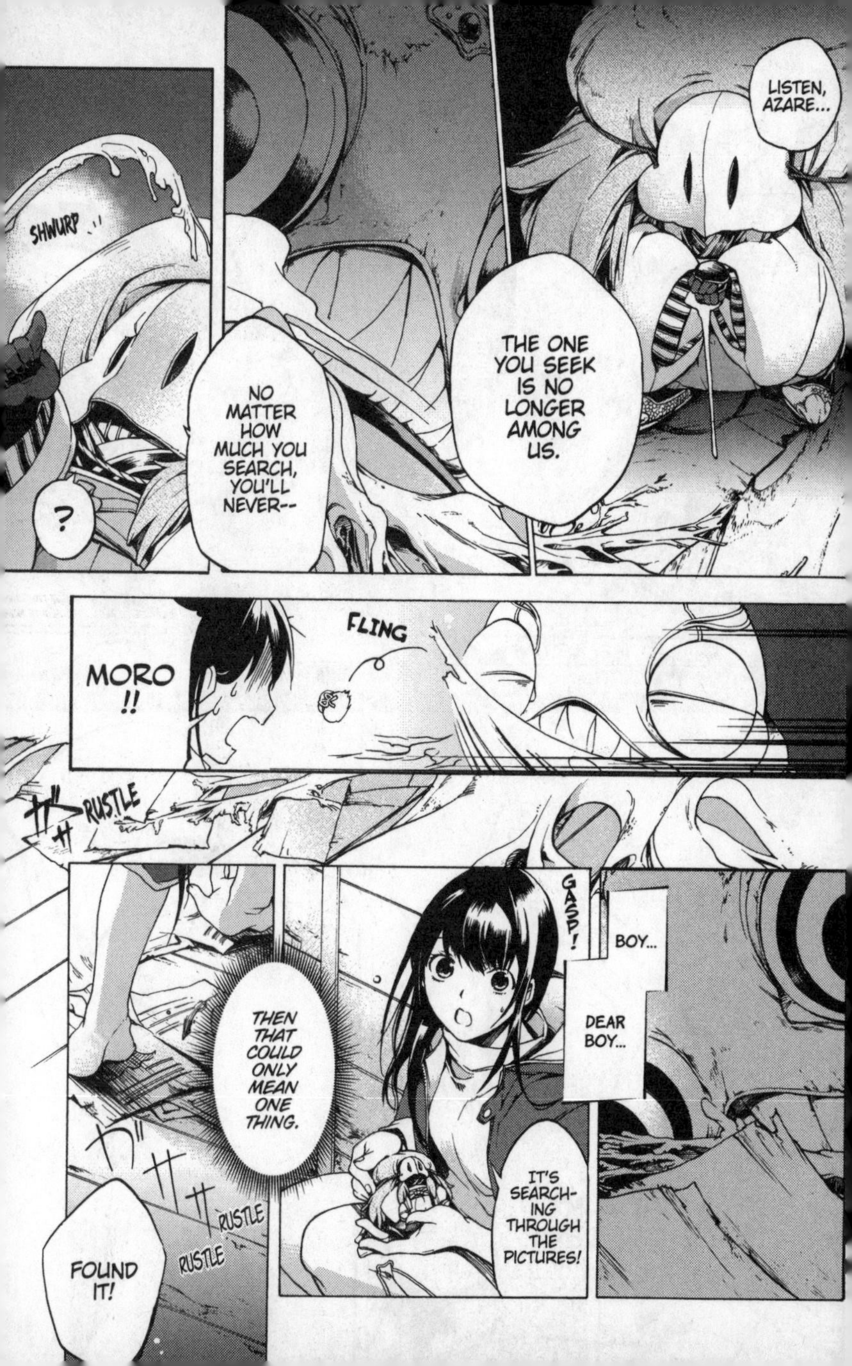
LISTEN, AZARE...
THE ONE YOU SEEK IS NO LONGER AMONG US.
SHWURP
NO MATTER HOW MUCH YOU SEARCH, YOU'LL NEVER--
?
FLING
MORO !!
RUSTLE
BOY...
DEAR BOY...
GASP!
IT'S SEARCHING THROUGH THE PICTURES!
THEN THAT COULD ONLY MEAN ONE THING.
RUSTLE
RUSTLE
FOUND IT!

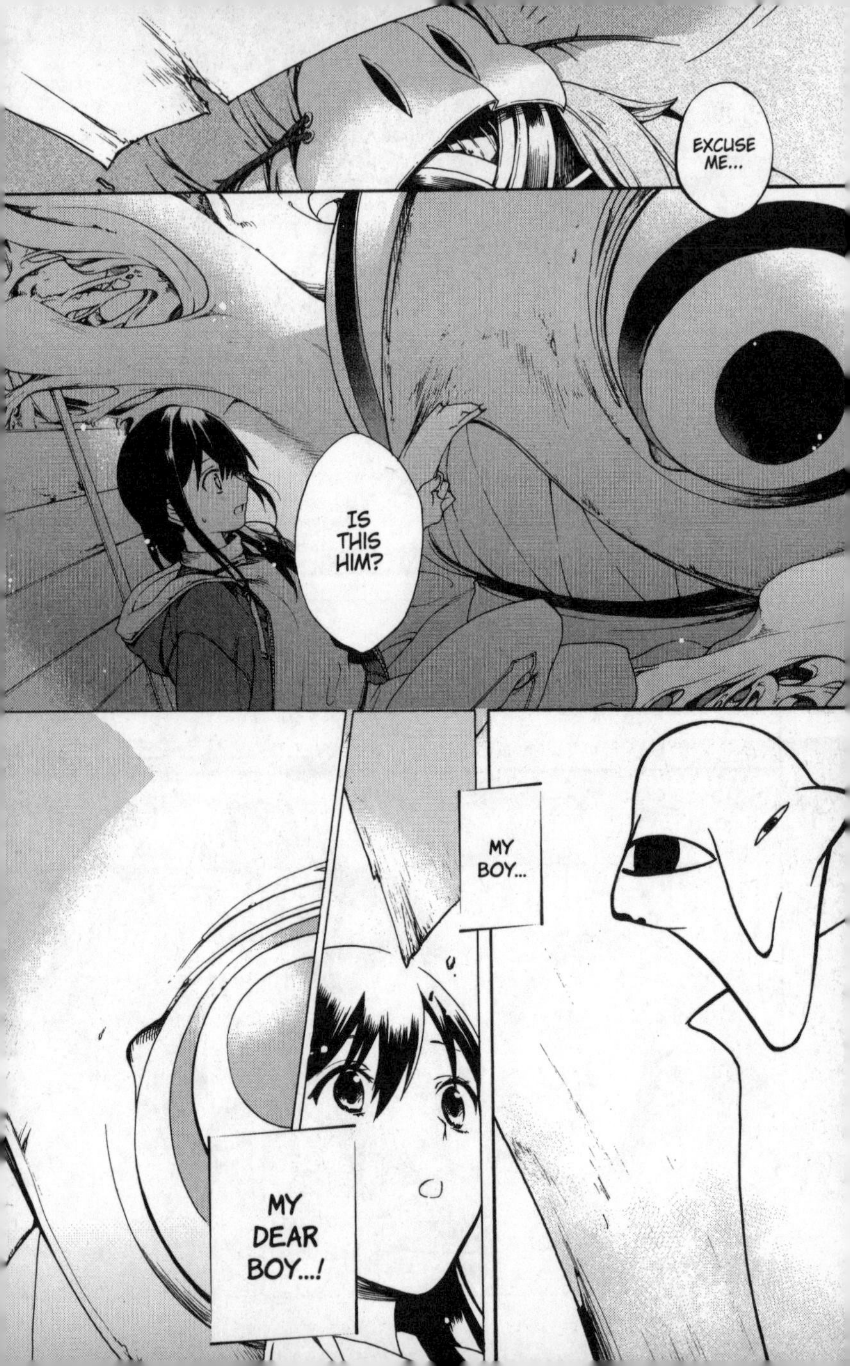
EXCUSE ME...
IS THIS HIM?
MY BOY...
MY DEAR BOY...!

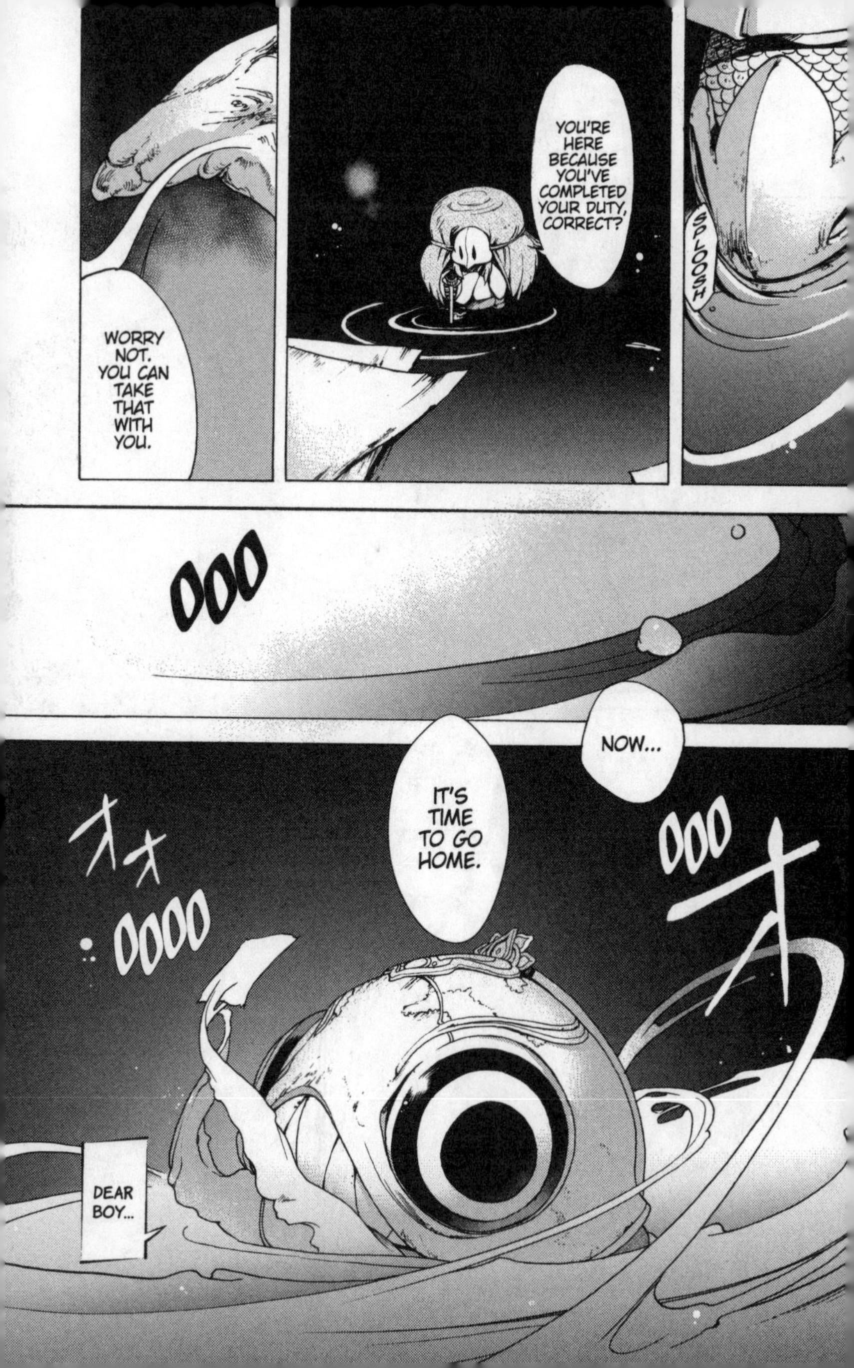
SPLOOSH
YOU'RE HERE BECAUSE YOU'VE COMPLETED YOUR DUTY, CORRECT?
WORRY NOT. YOU CAN TAKE THAT WITH YOU.
OOO
NOW...
IT'S TIME TO GO HOME.
OOO
オ
オオ
OOOO
DEAR BOY...

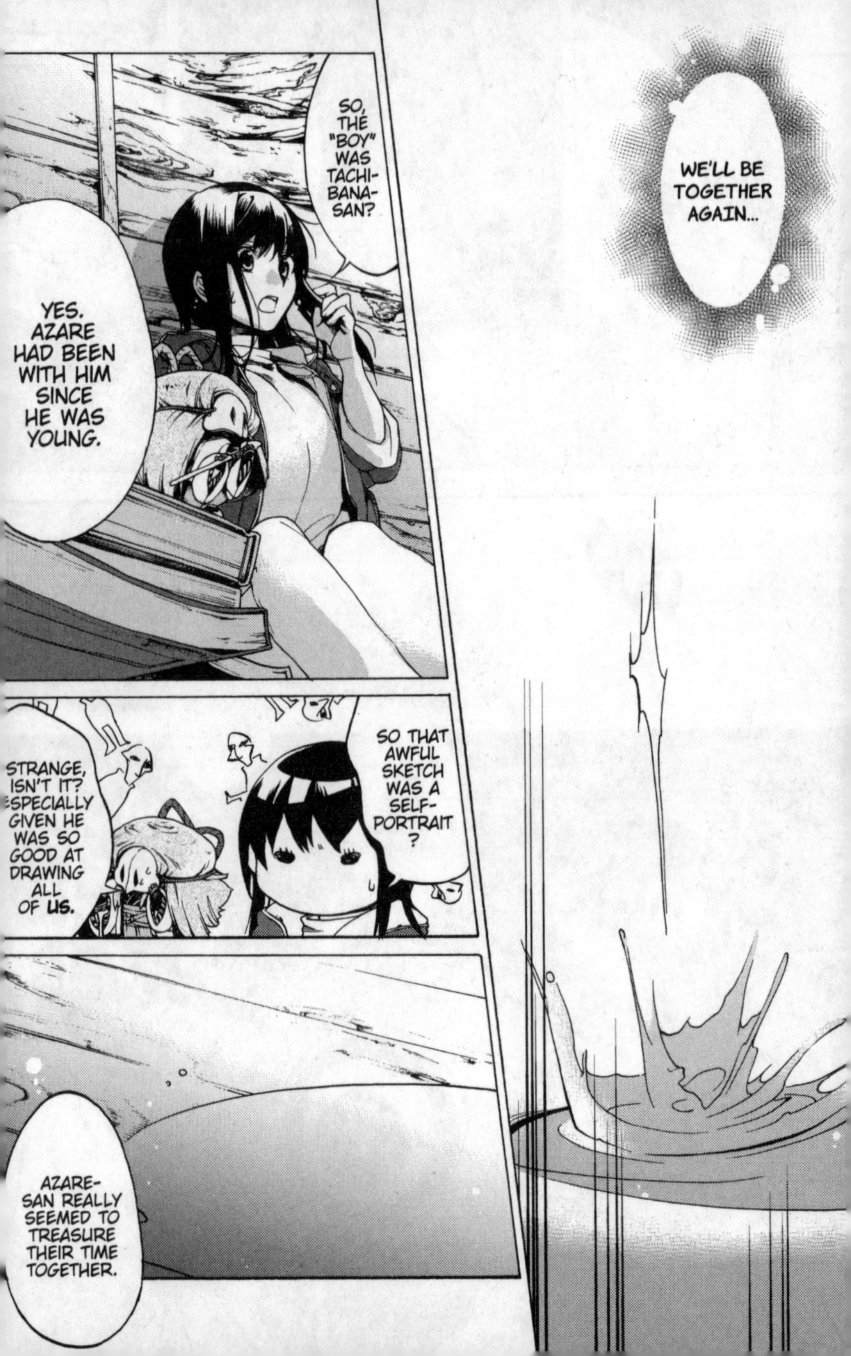
WE'LL BE TOGETHER AGAIN...
SO, THE "BOY" WAS TACHIBANA-SAN?
YES. AZARE HAD BEEN WITH HIM SINCE HE WAS YOUNG.
SO THAT AWFUL SKETCH WAS A SELF-PORTRAIT?
STRANGE, ISN'T IT? ESPECIALLY GIVEN HE WAS SO GOOD AT DRAWING ALL OF US.
AZARE-SAN REALLY SEEMED TO TREASURE THEIR TIME TOGETHER.

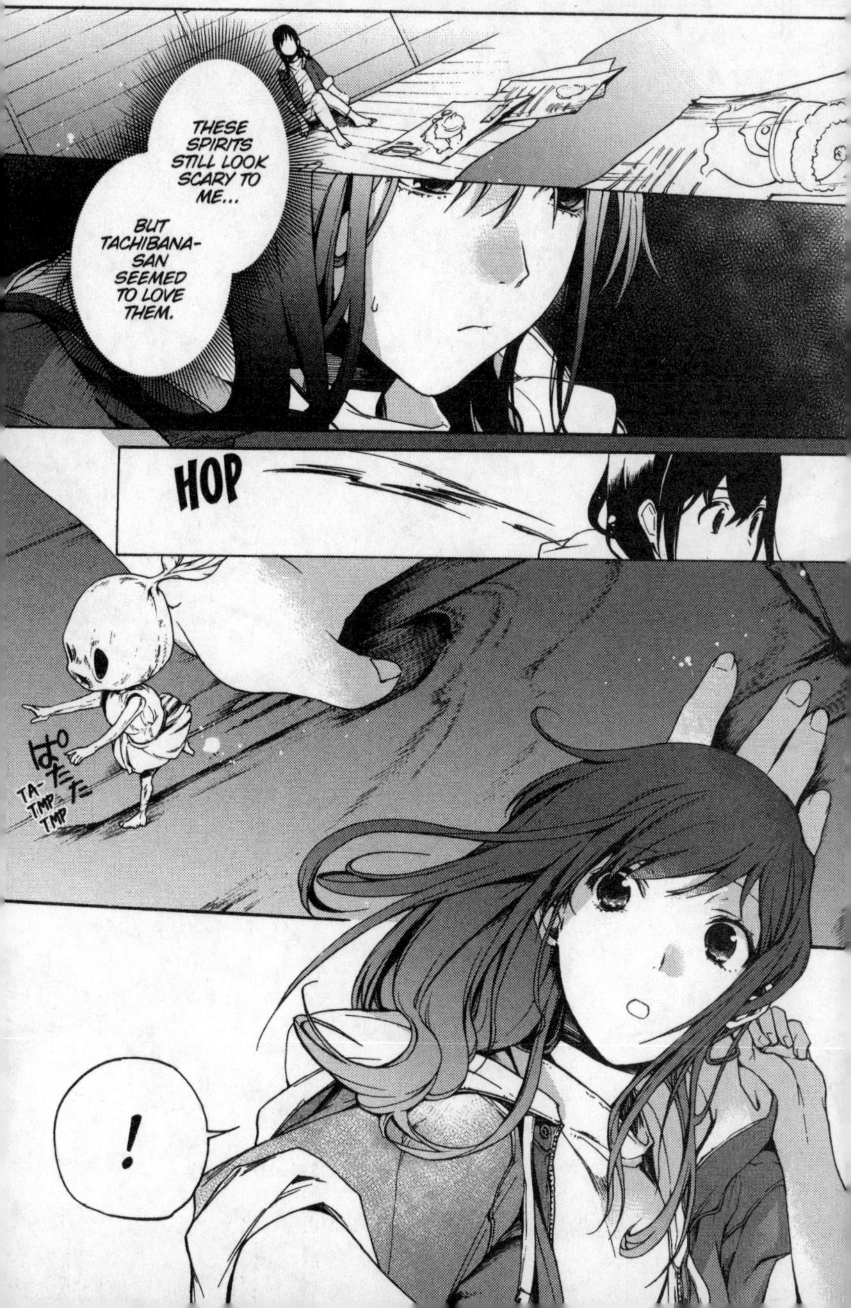
THESE SPIRITS STILL LOOK SCARY TO ME...
BUT TACHIBANA-SAN SEEMED TO LOVE THEM.
HOP
ぱたた
TA-TMP TMP
!

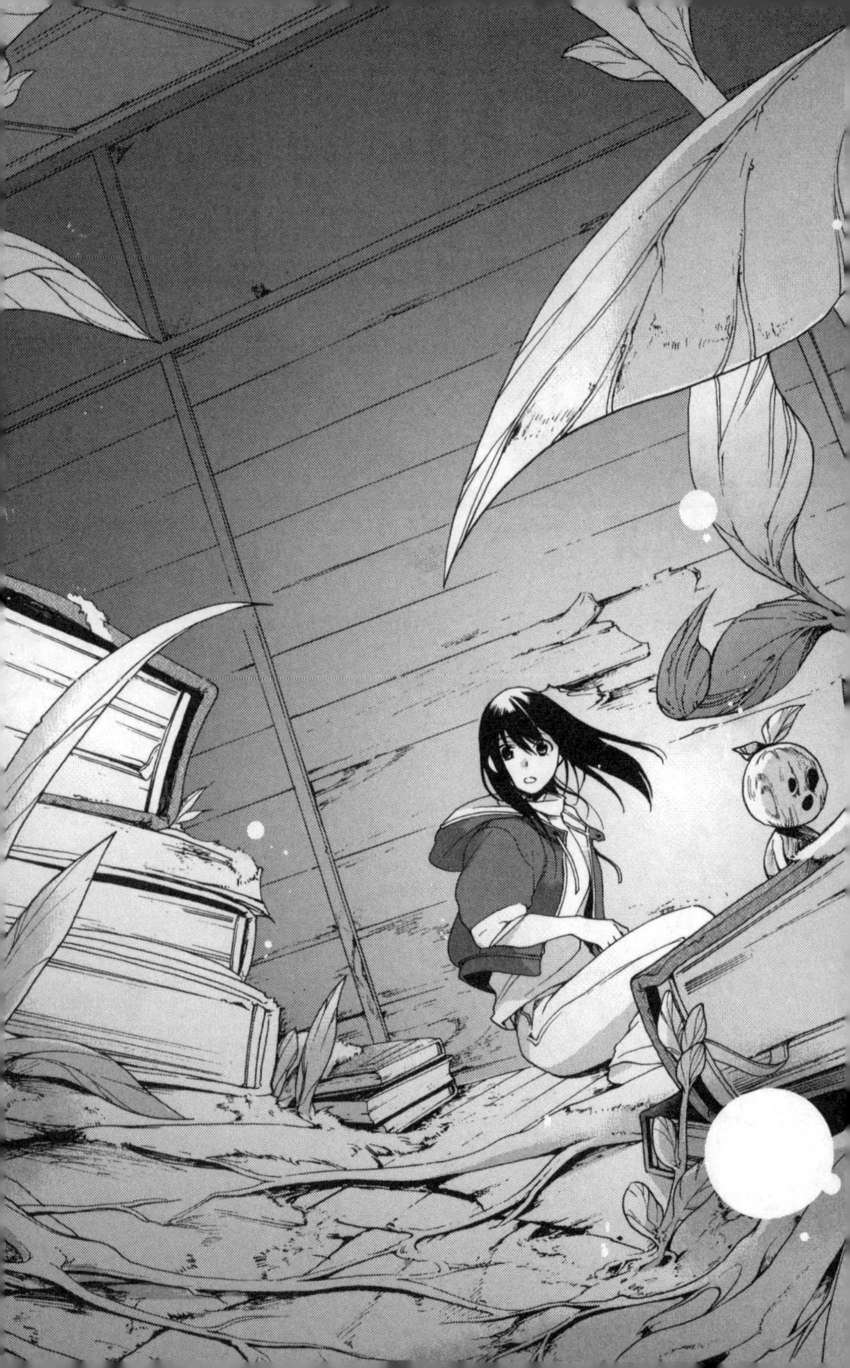

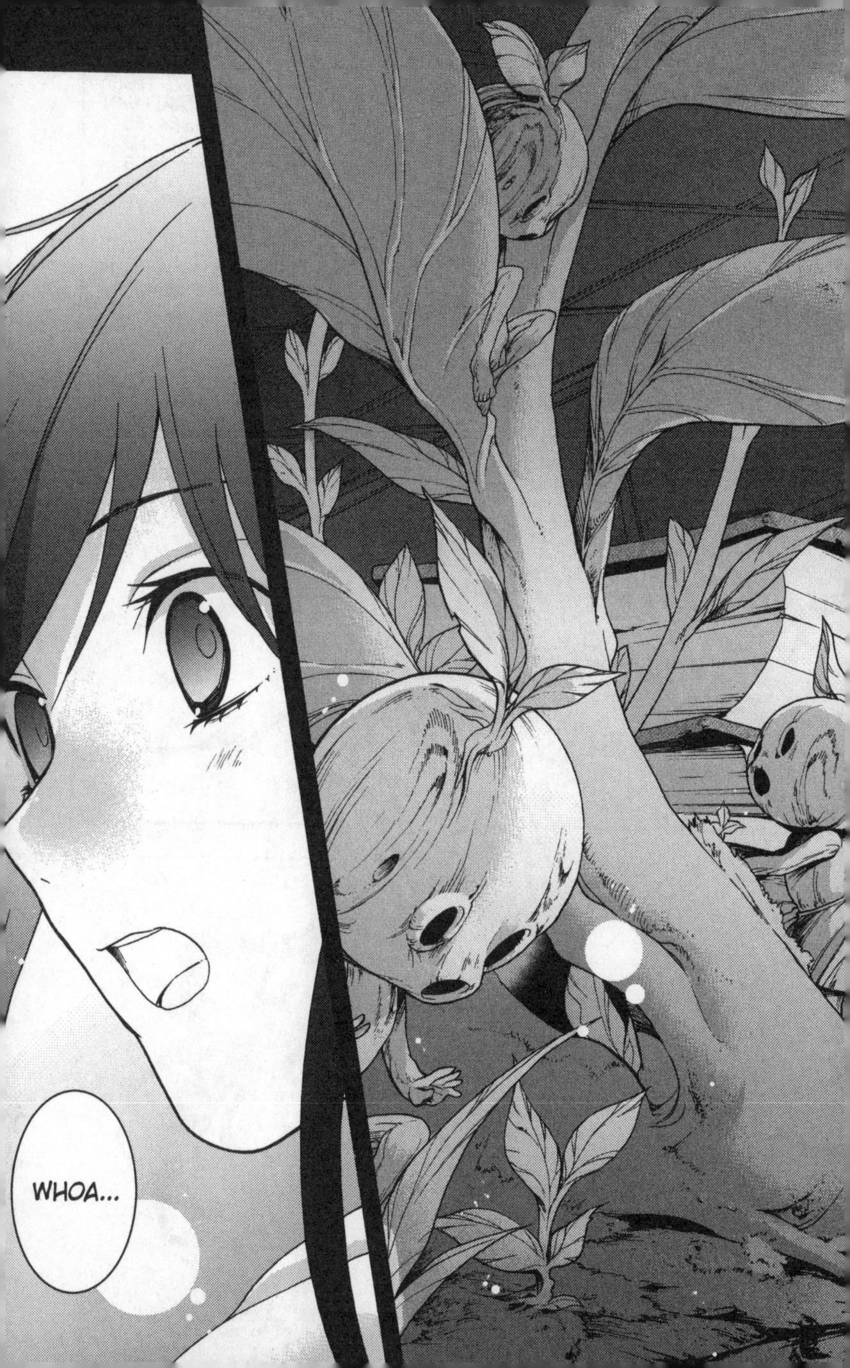
WHOA...

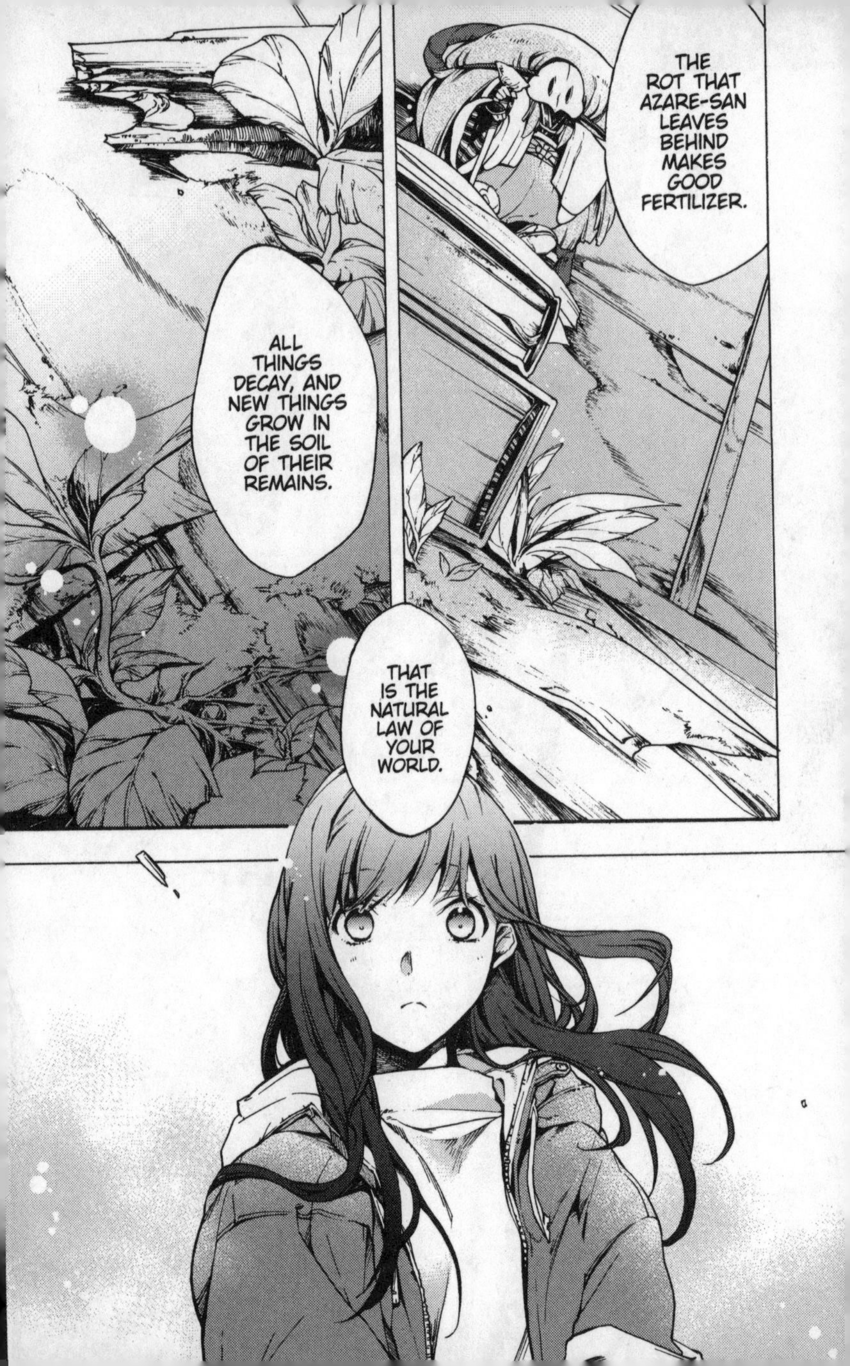
THE ROT THAT AZARE-SAN LEAVES BEHIND MAKES GOOD FERTILIZER.
ALL THINGS DECAY, AND NEW THINGS GROW IN THE SOIL OF THEIR REMAINS.
THAT IS THE NATURAL LAW OF YOUR WORLD.

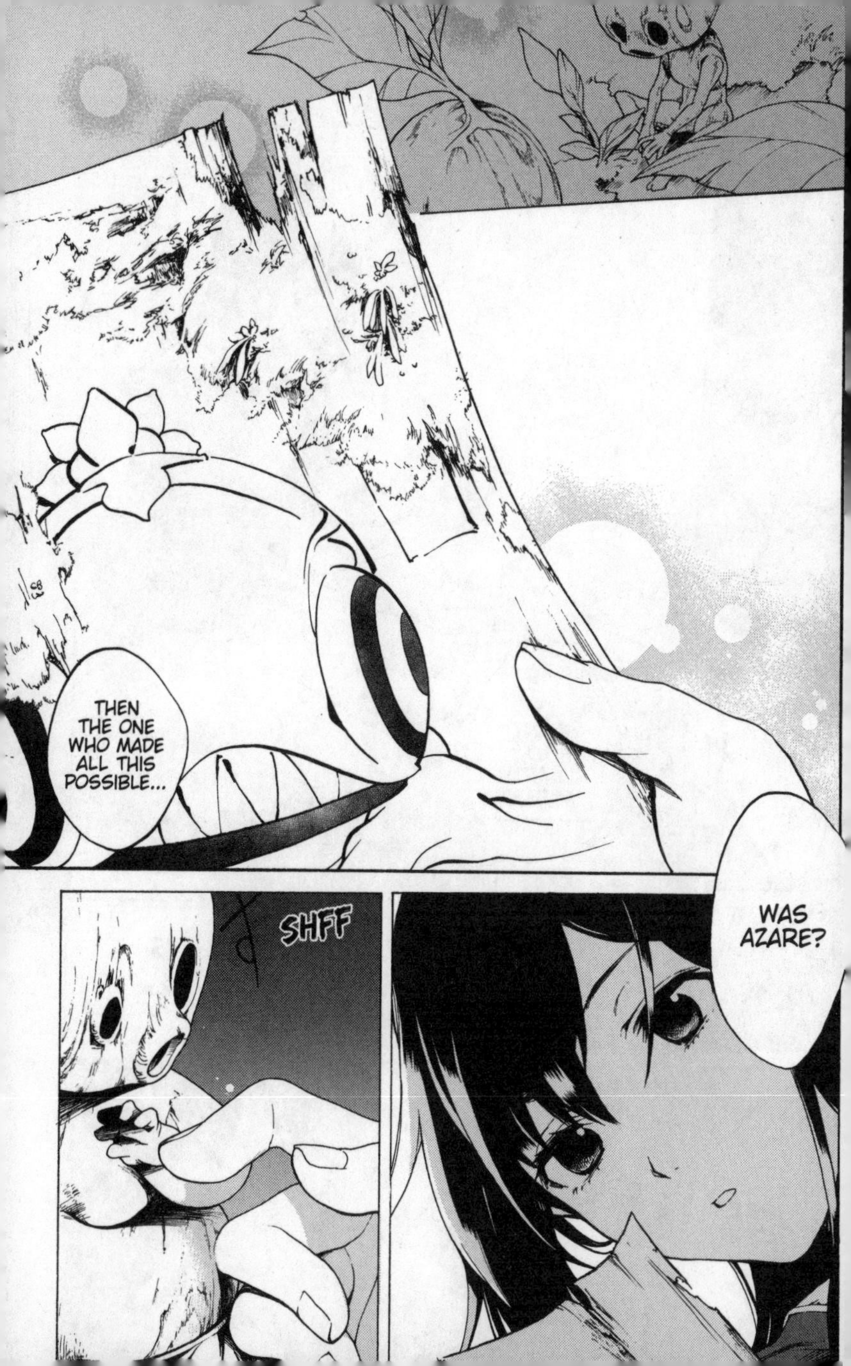
THEN THE ONE WHO MADE ALL THIS POSSIBLE...
WAS AZARE?
SHFF

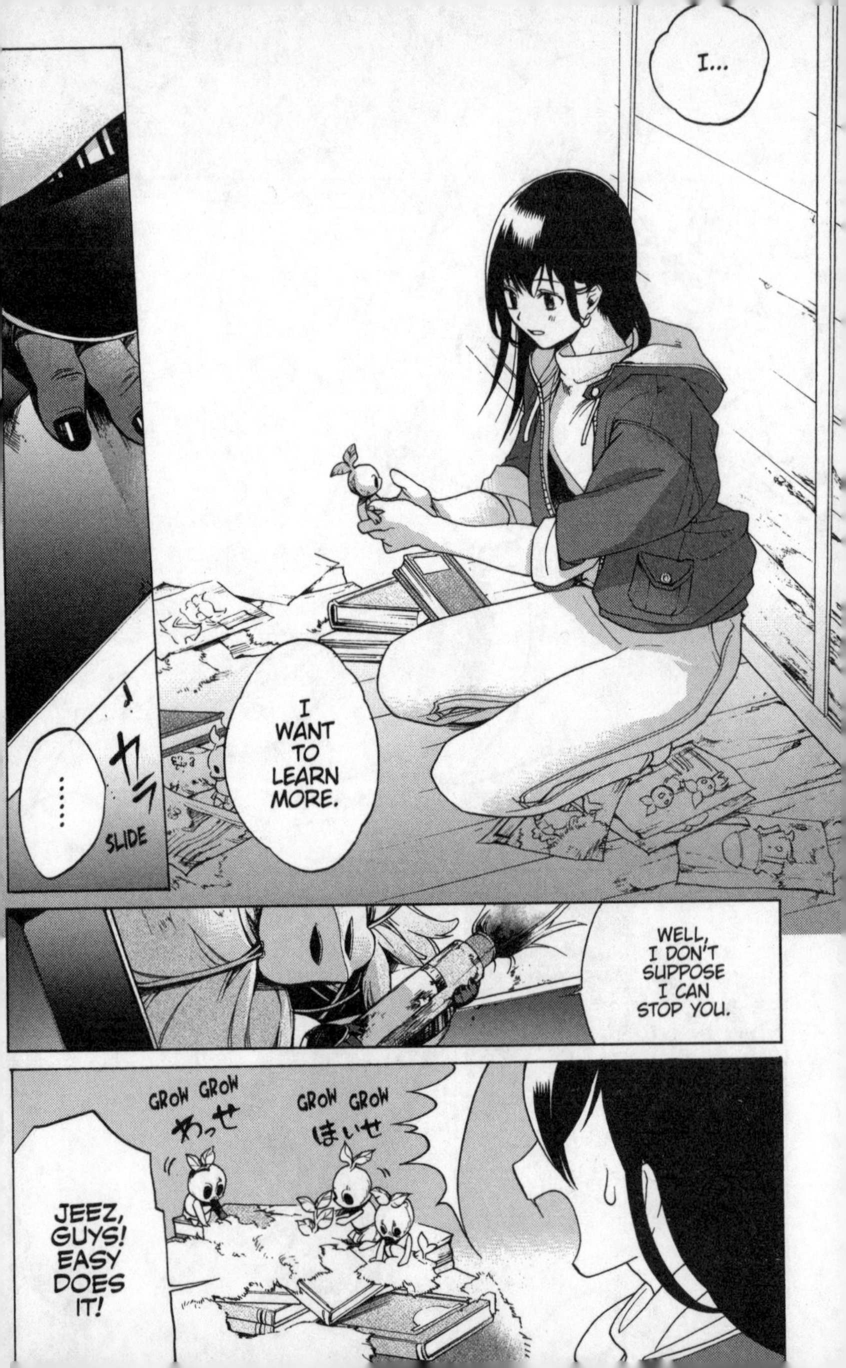

I...
I WANT TO LEARN MORE.
......
SLIDE
WELL, I DON'T SUPPOSE I CAN STOP YOU.
GROW GROW
ほいせ
GROW GROW
わっせ
JEEZ, GUYS! EASY DOES IT!

LATER...

SCRUB

SCRUB

SCRUB

SIGH...

HOMEOWNERS HAVE TO WORK,
EVEN ON THEIR DAY OFF.

Ghostly
Things

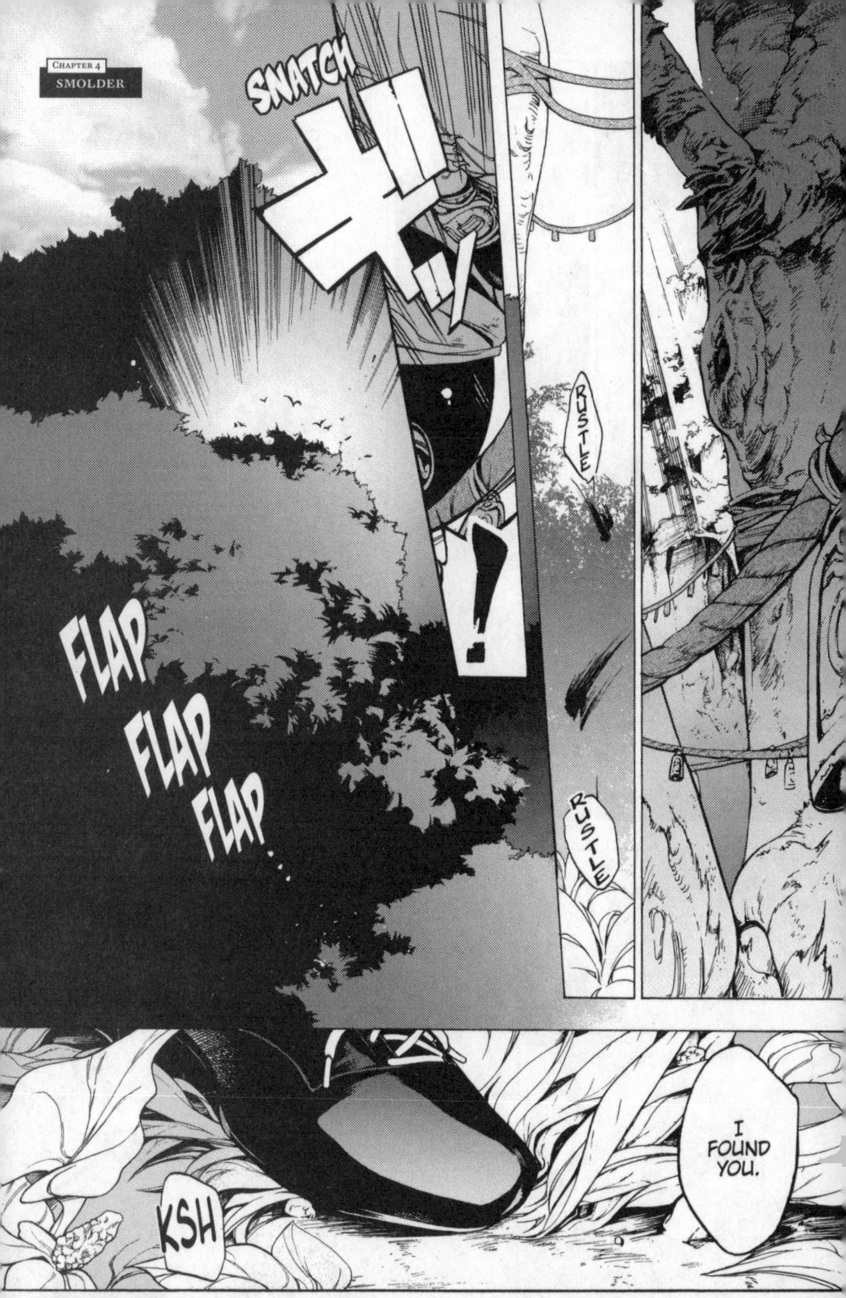
RUSTLE
RUSTLE
SNATCH
!
FLAP
FLAP
FLAP...
I FOUND YOU.
KSH

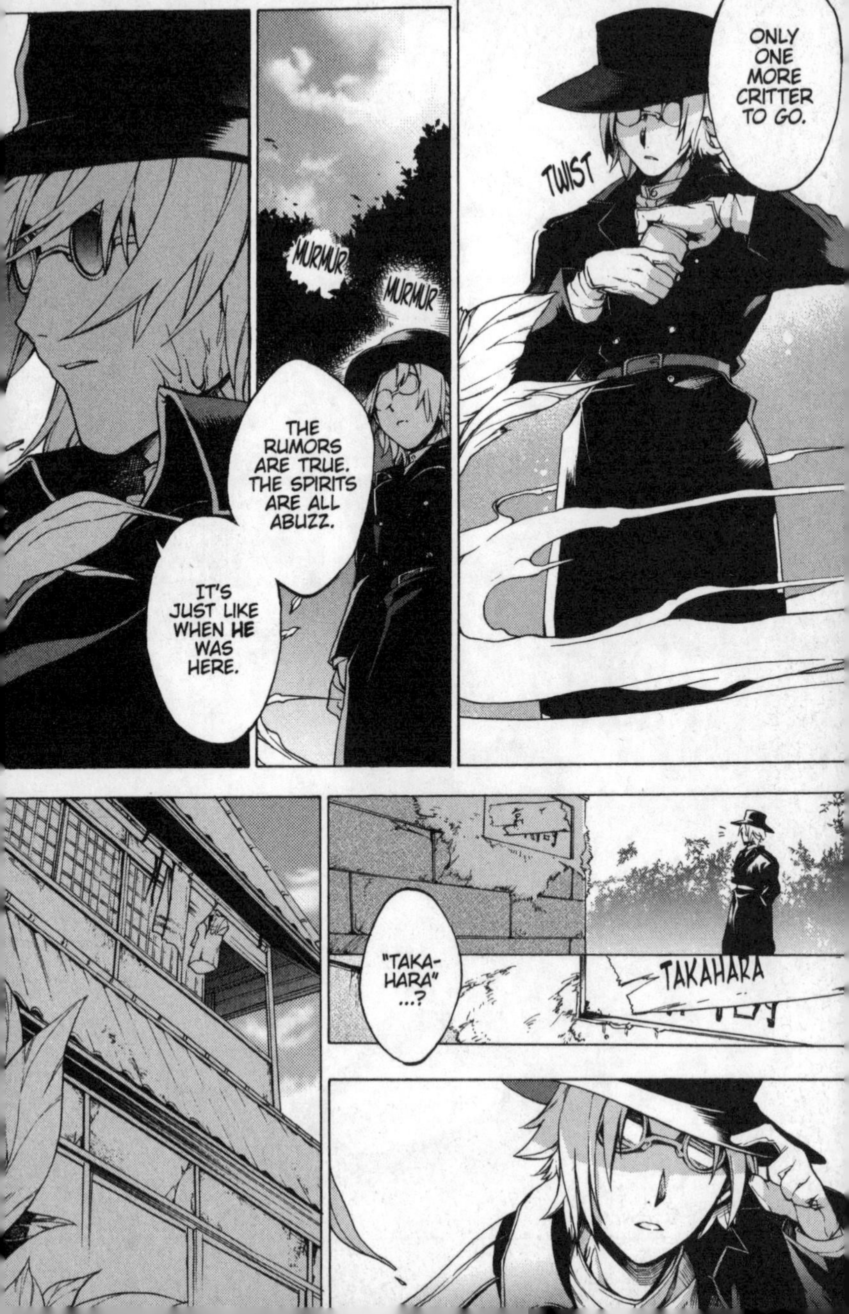
ONLY ONE MORE CRITTER TO GO.
TWIST
MURMUR
MURMUR
THE RUMORS ARE TRUE. THE SPIRITS ARE ALL ABUZZ.
IT'S JUST LIKE WHEN HE WAS HERE.
TAKAHARA
"TAKA-HARA" ...?

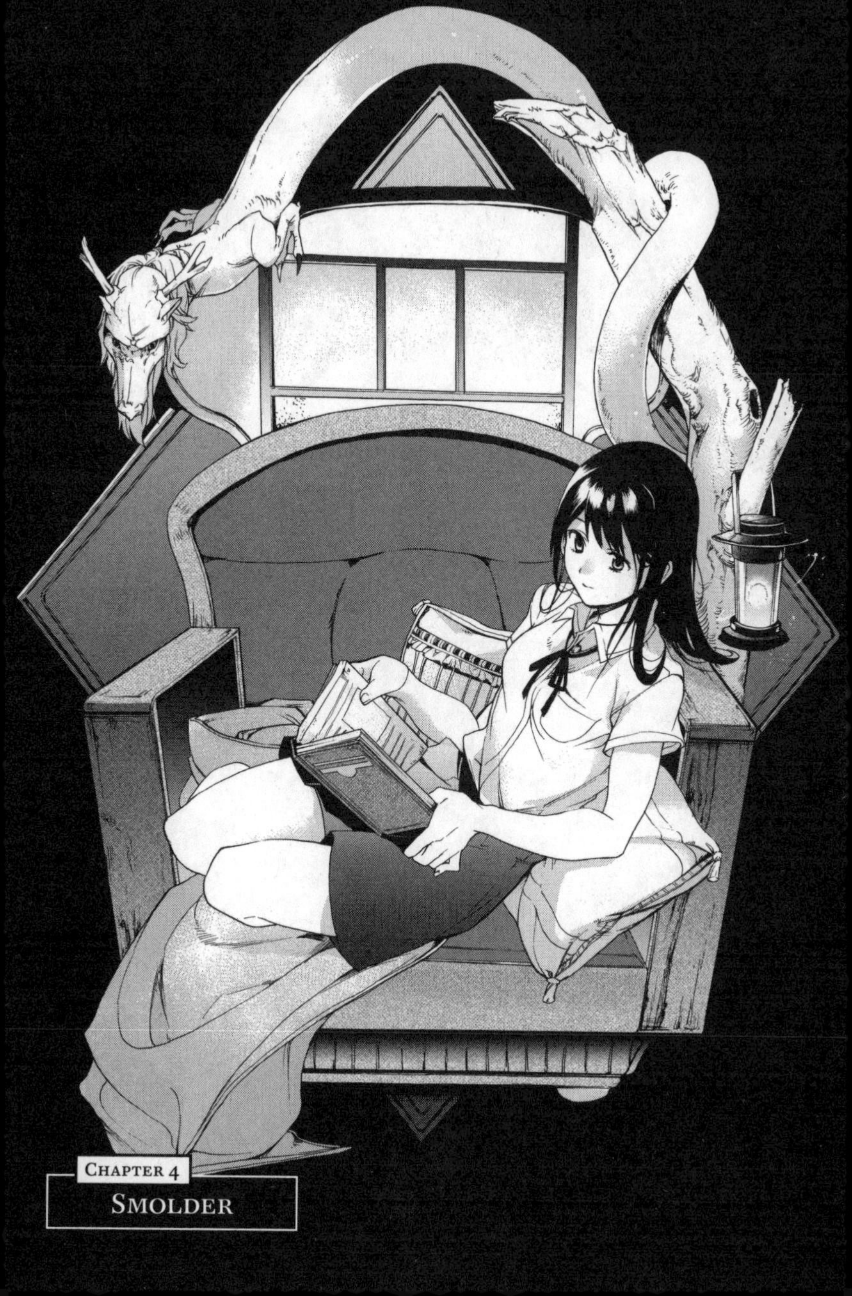

CHAPTER 4

SMOLDER

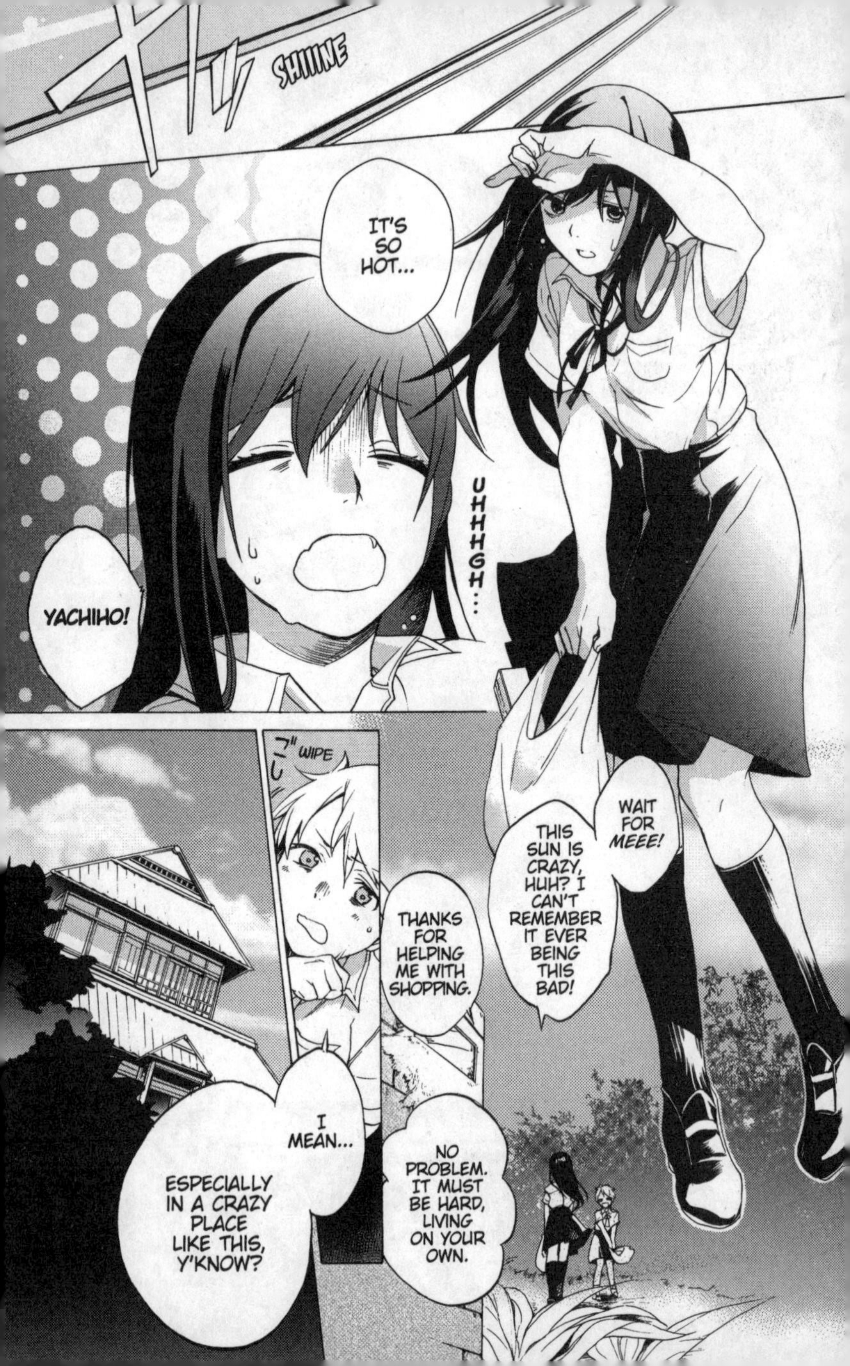
SHIIINE
IT'S SO HOT...
UHHHGH...
YACHIHO!
WAIT FOR MEEE!
THIS SUN IS CRAZY, HUH? I CAN'T REMEMBER IT EVER BEING THIS BAD!
WIPE
THANKS FOR HELPING ME WITH SHOPPING.
NO PROBLEM. IT MUST BE HARD, LIVING ON YOUR OWN.
I MEAN...
ESPECIALLY IN A CRAZY PLACE LIKE THIS, Y'KNOW?

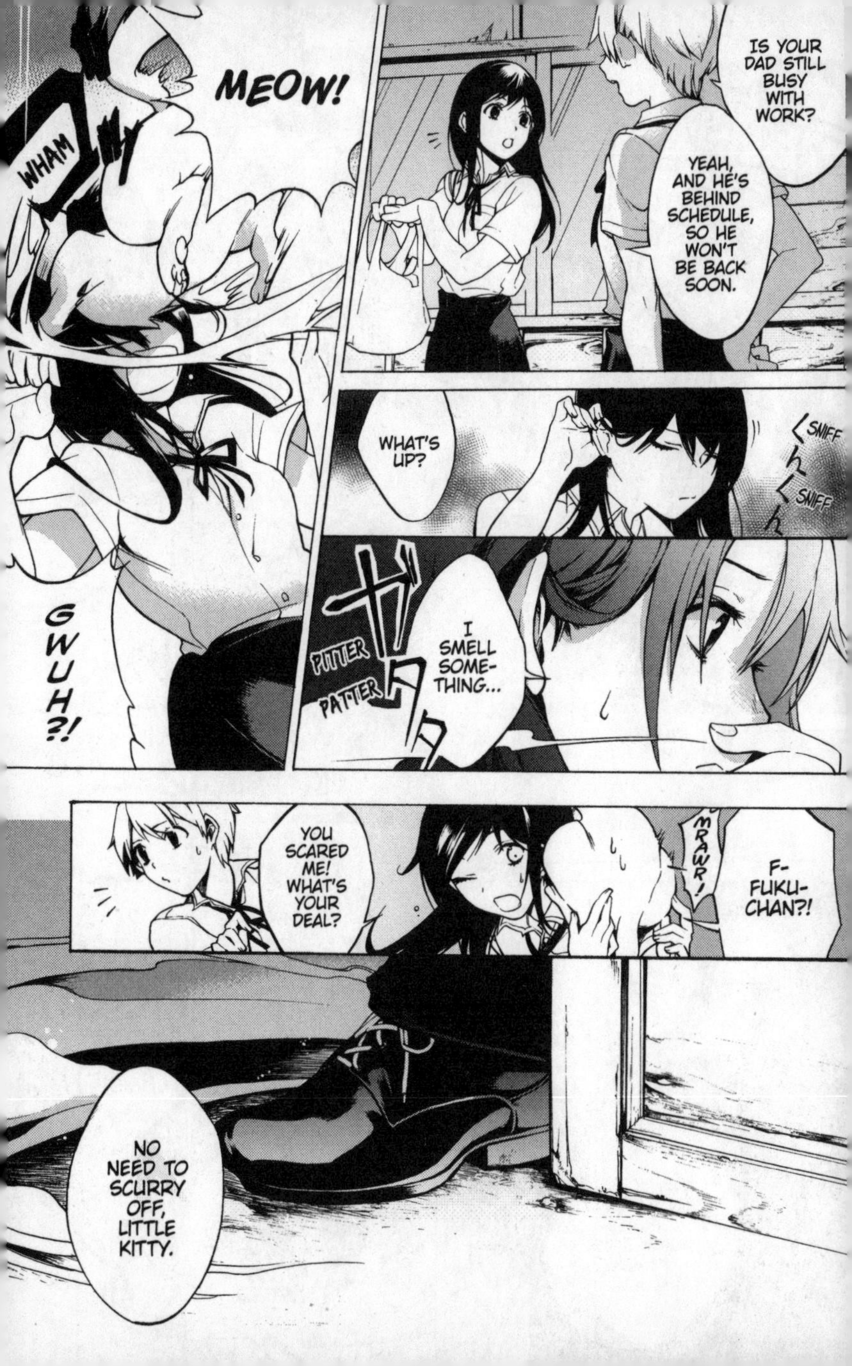
IS YOUR DAD STILL BUSY WITH WORK?
YEAH, AND HE'S BEHIND SCHEDULE, SO HE WON'T BE BACK SOON.
SNIFF
SNIFF
WHAT'S UP?
I SMELL SOME-THING...
PITTER
PATTER
MEOW!
WHAM
GWUH?!
F-FUKU-CHAN?!
MRAWR!
YOU SCARED ME! WHAT'S YOUR DEAL?
NO NEED TO SCURRY OFF, LITTLE KITTY.

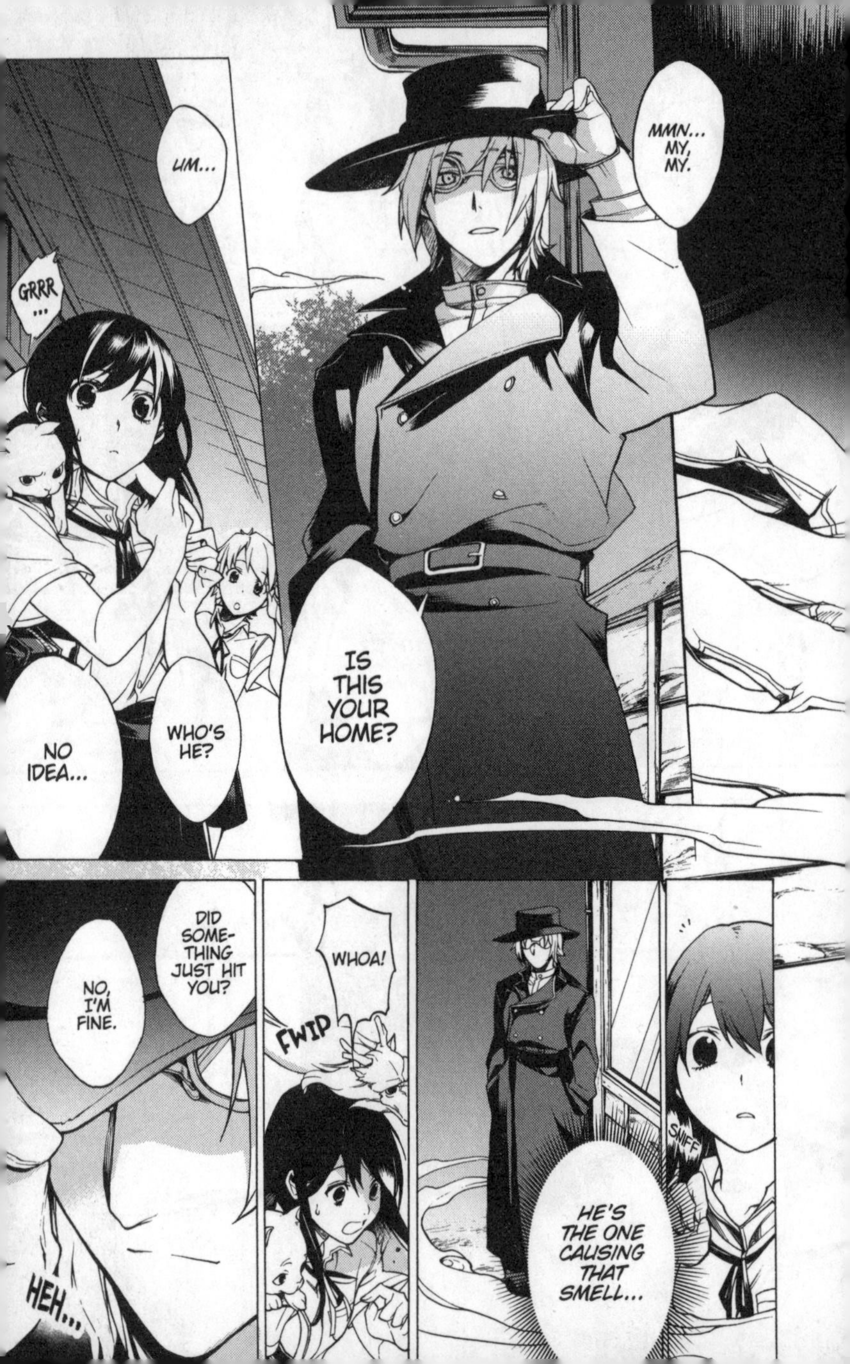
MMN... MY, MY.
IS THIS YOUR HOME?
UM...
GRRR...
WHO'S HE?
NO IDEA...
SNIFF
HE'S THE ONE CAUSING THAT SMELL...
WHOA!
FWIP
DID SOMETHING JUST HIT YOU?
NO, I'M FINE.
HEH...

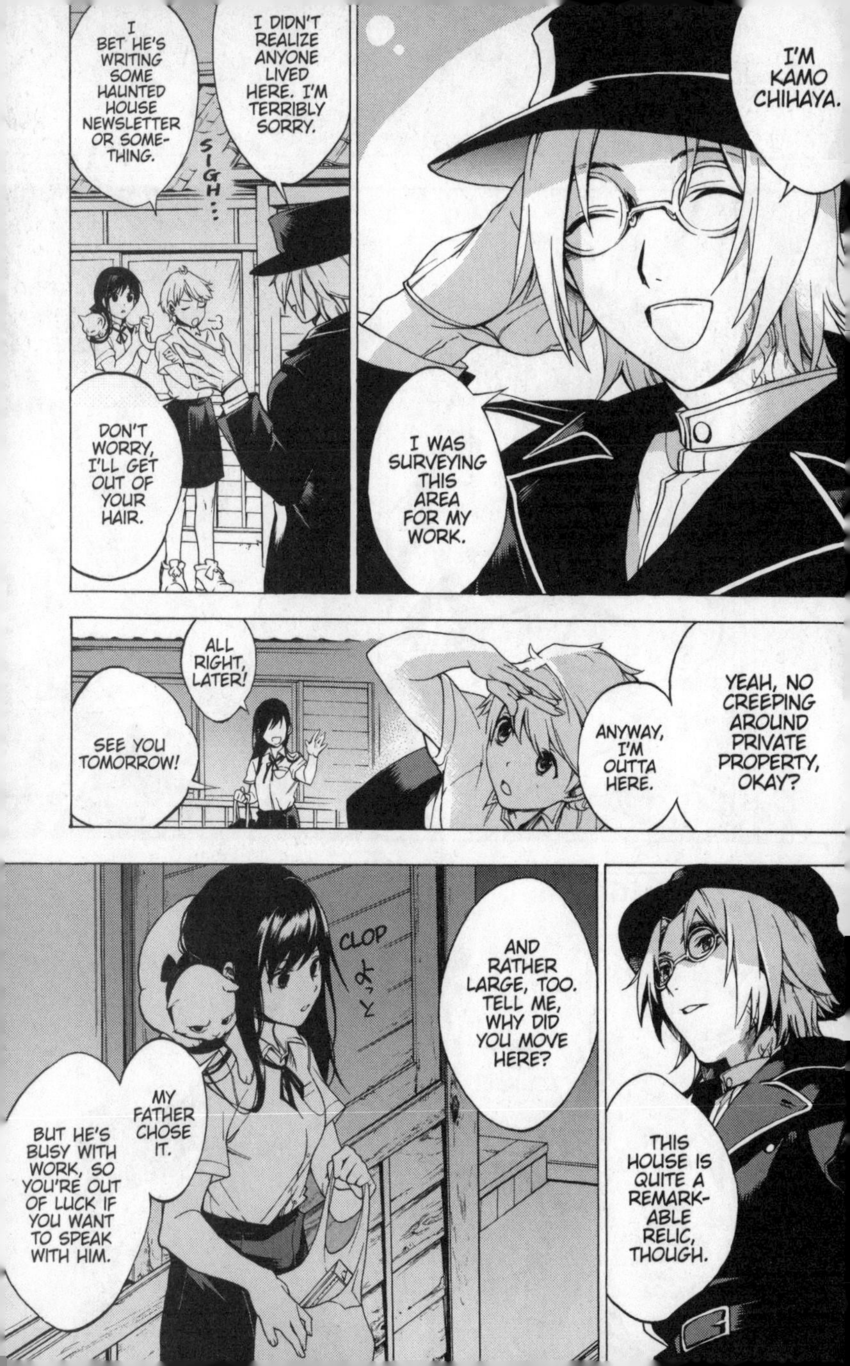
I'M KAMO CHIHAYA.
I WAS SURVEYING THIS AREA FOR MY WORK.
I DIDN'T REALIZE ANYONE LIVED HERE. I'M TERRIBLY SORRY.
SIGH...
I BET HE'S WRITING SOME HAUNTED HOUSE NEWSLETTER OR SOMETHING.
DON'T WORRY, I'LL GET OUT OF YOUR HAIR.
YEAH, NO CREEPING AROUND PRIVATE PROPERTY, OKAY?
ANYWAY, I'M OUTTA HERE.
ALL RIGHT, LATER!
SEE YOU TOMORROW!
THIS HOUSE IS QUITE A REMARKABLE RELIC, THOUGH.
AND RATHER LARGE, TOO. TELL ME, WHY DID YOU MOVE HERE?
CLOP
よっと
MY FATHER CHOSE IT.
BUT HE'S BUSY WITH WORK, SO YOU'RE OUT OF LUCK IF YOU WANT TO SPEAK WITH HIM.

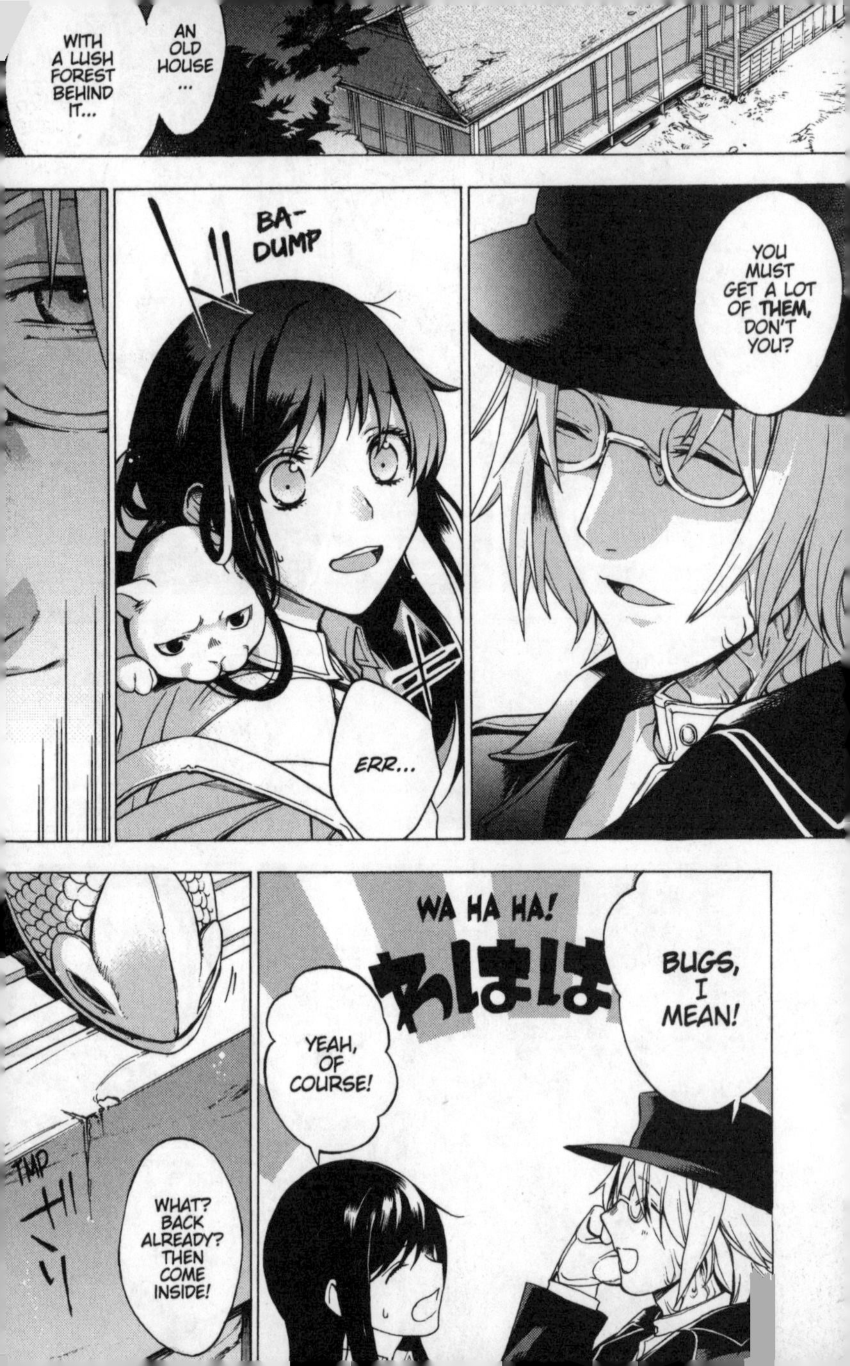
AN OLD HOUSE...
WITH A LUSH FOREST BEHIND IT...
YOU MUST GET A LOT OF THEM, DON'T YOU?
BA-DUMP
ERR...
BUGS, I MEAN!
WA HA HA!
わはは
YEAH, OF COURSE!
TMP
WHAT? BACK ALREADY? THEN COME INSIDE!

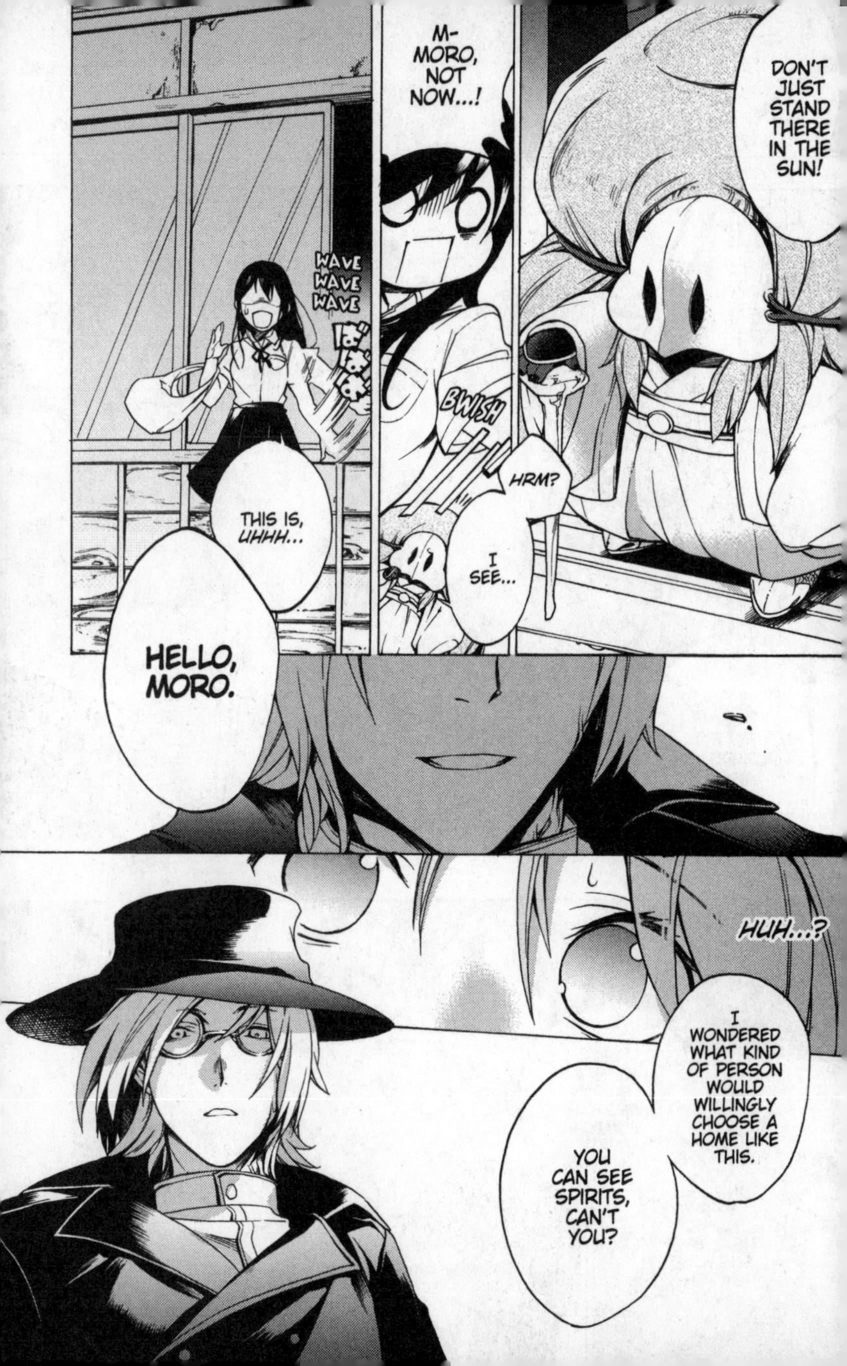
DON'T JUST STAND THERE IN THE SUN!
M-MORO, NOT NOW...!
BWISH
HRM?
I SEE...
WAVE WAVE WAVE
THIS IS, UHHH...
HELLO, MORO.
HUH...?
I WONDERED WHAT KIND OF PERSON WOULD WILLINGLY CHOOSE A HOME LIKE THIS.
YOU CAN SEE SPIRITS, CAN'T YOU?

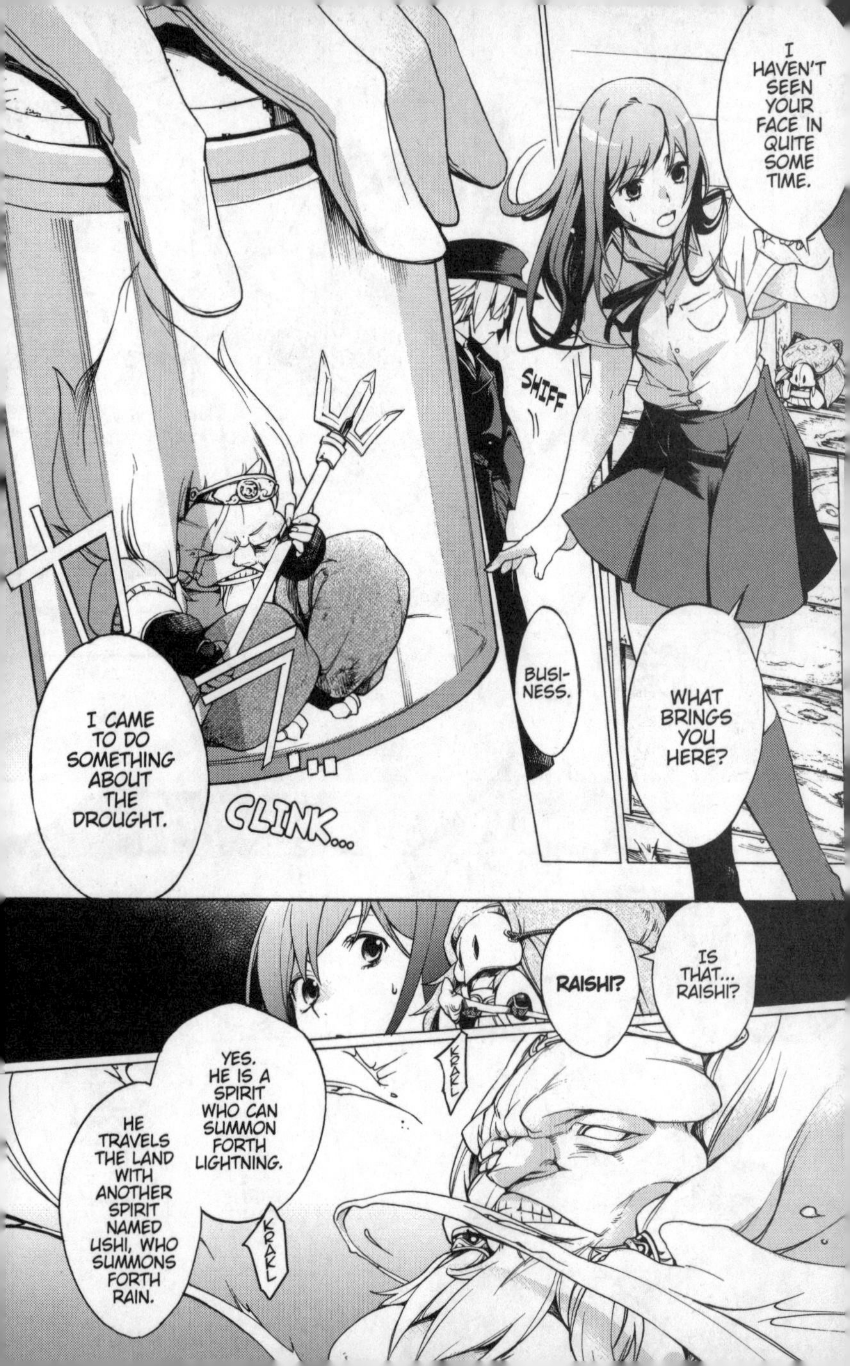
I HAVEN'T SEEN YOUR FACE IN QUITE SOME TIME.
SHIFF
WHAT BRINGS YOU HERE?
BUSINESS.
...
I CAME TO DO SOMETHING ABOUT THE DROUGHT.
CLINK...
IS THAT... RAISHI?
RAISHI?
KRAKL
YES. HE IS A SPIRIT WHO CAN SUMMON FORTH LIGHTNING.
KRAKL
HE TRAVELS THE LAND WITH ANOTHER SPIRIT NAMED USHI, WHO SUMMONS FORTH RAIN.

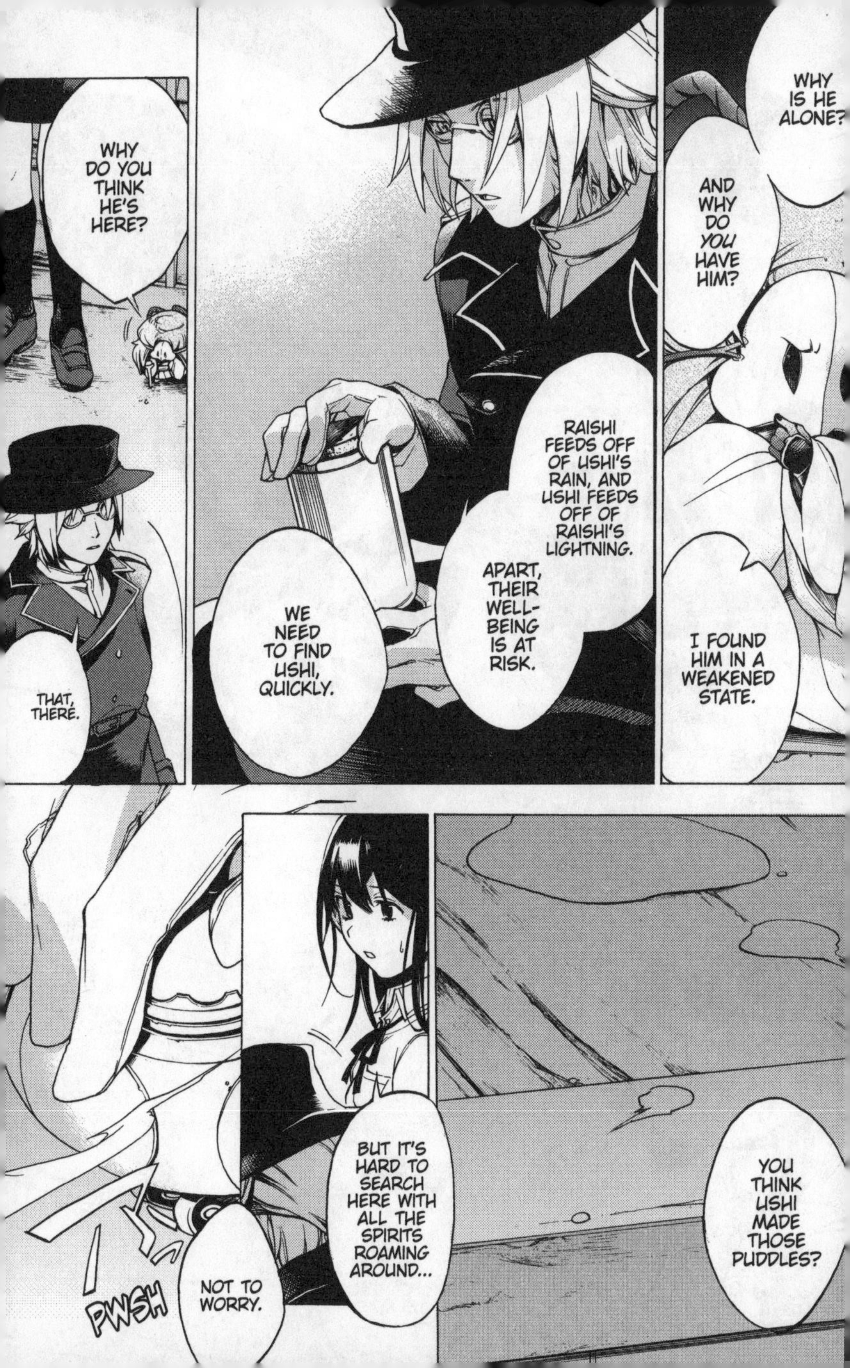
WHY IS HE ALONE?
AND WHY DO YOU HAVE HIM?
I FOUND HIM IN A WEAKENED STATE.
RAISHI FEEDS OFF OF USHI'S RAIN, AND USHI FEEDS OFF OF RAISHI'S LIGHTNING.
APART, THEIR WELL-BEING IS AT RISK.
WE NEED TO FIND USHI, QUICKLY.
WHY DO YOU THINK HE'S HERE?
THAT, THERE.
YOU THINK USHI MADE THOSE PUDDLES?
BUT IT'S HARD TO SEARCH HERE WITH ALL THE SPIRITS ROAMING AROUND...
NOT TO WORRY.
PWSH

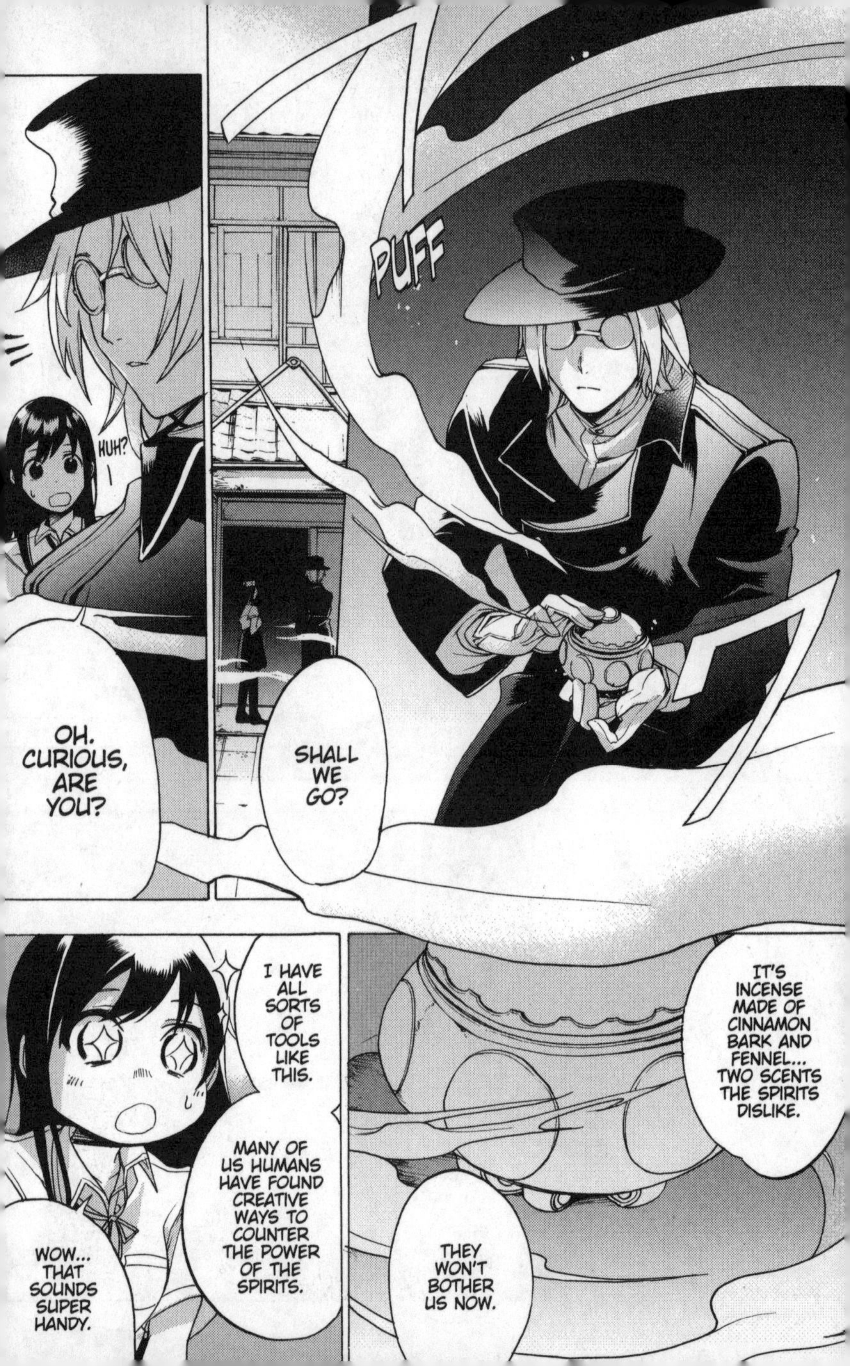
PUFF
SHALL WE GO?
HUH?
OH. CURIOUS, ARE YOU?
IT'S INCENSE MADE OF CINNAMON BARK AND FENNEL... TWO SCENTS THE SPIRITS DISLIKE.
THEY WON'T BOTHER US NOW.
I HAVE ALL SORTS OF TOOLS LIKE THIS.
MANY OF US HUMANS HAVE FOUND CREATIVE WAYS TO COUNTER THE POWER OF THE SPIRITS.
WOW... THAT SOUNDS SUPER HANDY.

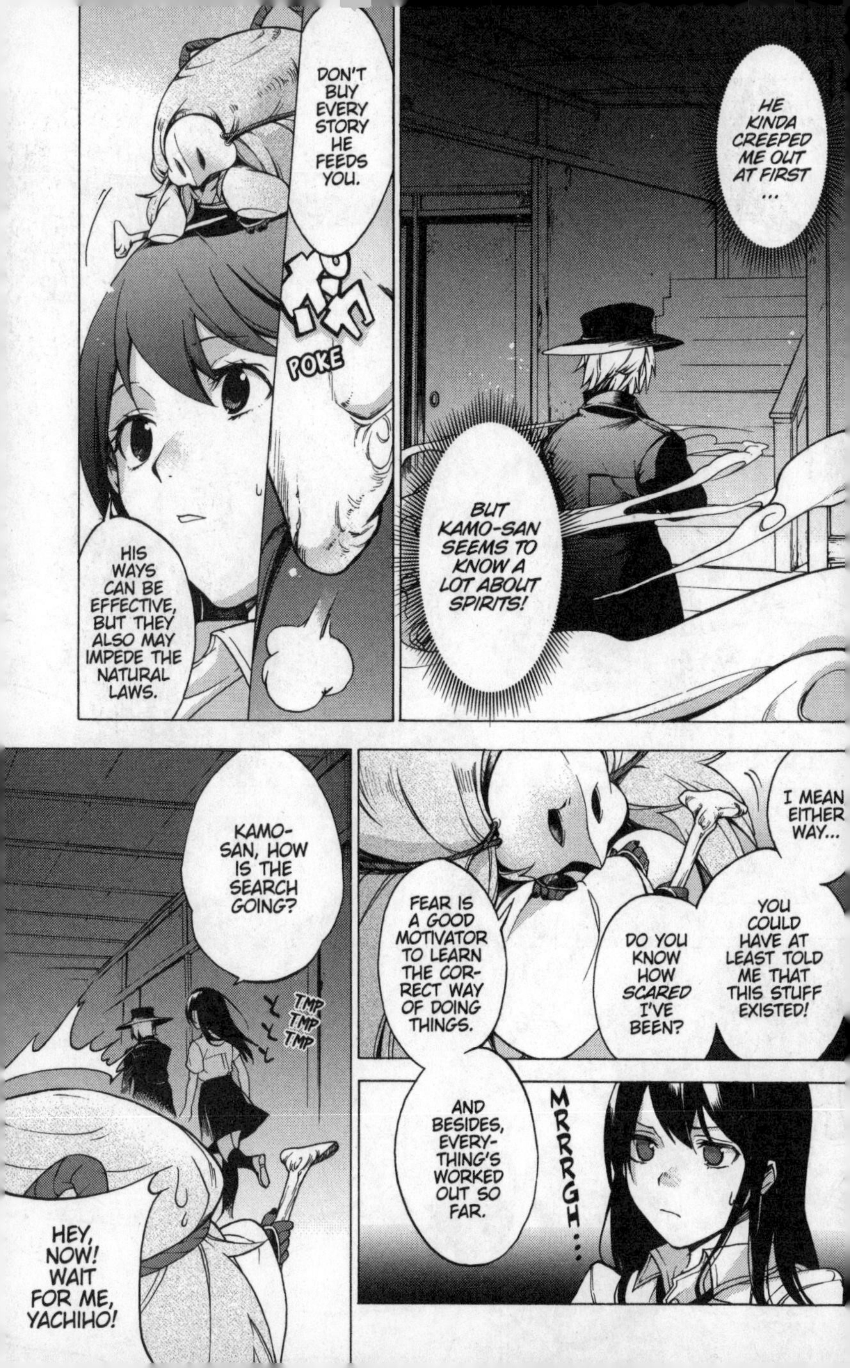
HE KINDA CREEPED ME OUT AT FIRST ...
BUT KAMO-SAN SEEMS TO KNOW A LOT ABOUT SPIRITS!
DON'T BUY EVERY STORY HE FEEDS YOU.
POKE
HIS WAYS CAN BE EFFECTIVE, BUT THEY ALSO MAY IMPEDE THE NATURAL LAWS.
I MEAN EITHER WAY...
YOU COULD HAVE AT LEAST TOLD ME THAT THIS STUFF EXISTED!
DO YOU KNOW HOW SCARED I'VE BEEN?
FEAR IS A GOOD MOTIVATOR TO LEARN THE CORRECT WAY OF DOING THINGS.
AND BESIDES, EVERYTHING'S WORKED OUT SO FAR.
MRRRGH...
KAMO-SAN, HOW IS THE SEARCH GOING?
TMP TMP TMP
HEY, NOW! WAIT FOR ME, YACHIHO!

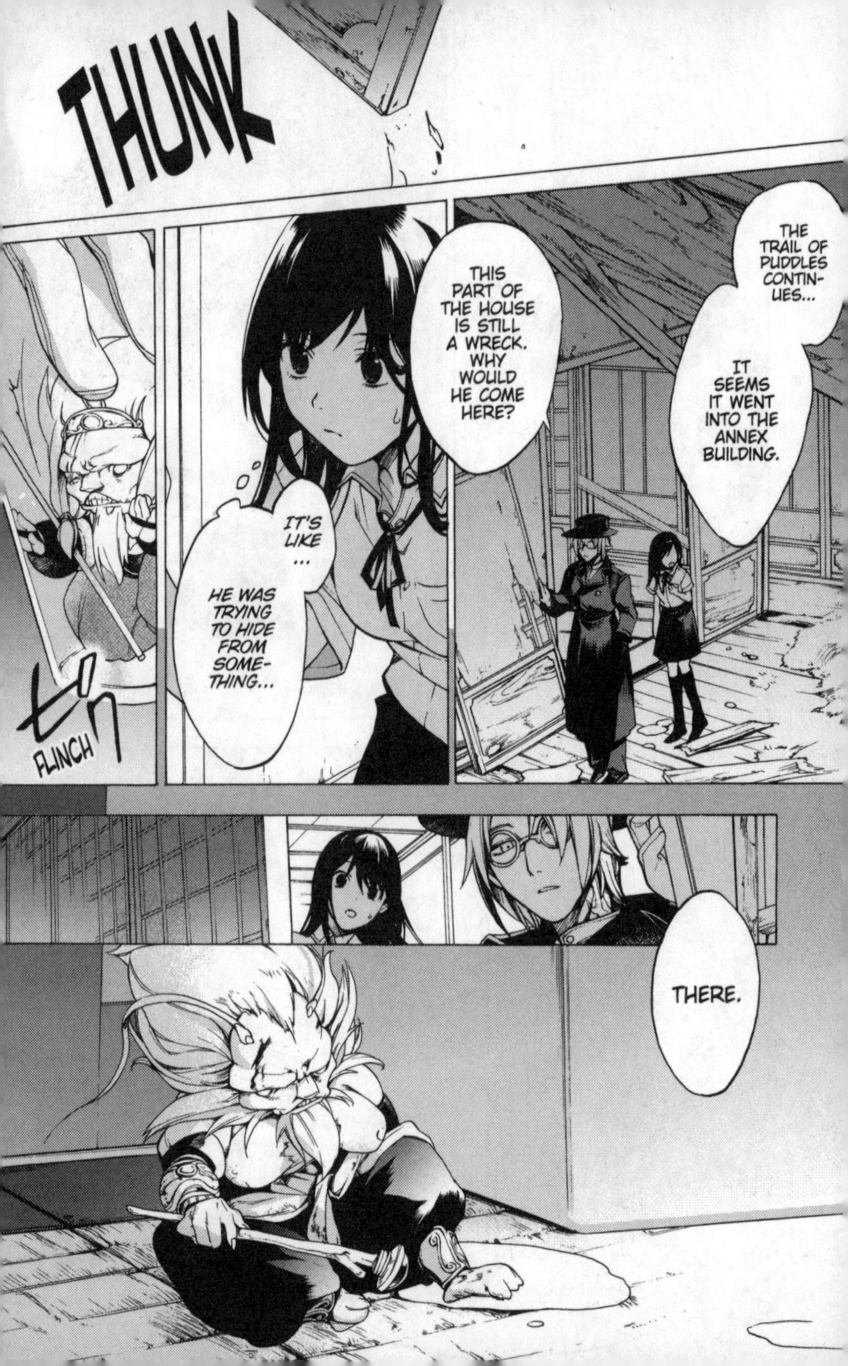
THUNK
THE TRAIL OF PUDDLES CONTIN-UES...
IT SEEMS IT WENT INTO THE ANNEX BUILDING.
THIS PART OF THE HOUSE IS STILL A WRECK. WHY WOULD HE COME HERE?
IT'S LIKE ...
HE WAS TRYING TO HIDE FROM SOME-THING...
FLINCH
THERE.

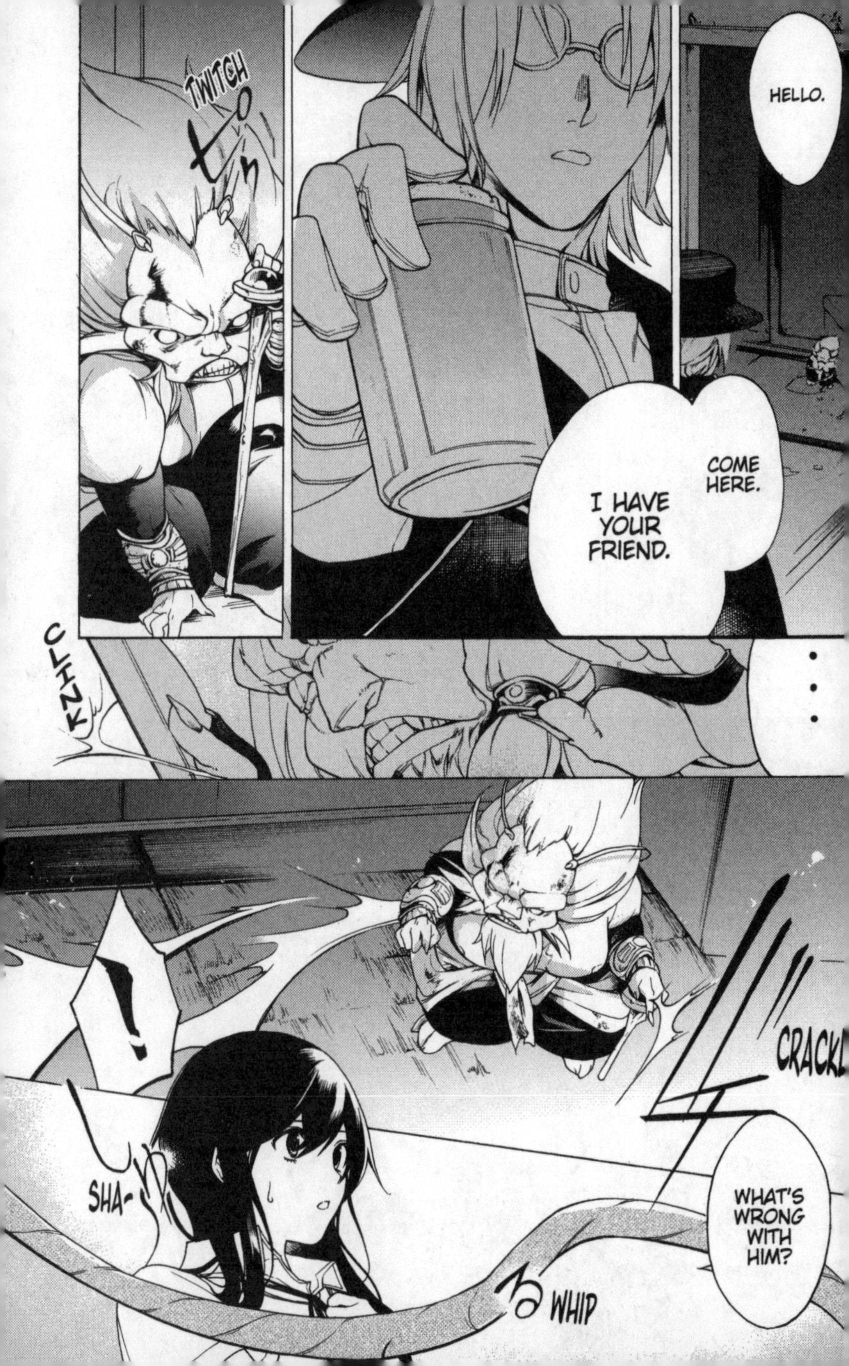
HELLO.
COME HERE.
I HAVE YOUR FRIEND.
TWITCH
...
CLINK
CRACKL
WHAT'S WRONG WITH HIM?
!
SHA-
WHIP

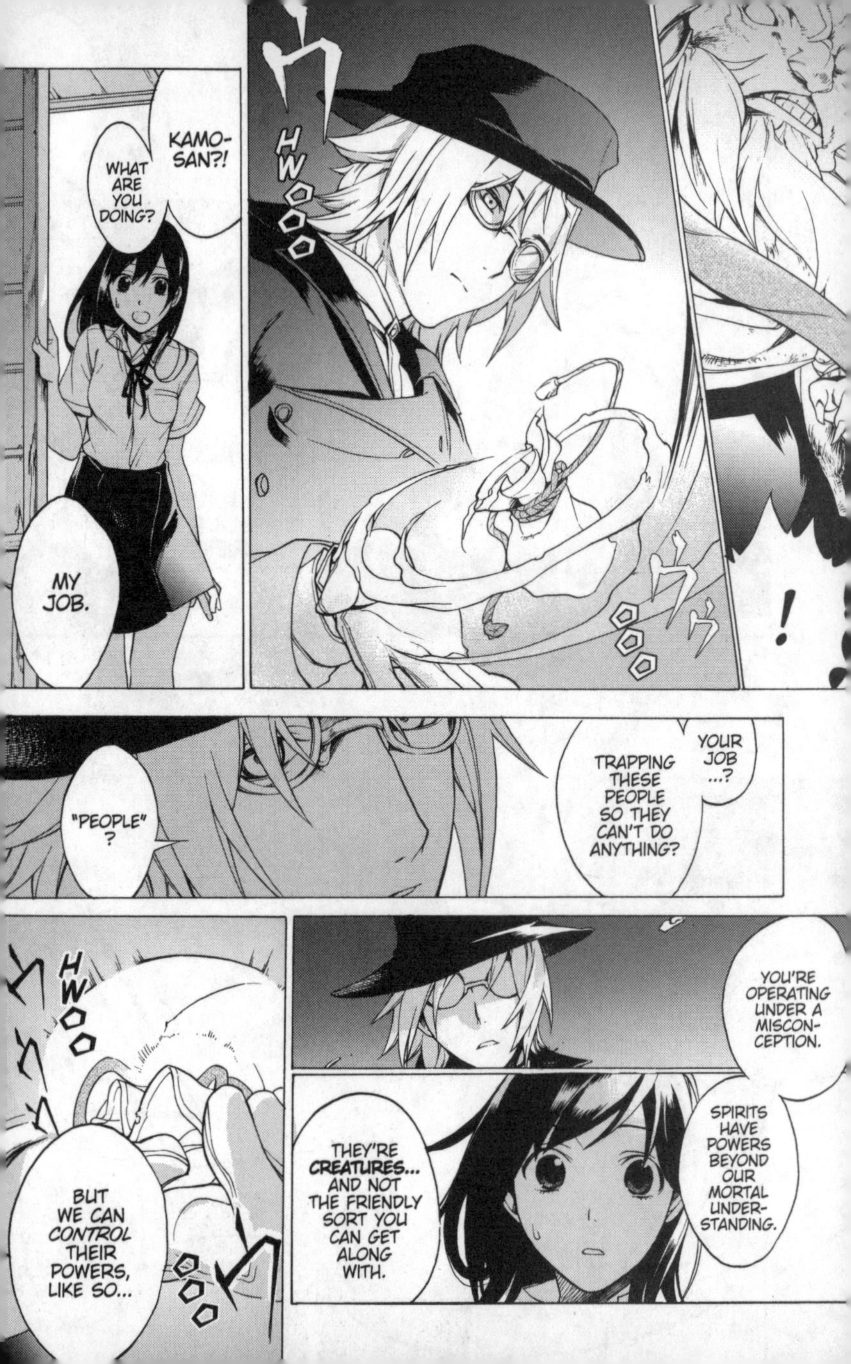
!
HWOOO
OOO
KAMO-SAN?!
WHAT ARE YOU DOING?
MY JOB.
YOUR JOB ...?
TRAPPING THESE PEOPLE SO THEY CAN'T DO ANYTHING?
"PEOPLE"?
YOU'RE OPERATING UNDER A MISCONCEPTION.
SPIRITS HAVE POWERS BEYOND OUR MORTAL UNDER-STANDING.
THEY'RE **CREATURES...** AND NOT THE FRIENDLY SORT YOU CAN GET ALONG WITH.
HWOOO
BUT WE CAN *CONTROL* THEIR POWERS, LIKE SO...
OOO

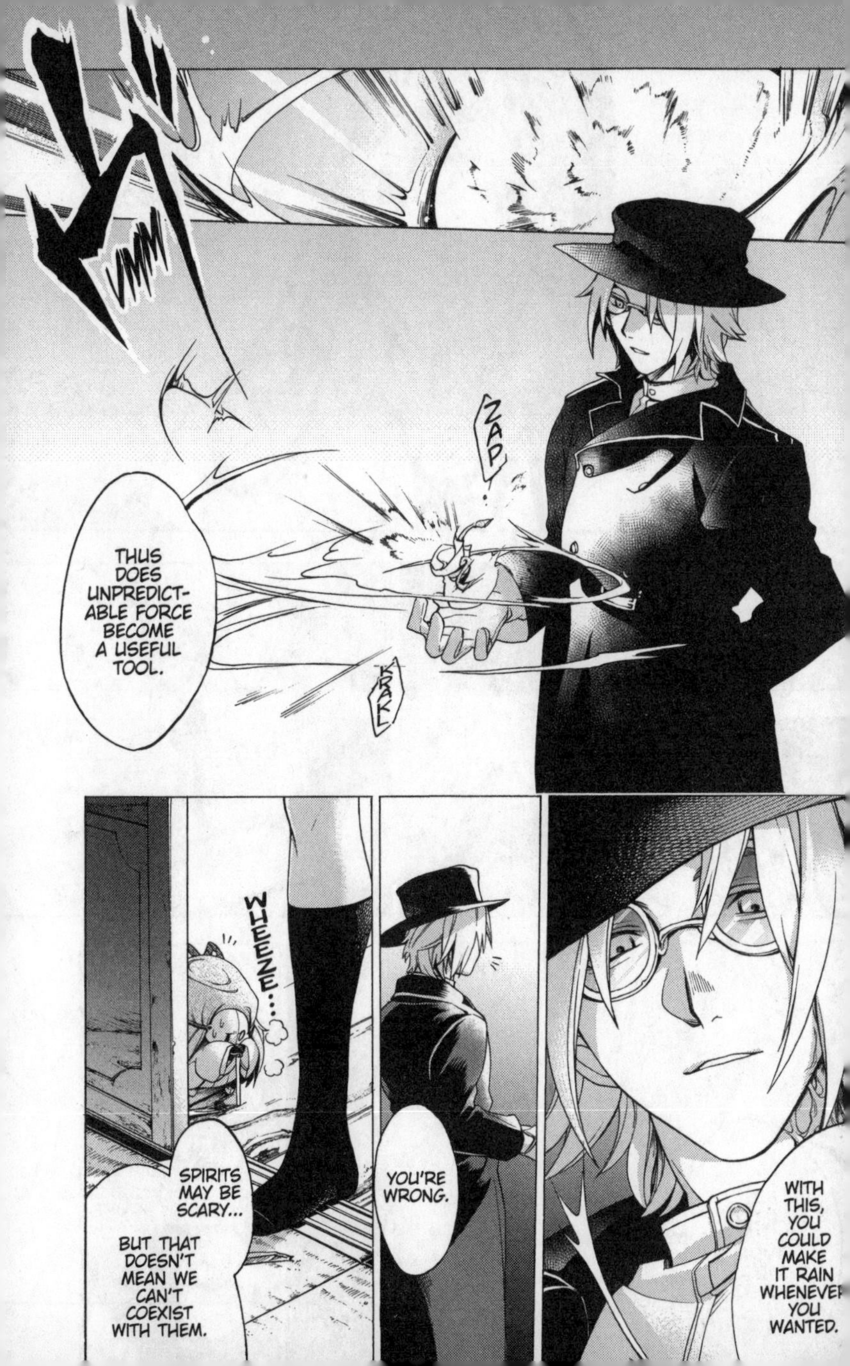
VMMM
ZAP
THUS DOES UNPREDICTABLE FORCE BECOME A USEFUL TOOL.
KRAKL
WITH THIS, YOU COULD MAKE IT RAIN WHENEVER YOU WANTED.
YOU'RE WRONG.
WHEEZE...
SPIRITS MAY BE SCARY...
BUT THAT DOESN'T MEAN WE CAN'T COEXIST WITH THEM.

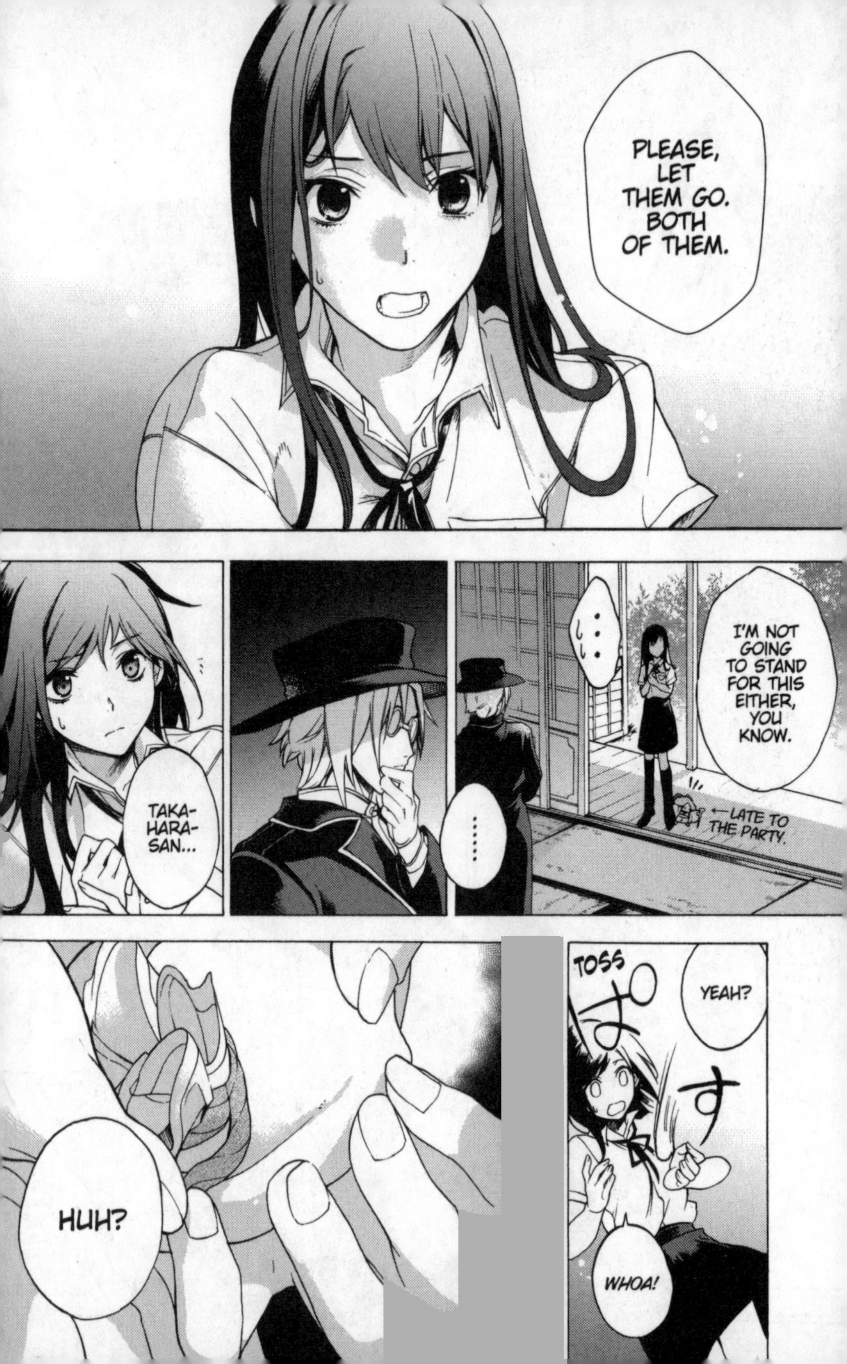
PLEASE, LET THEM GO. BOTH OF THEM.
I'M NOT GOING TO STAND FOR THIS EITHER, YOU KNOW.
...
←LATE TO THE PARTY.
......
TAKA-HARA-SAN...
YEAH?
TOSS
WHOA!
HUH?

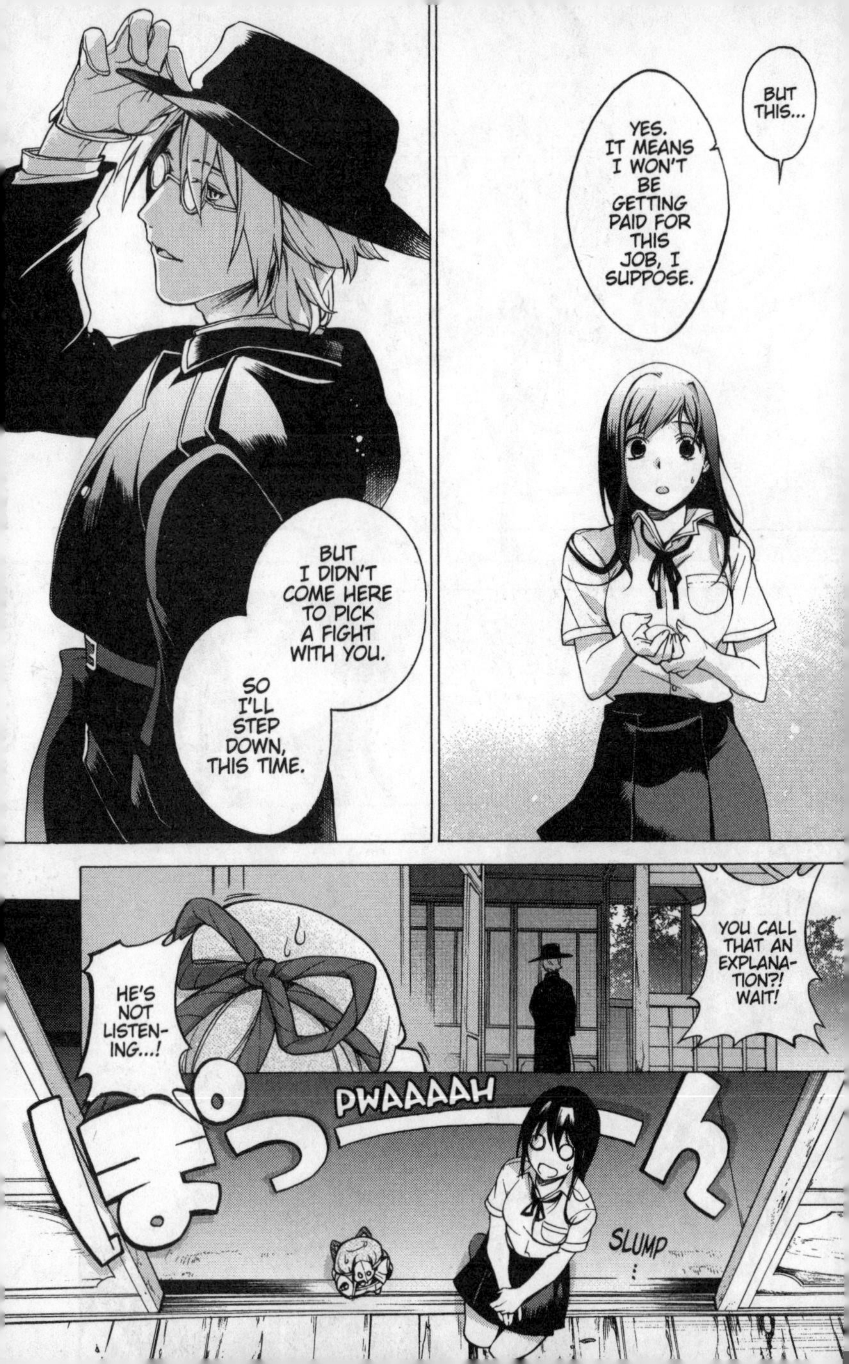
BUT THIS...
YES. IT MEANS I WON'T BE GETTING PAID FOR THIS JOB, I SUPPOSE.
BUT I DIDN'T COME HERE TO PICK A FIGHT WITH YOU.
SO I'LL STEP DOWN, THIS TIME.
YOU CALL THAT AN EXPLANA-TION?! WAIT!
HE'S NOT LISTEN-ING...!
PWAAAAH
ぽつーん
SLUMP

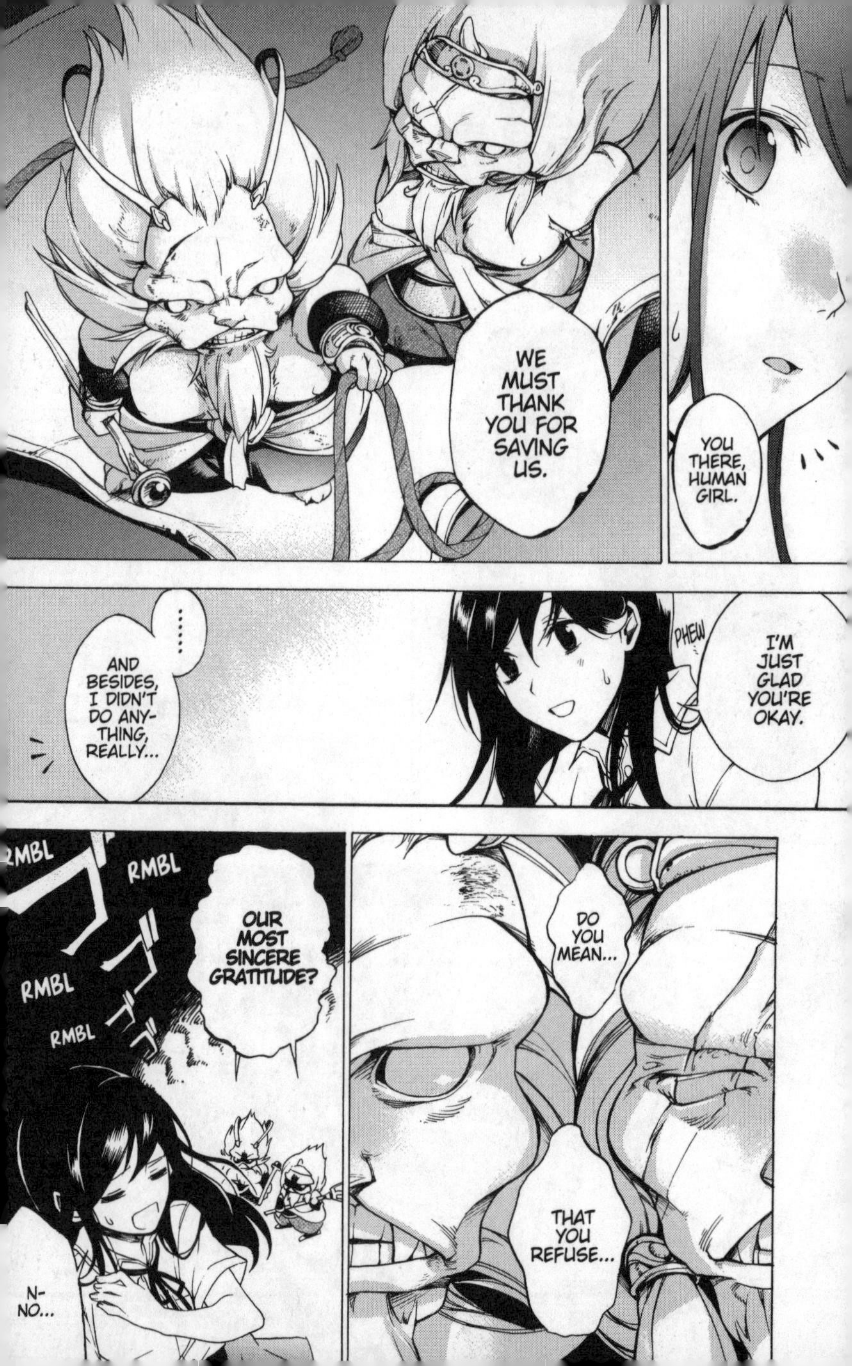
YOU THERE, HUMAN GIRL.
WE MUST THANK YOU FOR SAVING US.
PHEW
I'M JUST GLAD YOU'RE OKAY.
AND BESIDES, I DIDN'T DO ANY-THING, REALLY...
......
DO YOU MEAN...
THAT YOU REFUSE...
RMBL
RMBL
OUR MOST SINCERE GRATITUDE?
RMBL
RMBL
N-NO...

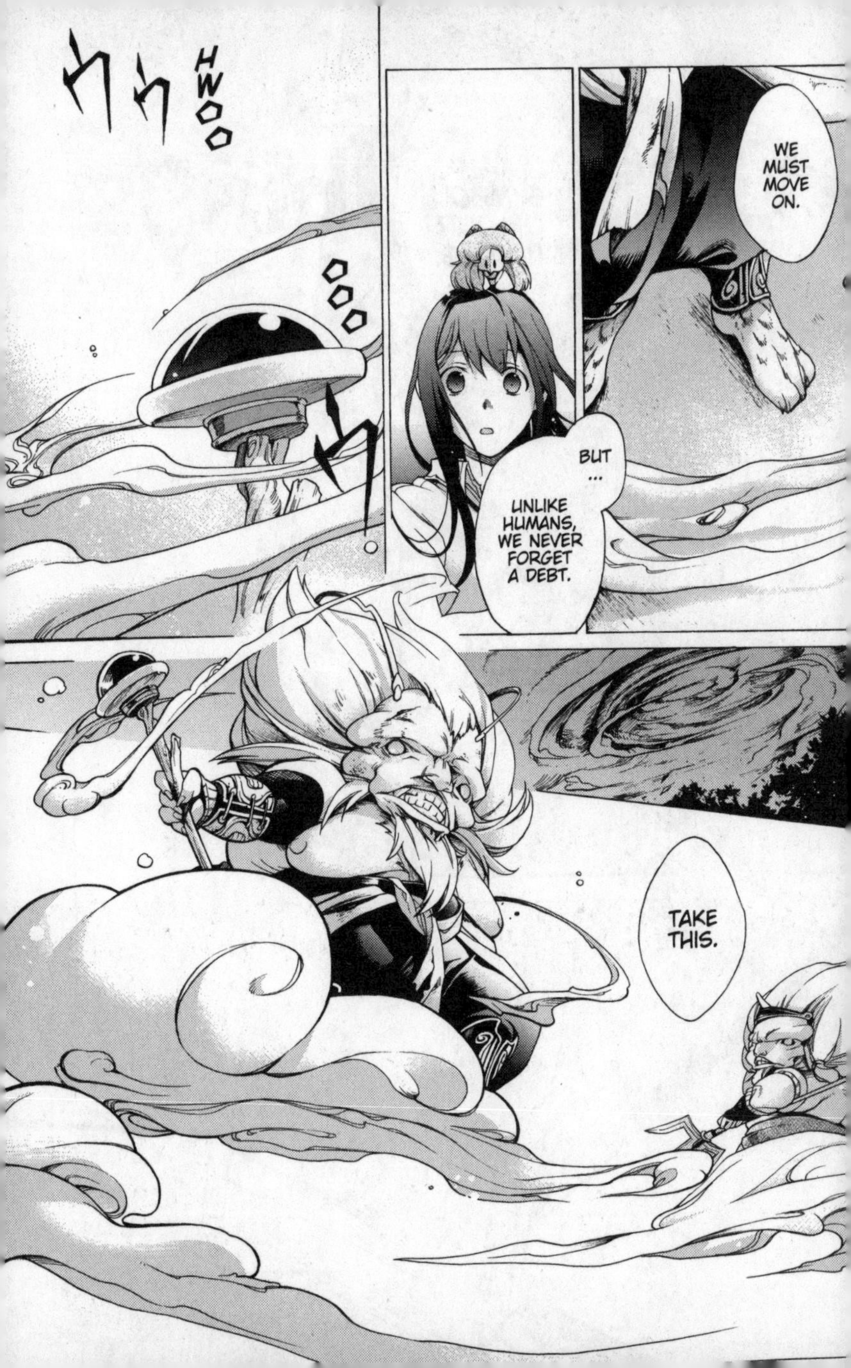
WE MUST MOVE ON.
BUT ...
UNLIKE HUMANS, WE NEVER FORGET A DEBT.
HWOO
OOO
TAKE THIS.

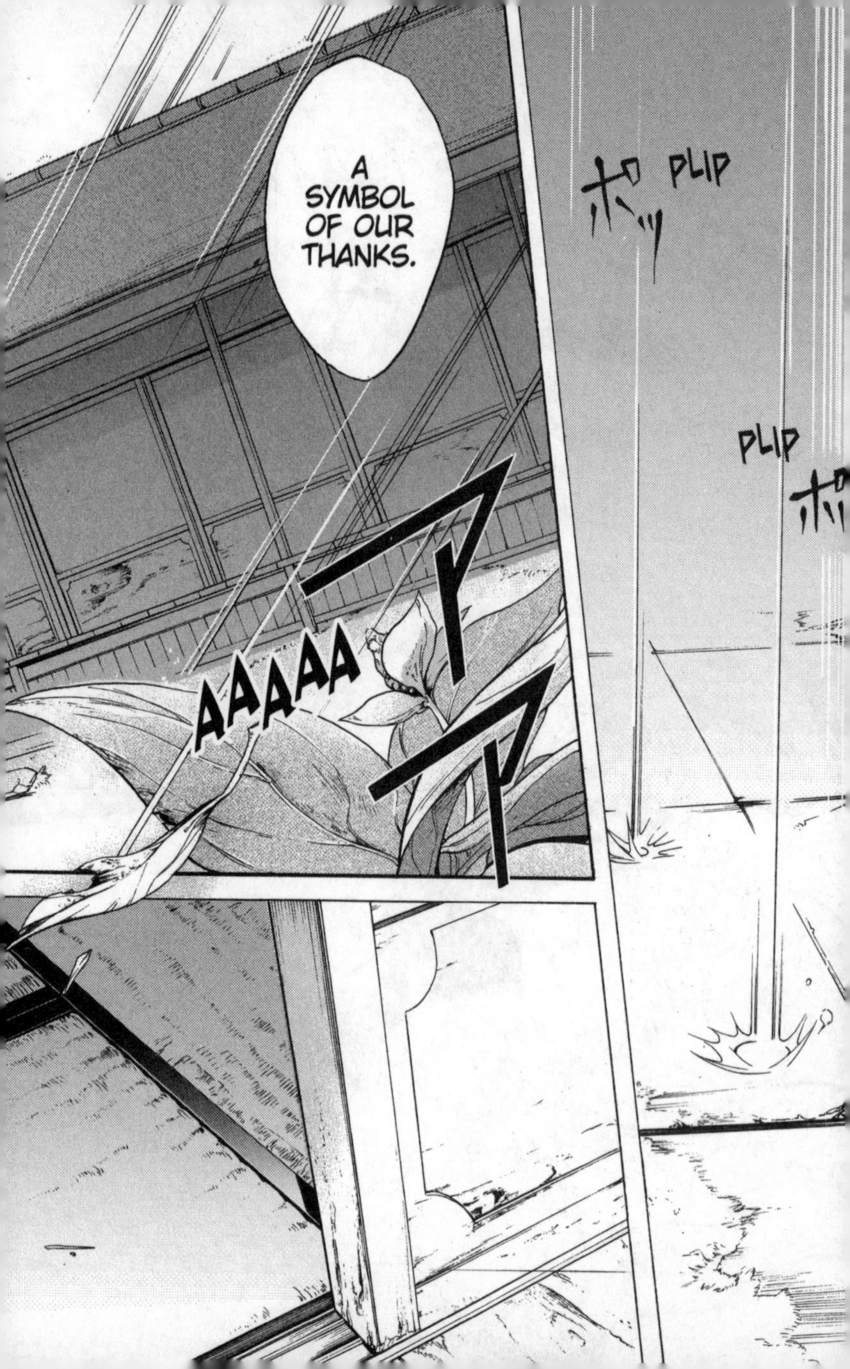
PLIP
ポッ
PLIP
ポッ
A SYMBOL OF OUR THANKS.
AAAAA
アァ

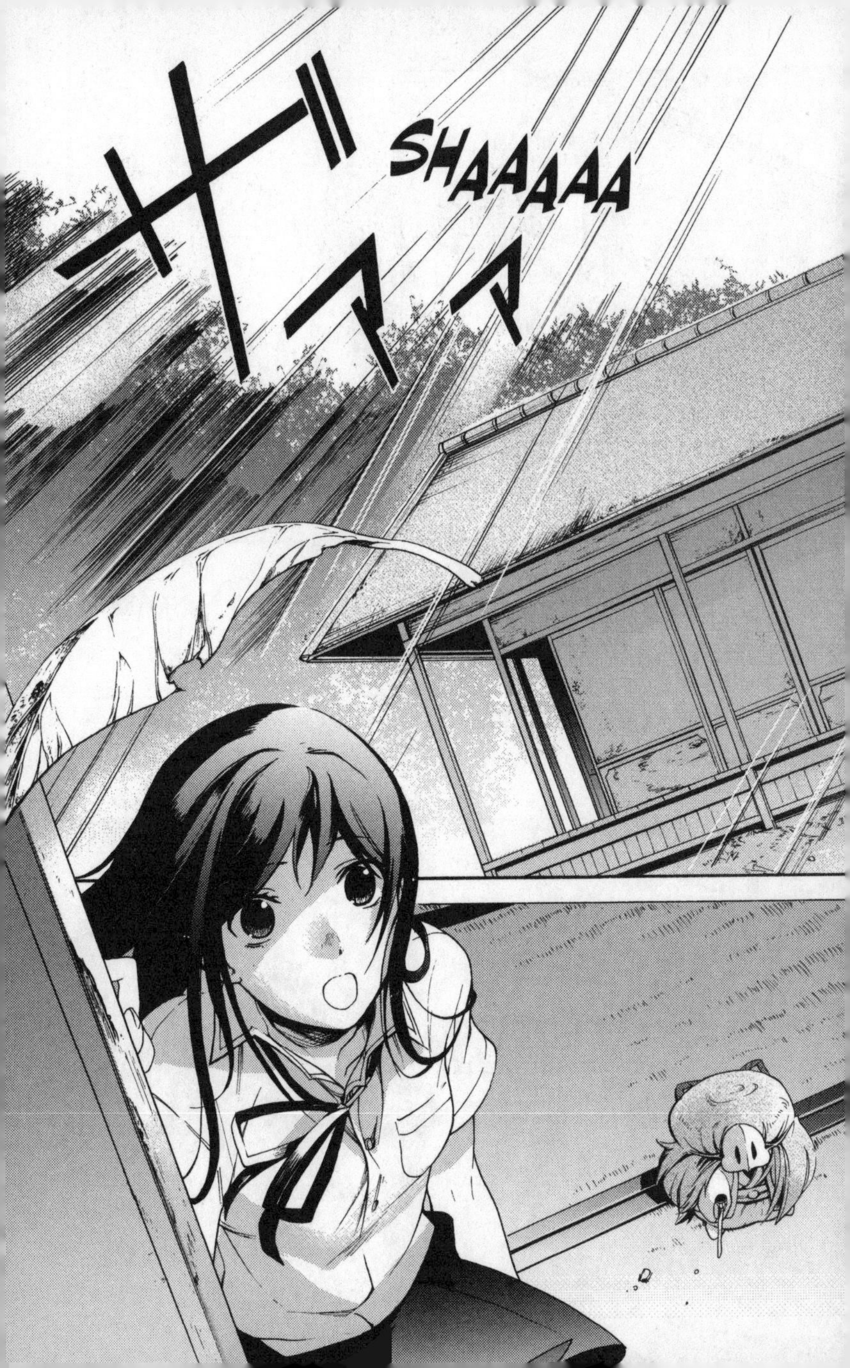
SHAAAAA

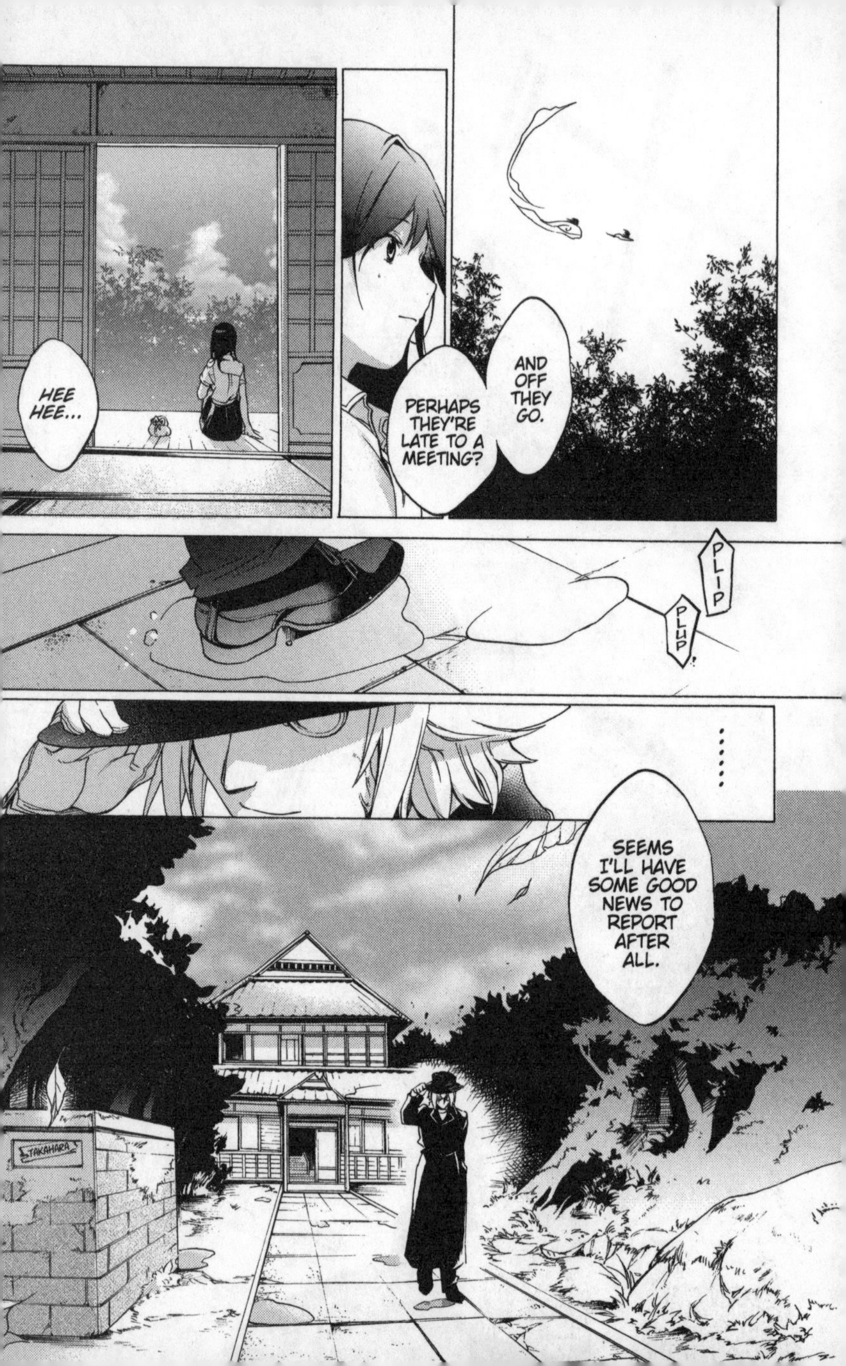
AND OFF THEY GO.
PERHAPS THEY'RE LATE TO A MEETING?
HEE HEE...
PLIP
PLUP
......
SEEMS I'LL HAVE SOME GOOD NEWS TO REPORT AFTER ALL.
TAKAHARA

THE ENCOUNTER

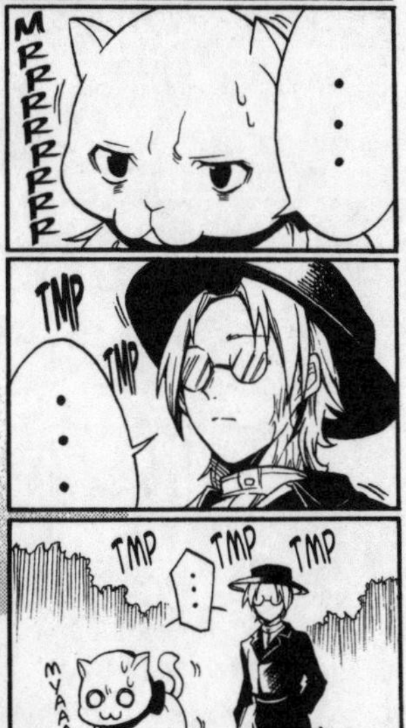
MRRRRRRRR
...
TMP
TMP
...
TMP
TMP
TMP
...
MYAAA!
DASH
MEOOOOW!
(THIS GUY IS CREEPY!)
KITTY...

THIS HAPPENED RIGHT BEFORE HIS BIG ENTRANCE.

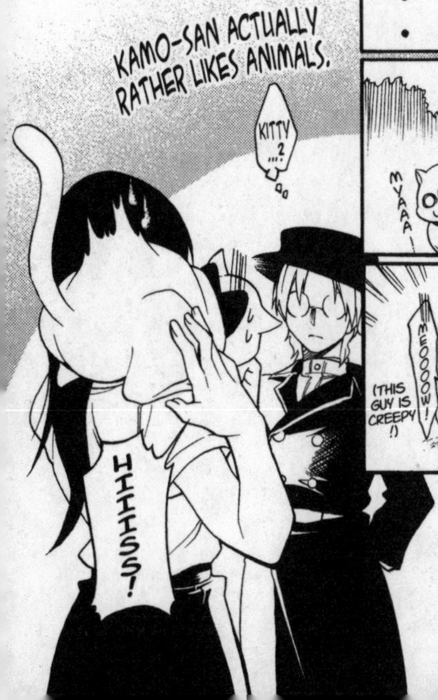
KAMO-SAN ACTUALLY RATHER LIKES ANIMALS.
KITTY ...?
HIIISS!

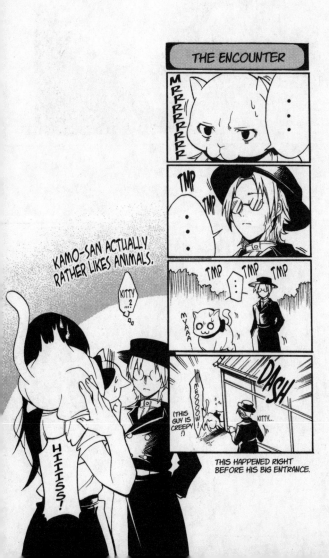

Ghostly
Things

Chapter 5

The Successor and the Venerable Verdant (Part 1)

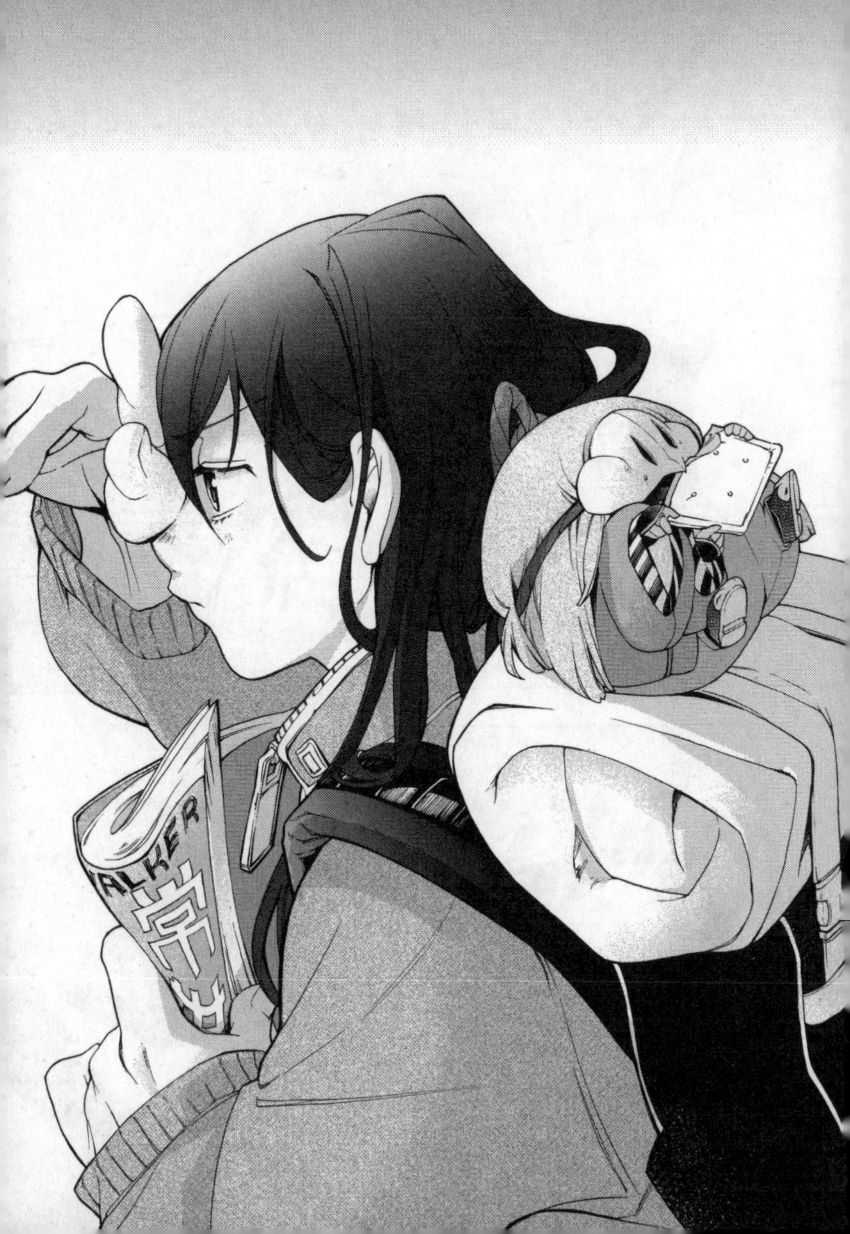
ALKER

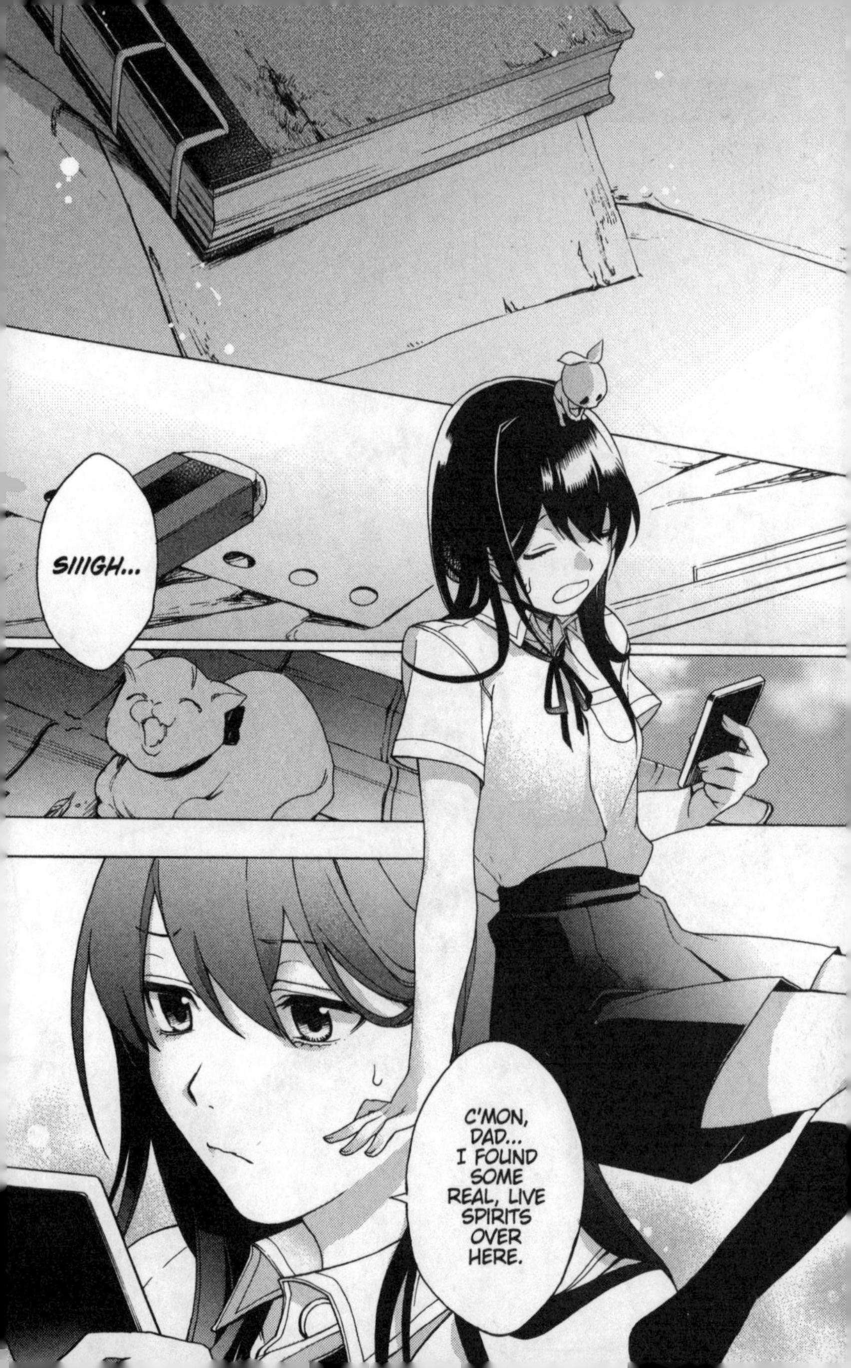
SIIIGH...
C'MON, DAD... I FOUND SOME REAL, LIVE SPIRITS OVER HERE.

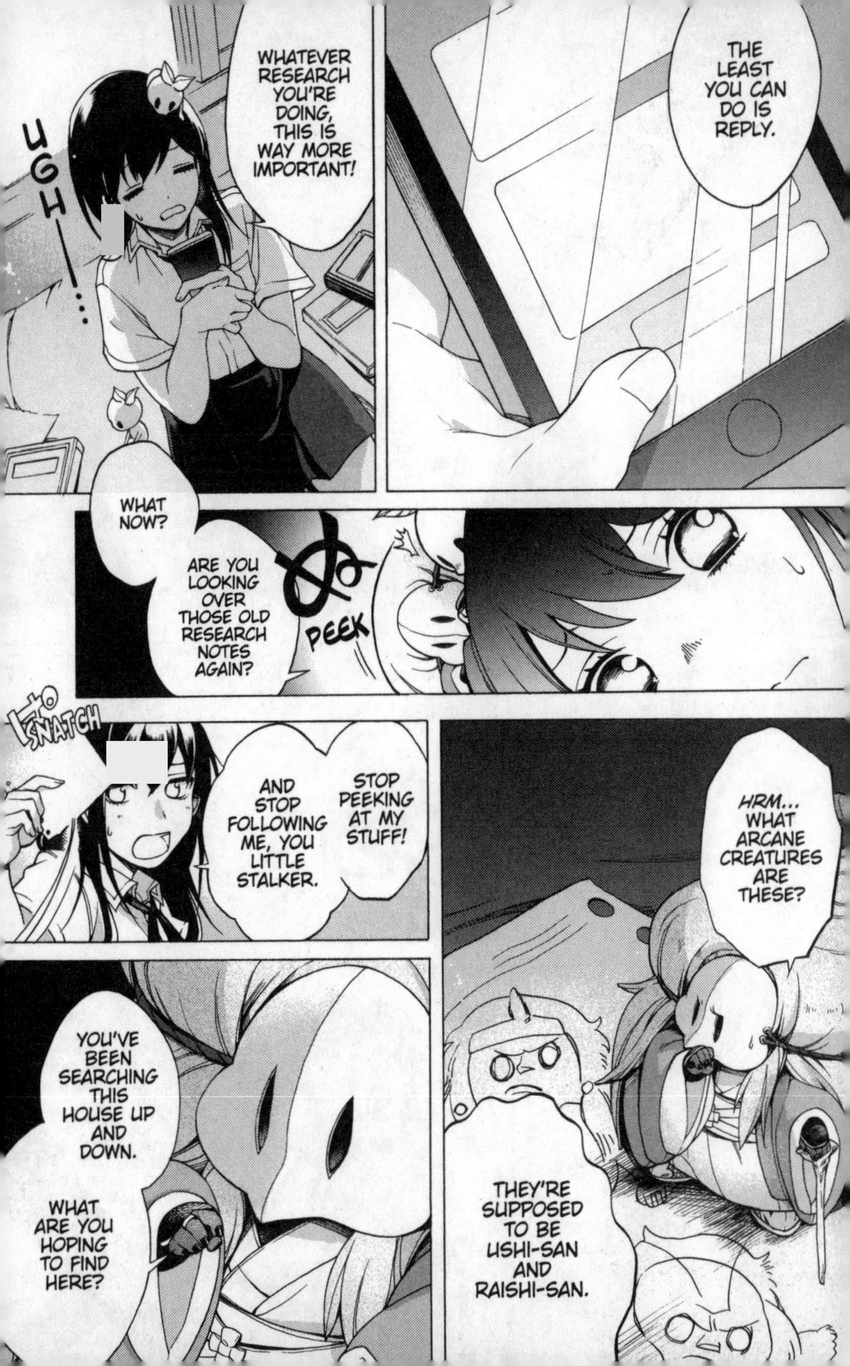
THE LEAST YOU CAN DO IS REPLY.
WHATEVER RESEARCH YOU'RE DOING, THIS IS WAY MORE IMPORTANT!
UGH...
WHAT NOW?
ARE YOU LOOKING OVER THOSE OLD RESEARCH NOTES AGAIN?
PEEK
HRM... WHAT ARCANE CREATURES ARE THESE?
THEY'RE SUPPOSED TO BE USHI-SAN AND RAISHI-SAN.
SNATCH
STOP PEEKING AT MY STUFF!
AND STOP FOLLOWING ME, YOU LITTLE STALKER.
YOU'VE BEEN SEARCHING THIS HOUSE UP AND DOWN.
WHAT ARE YOU HOPING TO FIND HERE?

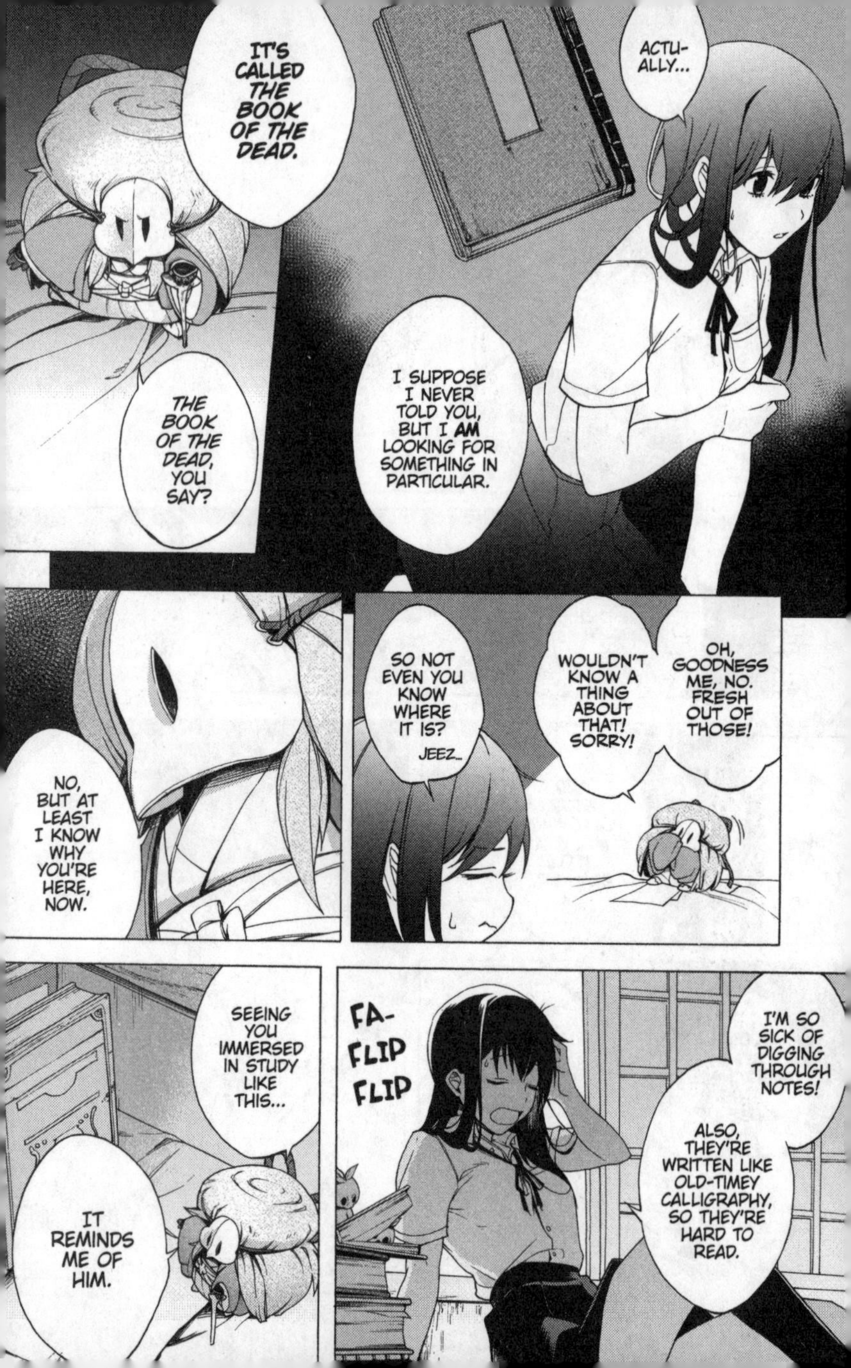
ACTUALLY...
I SUPPOSE I NEVER TOLD YOU, BUT I AM LOOKING FOR SOMETHING IN PARTICULAR.
IT'S CALLED THE BOOK OF THE DEAD.
THE BOOK OF THE DEAD, YOU SAY?
OH, GOODNESS ME, NO. FRESH OUT OF THOSE!
WOULDN'T KNOW A THING ABOUT THAT! SORRY!
SO NOT EVEN YOU KNOW WHERE IT IS?
JEEZ...
NO, BUT AT LEAST I KNOW WHY YOU'RE HERE, NOW.
I'M SO SICK OF DIGGING THROUGH NOTES!
ALSO, THEY'RE WRITTEN LIKE OLD-TIMEY CALLIGRAPHY, SO THEY'RE HARD TO READ.
FA-FLIP FLIP FLIP
SEEING YOU IMMERSED IN STUDY LIKE THIS...
IT REMINDS ME OF HIM.

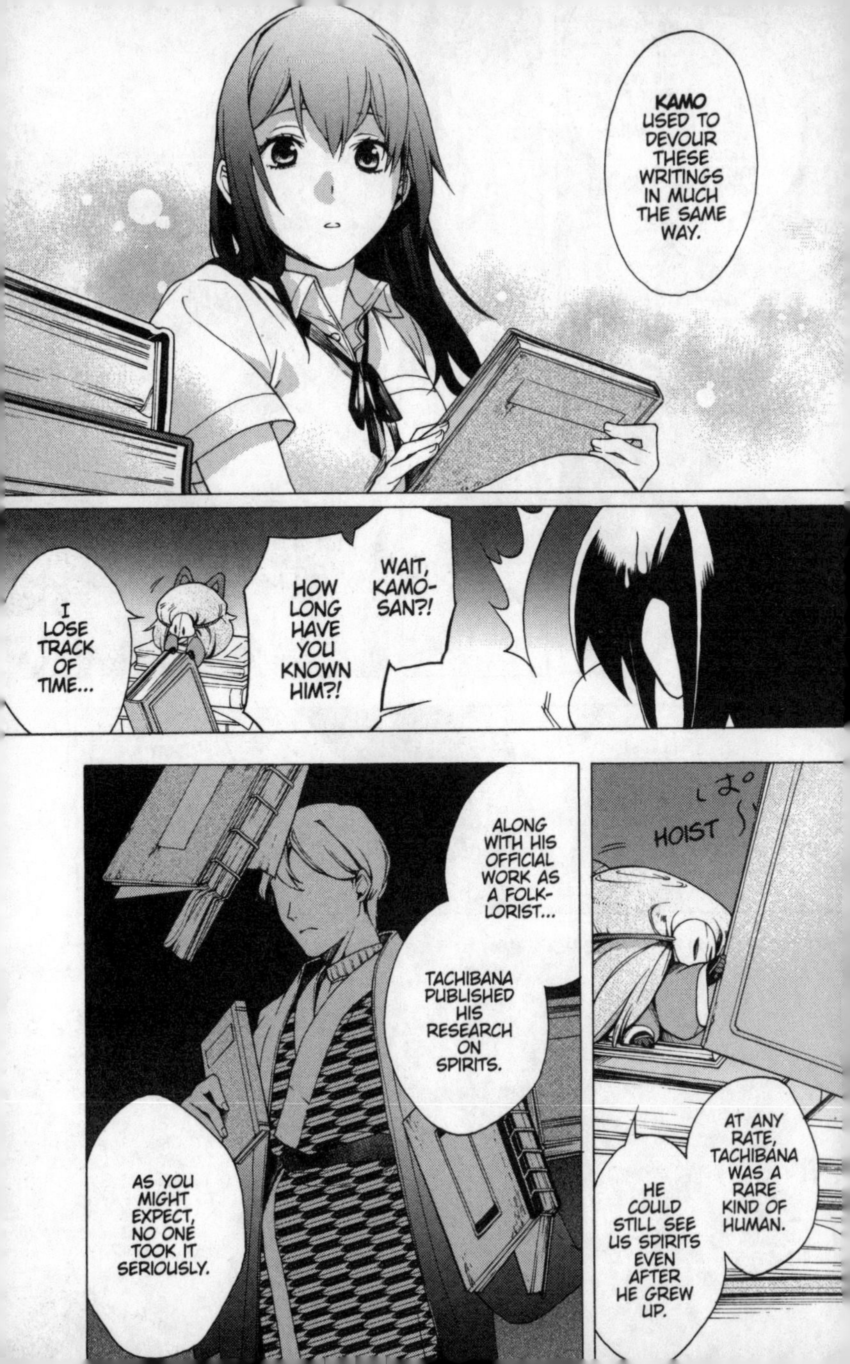
KAMO USED TO DEVOUR THESE WRITINGS IN MUCH THE SAME WAY.
WAIT, KAMO-SAN?!
HOW LONG HAVE YOU KNOWN HIM?!
I LOSE TRACK OF TIME...
HOIST
AT ANY RATE, TACHIBANA WAS A RARE KIND OF HUMAN.
HE COULD STILL SEE US SPIRITS EVEN AFTER HE GREW UP.
ALONG WITH HIS OFFICIAL WORK AS A FOLK-LORIST...
TACHIBANA PUBLISHED HIS RESEARCH ON SPIRITS.
AS YOU MIGHT EXPECT, NO ONE TOOK IT SERIOUSLY.

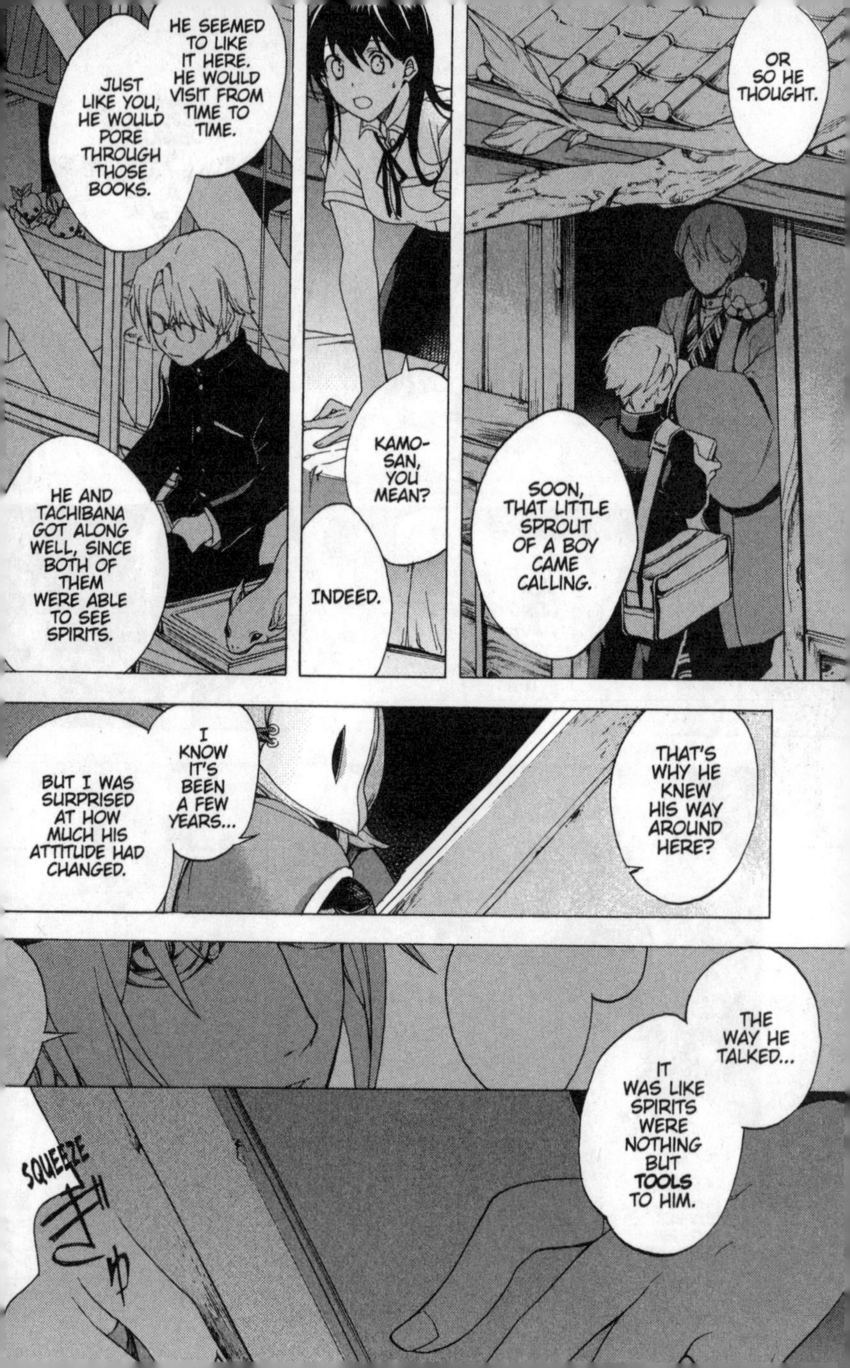
OR SO HE THOUGHT.
SOON, THAT LITTLE SPROUT OF A BOY CAME CALLING.
KAMO-SAN, YOU MEAN?
INDEED.
HE SEEMED TO LIKE IT HERE. HE WOULD VISIT FROM TIME TO TIME.
JUST LIKE YOU, HE WOULD PORE THROUGH THOSE BOOKS.
HE AND TACHIBANA GOT ALONG WELL, SINCE BOTH OF THEM WERE ABLE TO SEE SPIRITS.
THAT'S WHY HE KNEW HIS WAY AROUND HERE?
I KNOW IT'S BEEN A FEW YEARS...
BUT I WAS SURPRISED AT HOW MUCH HIS ATTITUDE HAD CHANGED.
THE WAY HE TALKED...
IT WAS LIKE SPIRITS WERE NOTHING BUT **TOOLS** TO HIM.
SQUEEZE

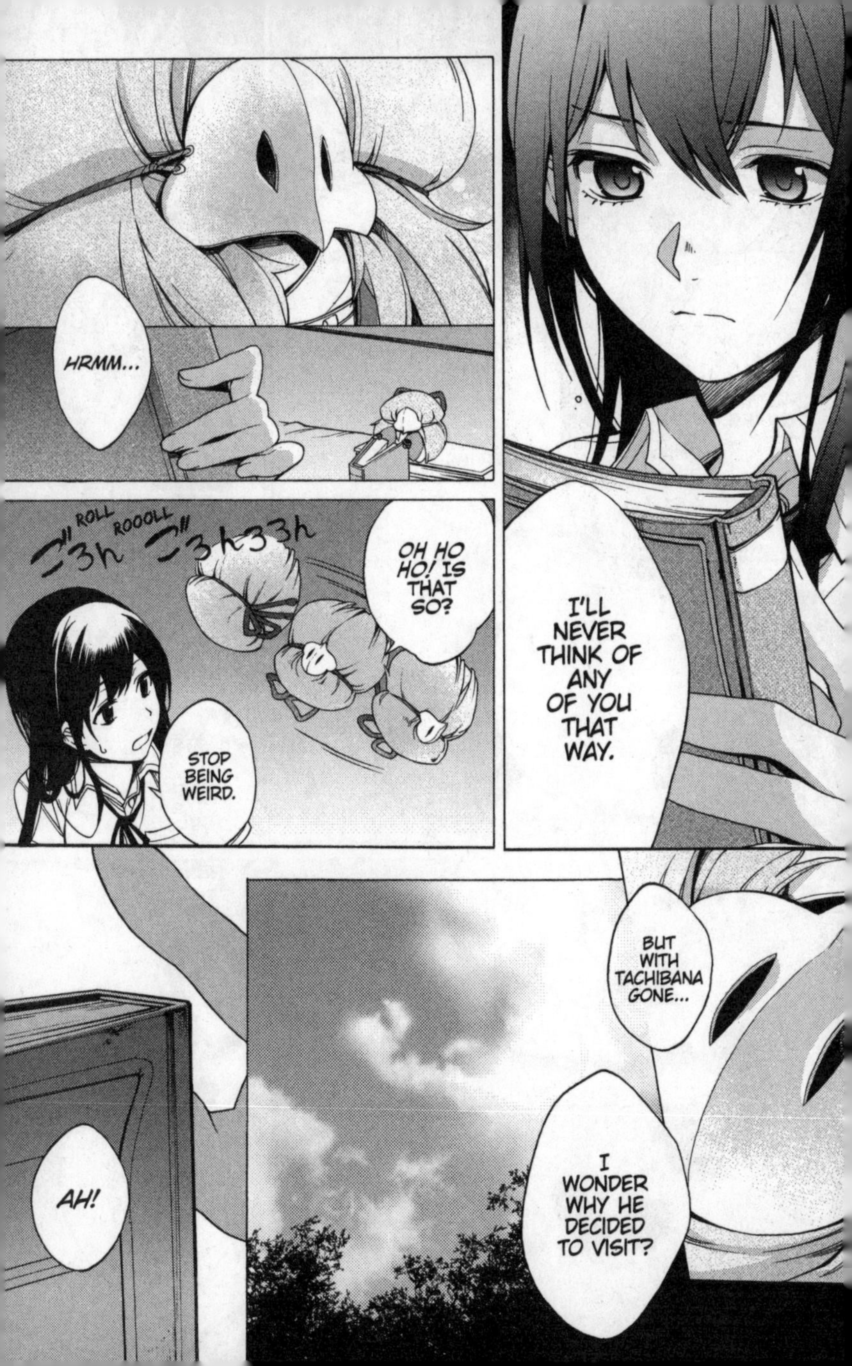
I'LL NEVER THINK OF ANY OF YOU THAT WAY.
HRMM...
ROLL ROOOLL
OH HO HO! IS THAT SO?
STOP BEING WEIRD.
BUT WITH TACHIBANA GONE...
I WONDER WHY HE DECIDED TO VISIT?
AH!

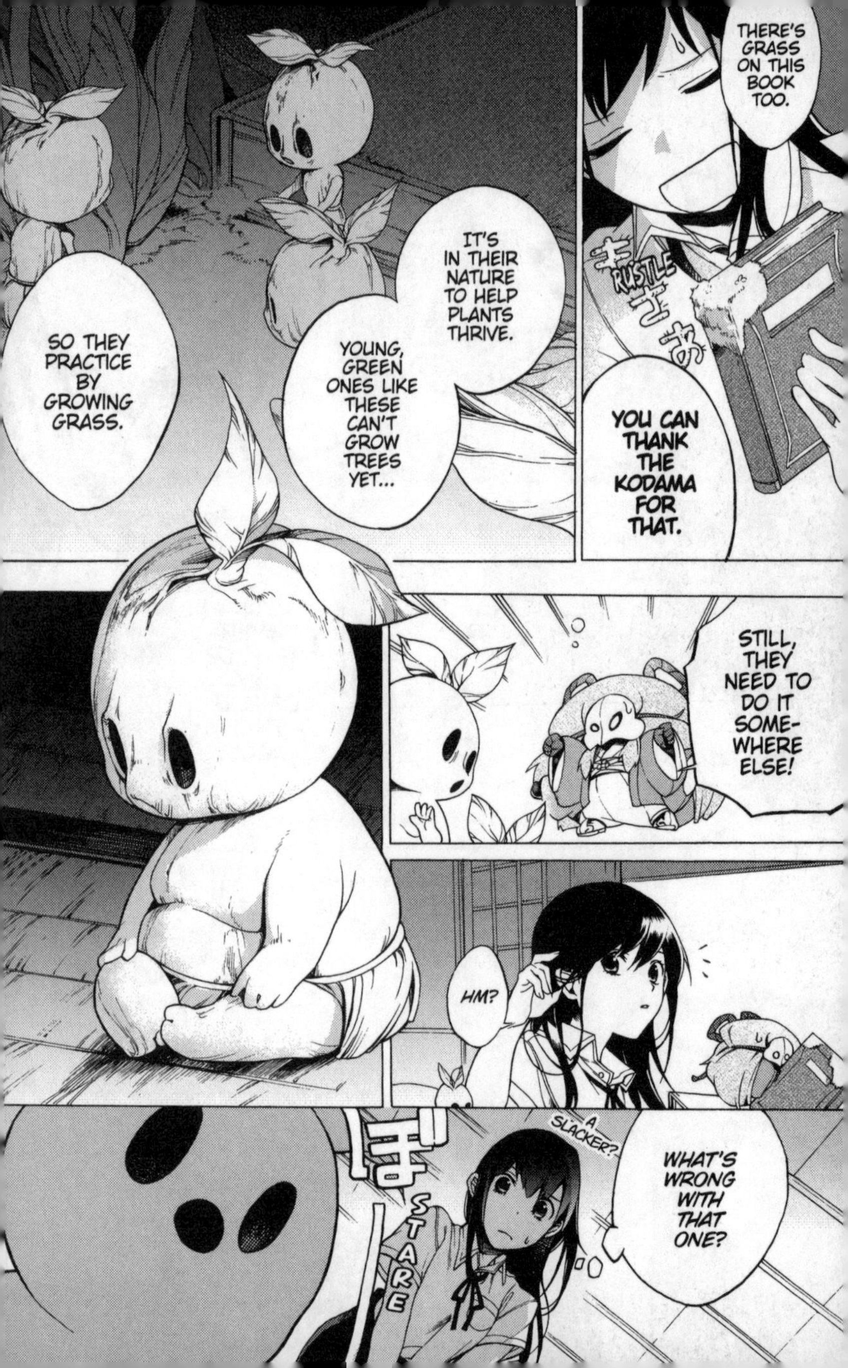
THERE'S GRASS ON THIS BOOK TOO.
RUSTLE
YOU CAN THANK THE KODAMA FOR THAT.
IT'S IN THEIR NATURE TO HELP PLANTS THRIVE.
YOUNG, GREEN ONES LIKE THESE CAN'T GROW TREES YET...
SO THEY PRACTICE BY GROWING GRASS.
STILL, THEY NEED TO DO IT SOME-WHERE ELSE!
HM?
WHAT'S WRONG WITH THAT ONE?
A SLACKER?
STARE

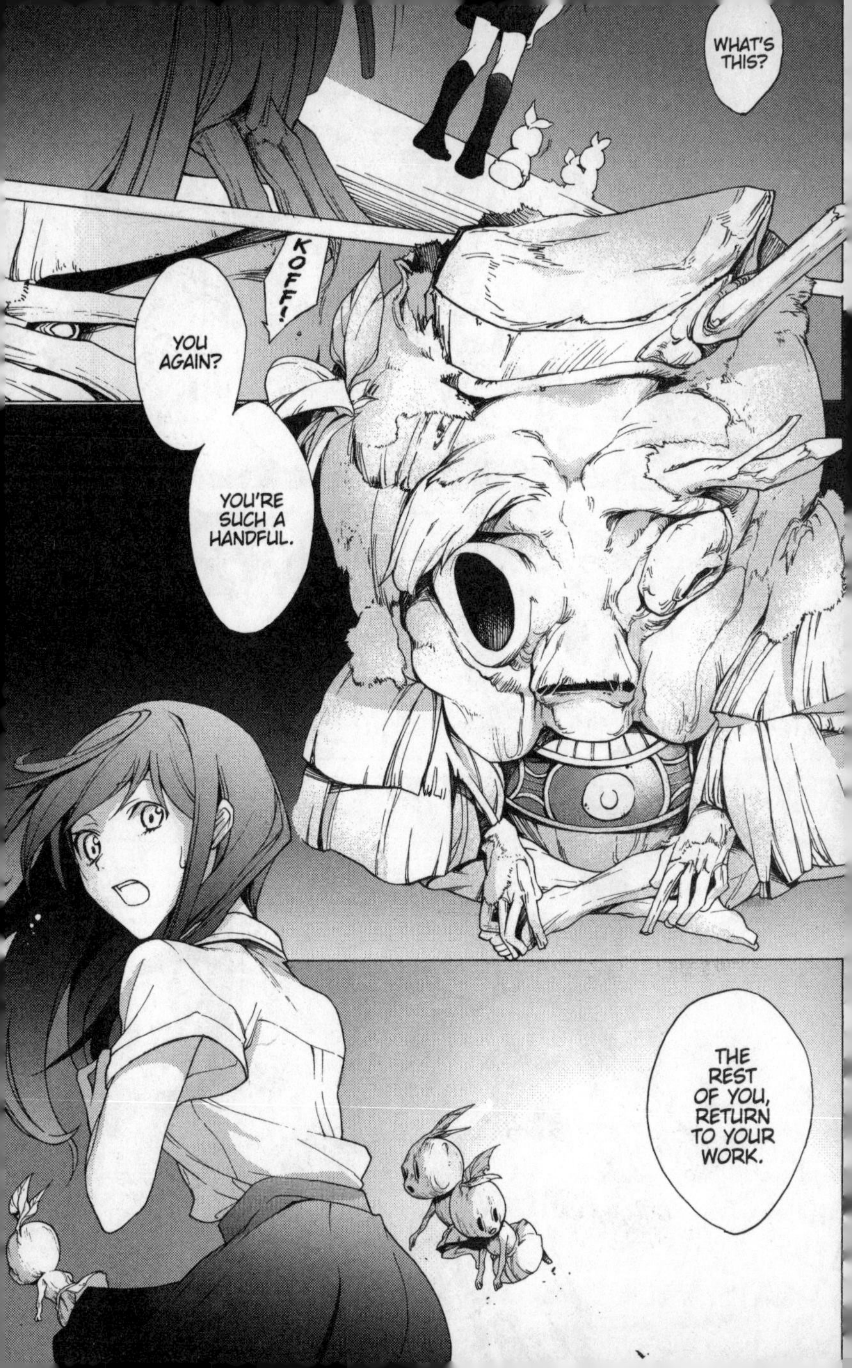
WHAT'S THIS?
KOFF!
YOU AGAIN?
YOU'RE SUCH A HANDFUL.
THE REST OF YOU, RETURN TO YOUR WORK.

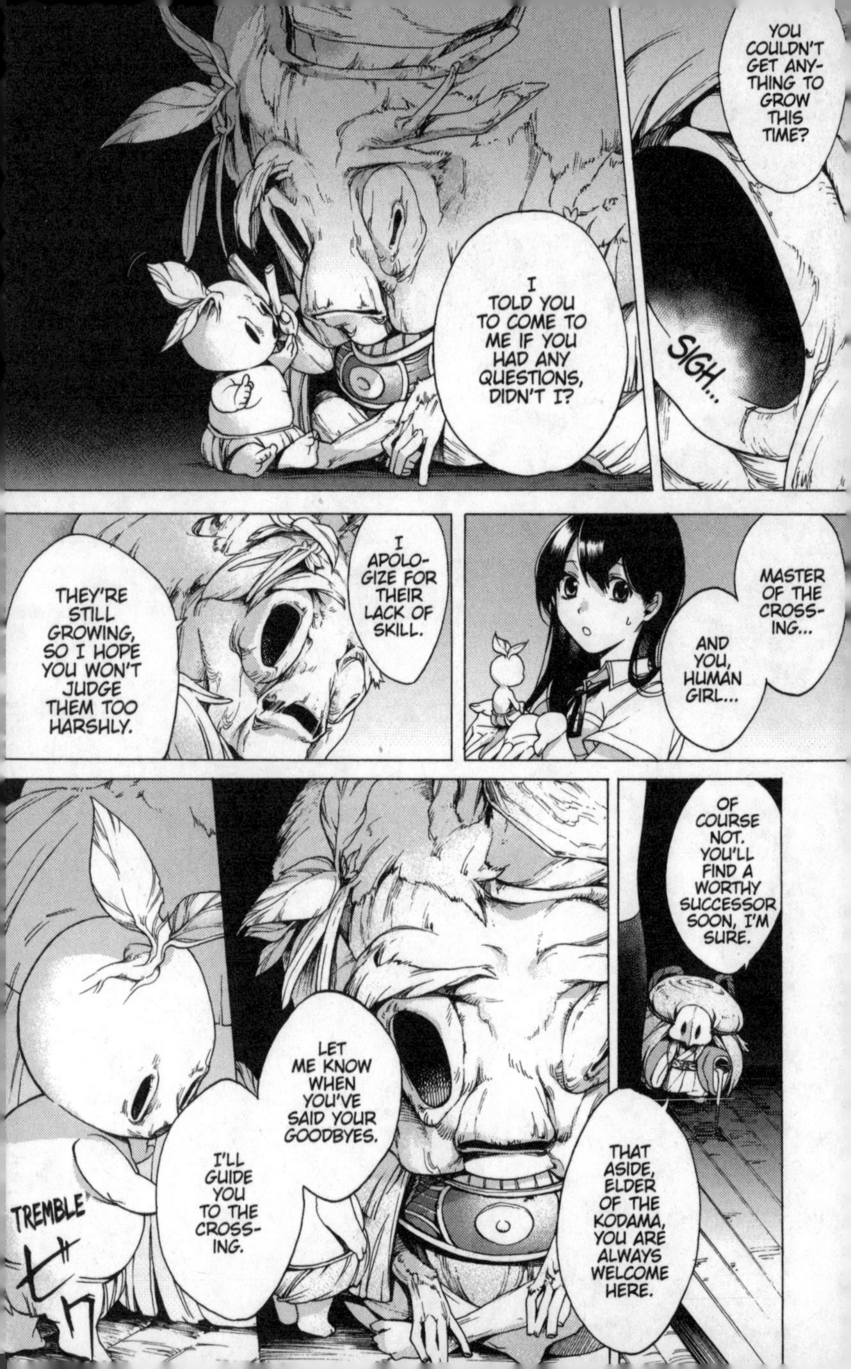
YOU COULDN'T GET ANY-THING TO GROW THIS TIME?
SIGH...
I TOLD YOU TO COME TO ME IF YOU HAD ANY QUESTIONS, DIDN'T I?
MASTER OF THE CROSS-ING...
AND YOU, HUMAN GIRL...
I APOLO-GIZE FOR THEIR LACK OF SKILL.
THEY'RE STILL GROWING, SO I HOPE YOU WON'T JUDGE THEM TOO HARSHLY.
OF COURSE NOT. YOU'LL FIND A WORTHY SUCCESSOR SOON, I'M SURE.
THAT ASIDE, ELDER OF THE KODAMA, YOU ARE ALWAYS WELCOME HERE.
LET ME KNOW WHEN YOU'VE SAID YOUR GOODBYES.
I'LL GUIDE YOU TO THE CROSS-ING.
TREMBLE

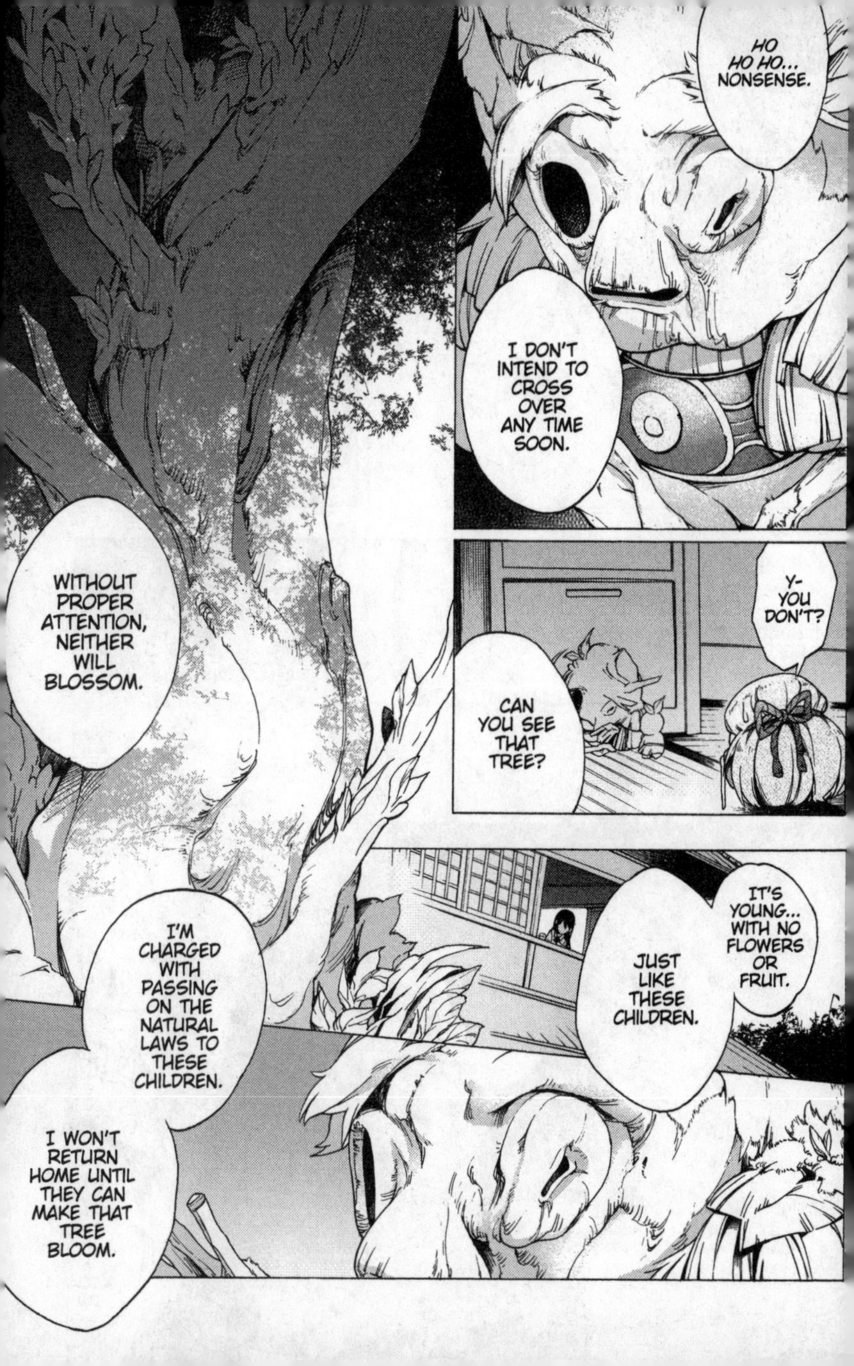
HO HO HO... NONSENSE.
I DON'T INTEND TO CROSS OVER ANY TIME SOON.
Y-YOU DON'T?
CAN YOU SEE THAT TREE?
IT'S YOUNG... WITH NO FLOWERS OR FRUIT.
JUST LIKE THESE CHILDREN.
WITHOUT PROPER ATTENTION, NEITHER WILL BLOSSOM.
I'M CHARGED WITH PASSING ON THE NATURAL LAWS TO THESE CHILDREN.
I WON'T RETURN HOME UNTIL THEY CAN MAKE THAT TREE BLOOM.

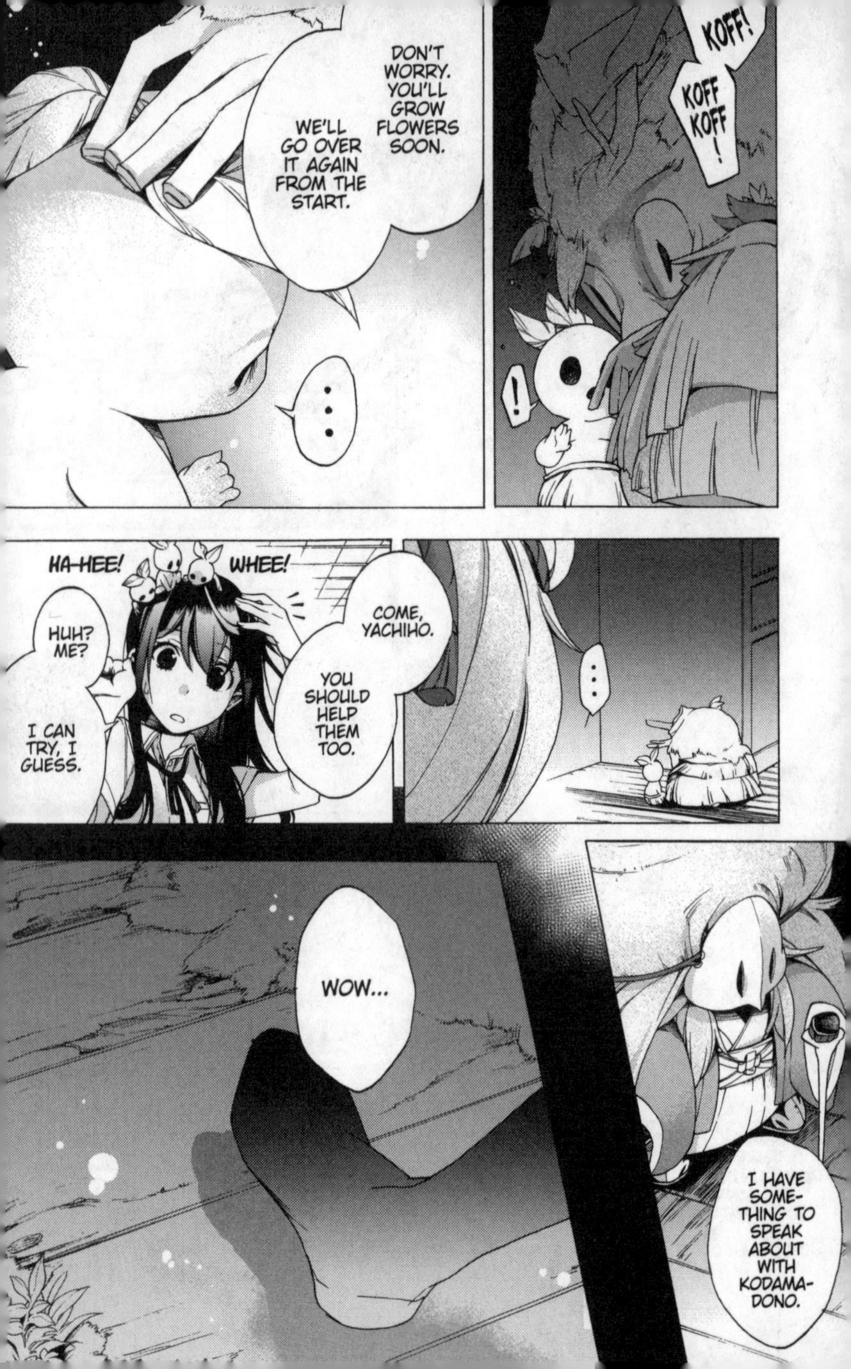
KOFF!
KOFF KOFF!
!
DON'T WORRY. YOU'LL GROW FLOWERS SOON.
WE'LL GO OVER IT AGAIN FROM THE START.
...
...
COME, YACHIHO.
YOU SHOULD HELP THEM TOO.
WHEE!
HA-HEE!
HUH? ME?
I CAN TRY, I GUESS.
I HAVE SOME-THING TO SPEAK ABOUT WITH KODAMA-DONO.
WOW...

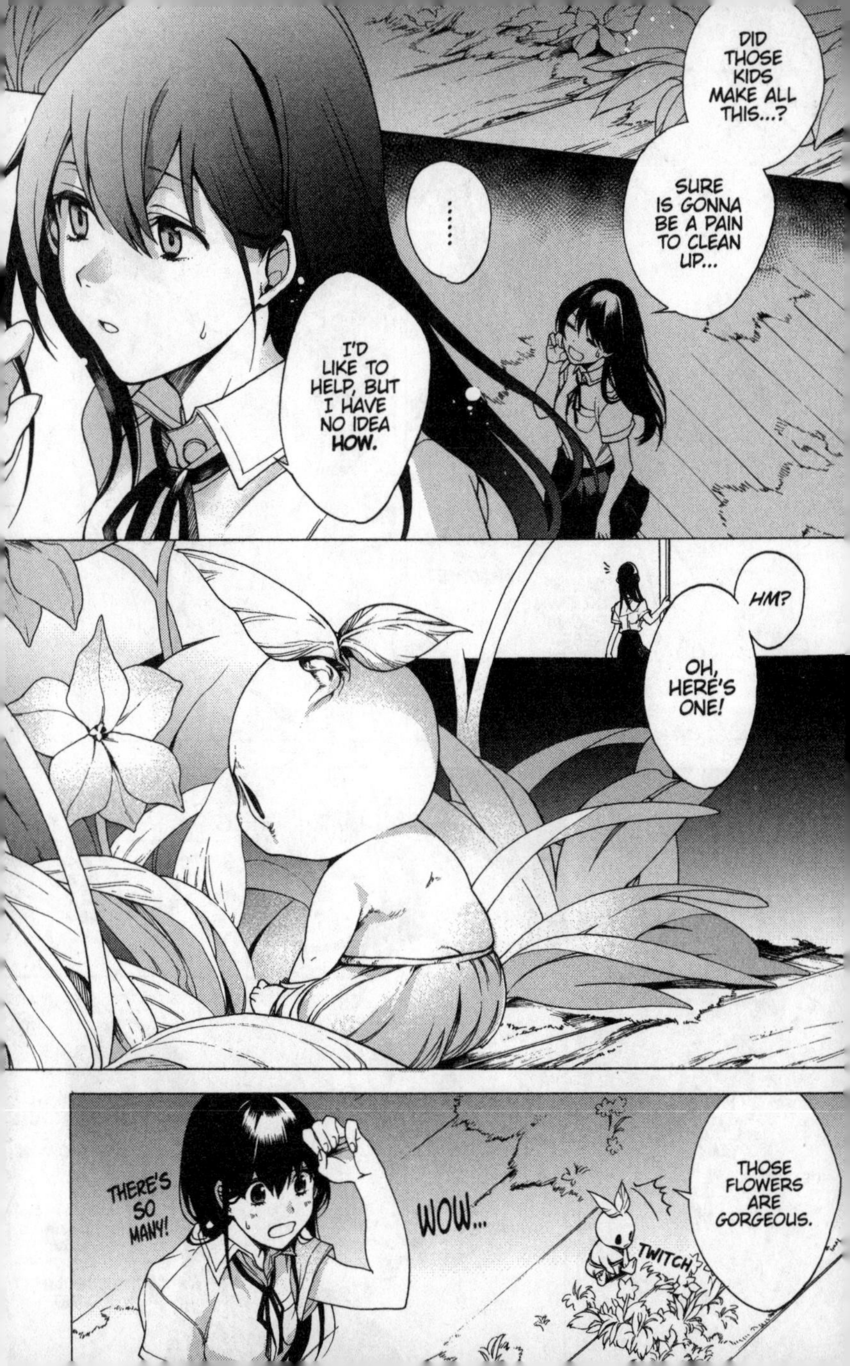
DID THOSE KIDS MAKE ALL THIS...?
SURE IS GONNA BE A PAIN TO CLEAN UP...
......
I'D LIKE TO HELP, BUT I HAVE NO IDEA HOW.
HM?
OH, HERE'S ONE!
THOSE FLOWERS ARE GORGEOUS.
TWITCH
WOW...
THERE'S SO MANY!

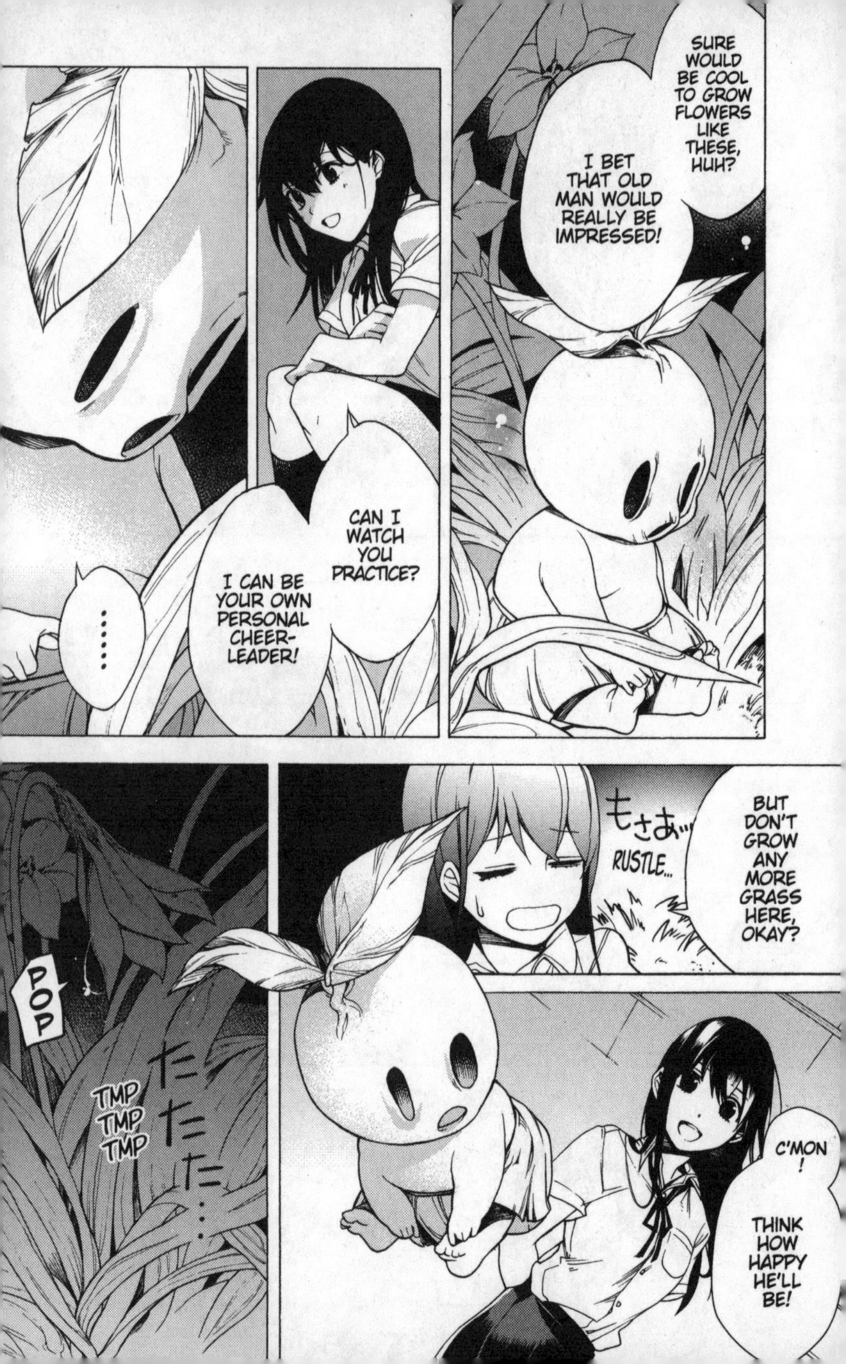
SURE WOULD BE COOL TO GROW FLOWERS LIKE THESE, HUH?
I BET THAT OLD MAN WOULD REALLY BE IMPRESSED!
CAN I WATCH YOU PRACTICE?
I CAN BE YOUR OWN PERSONAL CHEER-LEADER!
......
BUT DON'T GROW ANY MORE GRASS HERE, OKAY?
もさぁッ
RUSTLE...
C'MON!
THINK HOW HAPPY HE'LL BE!
POP
たたた…
TMP TMP TMP

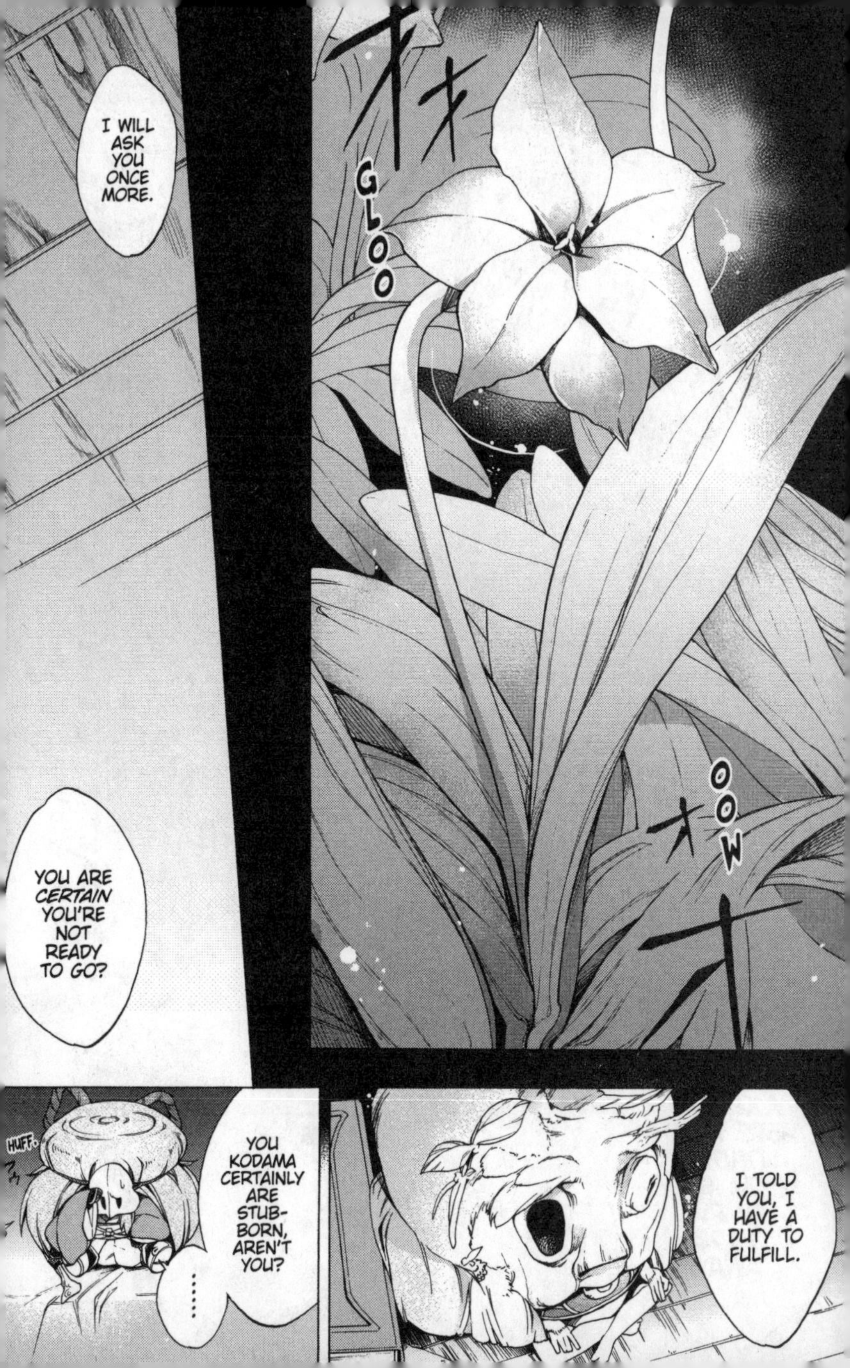
GLOO
OOW
I WILL ASK YOU ONCE MORE.
YOU ARE CERTAIN YOU'RE NOT READY TO GO?
I TOLD YOU, I HAVE A DUTY TO FULFILL.
HUFF.
YOU KODAMA CERTAINLY ARE STUBBORN, AREN'T YOU?
......

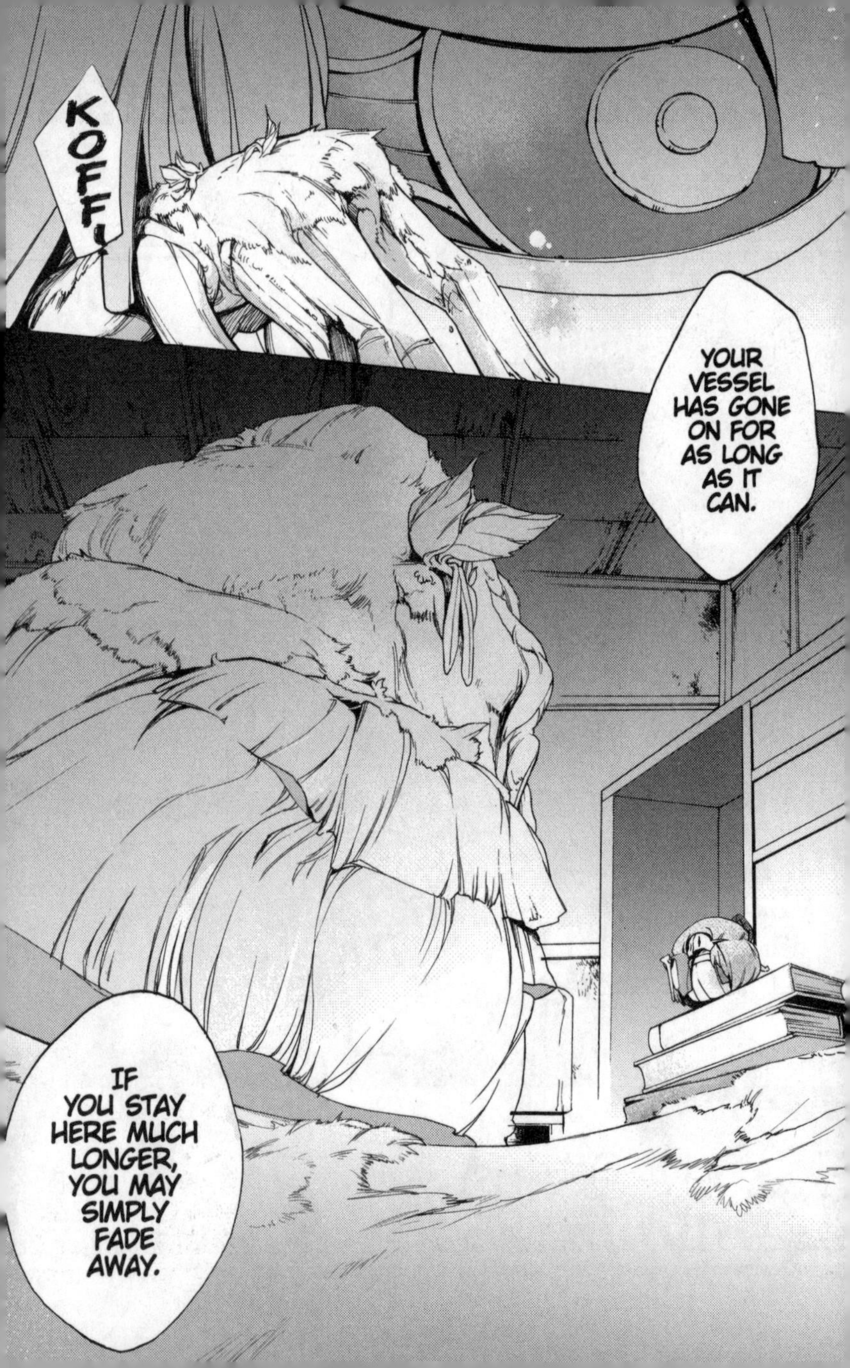
KOFF!
YOUR VESSEL HAS GONE ON FOR AS LONG AS IT CAN.
IF YOU STAY HERE MUCH LONGER, YOU MAY SIMPLY FADE AWAY.

Chapter 5

The Successor and the Venerable Verdant (Part 2)

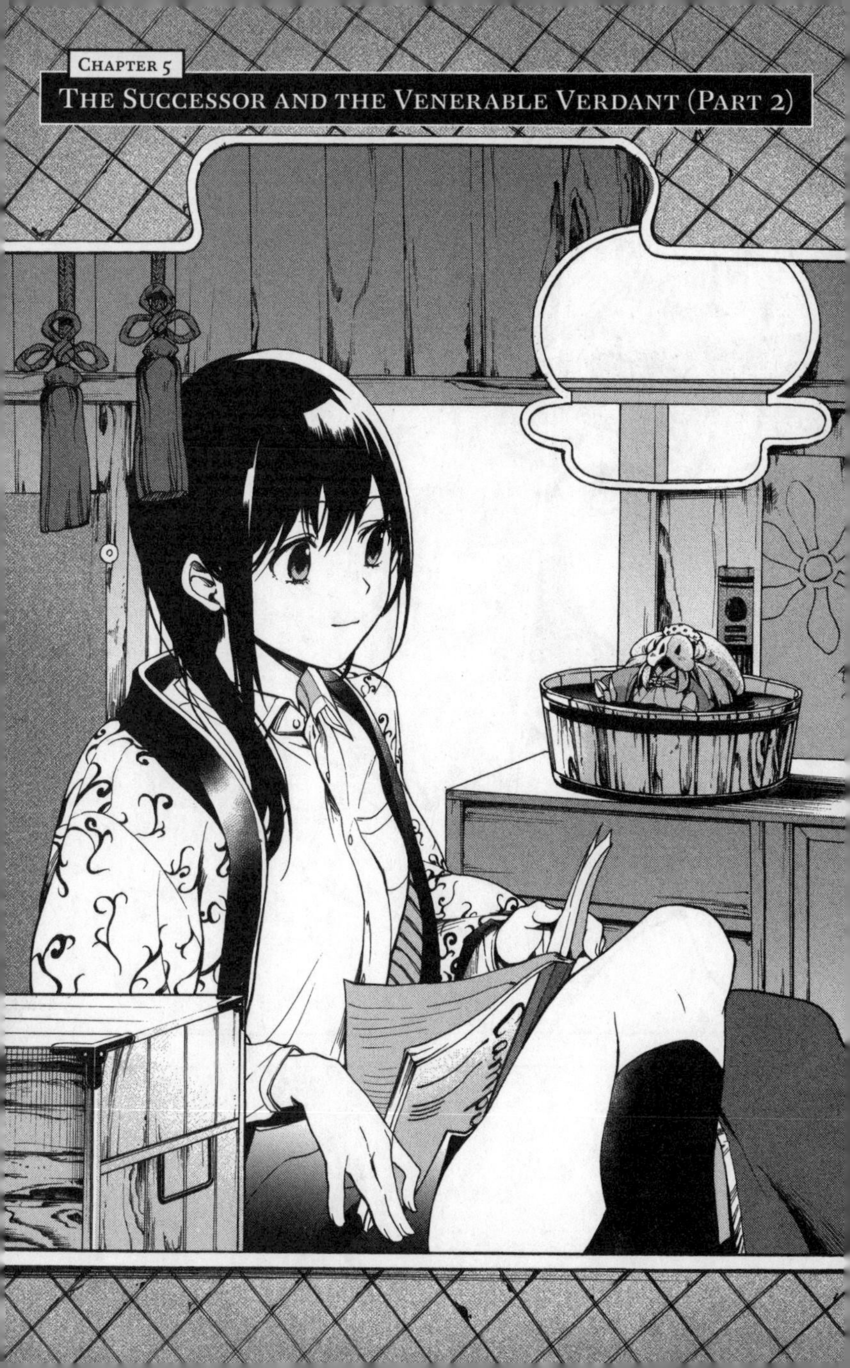

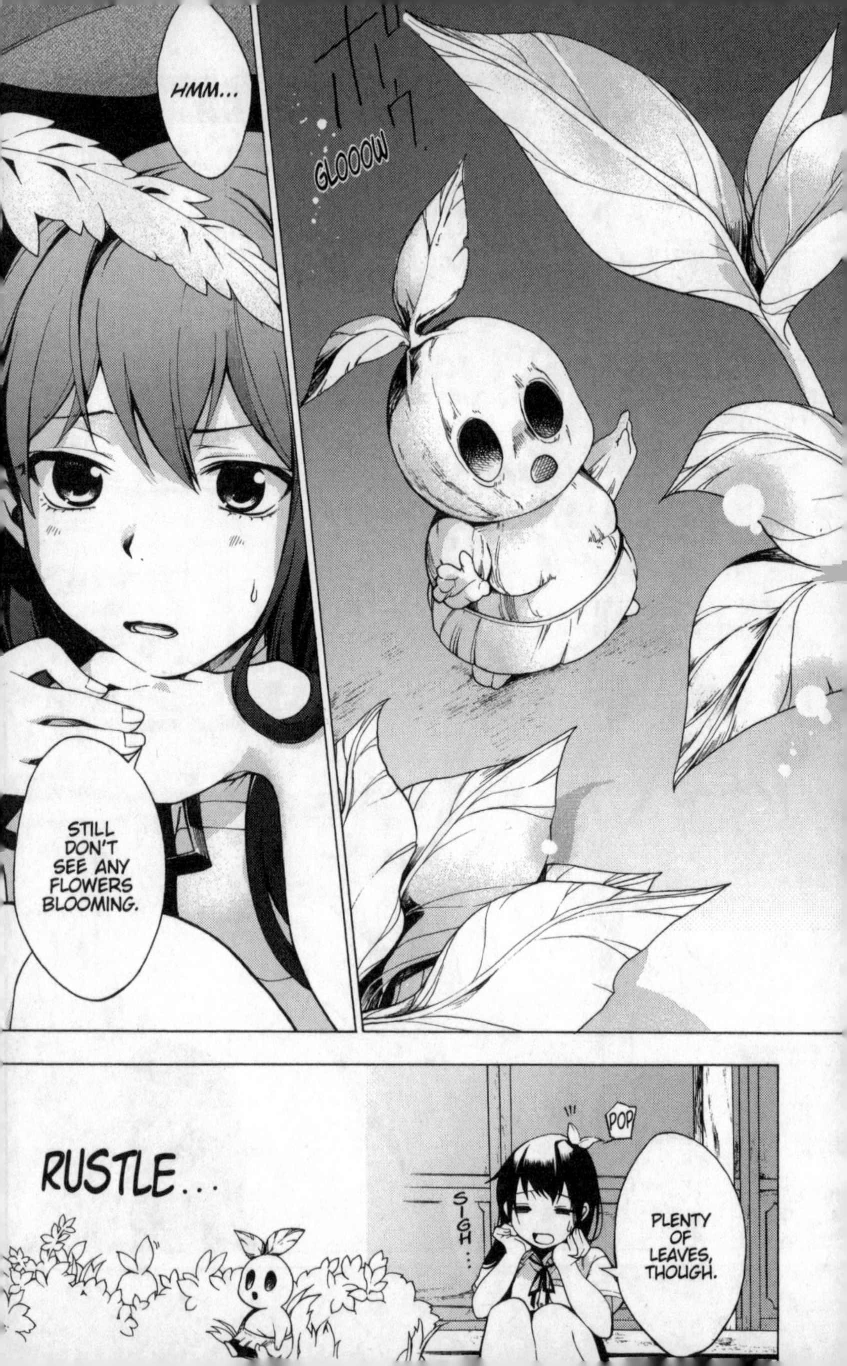
GLOOOW
HMM...
STILL DON'T SEE ANY FLOWERS BLOOMING.
POP
!!
PLENTY OF LEAVES, THOUGH.
SIGH...
RUSTLE...

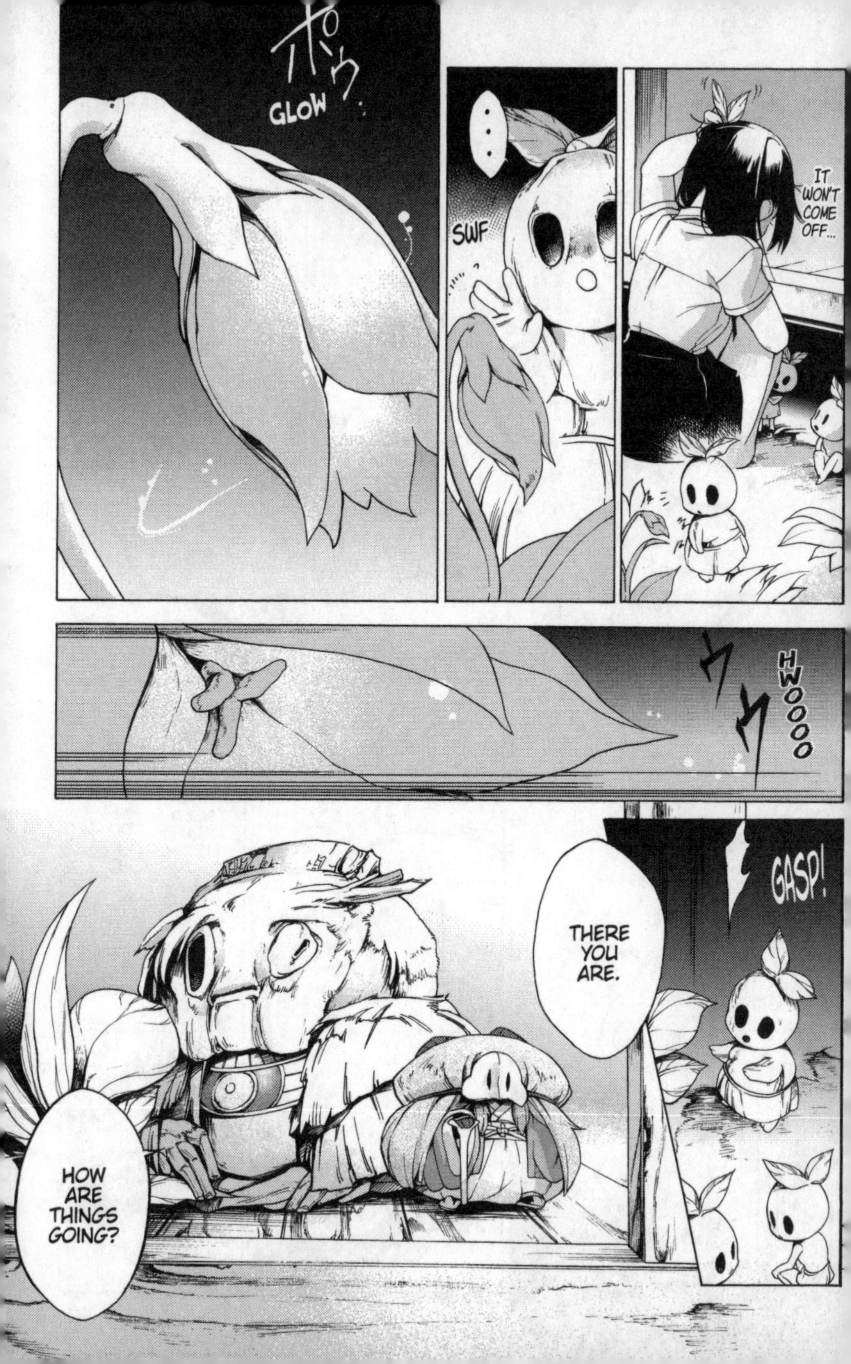
IT WON'T COME OFF...
...
SWF
ポウ
GLOW
ウウ
HWOOOO
GASP!
THERE YOU ARE.
HOW ARE THINGS GOING?

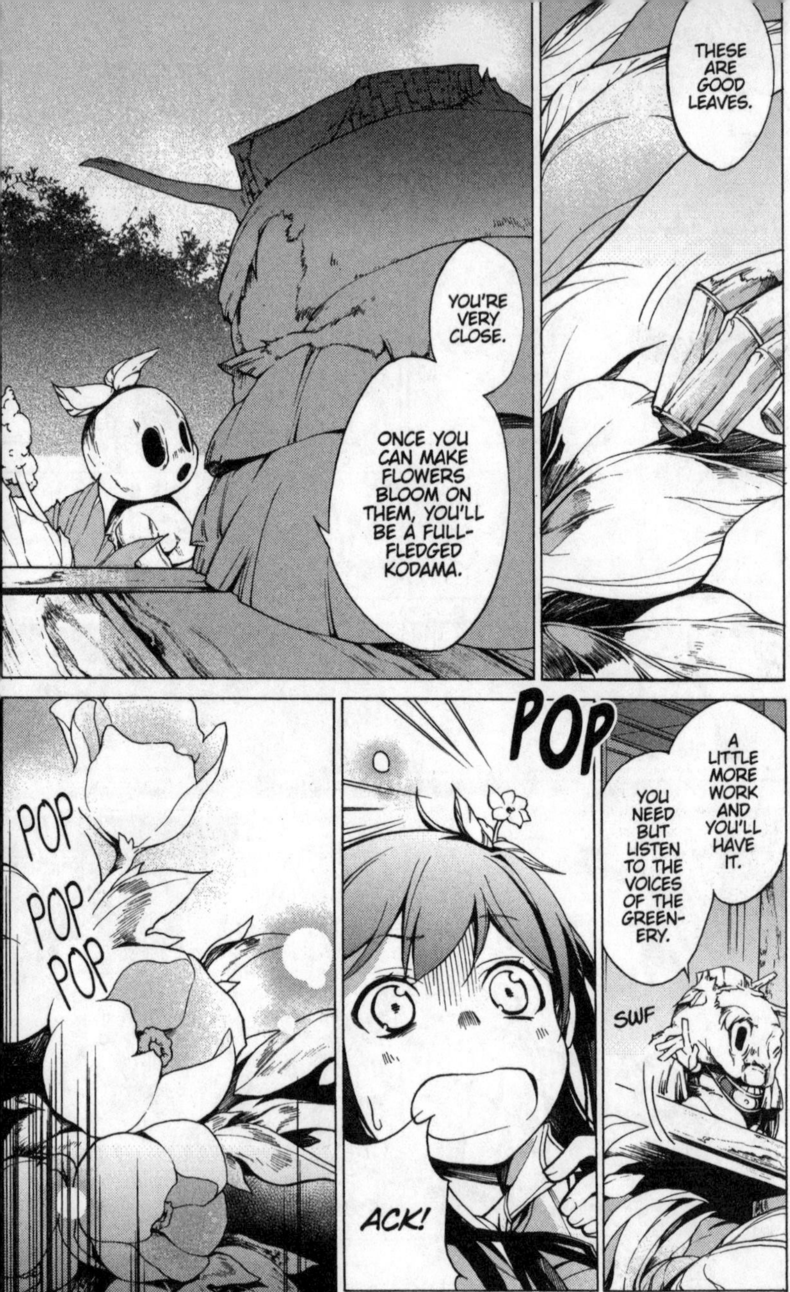
THESE ARE GOOD LEAVES.
YOU'RE VERY CLOSE.
ONCE YOU CAN MAKE FLOWERS BLOOM ON THEM, YOU'LL BE A FULL-FLEDGED KODAMA.
A LITTLE MORE WORK AND YOU'LL HAVE IT.
YOU NEED BUT LISTEN TO THE VOICES OF THE GREENERY.
SWF
POP
ACK!
POP
POP
POP

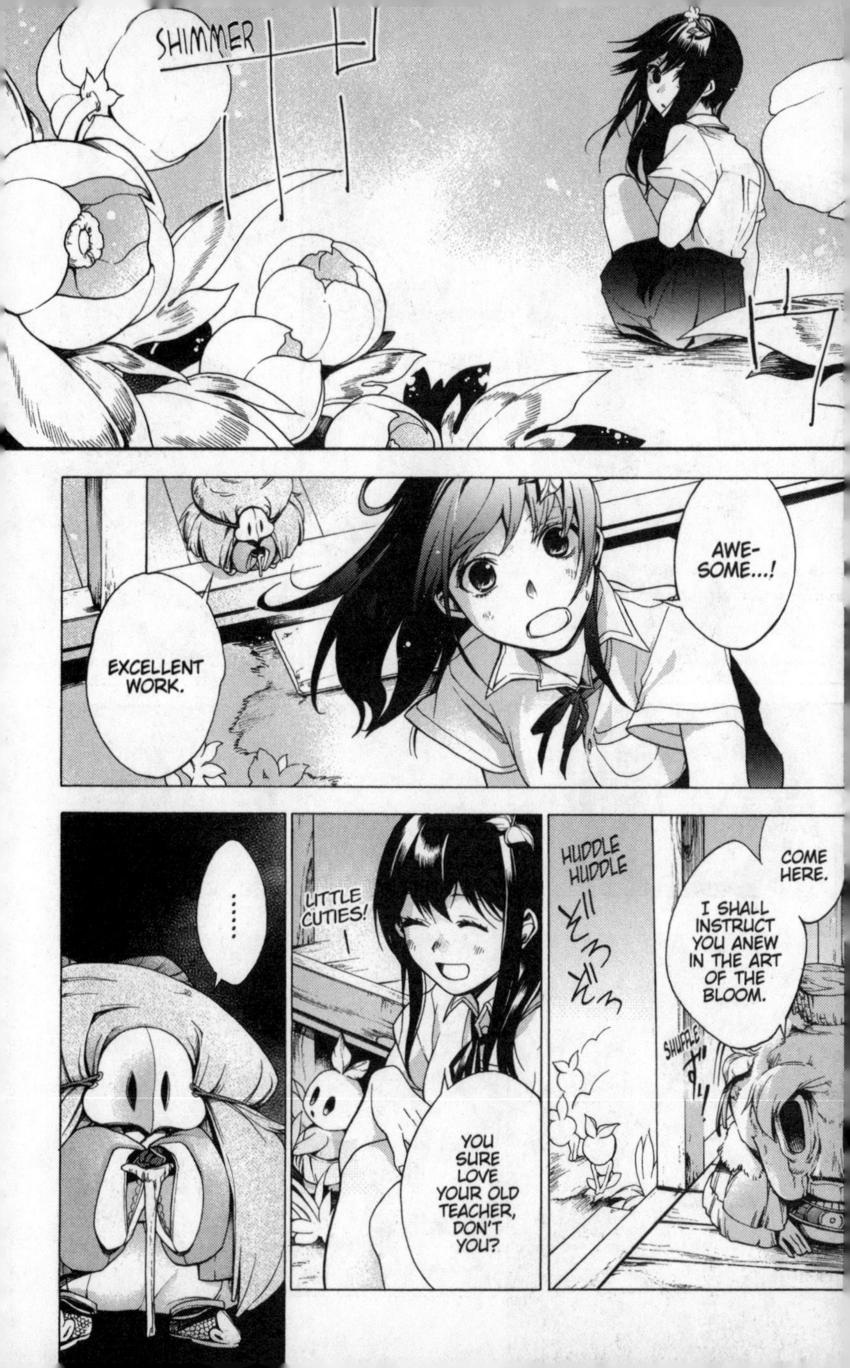
SHIMMER
AWE-SOME...!
EXCELLENT WORK.
COME HERE.
I SHALL INSTRUCT YOU ANEW IN THE ART OF THE BLOOM.
HUDDLE HUDDLE
SHUFFLE
LITTLE CUTIES!
YOU SURE LOVE YOUR OLD TEACHER, DON'T YOU?
......

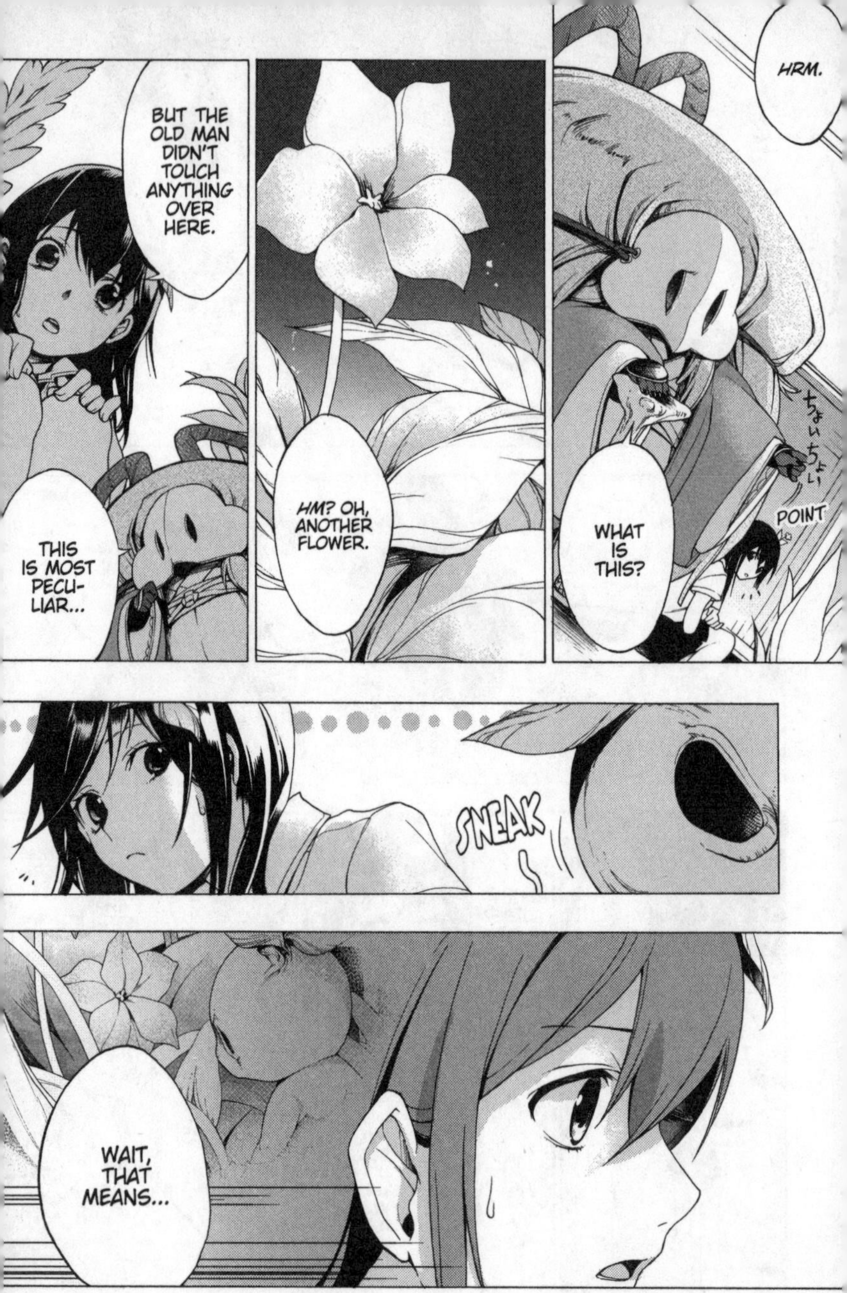
HRM.
ちょいちょい
POINT
WHAT IS THIS?
HM? OH, ANOTHER FLOWER.
BUT THE OLD MAN DIDN'T TOUCH ANYTHING OVER HERE.
THIS IS MOST PECULIAR...
SNEAK
WAIT, THAT MEANS...

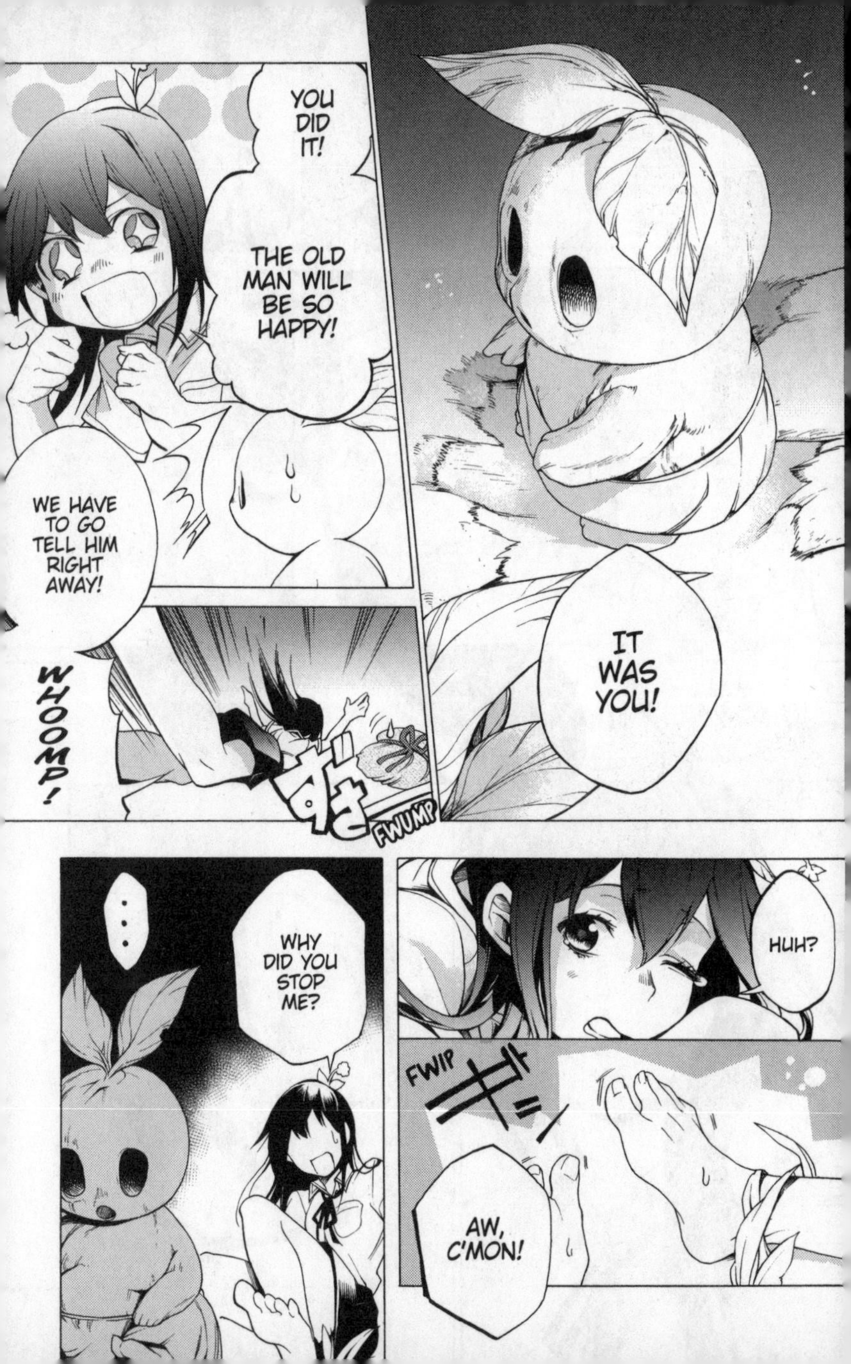
IT WAS YOU!
YOU DID IT!
THE OLD MAN WILL BE SO HAPPY!
WE HAVE TO GO TELL HIM RIGHT AWAY!
WHOOMP!
ずさ
FWUMP
HUH?
FWIP
AW, C'MON!
...
WHY DID YOU STOP ME?

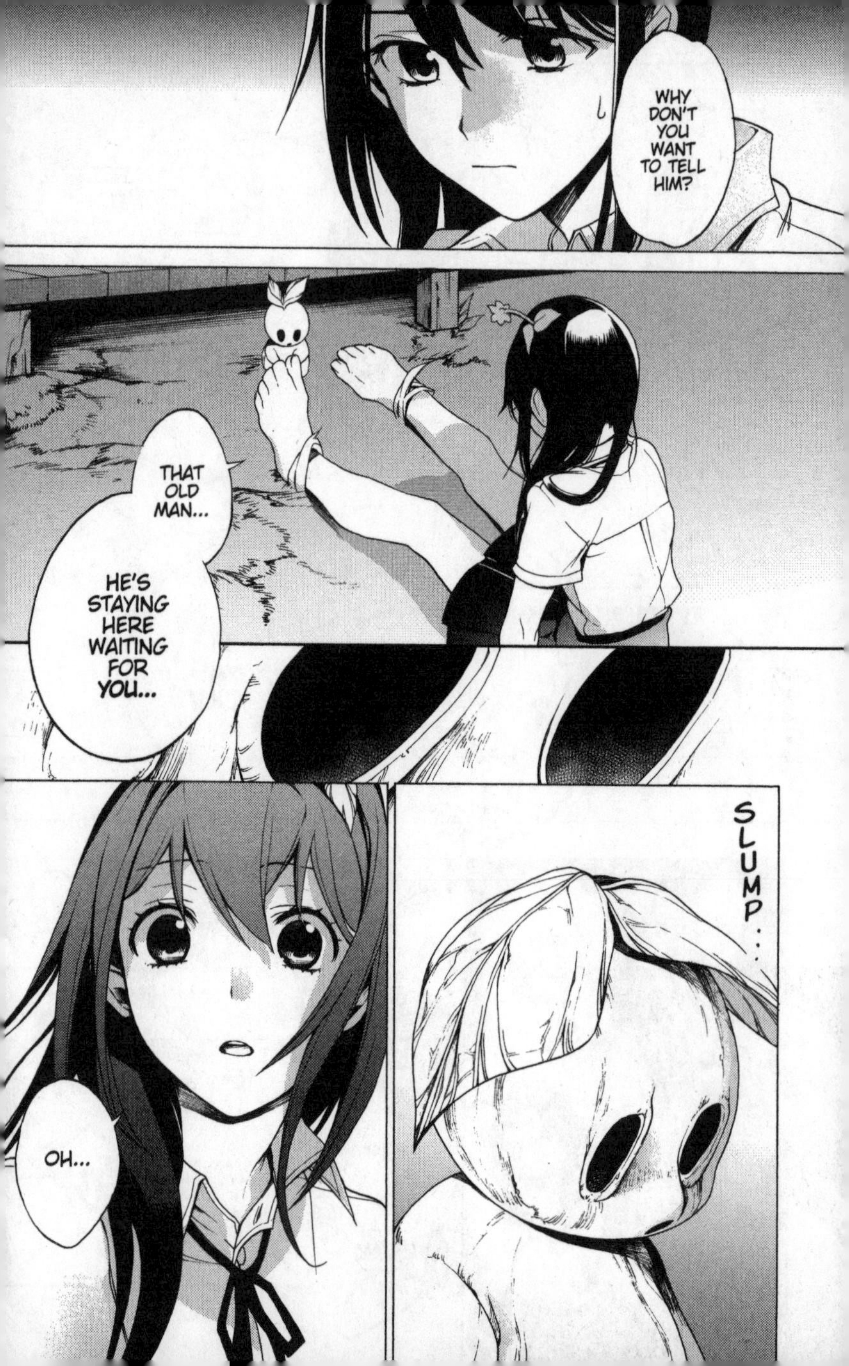
WHY DON'T YOU WANT TO TELL HIM?
THAT OLD MAN...
HE'S STAYING HERE WAITING FOR YOU...
SLUMP...
OH...

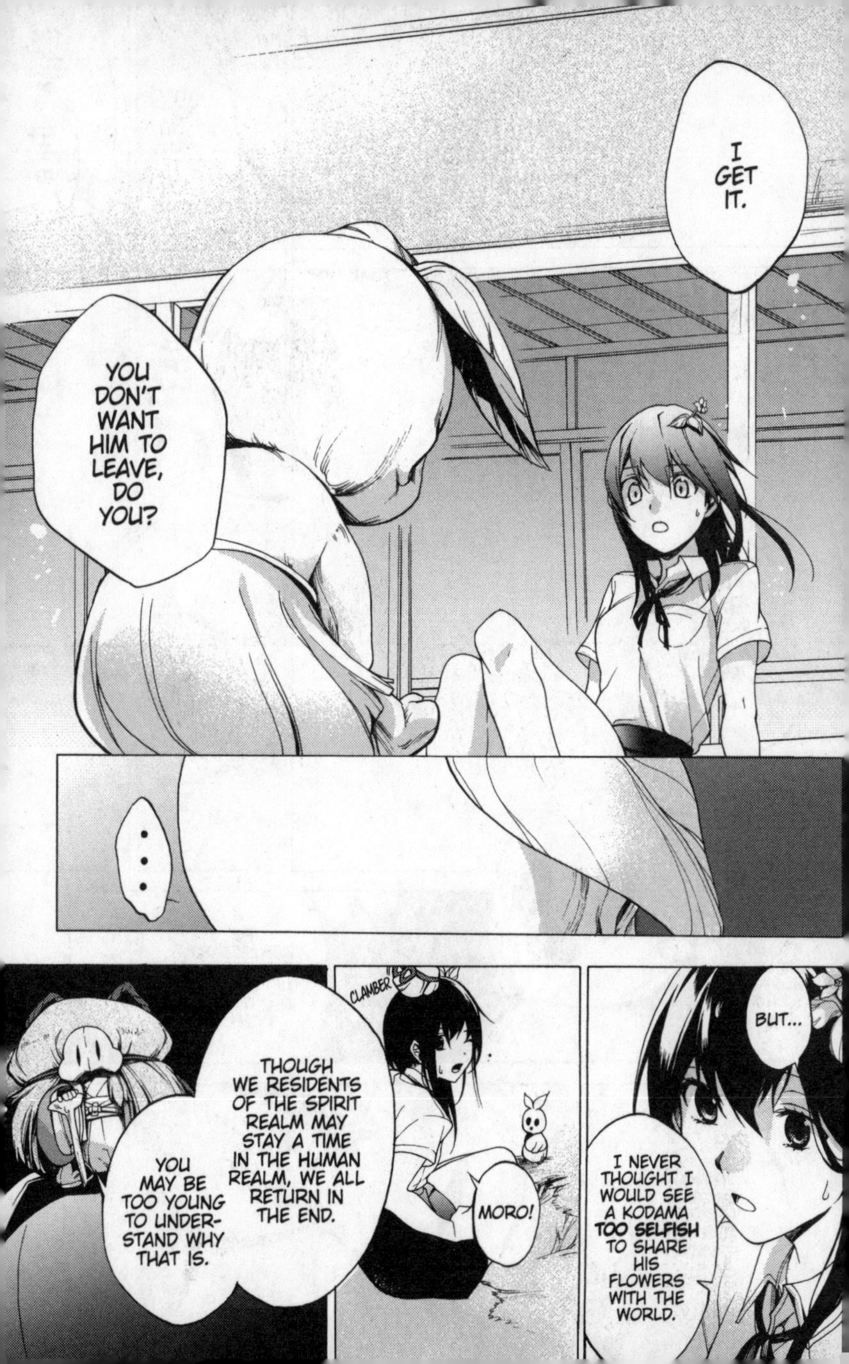
I GET IT.
YOU DON'T WANT HIM TO LEAVE, DO YOU?
...
BUT...
I NEVER THOUGHT I WOULD SEE A KODAMA **TOO SELFISH** TO SHARE HIS FLOWERS WITH THE WORLD.
CLAMBER
MORO!
THOUGH WE RESIDENTS OF THE SPIRIT REALM MAY STAY A TIME IN THE HUMAN REALM, WE ALL RETURN IN THE END.
YOU MAY BE TOO YOUNG TO UNDER-STAND WHY THAT IS.

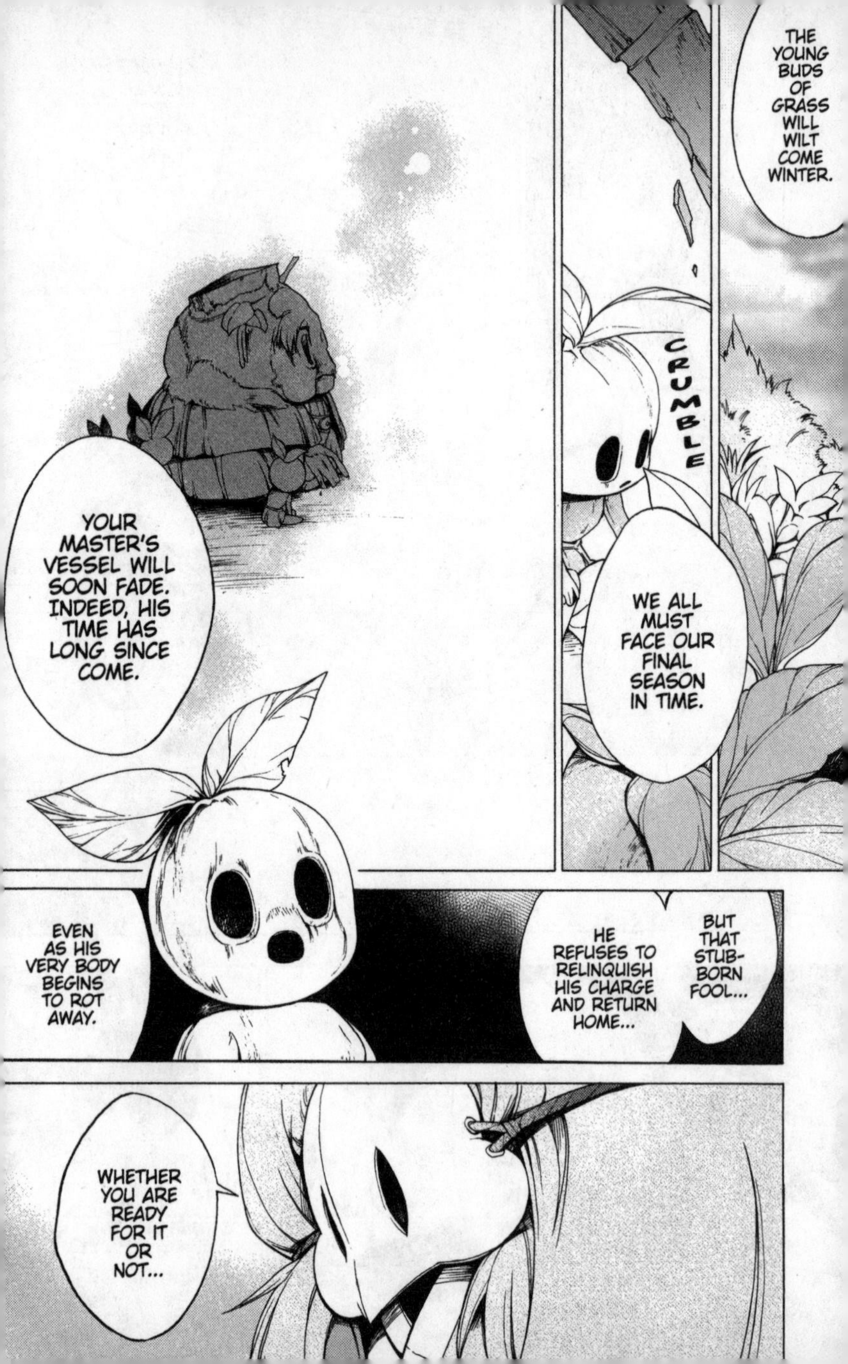
THE YOUNG BUDS OF GRASS WILL WILT COME WINTER.
CRUMBLE
WE ALL MUST FACE OUR FINAL SEASON IN TIME.
YOUR MASTER'S VESSEL WILL SOON FADE. INDEED, HIS TIME HAS LONG SINCE COME.
BUT THAT STUB-BORN FOOL...
HE REFUSES TO RELINQUISH HIS CHARGE AND RETURN HOME...
EVEN AS HIS VERY BODY BEGINS TO ROT AWAY.
WHETHER YOU ARE READY FOR IT OR NOT...

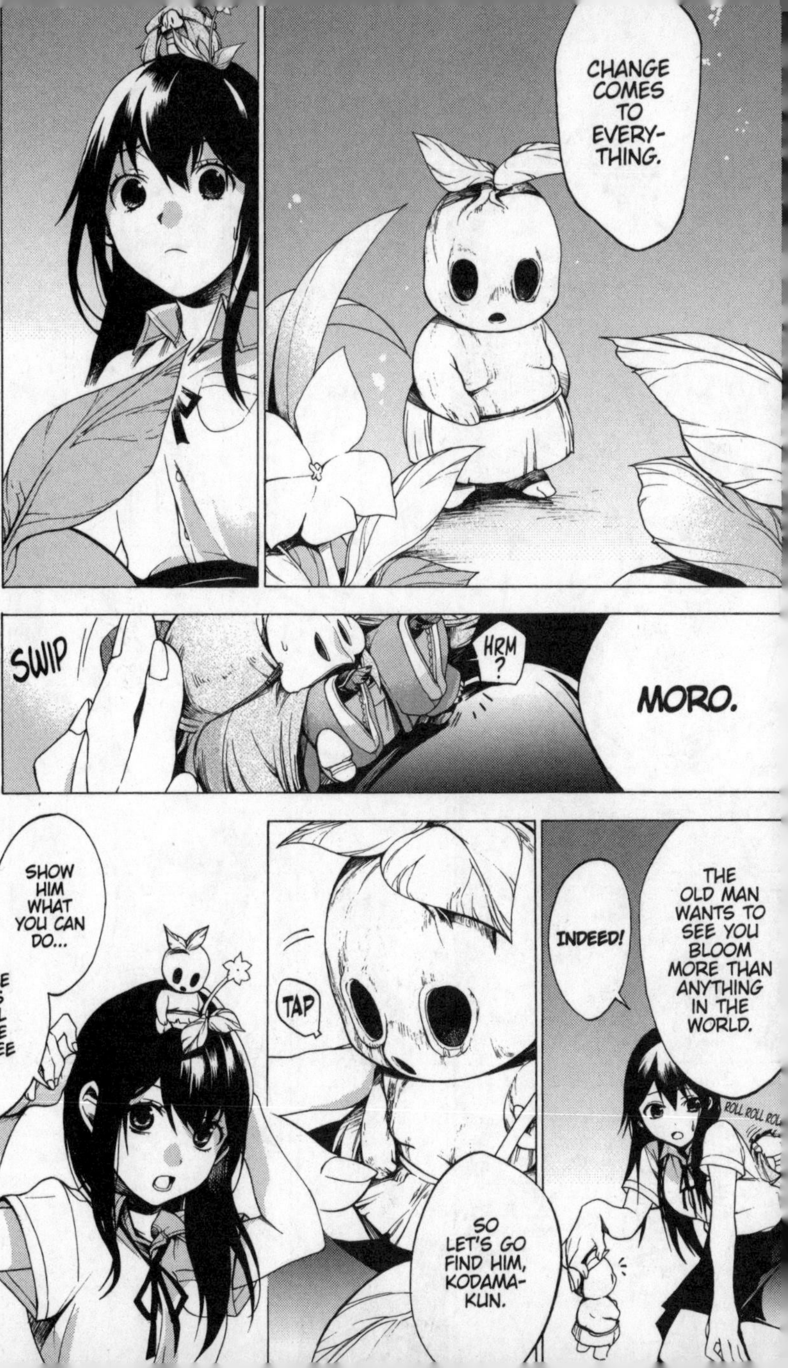
CHANGE COMES TO EVERY-THING.
MORO.
HRM?
SWIP
THE OLD MAN WANTS TO SEE YOU BLOOM MORE THAN ANYTHING IN THE WORLD.
INDEED!
ROLL ROLL
TAP
SO LET'S GO FIND HIM, KODAMA-KUN.
SHOW HIM WHAT YOU CAN DO...
WHILE HE'S STILL HERE TO SEE IT!

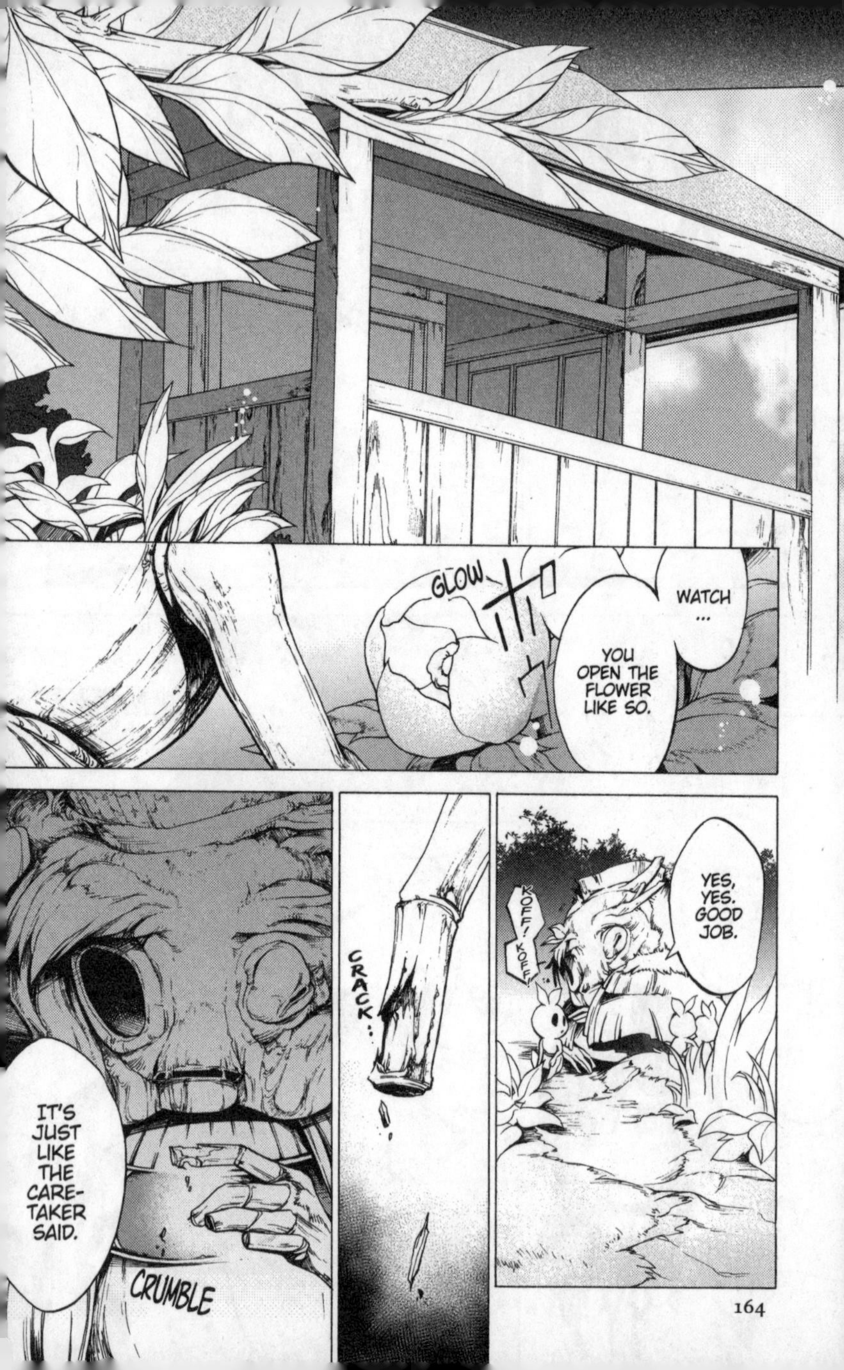
WATCH...
YOU OPEN THE FLOWER LIKE SO.
GLOW
YES, YES. GOOD JOB.
KOFF! KOFF!
CRACK...
IT'S JUST LIKE THE CARE-TAKER SAID.
CRUMBLE

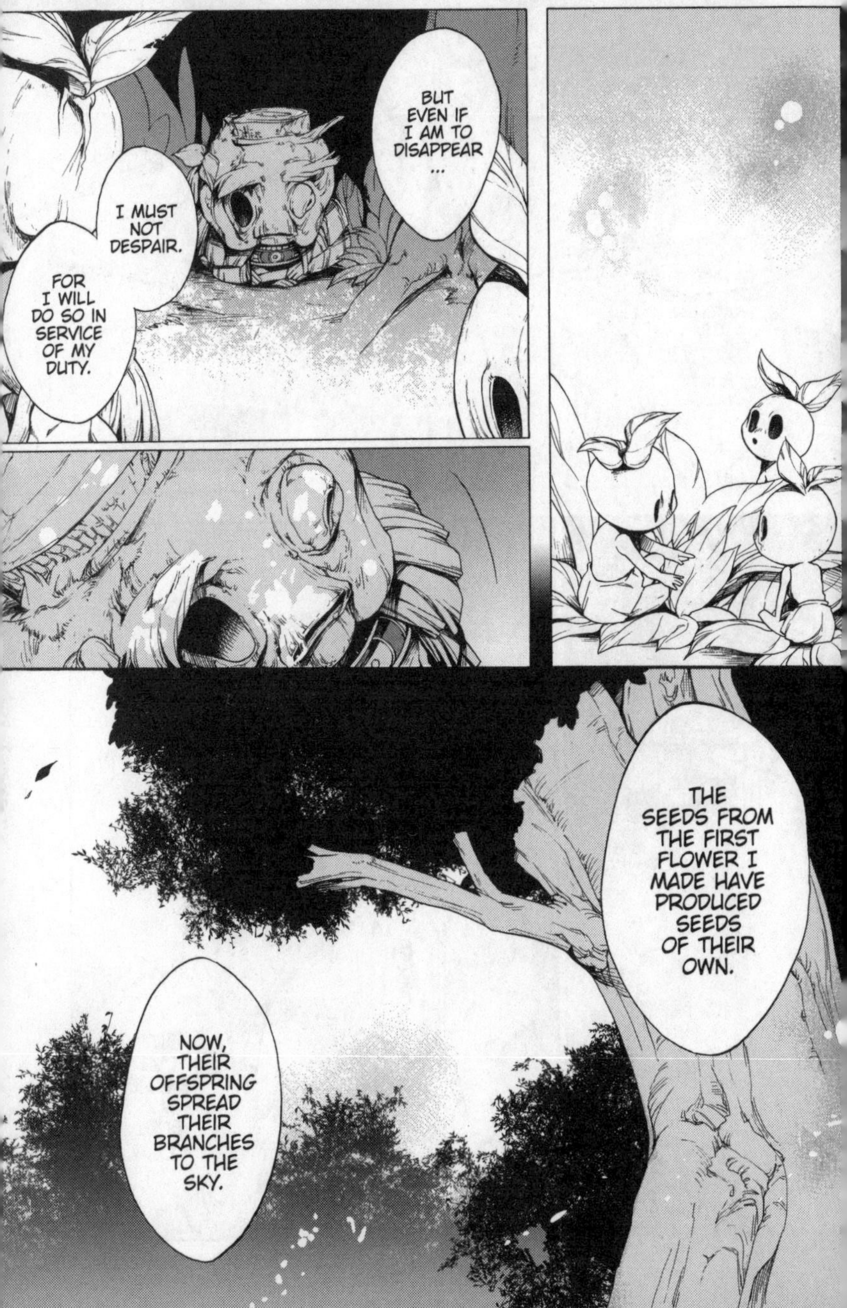
BUT EVEN IF I AM TO DISAPPEAR ...
I MUST NOT DESPAIR.
FOR I WILL DO SO IN SERVICE OF MY DUTY.
THE SEEDS FROM THE FIRST FLOWER I MADE HAVE PRODUCED SEEDS OF THEIR OWN.
NOW, THEIR OFFSPRING SPREAD THEIR BRANCHES TO THE SKY.

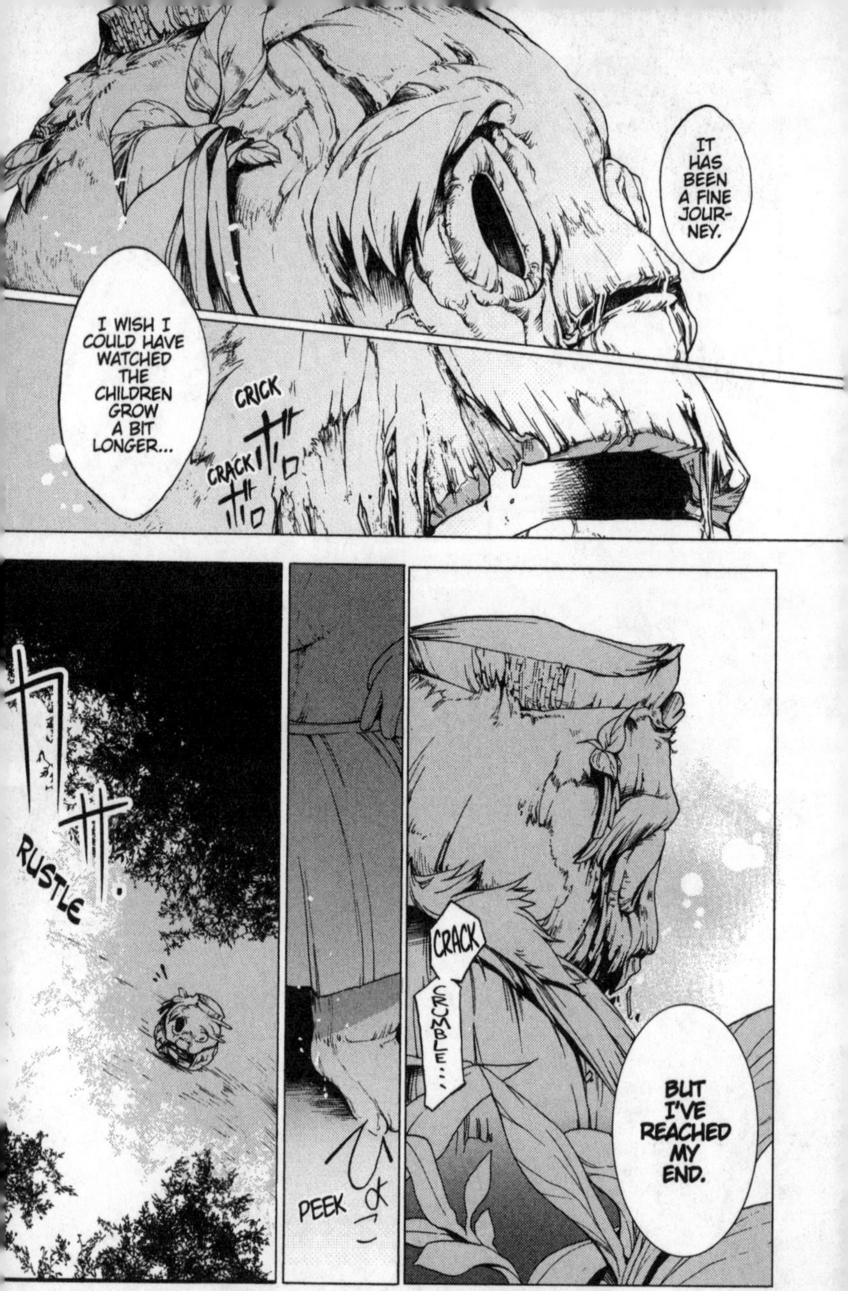
IT HAS BEEN A FINE JOURNEY.
I WISH I COULD HAVE WATCHED THE CHILDREN GROW A BIT LONGER...
CRICK
CRACK
CRACK
CRUMBLE...
BUT I'VE REACHED MY END.
PEEK
RUSTLE

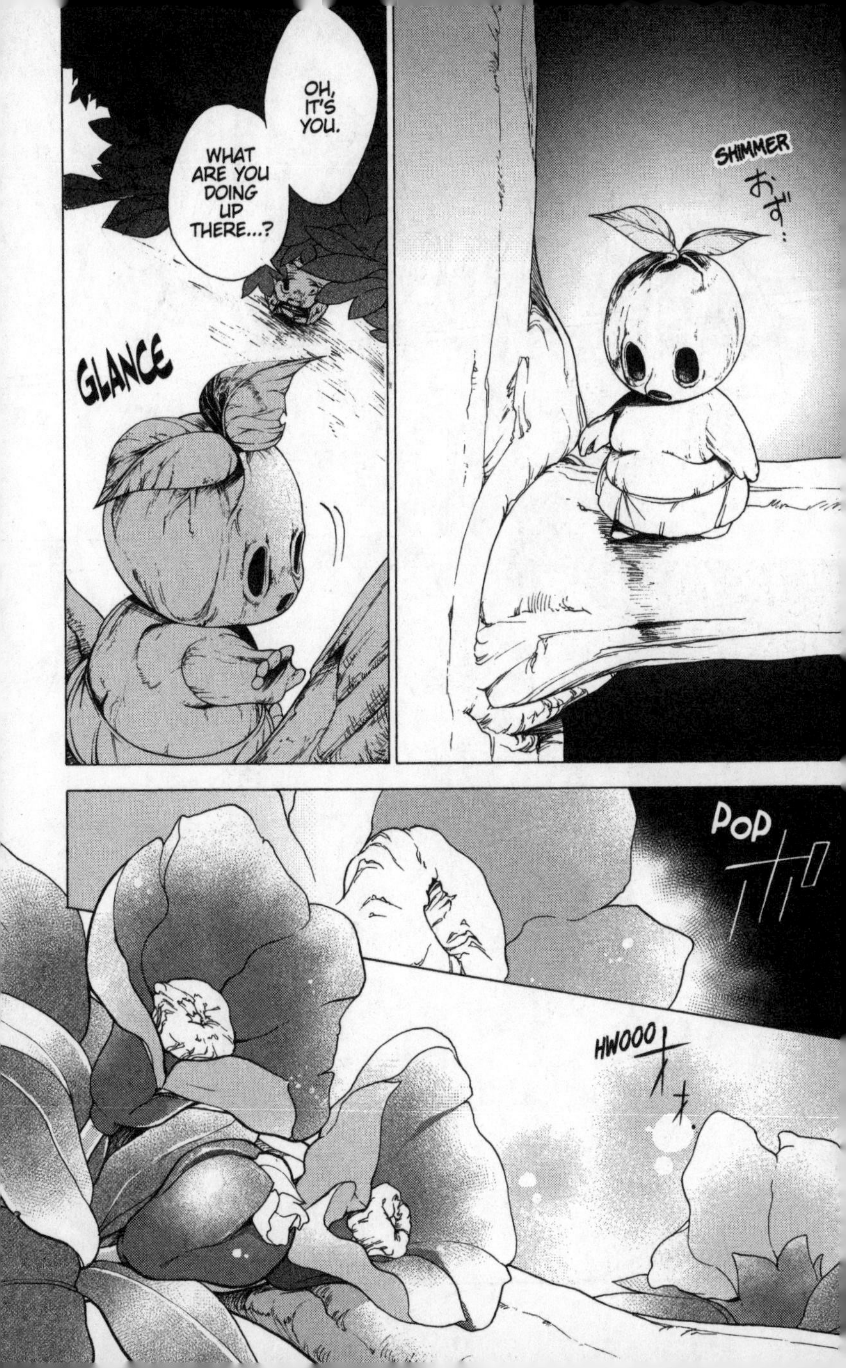
SHIMMER
おず…
OH, IT'S YOU.
WHAT ARE YOU DOING UP THERE...?
GLANCE
POP
HWOOO

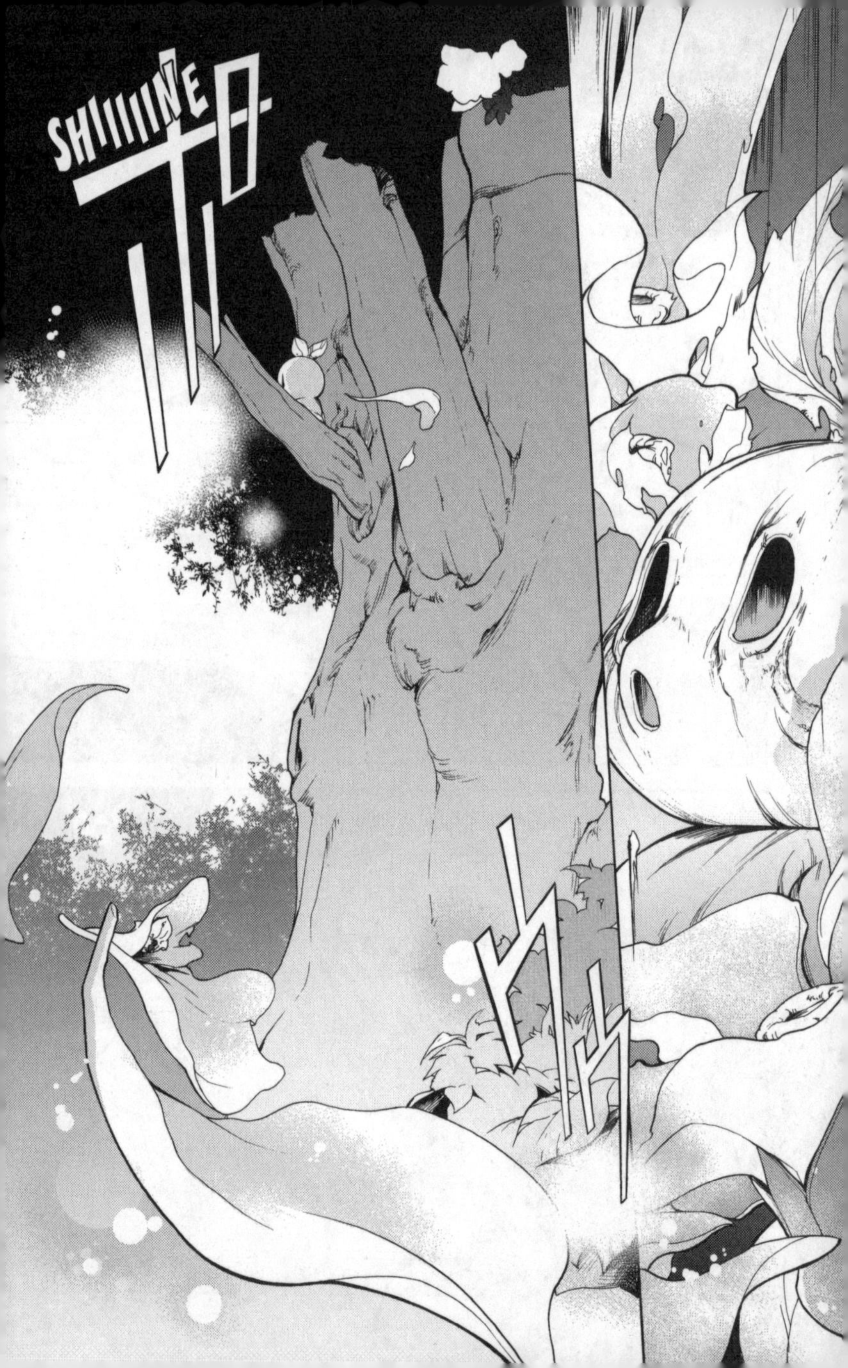
SHIIIIINE

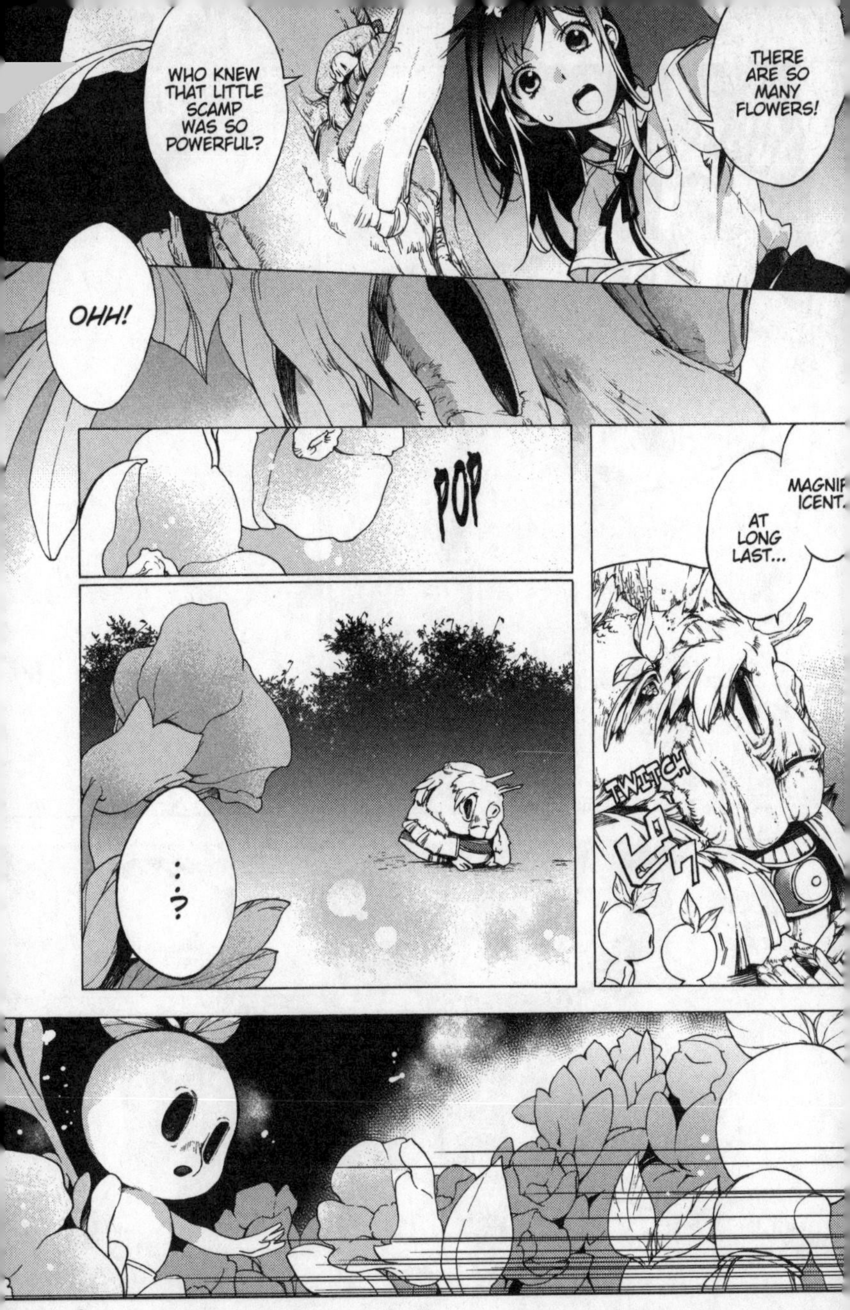
THERE ARE SO MANY FLOWERS!
WHO KNEW THAT LITTLE SCAMP WAS SO POWERFUL?
OHH!
MAGNIFICENT.
AT LONG LAST...
TWITCH
POP
...?

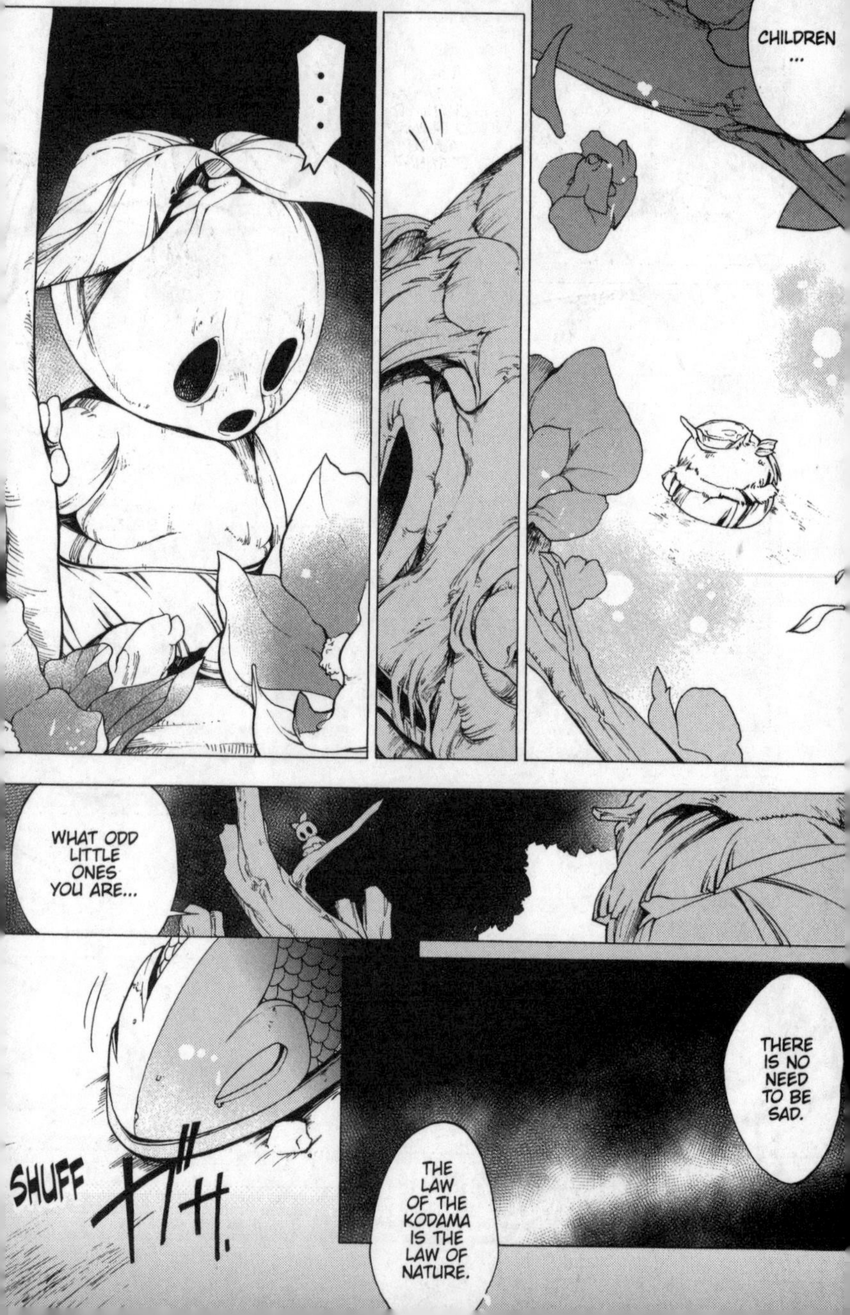
CHILDREN ...
!...
WHAT ODD LITTLE ONES YOU ARE...
THERE IS NO NEED TO BE SAD.
THE LAW OF THE KODAMA IS THE LAW OF NATURE.
SHUFF

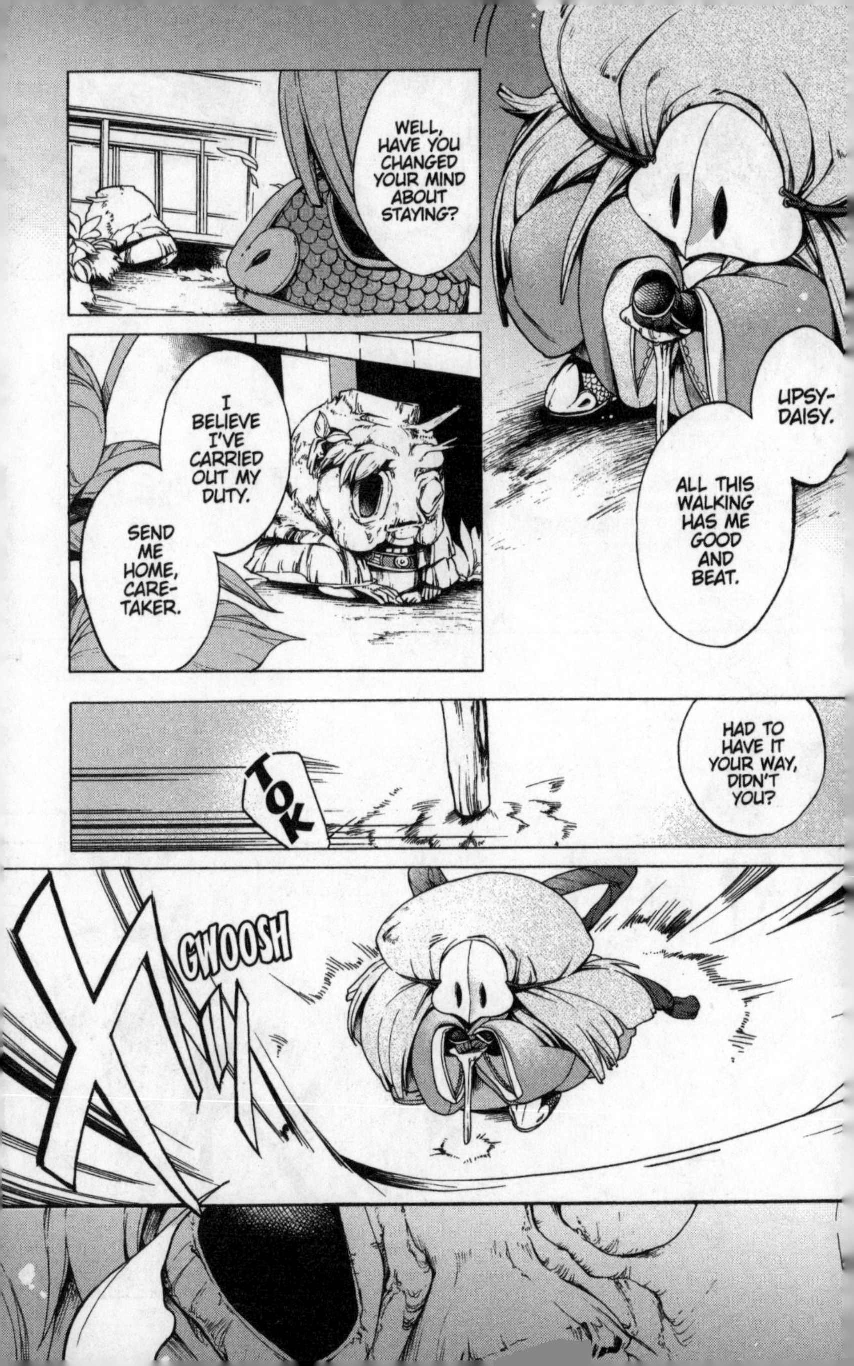
UPSY-DAISY.
ALL THIS WALKING HAS ME GOOD AND BEAT.
WELL, HAVE YOU CHANGED YOUR MIND ABOUT STAYING?
I BELIEVE I'VE CARRIED OUT MY DUTY.
SEND ME HOME, CARE-TAKER.
HAD TO HAVE IT YOUR WAY, DIDN'T YOU?
TOK
GWOOSH

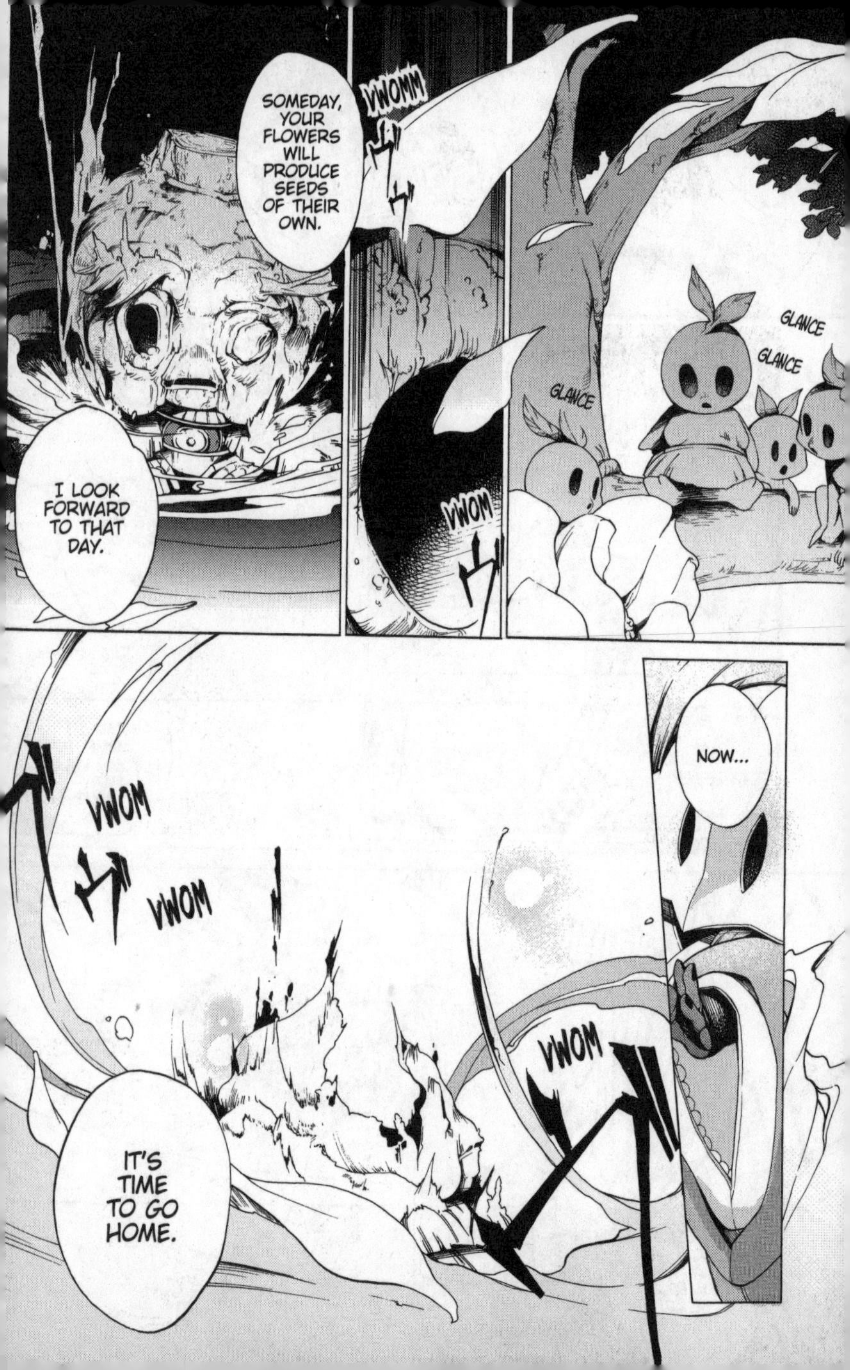
GLANCE
GLANCE
GLANCE
VWOMM
VWOM
SOMEDAY, YOUR FLOWERS WILL PRODUCE SEEDS OF THEIR OWN.
I LOOK FORWARD TO THAT DAY.
NOW...
VWOM
VWOM
VWOM
IT'S TIME TO GO HOME.

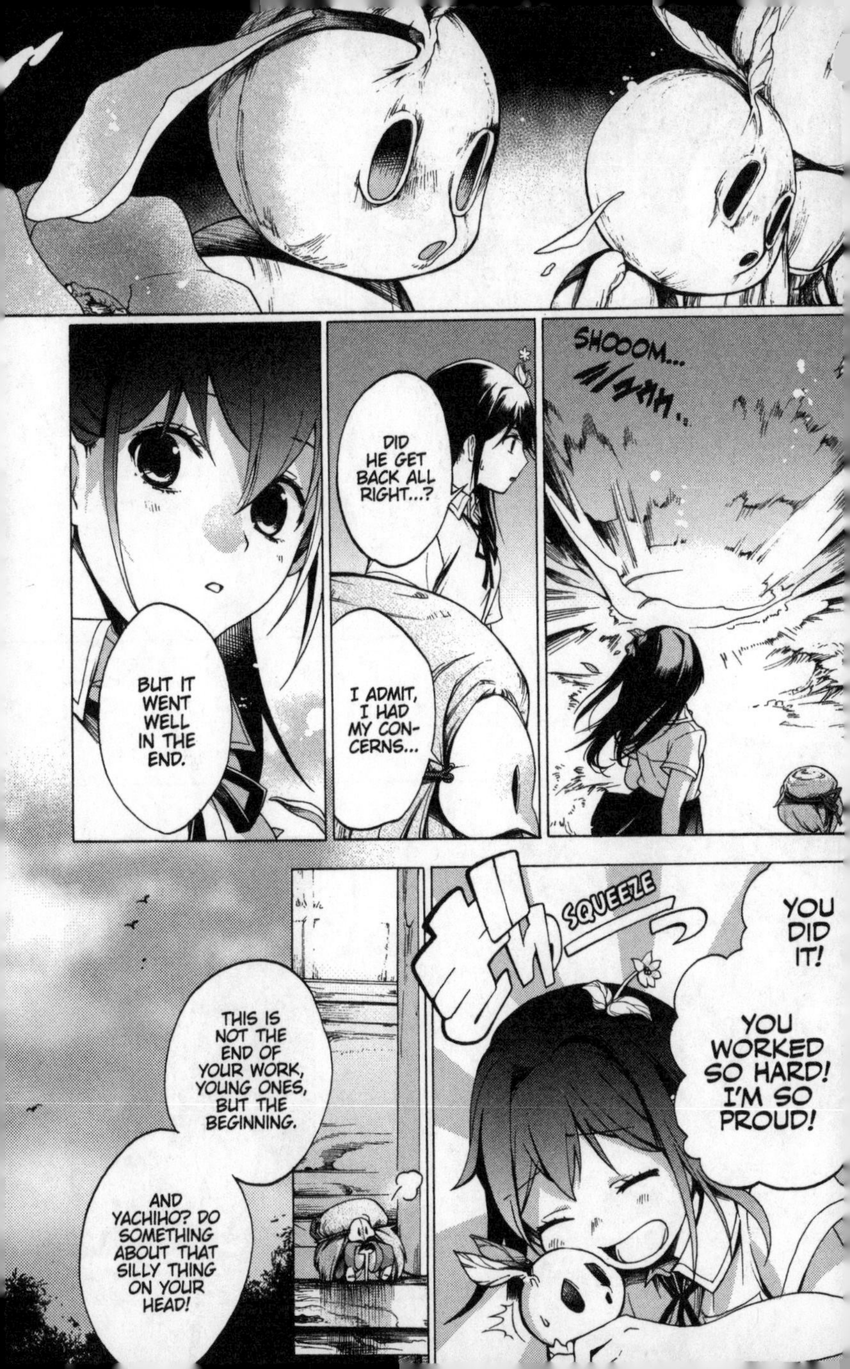
SHOOOM...
DID HE GET BACK ALL RIGHT...?
I ADMIT, I HAD MY CON-CERNS...
BUT IT WENT WELL IN THE END.
SQUEEZE
YOU DID IT!
YOU WORKED SO HARD! I'M SO PROUD!
THIS IS NOT THE END OF YOUR WORK, YOUNG ONES, BUT THE BEGINNING.
AND YACHIHO? DO SOMETHING ABOUT THAT SILLY THING ON YOUR HEAD!

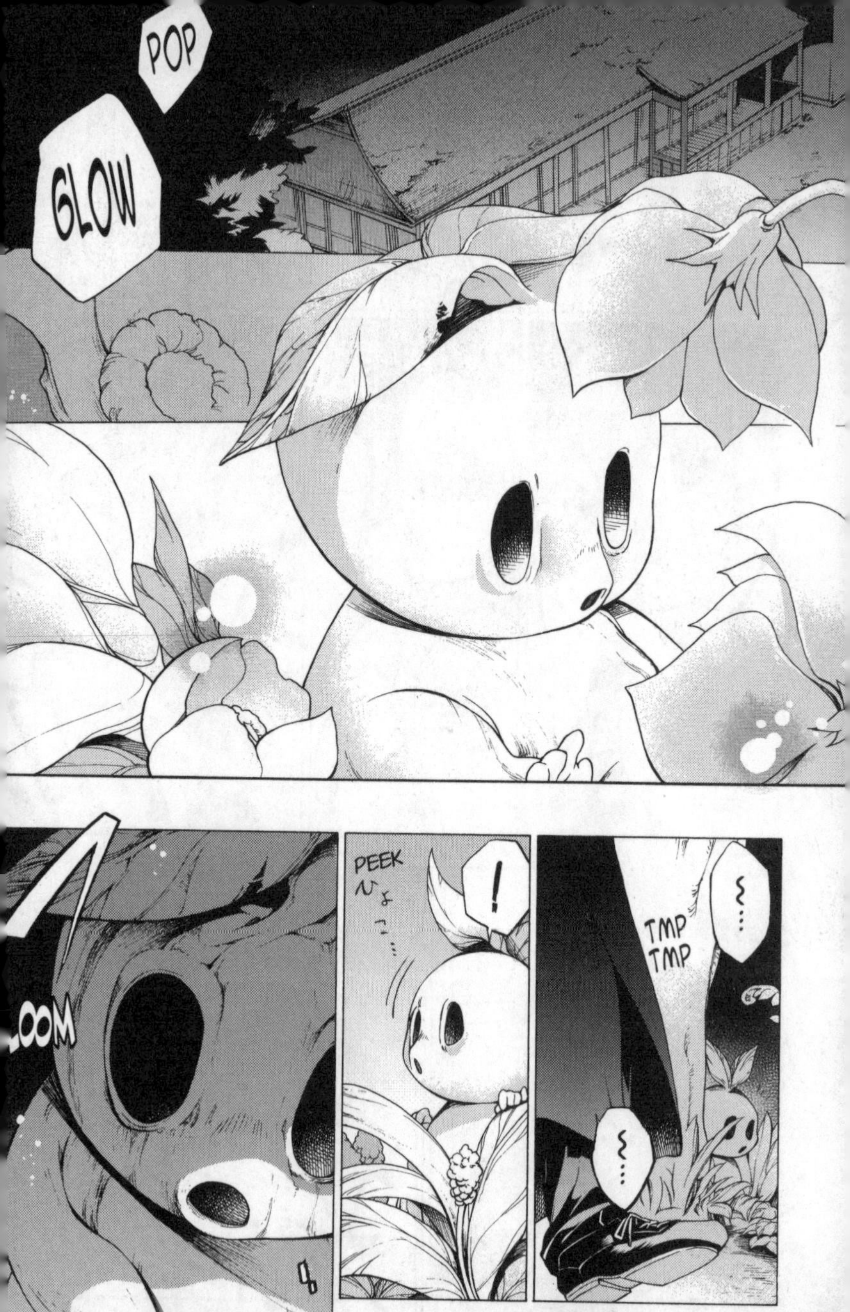
POP
GLOW
~...
TMP TMP
~...
!
PEEK
ひょこ...
LOOM

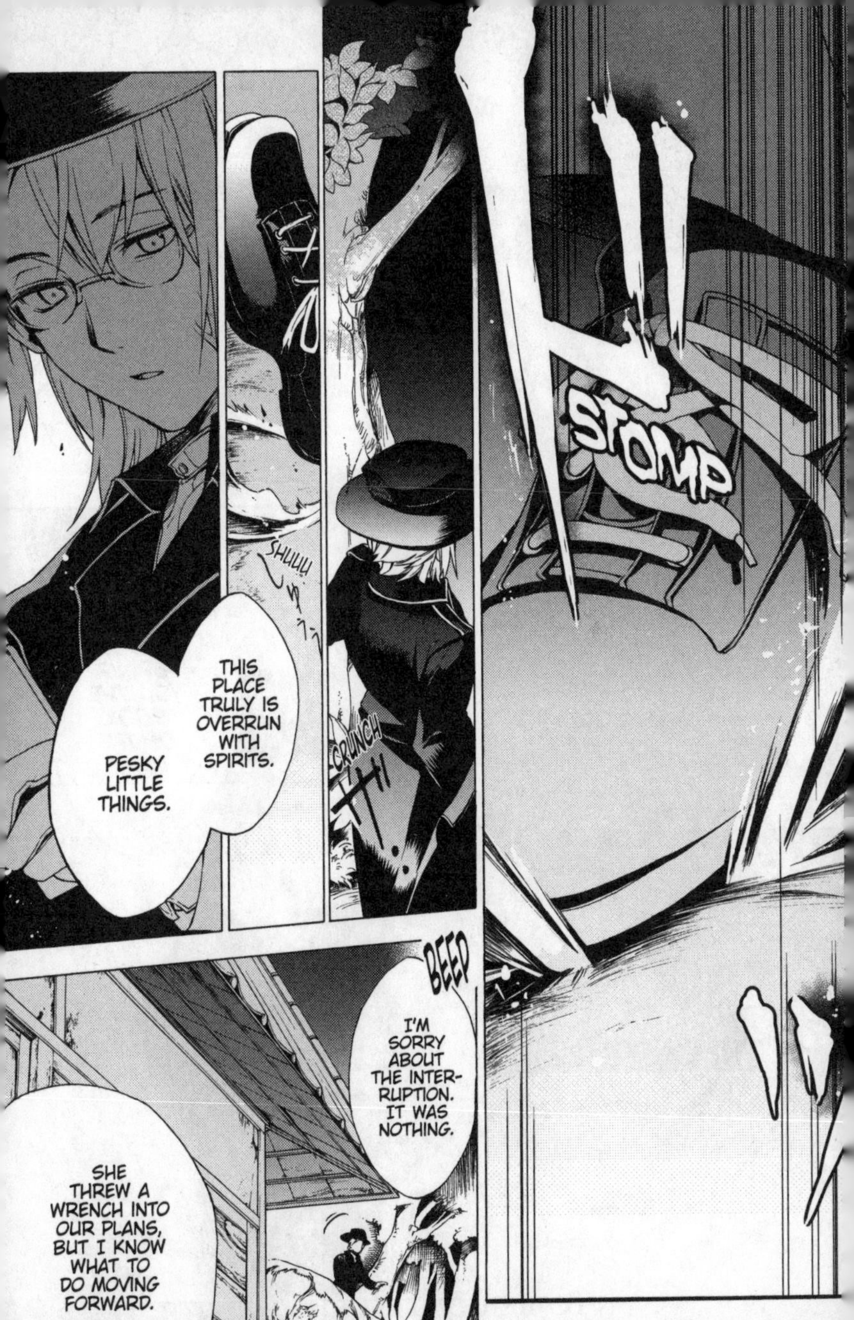
STOMP
CRUNCH
SHUUU
THIS PLACE TRULY IS OVERRUN WITH SPIRITS.
PESKY LITTLE THINGS.
BEEP
I'M SORRY ABOUT THE INTER-RUPTION. IT WAS NOTHING.
SHE THREW A WRENCH INTO OUR PLANS, BUT I KNOW WHAT TO DO MOVING FORWARD.

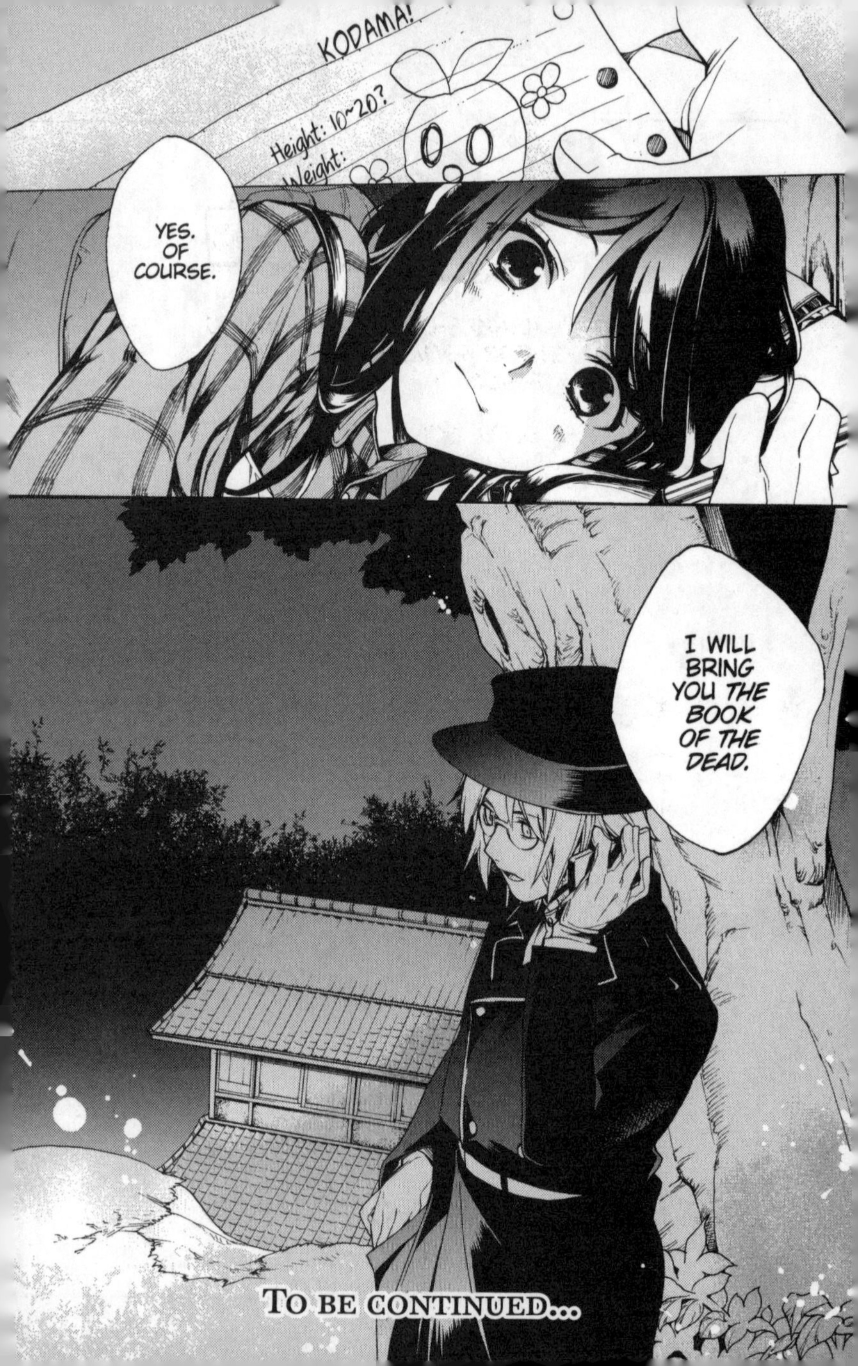
KODAMA!
Height: 10~20?
Weight:
YES. OF COURSE.
I WILL BRING YOU THE BOOK OF THE DEAD.
TO BE CONTINUED...

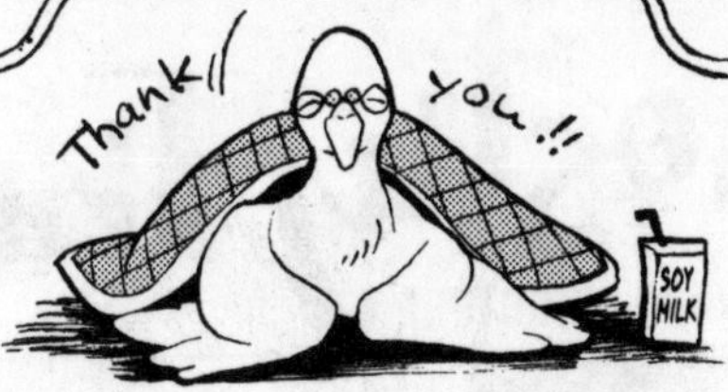
Thank you!!
SOY MILK

HELLO, I'M USHIO SHIROTORI. THANK YOU VERY MUCH FOR BUYING VOLUME 1 OF GHOSTLY THINGS.

IT'S BEEN SLOW GOING, BUT NOW THAT THE VOLUME HAS BEEN RELEASED, I'M BOTH HAPPY AND RELIEVED. ANYWAY, I HOPE YOU ENJOYED IT!!

2018.9, USHIO SHIROTORI

SPECIAL THANX TO EVERYONE INVOLVED!

* *

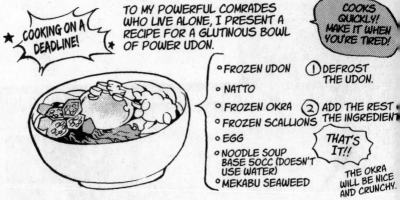

★ COOKING ON A DEADLINE! ★

TO MY POWERFUL COMRADES WHO LIVE ALONE, I PRESENT A RECIPE FOR A GLUTINOUS BOWL OF POWER UDON.

COOKS QUICKLY! MAKE IT WHEN YOU'RE TIRED!

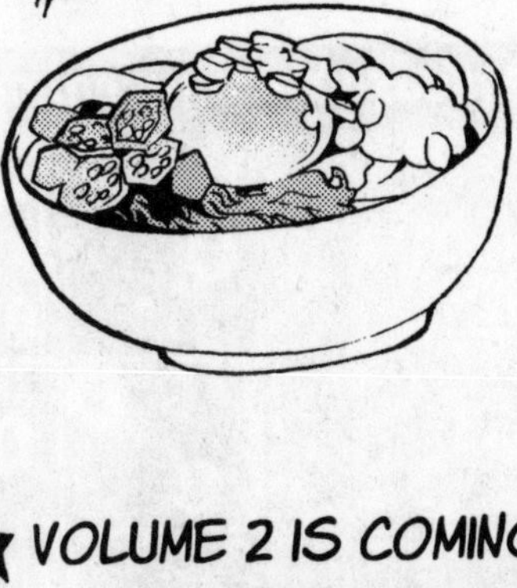

- FROZEN UDON
- NATTO
- FROZEN OKRA
- FROZEN SCALLIONS
- EGG
- NOODLE SOUP BASE 50CC (DOESN'T USE WATER)
- MEKABU SEAWEED

① DEFROST THE UDON.

② ADD THE REST THE INGREDIEN

THAT'S IT!!

THE OKRA WILL BE NICE AND CRUNCHY.

★ VOLUME 2 IS COMING SOON!

THE STORY MAKES ITS WAY TO SCHOOL...! PLEASE LOOK FORWARD TO IT!

SEVEN SEAS ENTERTAINMENT PRESENTS

Ghostly Things Vol. 1

story and art by USHIO SHIROTORI

TRANSLATION
Nova Skipper

ADAPTATION
Clint Bickham

LETTERING AND RETOUCH
Rina Mapa

COVER DESIGN
KC Fabellon

PROOFREADER
Brett Hallahan
Danielle King

EDITOR
J.P. Sullivan

PRODUCTION MANAGER
Lissa Pattillo

MANAGING EDITOR
Julie Davis

EDITOR-IN-CHIEF
Adam Arnold

PUBLISHER
Jason DeAngelis

AYASHIKOTO-GATARI VOL. 1
© Ushio Shirotori 2018
Originally published in Japan in 2018 by MAG Garden Corporation, Tokyo.
English translation rights arranged through TOHAN CORPORATION, Tokyo.

Seven Seas press and purchase enquiries can be sent to Marketing Manager
Lianne Sentar at press@gomanga.com. Information regarding the distribution
and purchase of digital editions is available from Digital Manager CK Russell
at digital@gomanga.com.

Seven Seas and the Seven Seas logo are trademarks of
Seven Seas Entertainment. All rights reserved.

ISBN: 978-1-64275-710-1

Printed in Canada

First Printing: October 2019

10 9 8 7 6 5 4 3 2 1

FOLLOW US ONLINE: *www.sevenseasentertainment.com*

READING DIRECTIONS

This book reads from *right to left*, Japanese style.
If this is your first time reading manga, you start
reading from the top right panel on each page and
take it from there. If you get lost, just follow the
numbered diagram here. It may seem backwards at
first, but you'll get the hang of it! Have fun!!

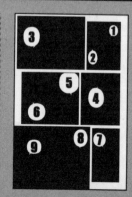